POSUKA DEMIZU

The hunting ground arc is finally completed!

It looks like the kids can't let their guards down, but now with more friends, they can begin planning the rescue of Phil and the others.

This volume ended at chapter 97, so in volume 12 we'll reach 100 chapters!

We've actually already reached it in the pages of *Shonen Jump*, and chapter 100 being that specific story is all due to Shirai Sensei's calculation.

See you again soon!

KAIU SHIRAI

Writer Shirai's personal highlights for *The Promised Neverland* fanatics, part 8!

1. Leuvis is the fifth son of a demon king.

2. For page 104, Demizu Sensei drew a different version just in case. (But we went with the original despite the other option.)

3. Somewhere in the chapters you can find Koro Sensei. (Thank you, Matsui Sensei!)

Please enjoy this volume!

Posuka Demizu debuted as a manga artist with the 2013 *CoroCoro* series *Oreca Monster Bouken Retsuden*. A collection of illustrations, *The Art of Posuka Demizu,* was released in 2016 by PIE International.

Kaiu Shirai debuted in 2015 with *Ashley Gate no Yukue* on the *Shonen Jump+* website. Shirai first worked with Posuka Demizu on the two-shot *Poppy no Negai*, which was released in February 2016.

THE PROMISED NEVERLAND

VOLUME 11
SHONEN JUMP Manga Edition

STORY BY KAIU SHIRAI
ART BY POSUKA DEMIZU

Translation/Satsuki Yamashita
Touch-Up Art & Lettering/Mark McMurray
Design/Julian [JR] Robinson
Editor/Alexis Kirsch

YAKUSOKU NO NEVERLAND © 2016 by Kaiu Shirai, Posuka Demizu
All rights reserved.
First published in Japan in 2016 by SHUEISHA Inc., Tokyo.
English translation rights arranged by SHUEISHA Inc.

Printed in the U.S.A.

Published by VIZ Media, LLC
P.O. Box 77010
San Francisco, CA 94107

10 9 8 7 6 5 4 3 2 1
First printing, August 2019

VIZ MEDIA
viz.com

PARENTAL ADVISORY
THE PROMISED NEVERLAND is rated T+ and is recommended for ages 16 and up. This volume contains fantasy violence and adult themes.

RATED T+ OLDER TEEN ratings.viz.com

SHONEN JUMP
shonenjump.com

THE PROMISED NEVERLAND

11

The End

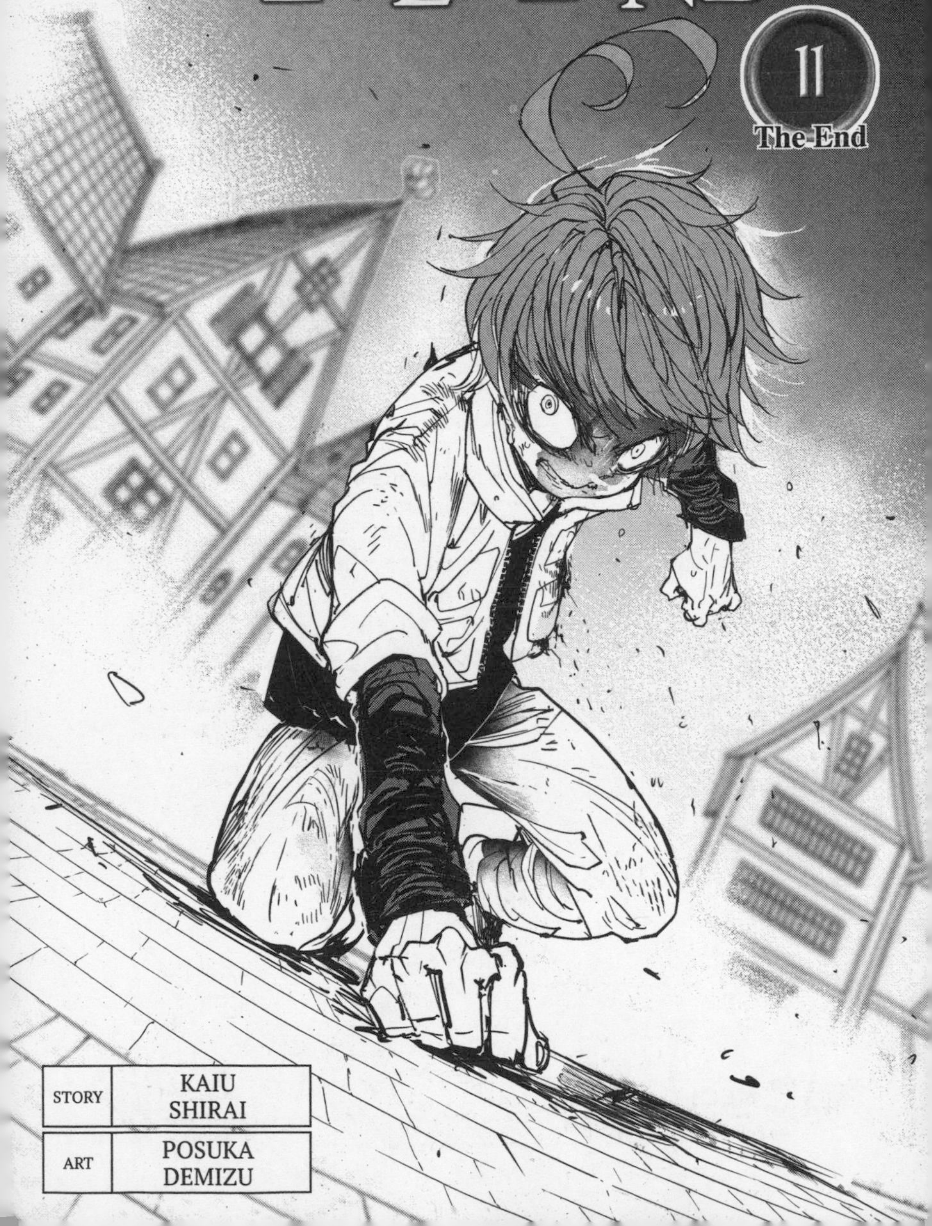

STORY	KAIU SHIRAI
ART	POSUKA DEMIZU

CHARACTERS

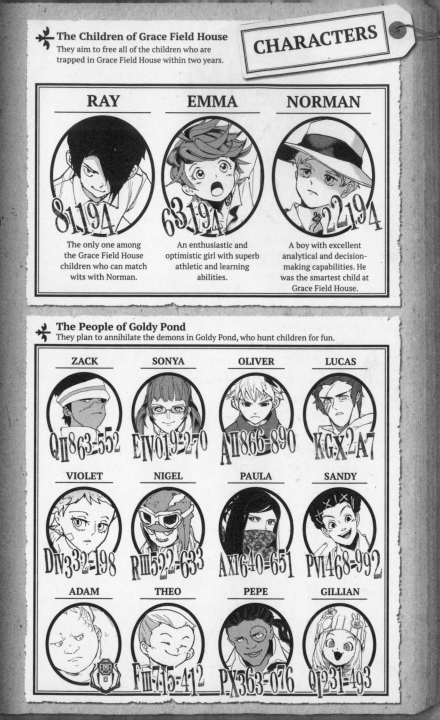

The Children of Grace Field House

They aim to free all of the children who are trapped in Grace Field House within two years.

RAY

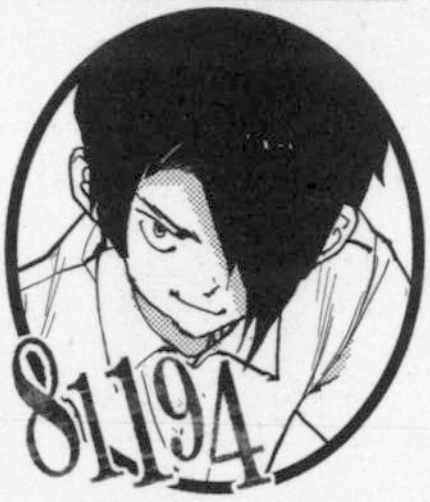
81194

The only one among the Grace Field House children who can match wits with Norman.

EMMA

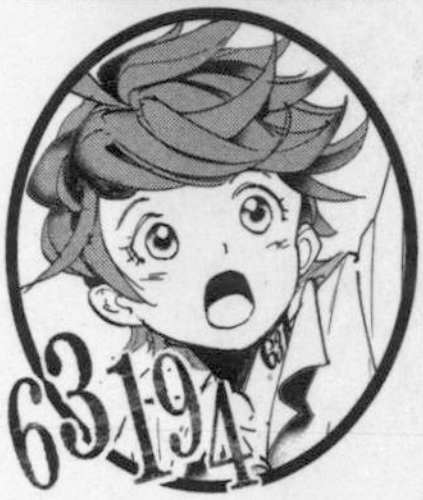
63194

An enthusiastic and optimistic girl with superb athletic and learning abilities.

NORMAN

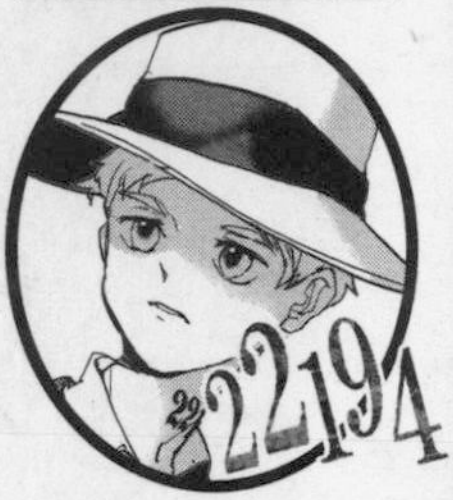
22194

A boy with excellent analytical and decision-making capabilities. He was the smartest child at Grace Field House.

The People of Goldy Pond

They plan to annihilate the demons in Goldy Pond, who hunt children for fun.

ZACK

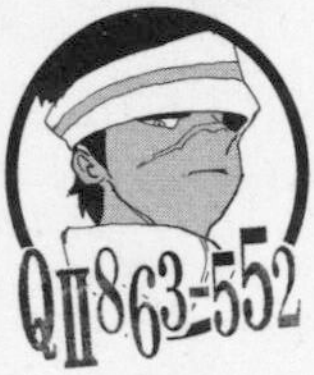
QII863-552

SONYA

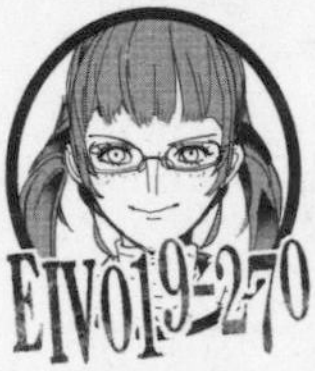
EIV019-270

OLIVER

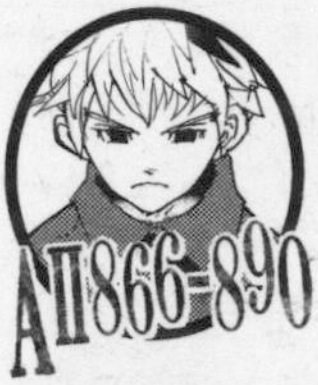
AII866-890

LUCAS

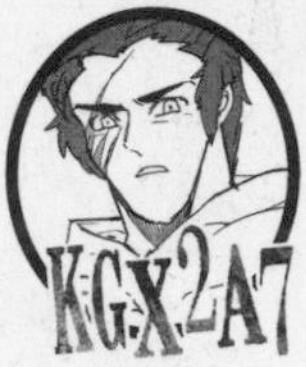
KGX2A7

VIOLET

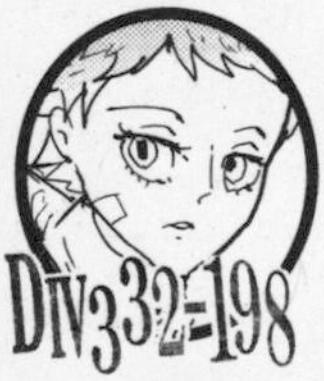
DIV332-198

NIGEL

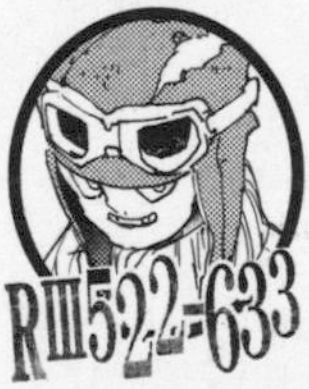
RIII522-633

PAULA

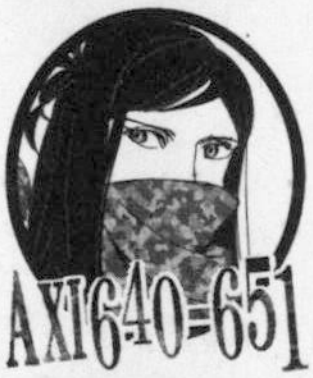
AXI640-651

SANDY

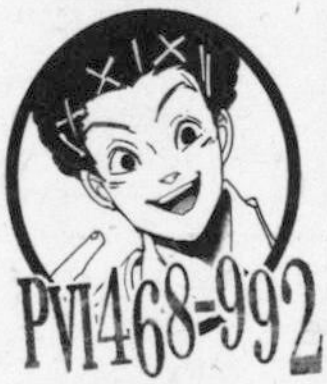
PVI468-992

ADAM

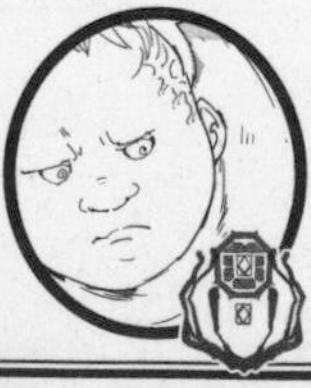

THEO

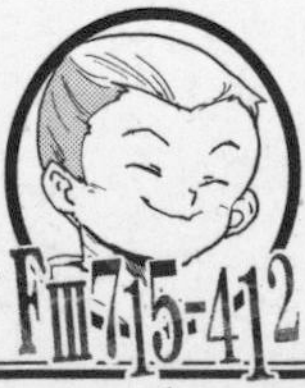
FIII715-412

PEPE

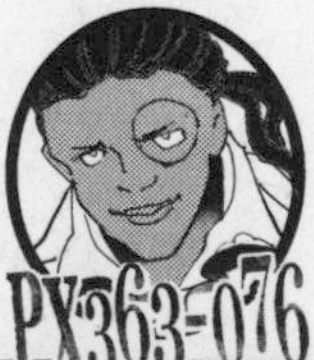
PX363-076

GILLIAN

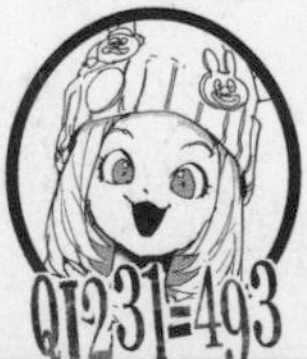
QI231-493

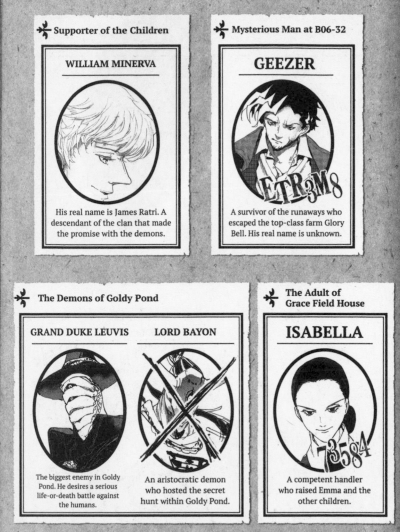

Supporter of the Children

WILLIAM MINERVA

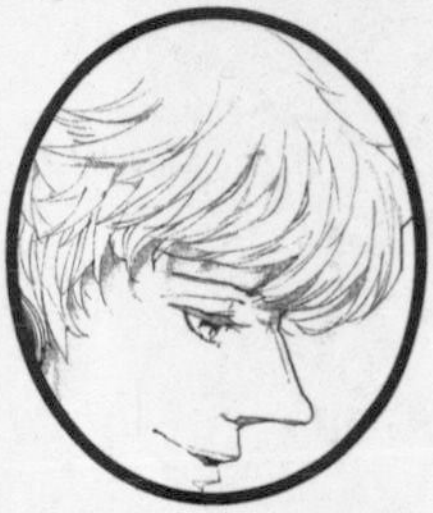

His real name is James Ratri. A descendant of the clan that made the promise with the demons.

Mysterious Man at B06-32

GEEZER

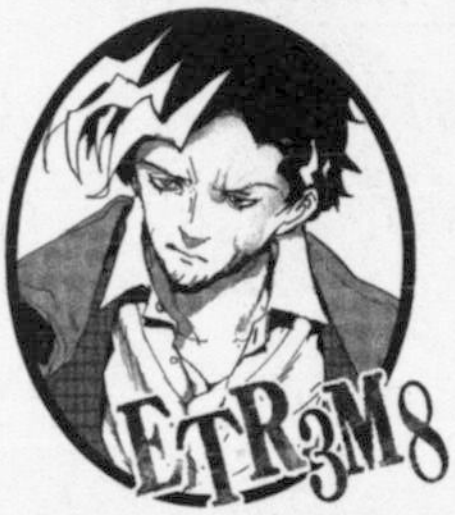
ETR3M8

A survivor of the runaways who escaped the top-class farm Glory Bell. His real name is unknown.

The Demons of Goldy Pond

GRAND DUKE LEUVIS

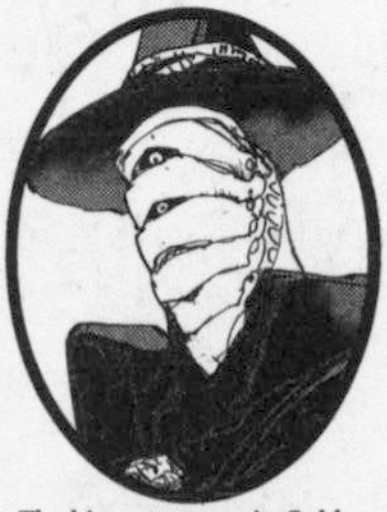

The biggest enemy in Goldy Pond. He desires a serious life-or-death battle against the humans.

LORD BAYON

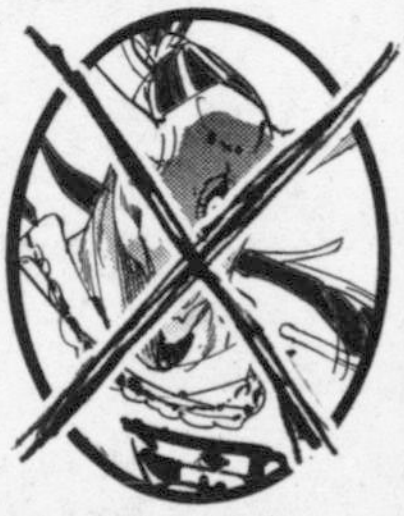

An aristocratic demon who hosted the secret hunt within Goldy Pond.

The Adult of Grace Field House

ISABELLA

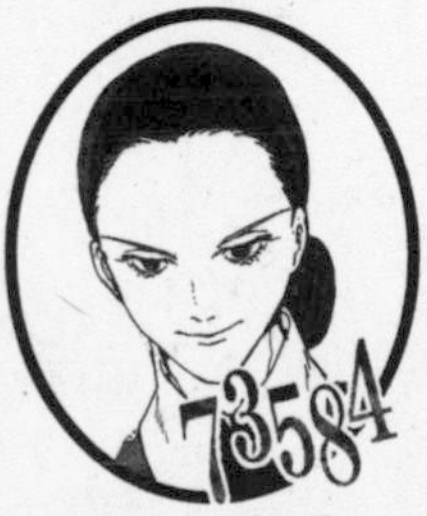
73584

A competent handler who raised Emma and the other children.

The Story So Far

Emma is living happily at Grace Field House with her foster siblings. One day, she realizes that they are being bred as food for demons and decides to escape with a group of other children. At a safe shelter, she meets a man who guides her and Ray to Goldy Pond, a location Minerva indicated in a letter. But Emma is kidnapped on the way and suddenly finds herself inside Goldy Pond. There, she meets other humans who are planning to destroy the demons that hunt them. Unforeseen circumstances force the humans to change their plans, but they're able to work together to defeat the demons one by one. With Ray and the man joining the fight, Emma faces the final enemy, Leuvis!

THE PROMISED NEVERLAND 11

The End

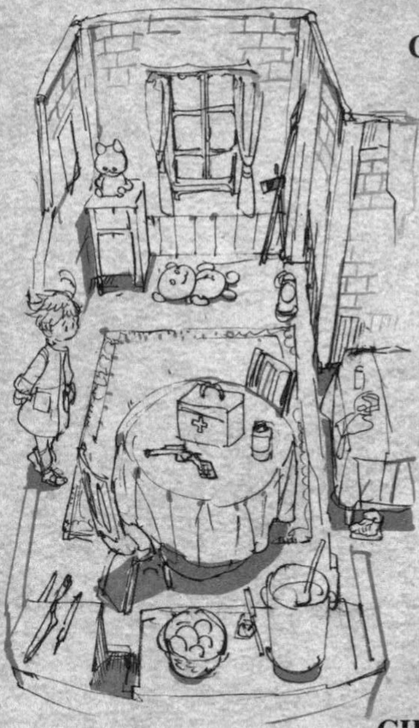

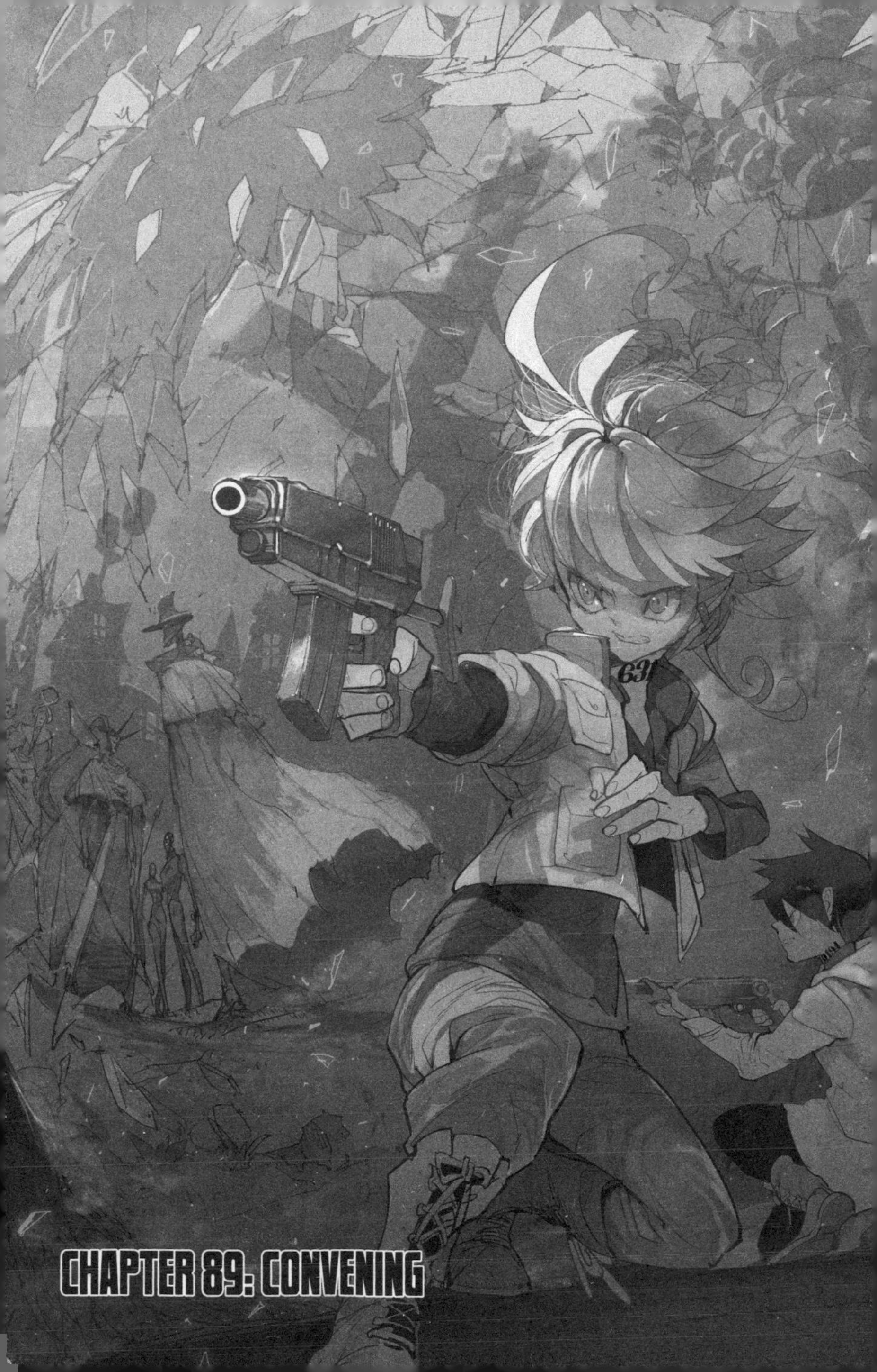
CHAPTER 89: CONVENING

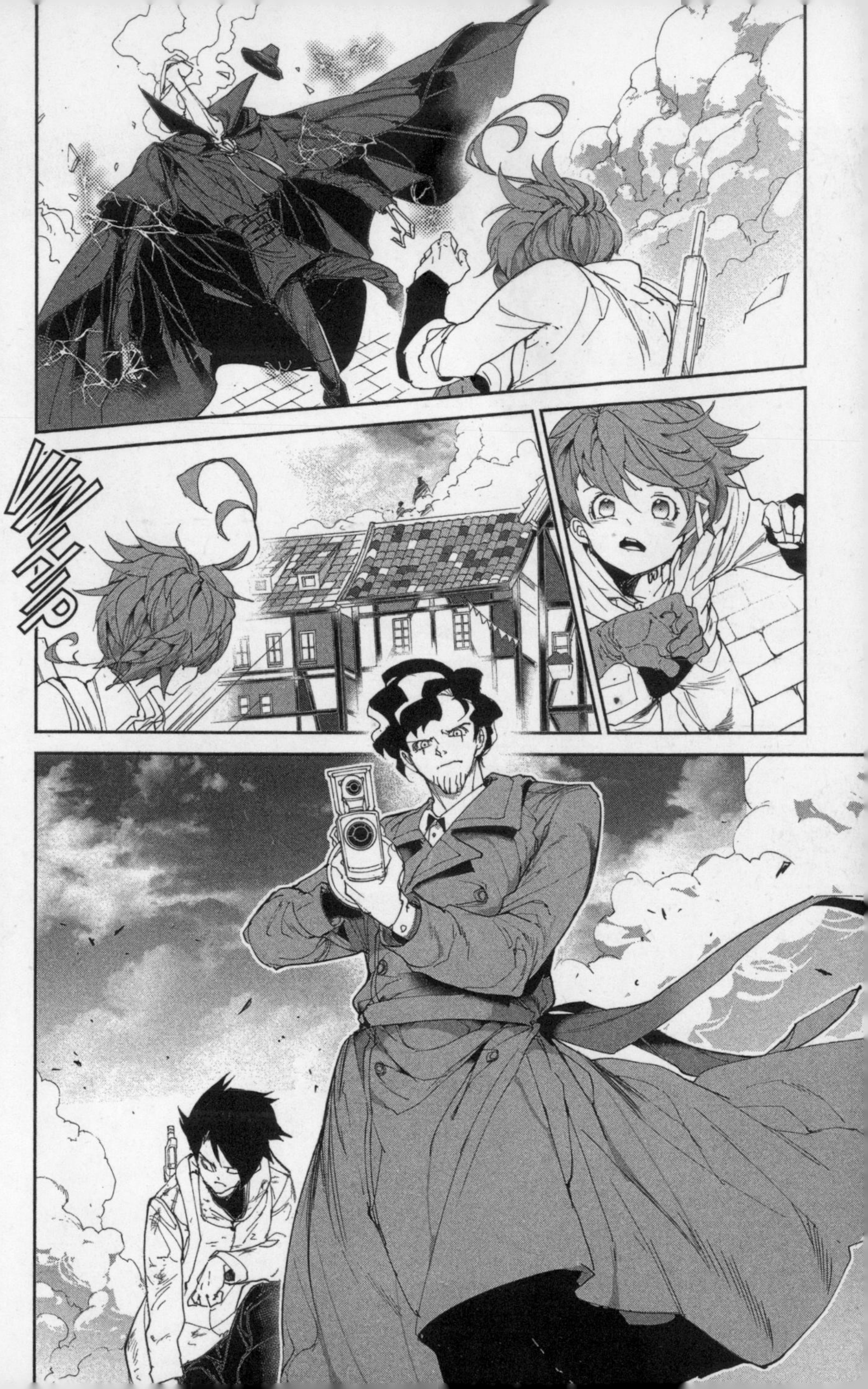
WHIP

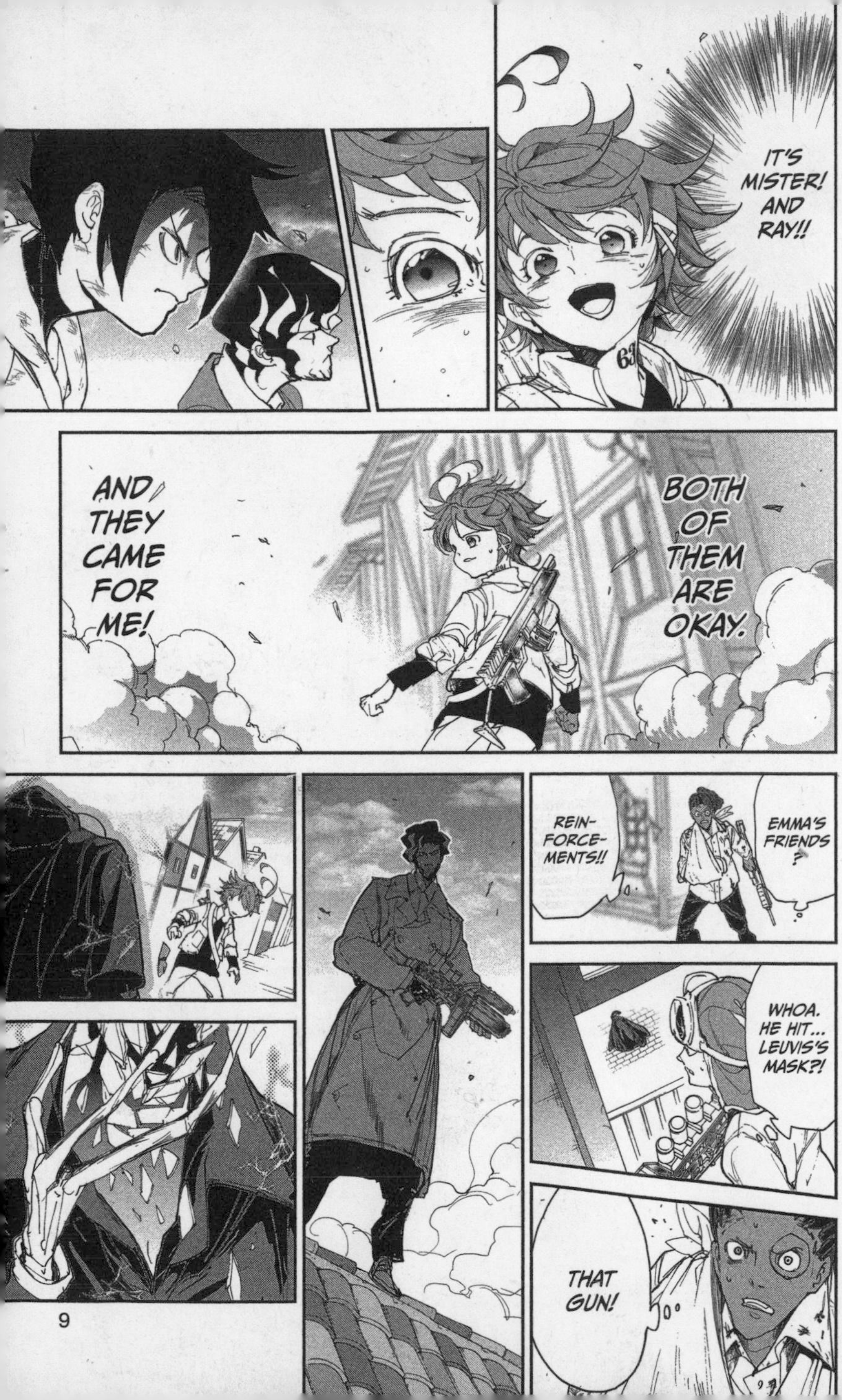
IT'S MISTER! AND RAY!!
BOTH OF THEM ARE OKAY.
AND THEY CAME FOR ME!
EMMA'S FRIENDS?
REIN-FORCE-MENTS!!
WHOA. HE HIT... LEUVIS'S MASK?!
THAT GUN!

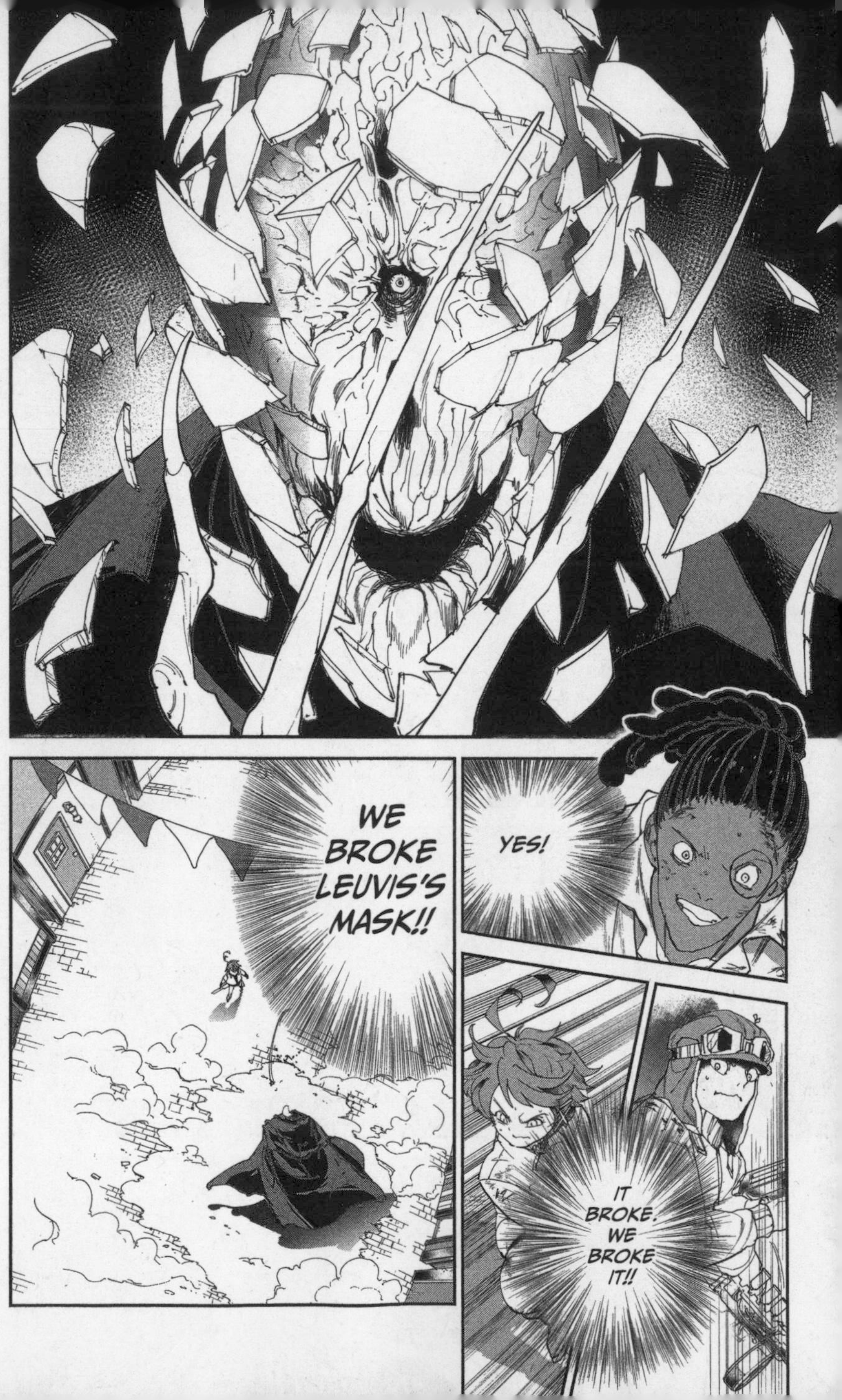
YES!
IT BROKE. WE BROKE IT!!
WE BROKE LEUVIS'S MASK!!

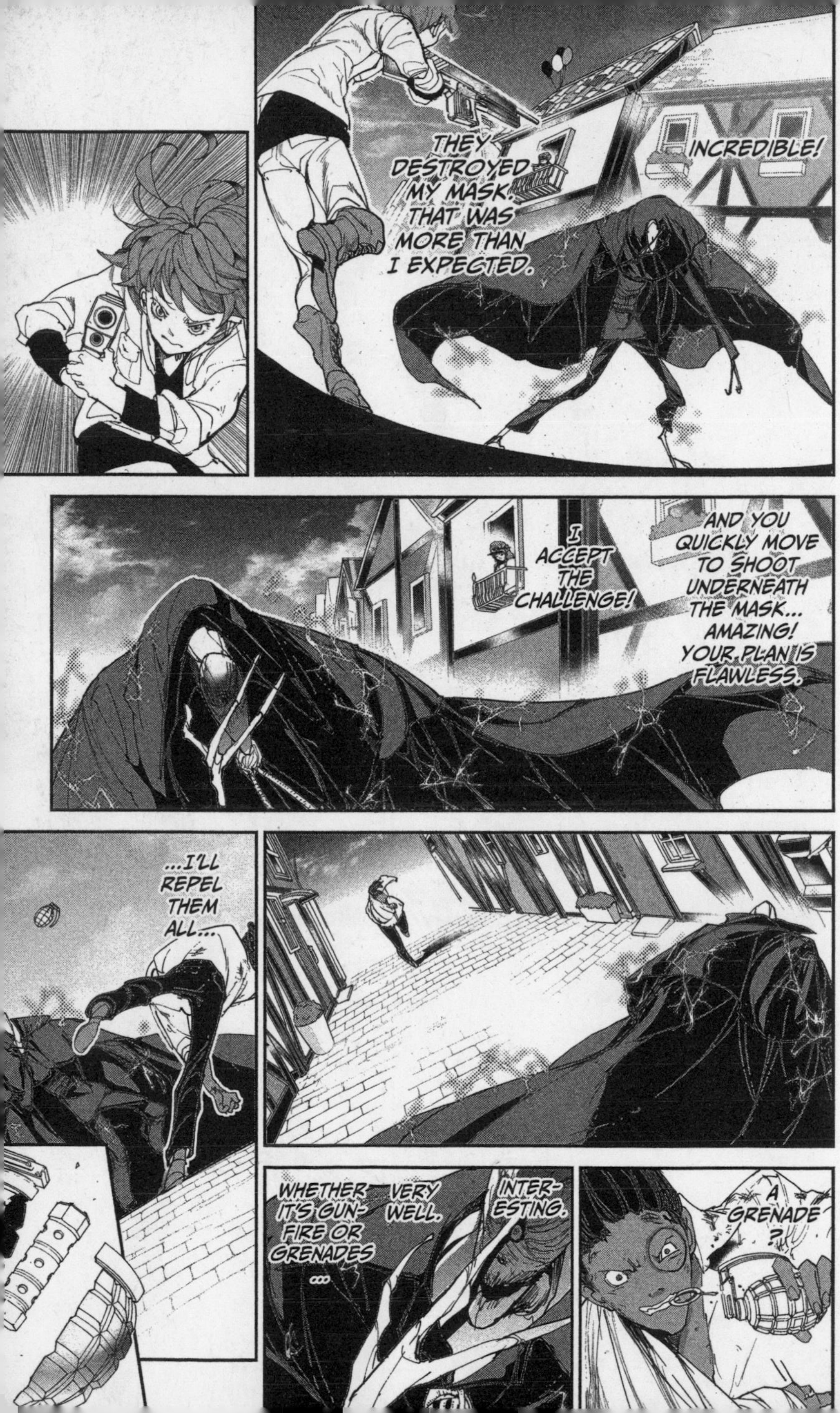
INCREDIBLE!
THEY DESTROYED MY MASK. THAT WAS MORE THAN I EXPECTED.
AND YOU QUICKLY MOVE TO SHOOT UNDERNEATH THE MASK... AMAZING! YOUR PLAN IS FLAWLESS.
I ACCEPT THE CHALLENGE!
...I'LL REPEL THEM ALL...
A GRENADE?
INTERESTING.
VERY WELL.
WHETHER IT'S GUNFIRE OR GRENADES...

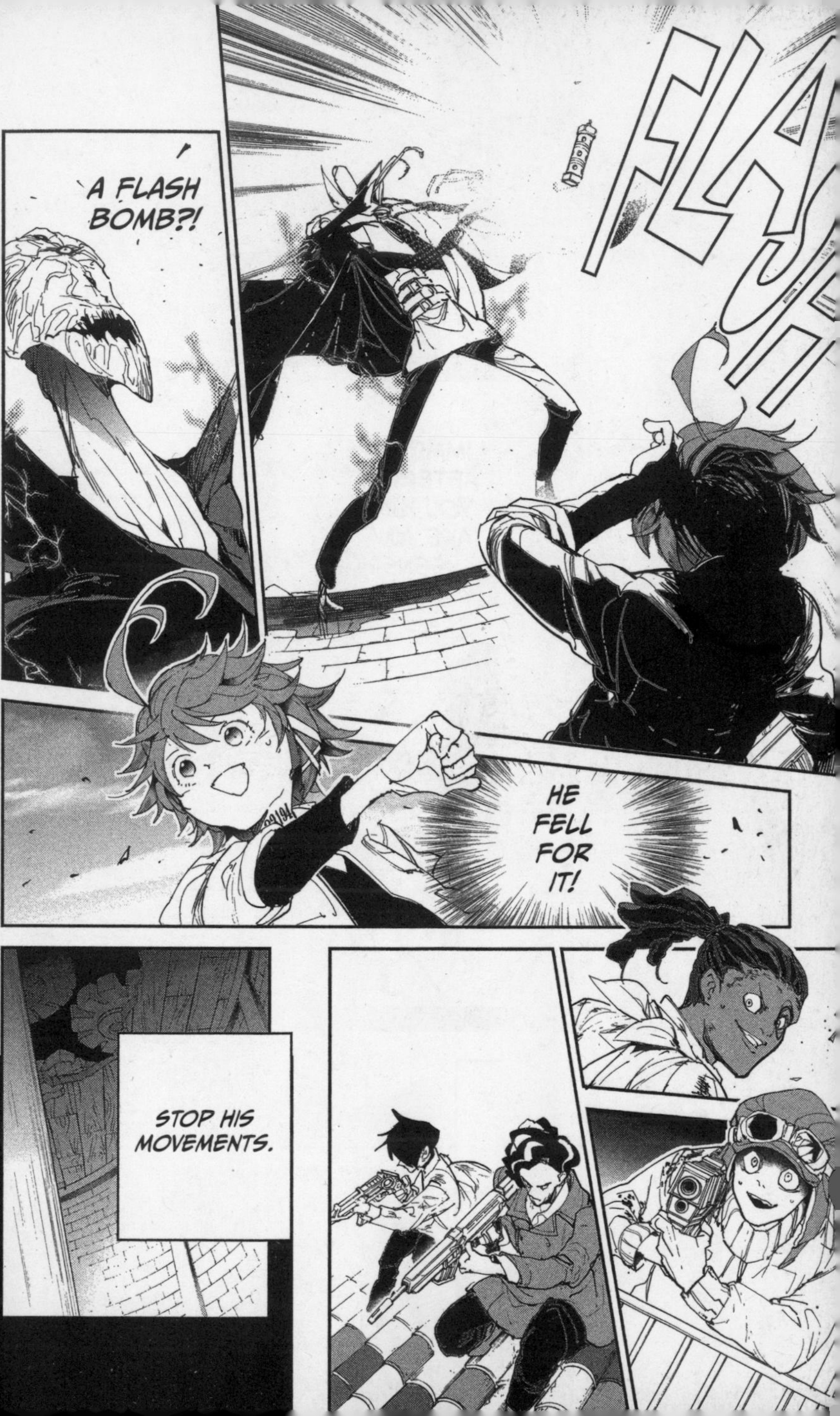
FLASH
A FLASH BOMB?!
HE FELL FOR IT!
STOP HIS MOVEMENTS.

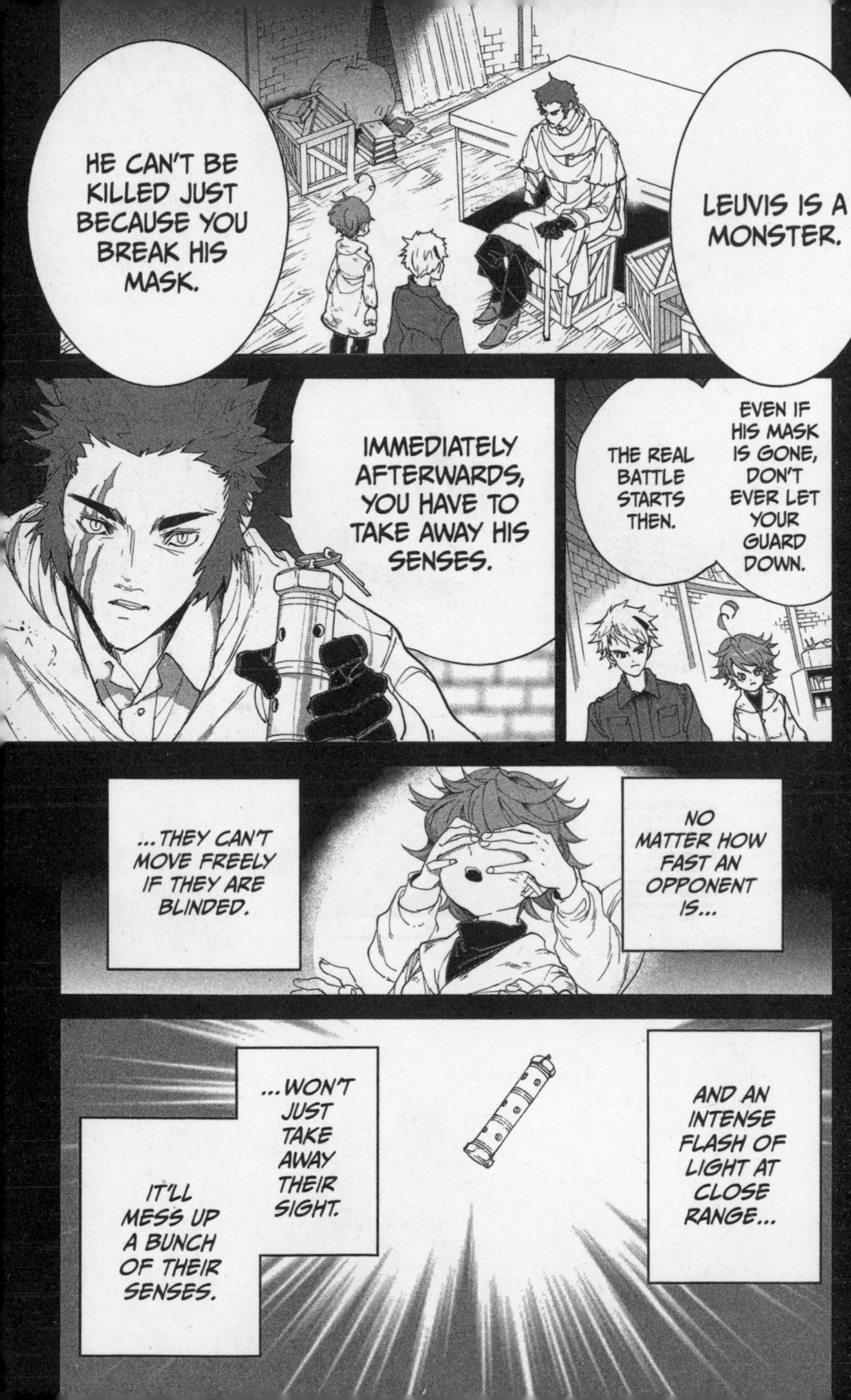
LEUVIS IS A MONSTER.
HE CAN'T BE KILLED JUST BECAUSE YOU BREAK HIS MASK.
EVEN IF HIS MASK IS GONE, DON'T EVER LET YOUR GUARD DOWN.
THE REAL BATTLE STARTS THEN.
IMMEDIATELY AFTERWARDS, YOU HAVE TO TAKE AWAY HIS SENSES.
NO MATTER HOW FAST AN OPPONENT IS...
...THEY CAN'T MOVE FREELY IF THEY ARE BLINDED.
AND AN INTENSE FLASH OF LIGHT AT CLOSE RANGE...
...WON'T JUST TAKE AWAY THEIR SIGHT.
IT'LL MESS UP A BUNCH OF THEIR SENSES.

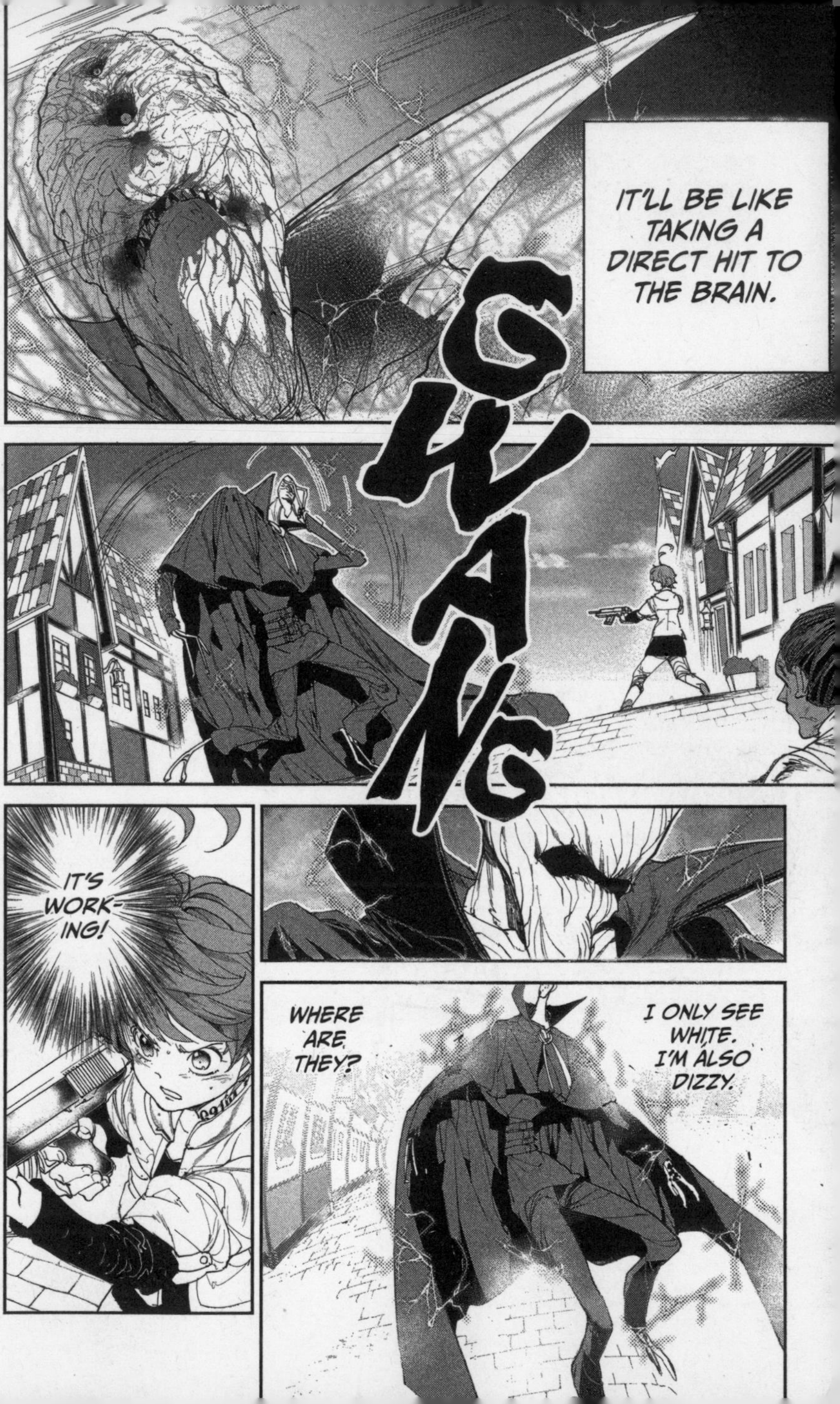
IT'LL BE LIKE TAKING A DIRECT HIT TO THE BRAIN.
GWANG
I ONLY SEE WHITE. I'M ALSO DIZZY.
WHERE ARE THEY?
IT'S WORK-ING!

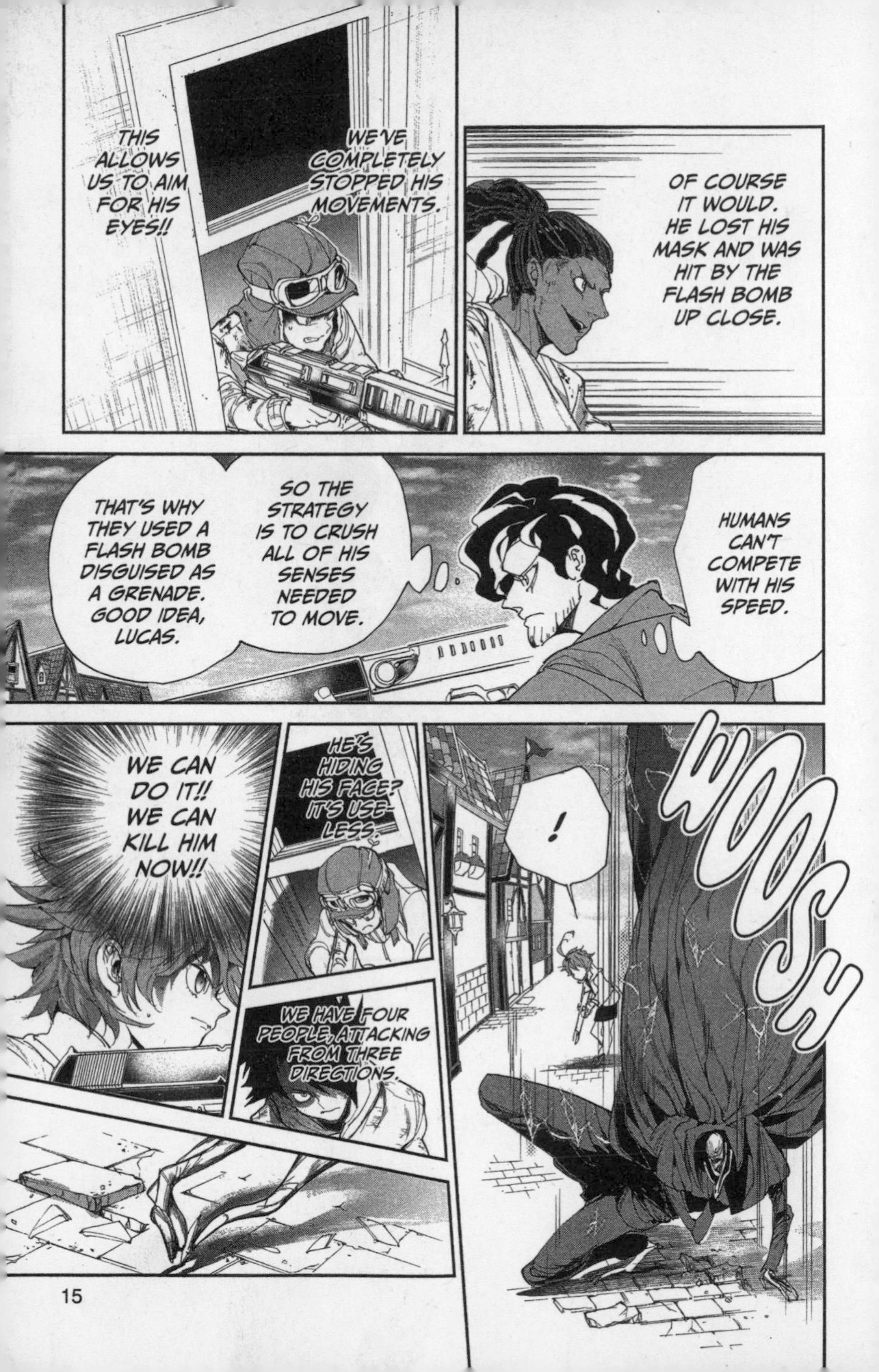
OF COURSE IT WOULD. HE LOST HIS MASK AND WAS HIT BY THE FLASH BOMB UP CLOSE.
WE'VE COMPLETELY STOPPED HIS MOVEMENTS.
THIS ALLOWS US TO AIM FOR HIS EYES!!
HUMANS CAN'T COMPETE WITH HIS SPEED.
SO THE STRATEGY IS TO CRUSH ALL OF HIS SENSES NEEDED TO MOVE.
THAT'S WHY THEY USED A FLASH BOMB DISGUISED AS A GRENADE. GOOD IDEA, LUCAS.
WOOSH
!
HE'S HIDING HIS FACE? IT'S USELESS.
WE HAVE FOUR PEOPLE, ATTACKING FROM THREE DIRECTIONS.
WE CAN DO IT!! WE CAN KILL HIM NOW!!

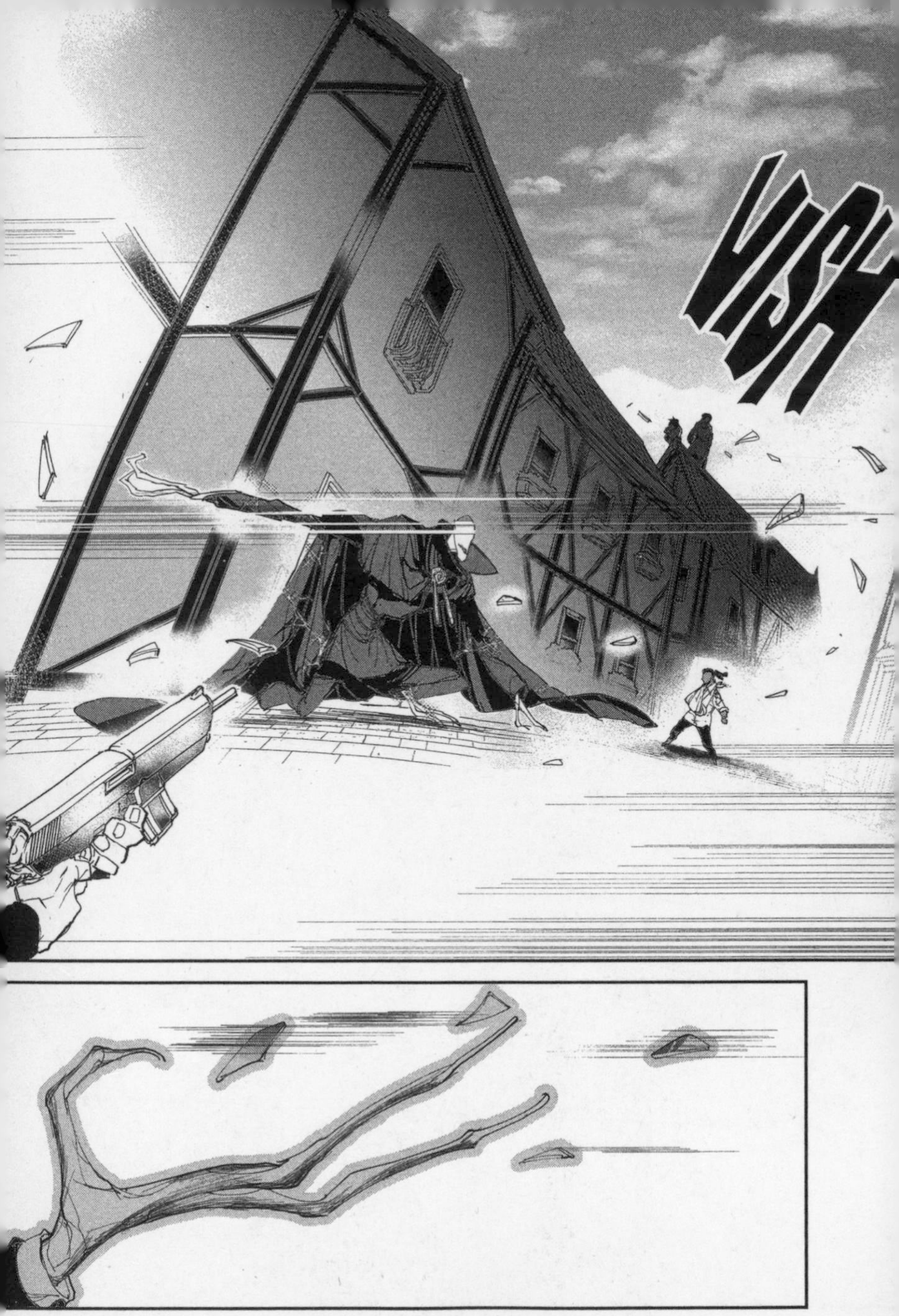
VISH

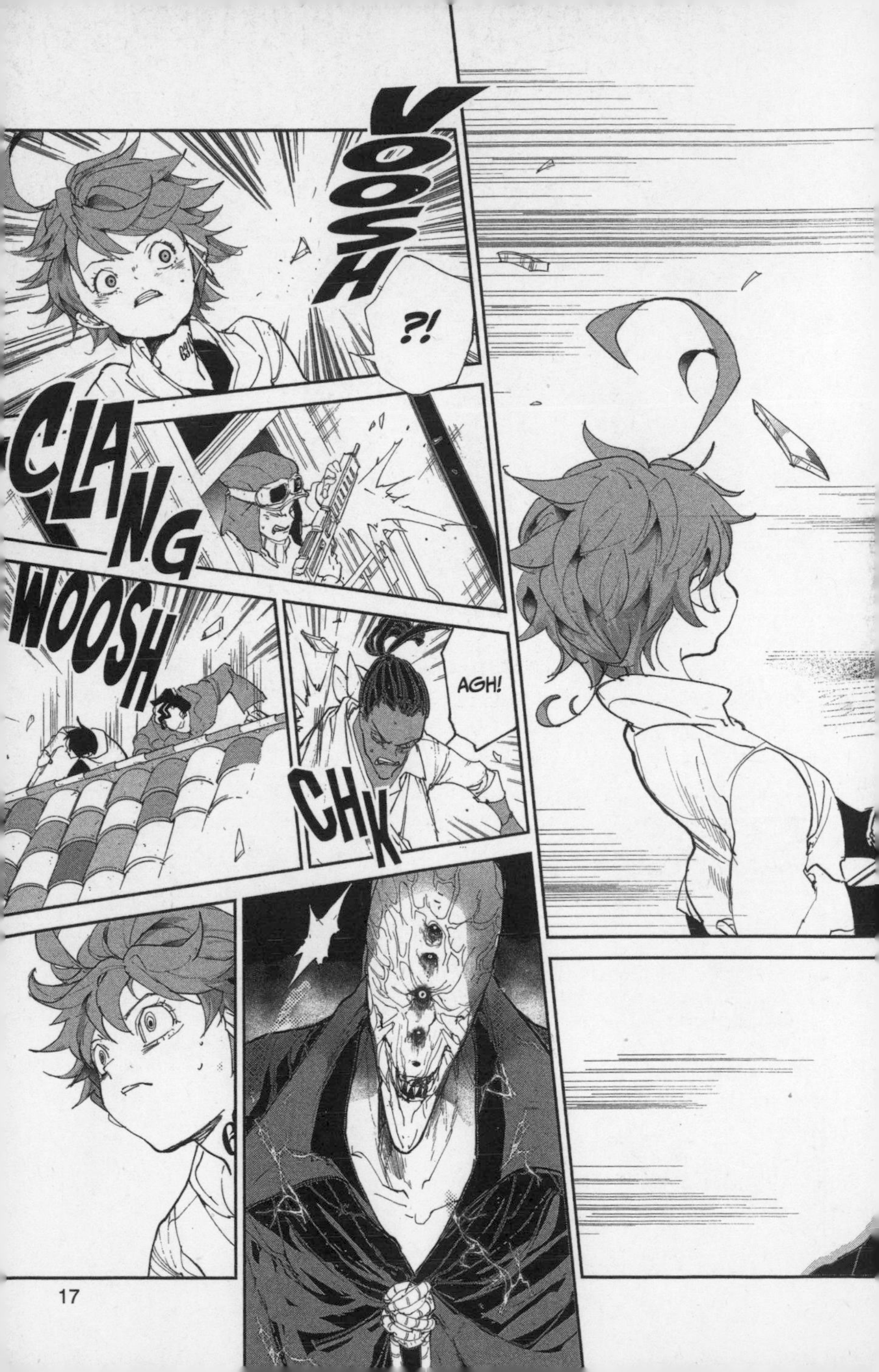
VOOSH
?!
CLANG
AGH!
CHK
WOOSH

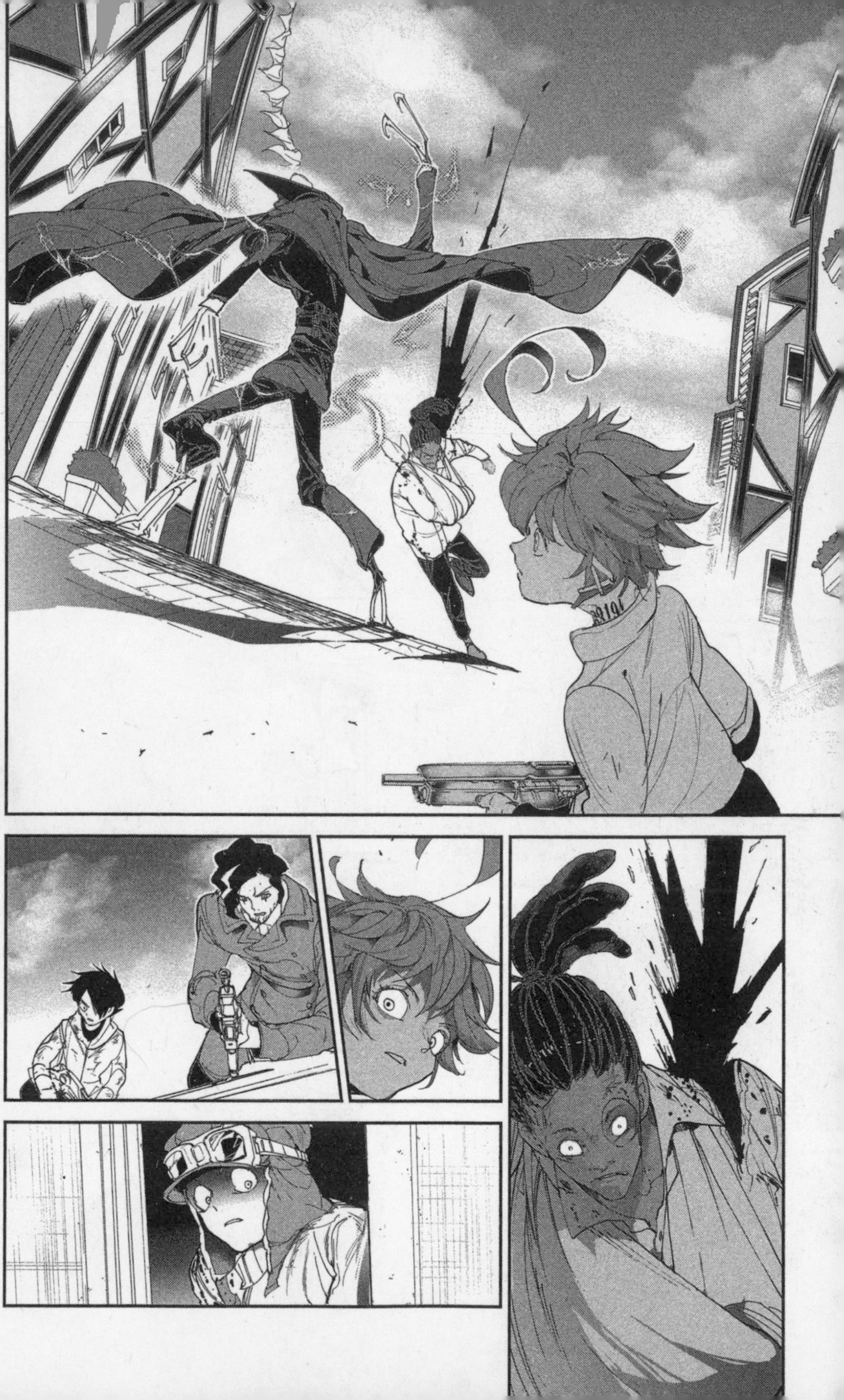

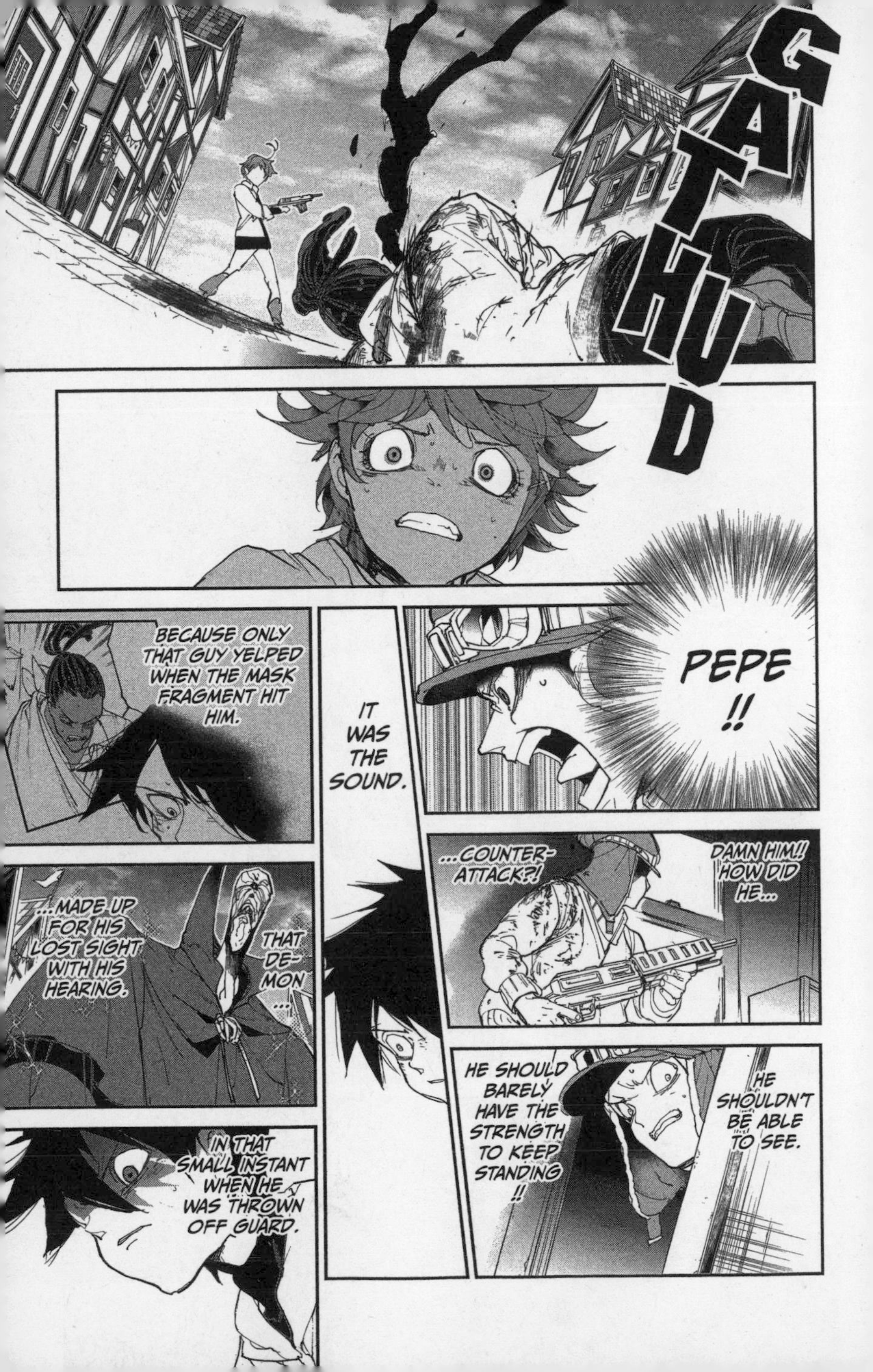
GATHUD
PEPE!!
DAMN HIM!! HOW DID HE...
...COUNTER-ATTACK?!
HE SHOULDN'T BE ABLE TO SEE.
HE SHOULD BARELY HAVE THE STRENGTH TO KEEP STANDING!!
IT WAS THE SOUND.
BECAUSE ONLY THAT GUY YELPED WHEN THE MASK FRAGMENT HIT HIM.
THAT DEMON...
...MADE UP FOR HIS LOST SIGHT WITH HIS HEARING.
IN THAT SMALL INSTANT WHEN HE WAS THROWN OFF GUARD.

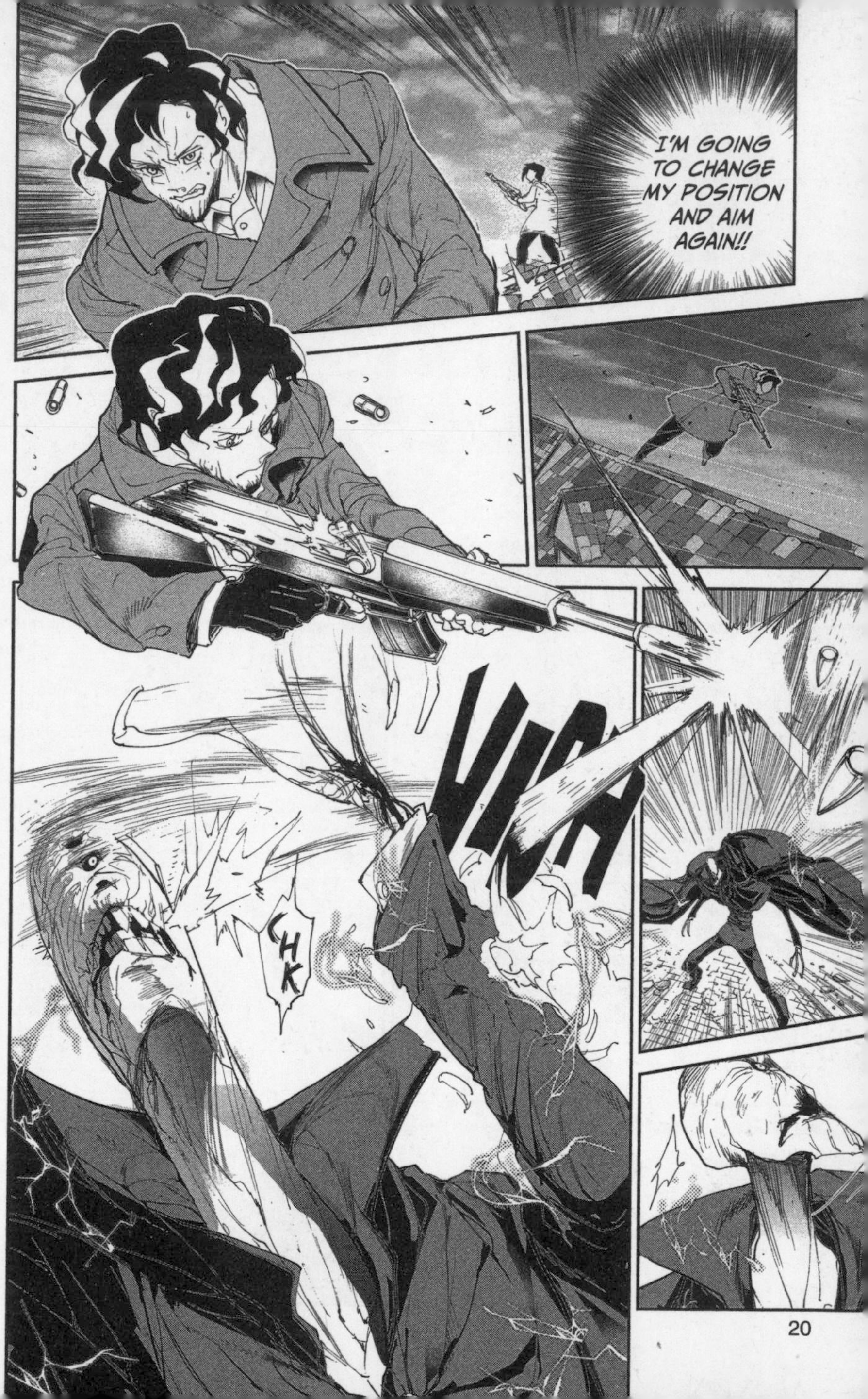
I'M GOING TO CHANGE MY POSITION AND AIM AGAIN!!
CHK

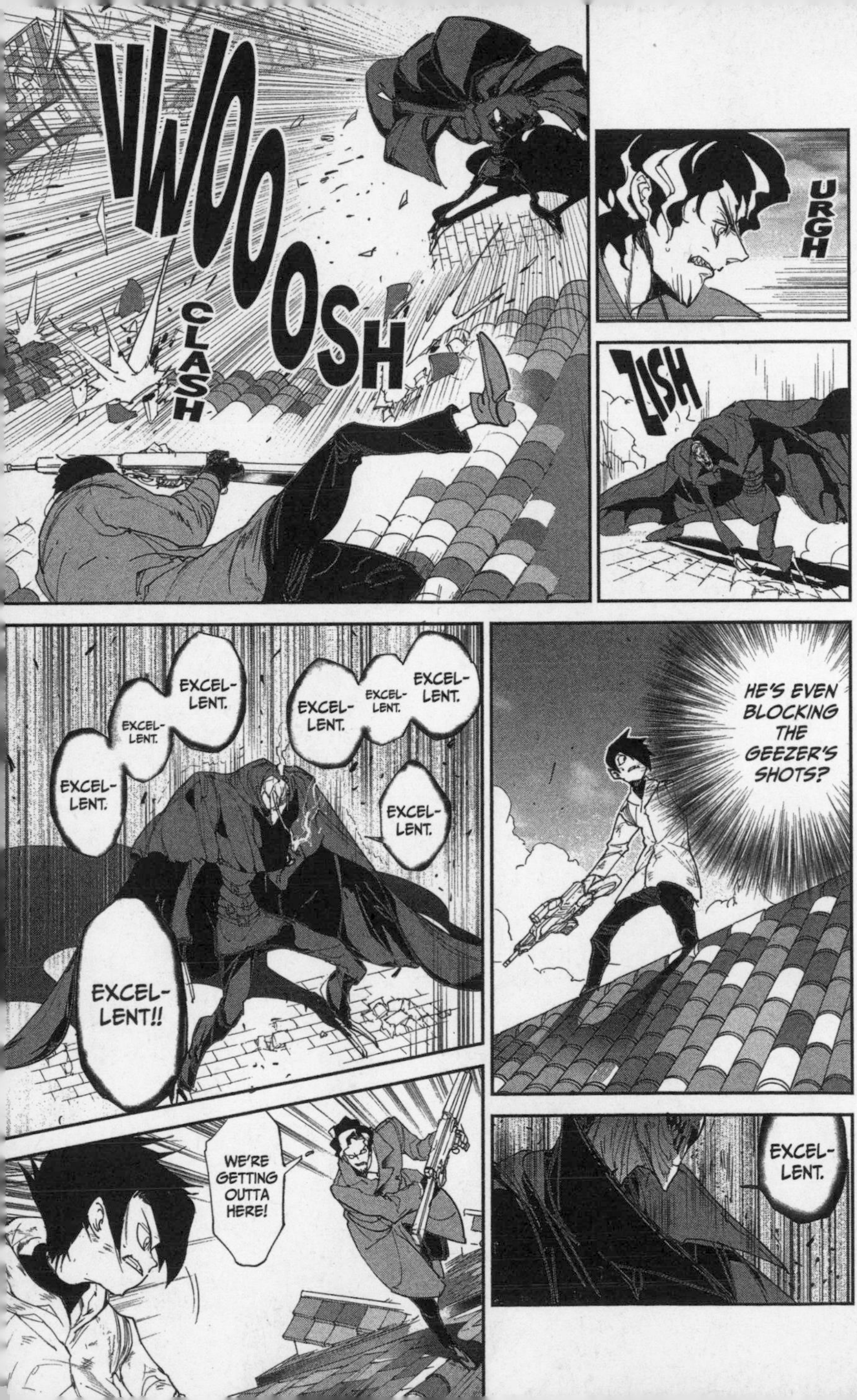
URGH
ZISH
VWOOOSH
CLASH
HE'S EVEN BLOCKING THE GEEZER'S SHOTS?
EXCEL-LENT.
EXCEL-LENT.
EXCEL-LENT.
EXCEL-LENT.
EXCEL-LENT.
EXCEL-LENT.
EXCEL-LENT.
EXCEL-LENT.
EXCEL-LENT!!
WE'RE GETTING OUTTA HERE!

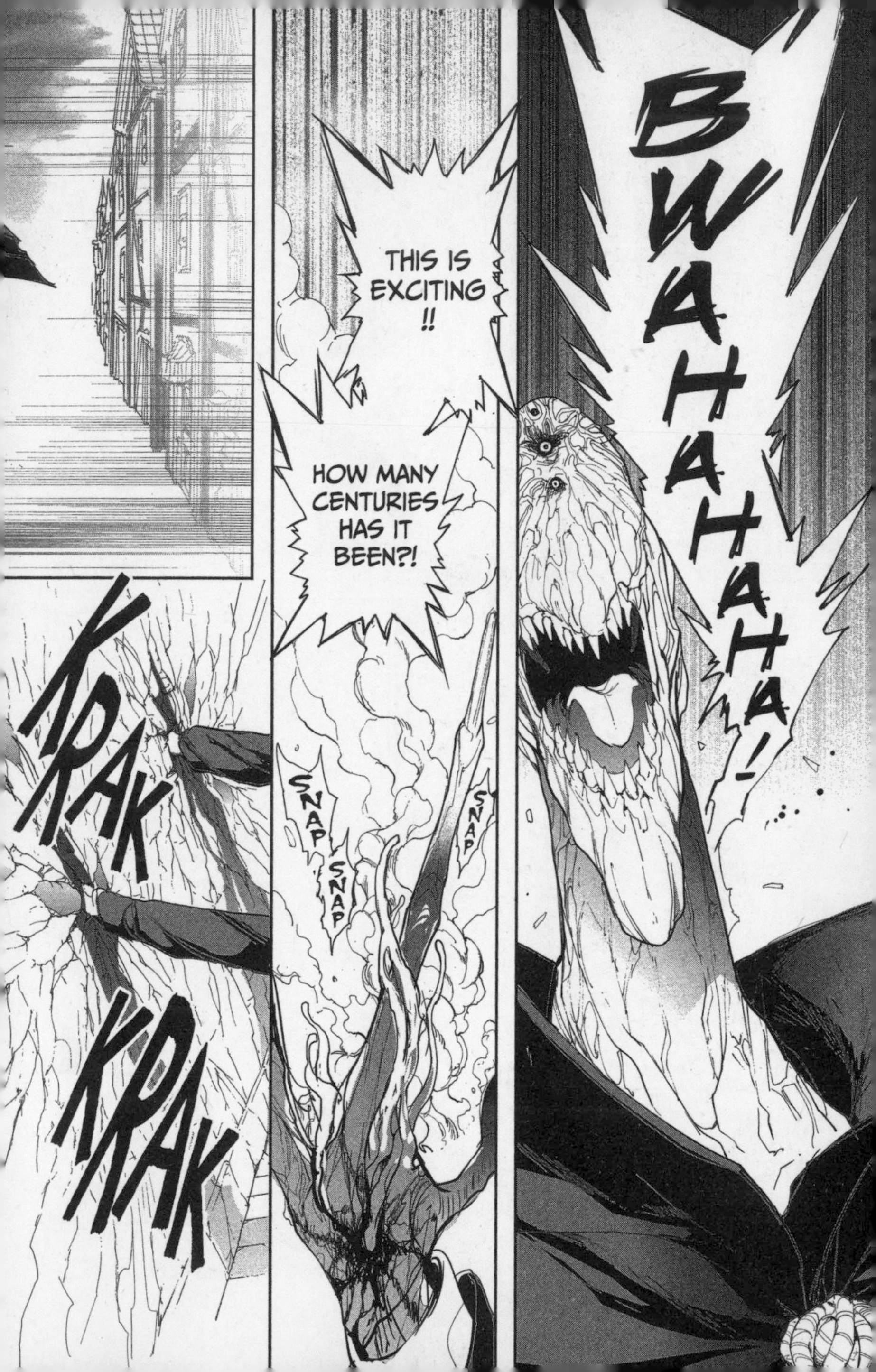
BWAHAHAHA!
THIS IS EXCITING!!
HOW MANY CENTURIES HAS IT BEEN?!
SNAP
SNAP
SNAP
KRAK
KRAK

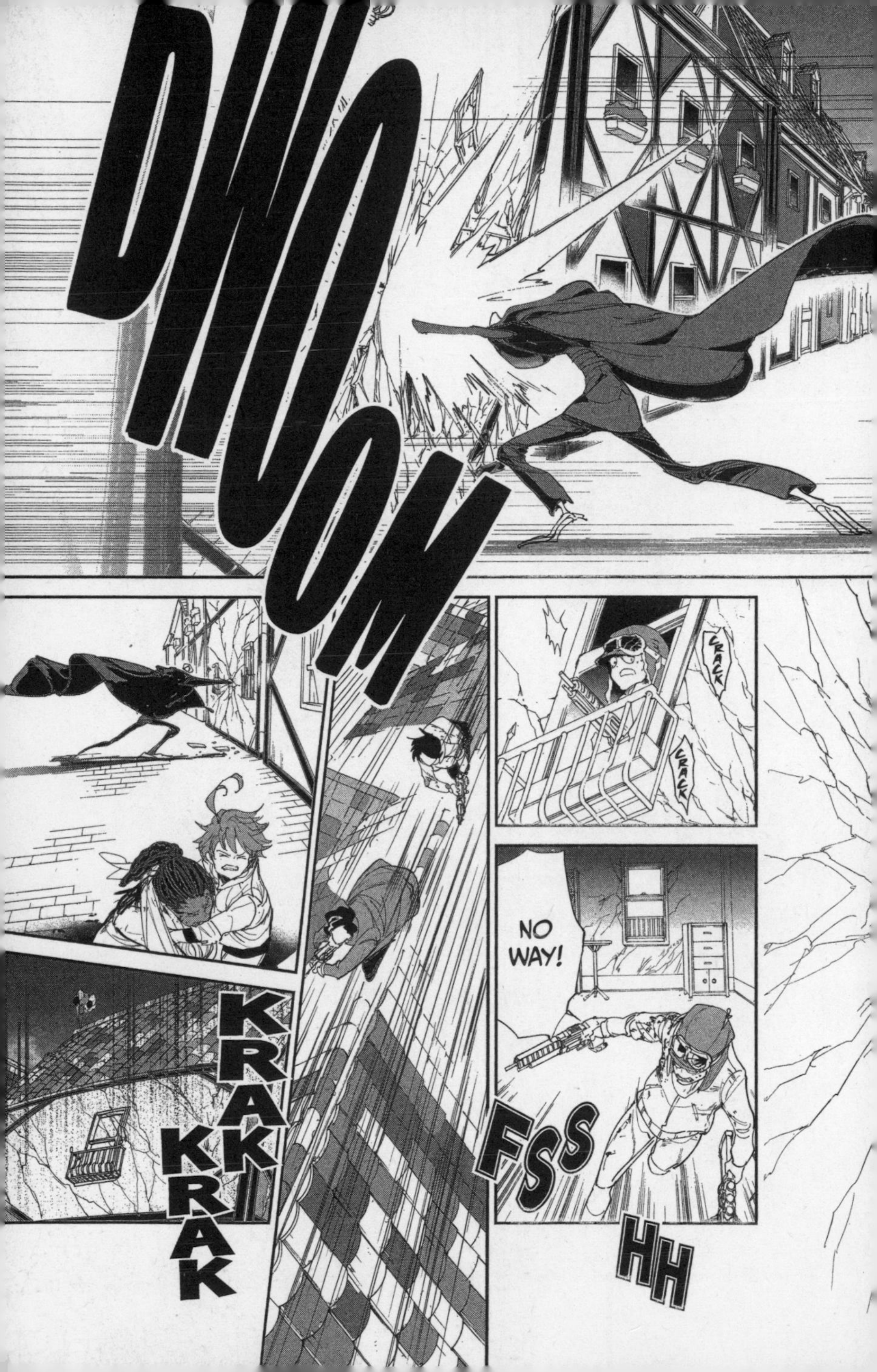
DHOOOM
CRACK
CRACK
NO WAY!
FSSHH
KRAK
KRAK

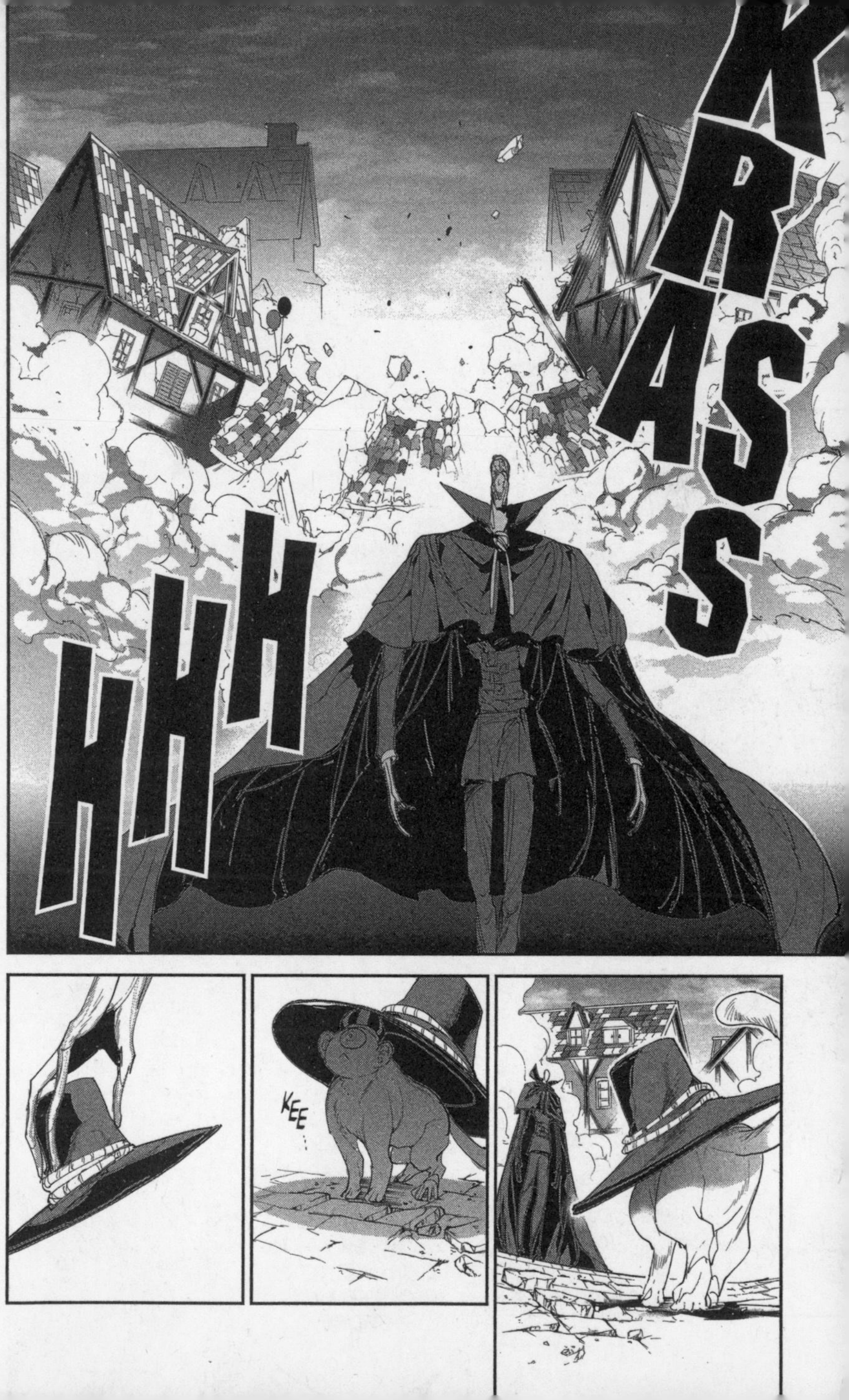
KRASS
HHHH
KEE...

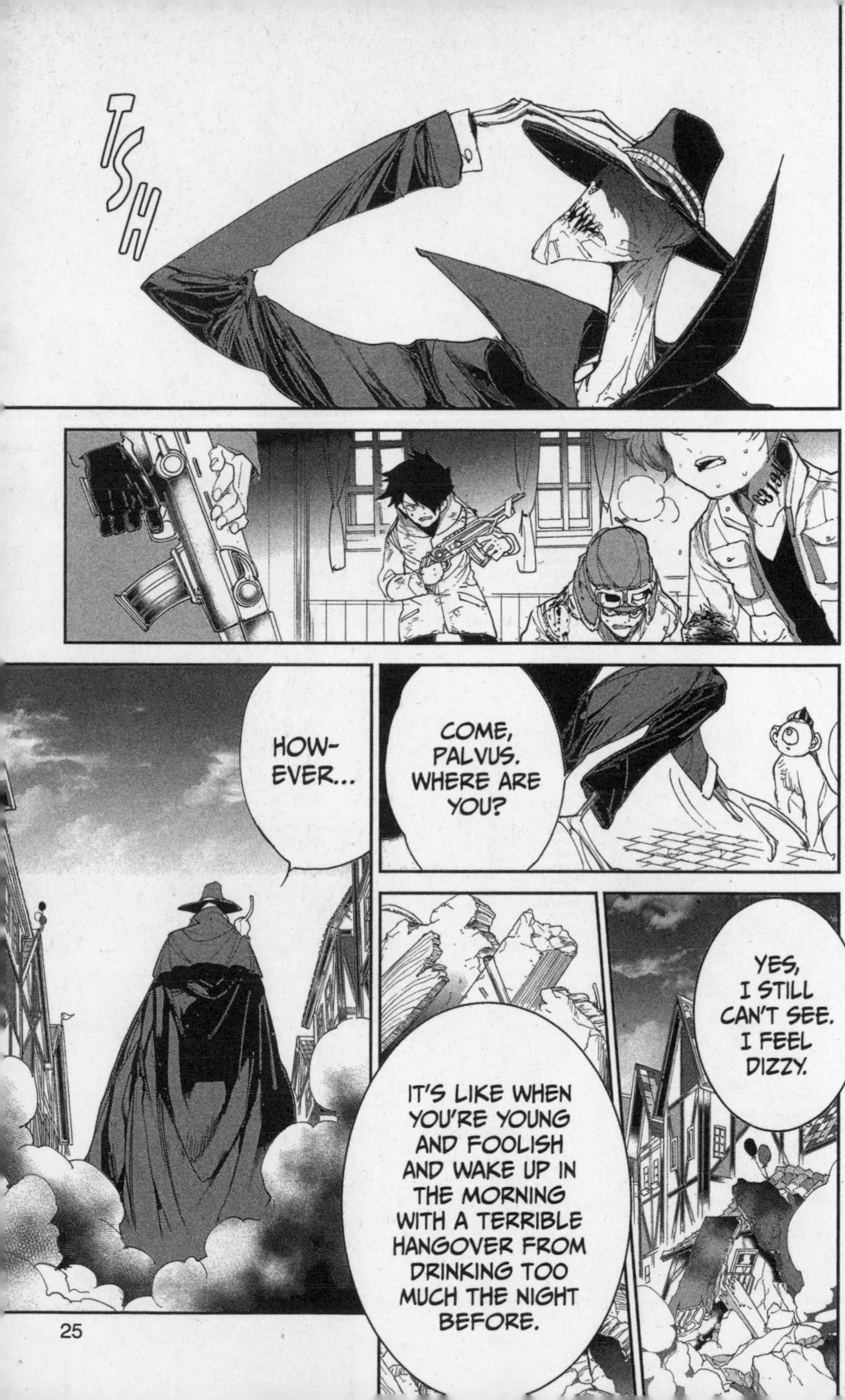
TSH
COME, PALVUS. WHERE ARE YOU?
YES, I STILL CAN'T SEE. I FEEL DIZZY.
IT'S LIKE WHEN YOU'RE YOUNG AND FOOLISH AND WAKE UP IN THE MORNING WITH A TERRIBLE HANGOVER FROM DRINKING TOO MUCH THE NIGHT BEFORE.
HOW-EVER...

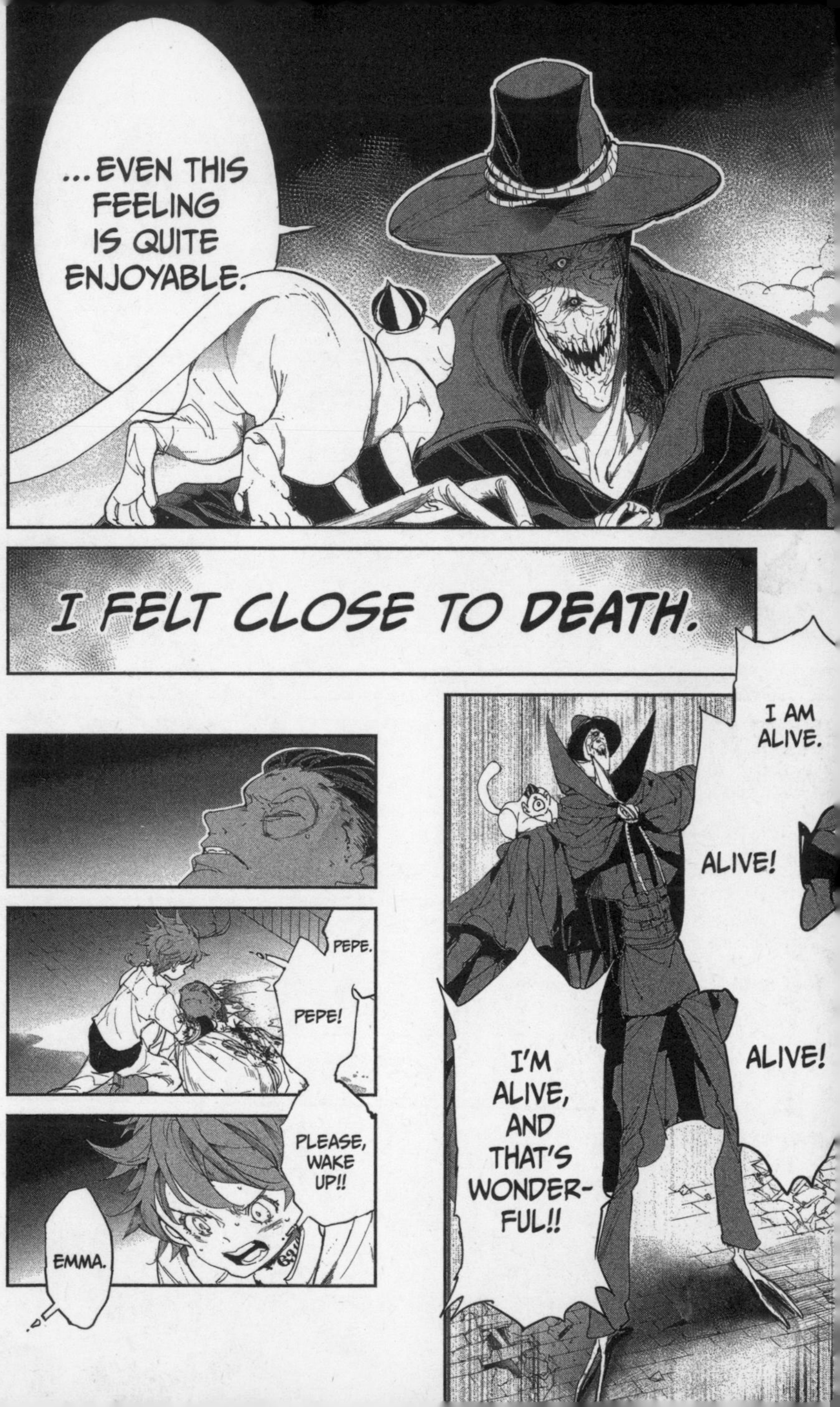
...EVEN THIS FEELING IS QUITE ENJOYABLE.
I FELT CLOSE TO DEATH.
I AM ALIVE.
ALIVE!
ALIVE!
I'M ALIVE, AND THAT'S WONDERFUL!!
PEPE.
PEPE!
PLEASE, WAKE UP!!
EMMA.

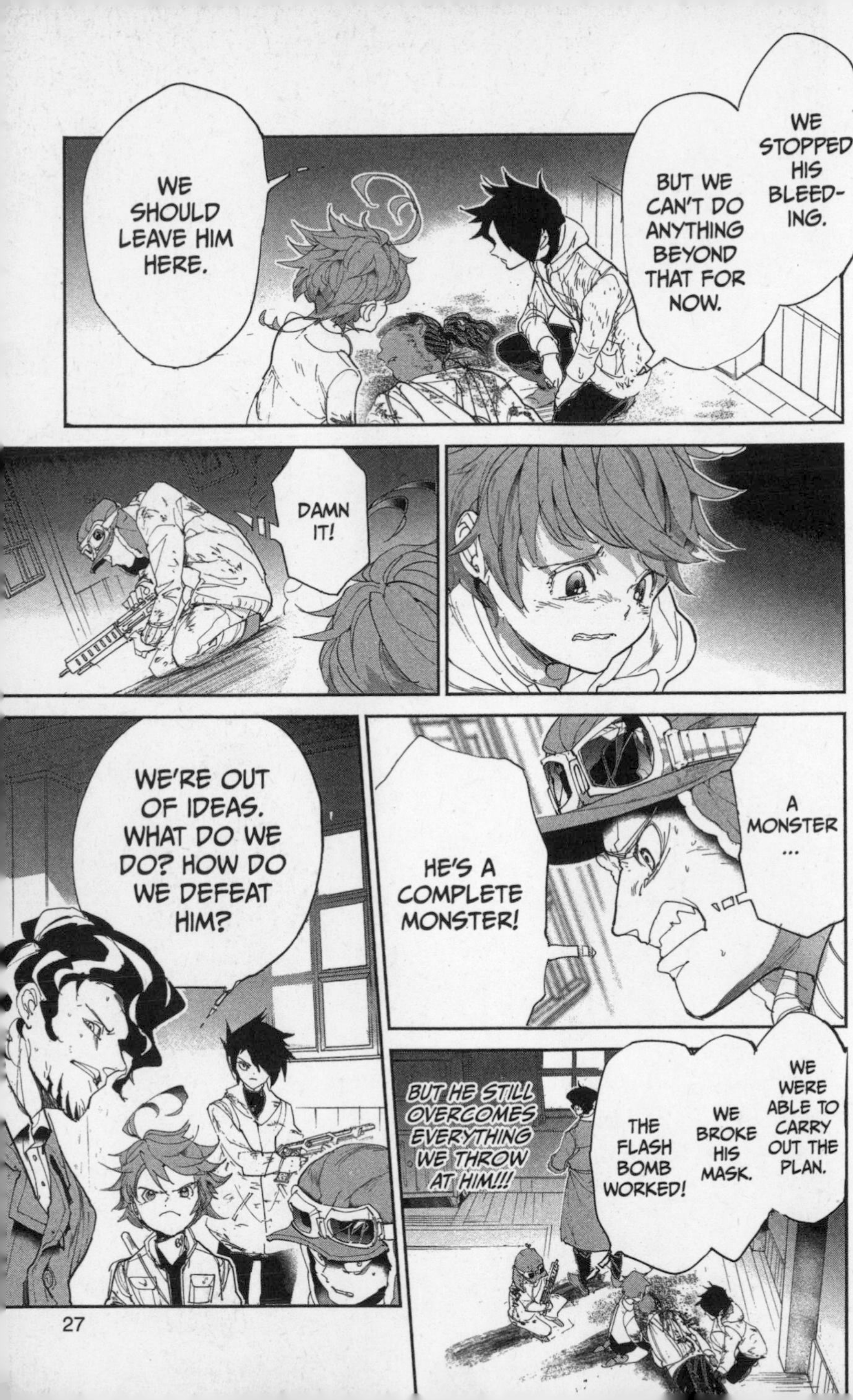
WE STOPPED HIS BLEED-ING.
BUT WE CAN'T DO ANYTHING BEYOND THAT FOR NOW.
WE SHOULD LEAVE HIM HERE.
DAMN IT!
A MONSTER...
HE'S A COMPLETE MONSTER!
WE WERE ABLE TO CARRY OUT THE PLAN.
WE BROKE HIS MASK.
THE FLASH BOMB WORKED!
BUT HE STILL OVERCOMES EVERYTHING WE THROW AT HIM!!!
WE'RE OUT OF IDEAS. WHAT DO WE DO? HOW DO WE DEFEAT HIM?

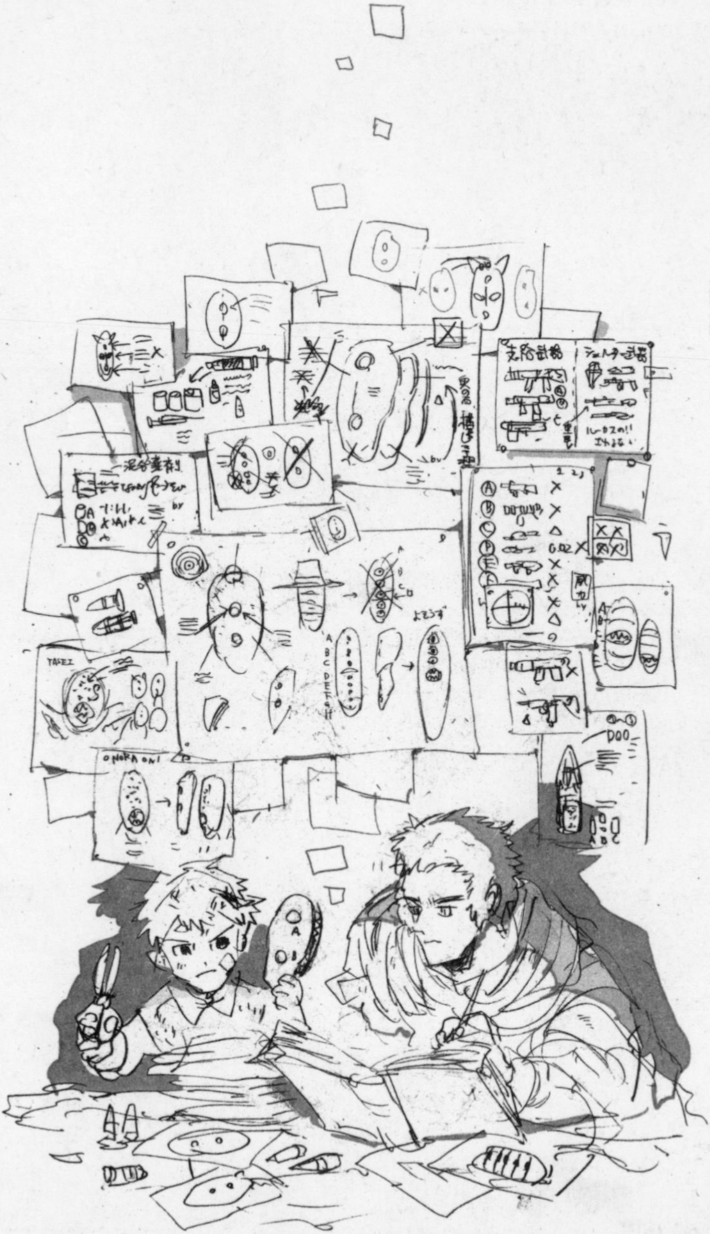

CHAPTER 90: LET'S WIN

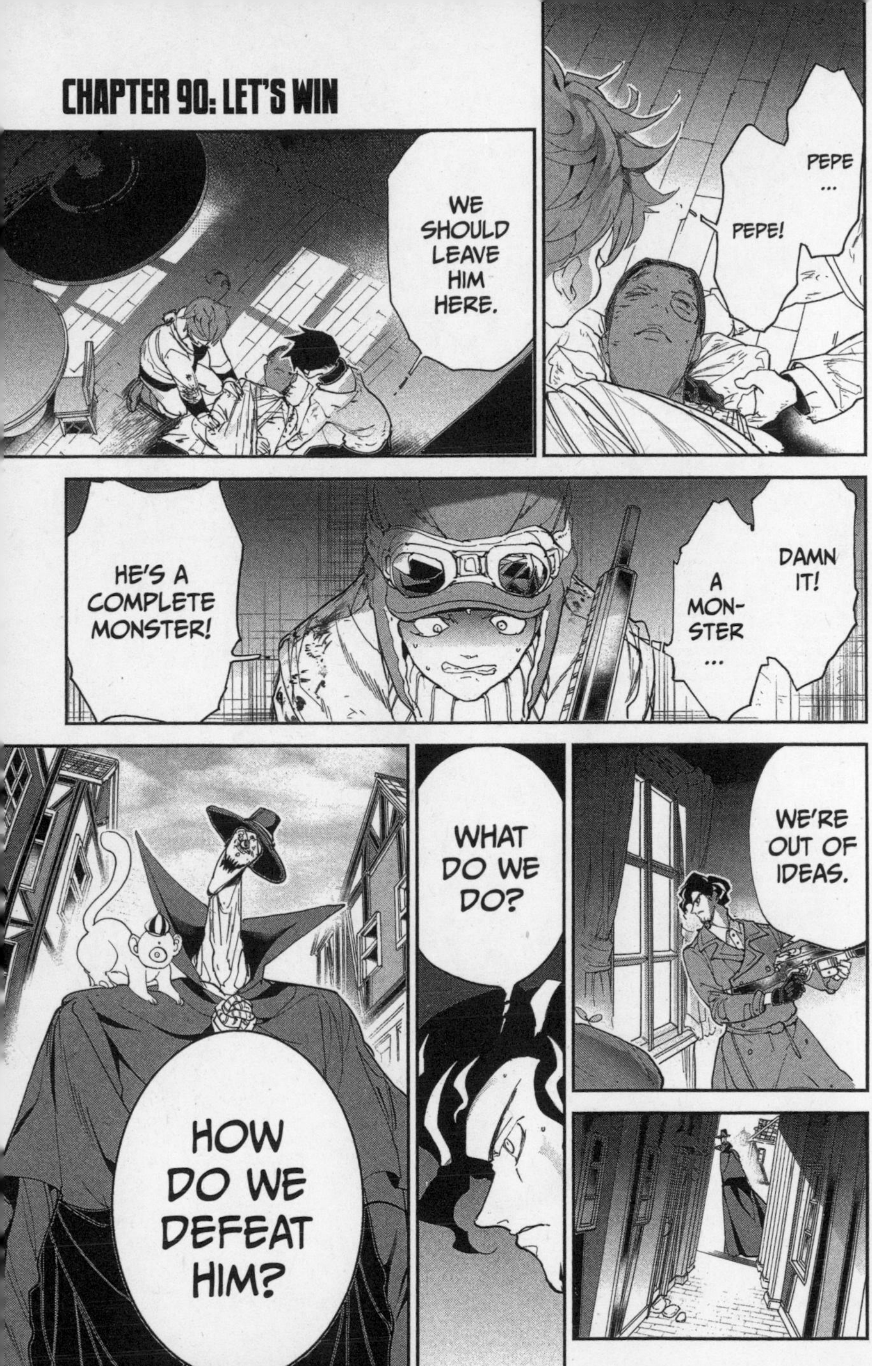

PEPE ...
PEPE!
WE SHOULD LEAVE HIM HERE.
DAMN IT!
A MON-STER ...
HE'S A COMPLETE MONSTER!
WE'RE OUT OF IDEAS.
WHAT DO WE DO?
HOW DO WE DEFEAT HIM?

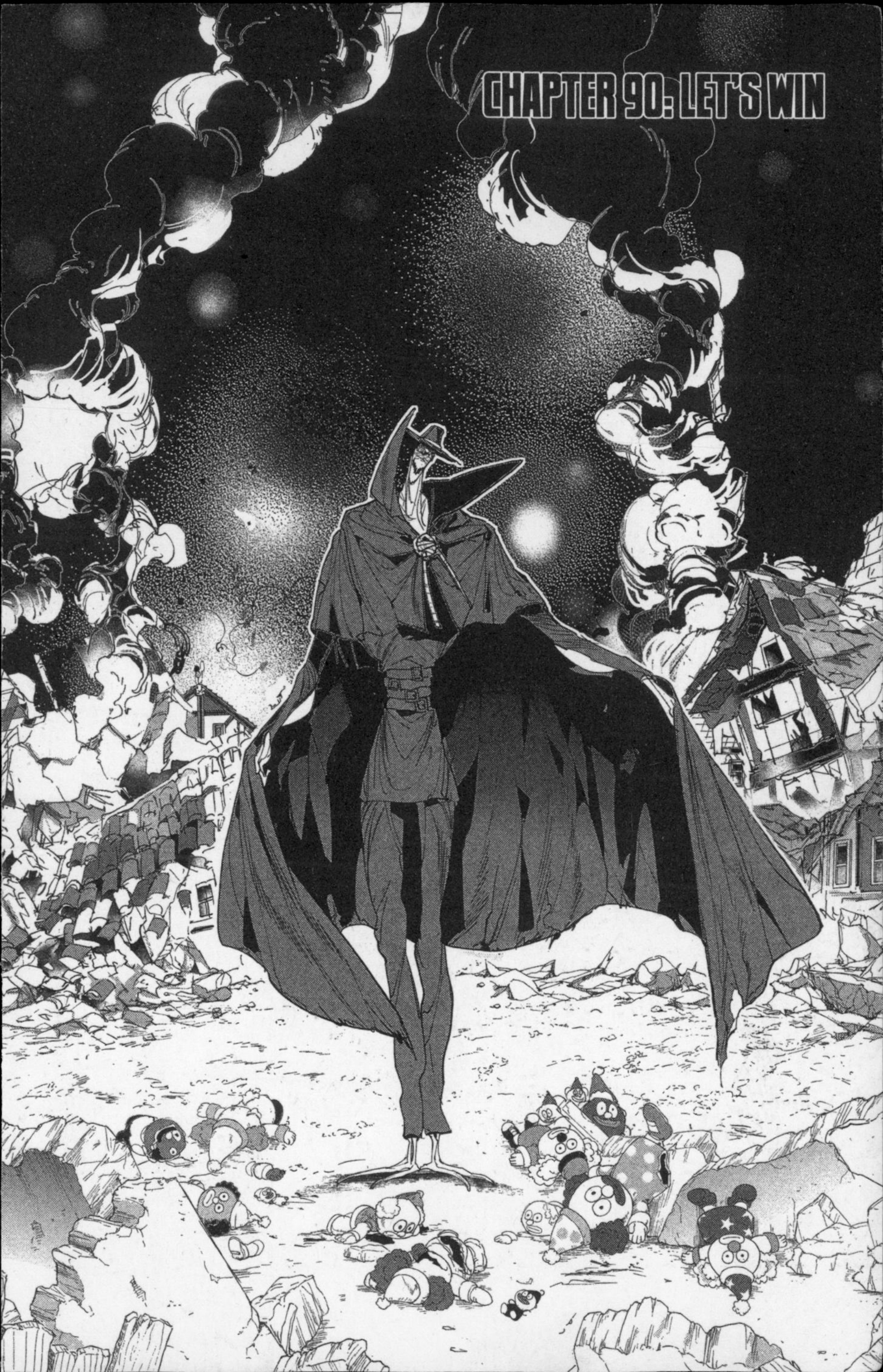
CHAPTER 90: LET'S WIN

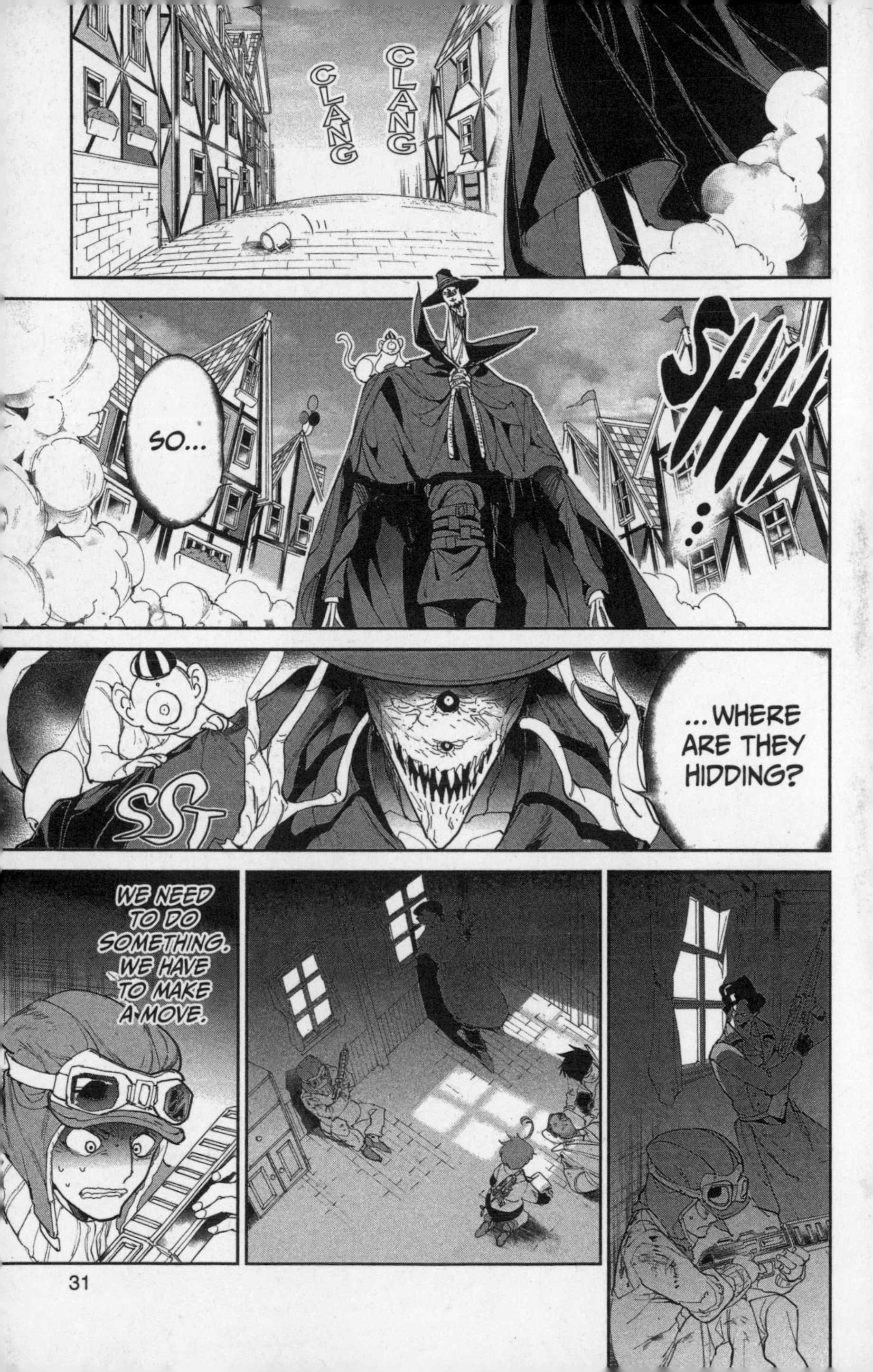
CLANG
CLANG
SHH...
SO...
...WHERE ARE THEY HIDDING?
SST
WE NEED TO DO SOMETHING. WE HAVE TO MAKE A MOVE.

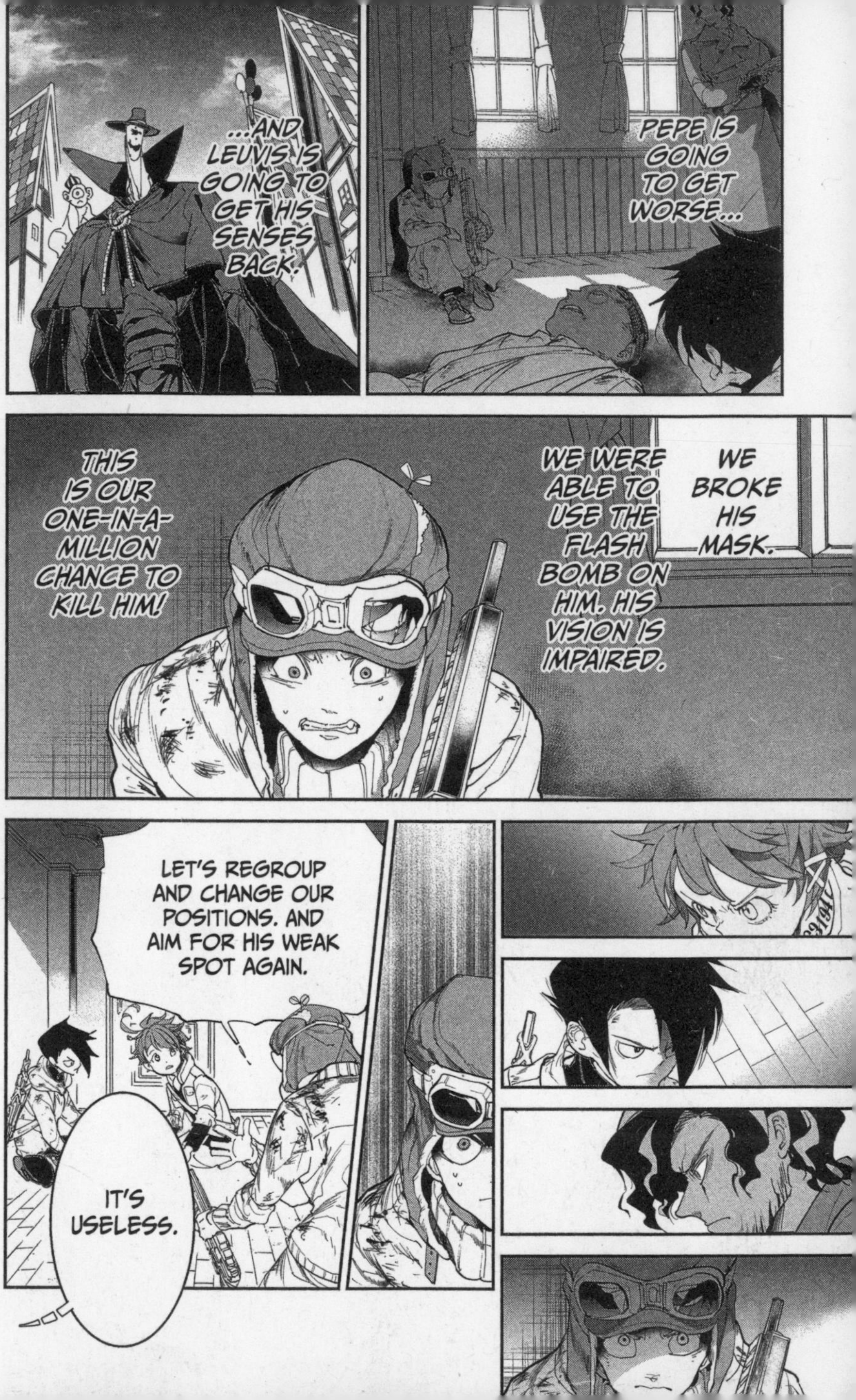
PEPE IS GOING TO GET WORSE...
...AND LEUVIS IS GOING TO GET HIS SENSES BACK.
WE BROKE HIS MASK.
WE WERE ABLE TO USE THE FLASH BOMB ON HIM. HIS VISION IS IMPAIRED.
THIS IS OUR ONE-IN-A-MILLION CHANCE TO KILL HIM!
LET'S REGROUP AND CHANGE OUR POSITIONS. AND AIM FOR HIS WEAK SPOT AGAIN.
IT'S USELESS.

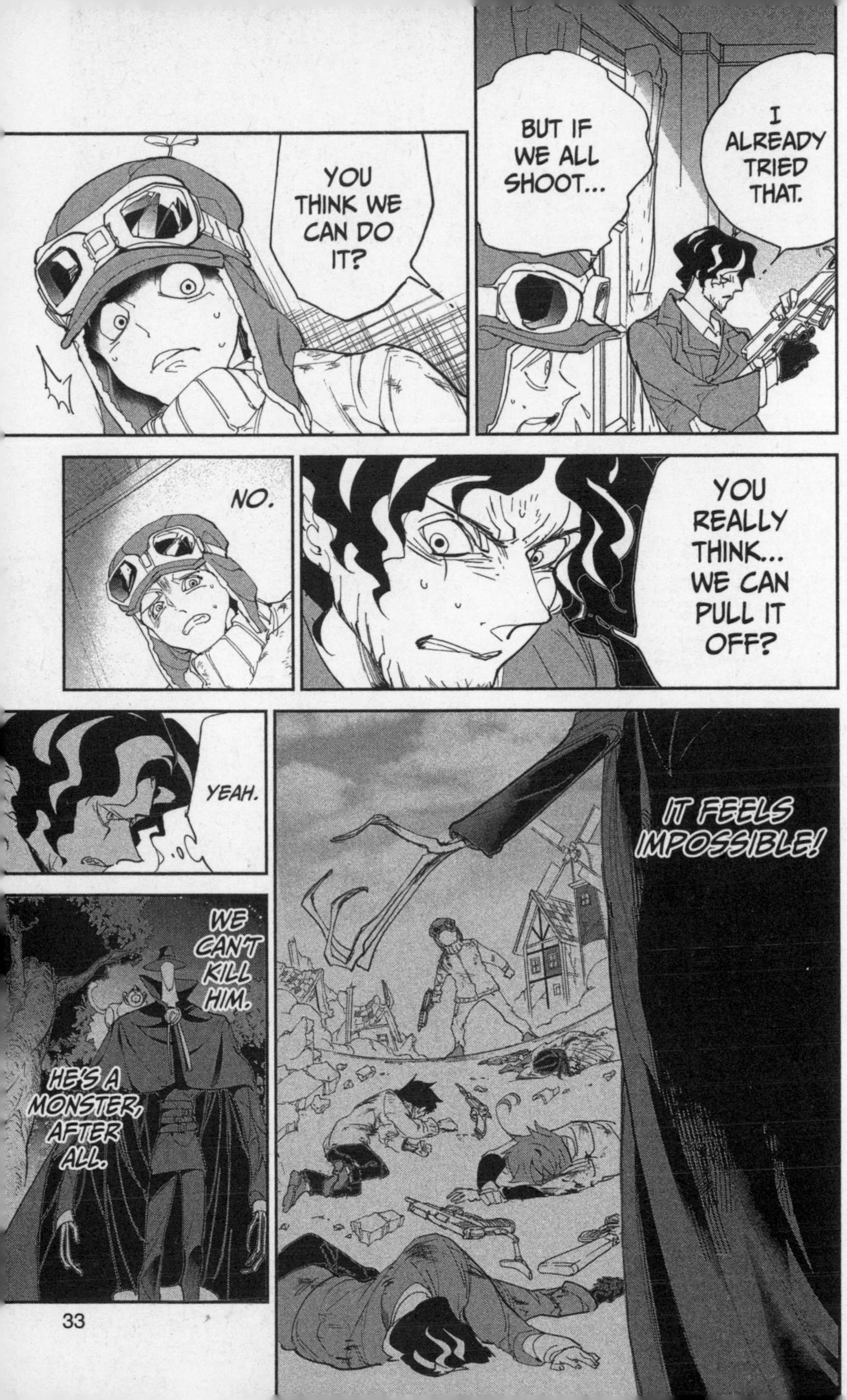
BUT IF WE ALL SHOOT...
I ALREADY TRIED THAT.
YOU THINK WE CAN DO IT?
YOU REALLY THINK... WE CAN PULL IT OFF?
NO.
IT FEELS IMPOSSIBLE!
YEAH.
WE CAN'T KILL HIM.
HE'S A MONSTER, AFTER ALL.

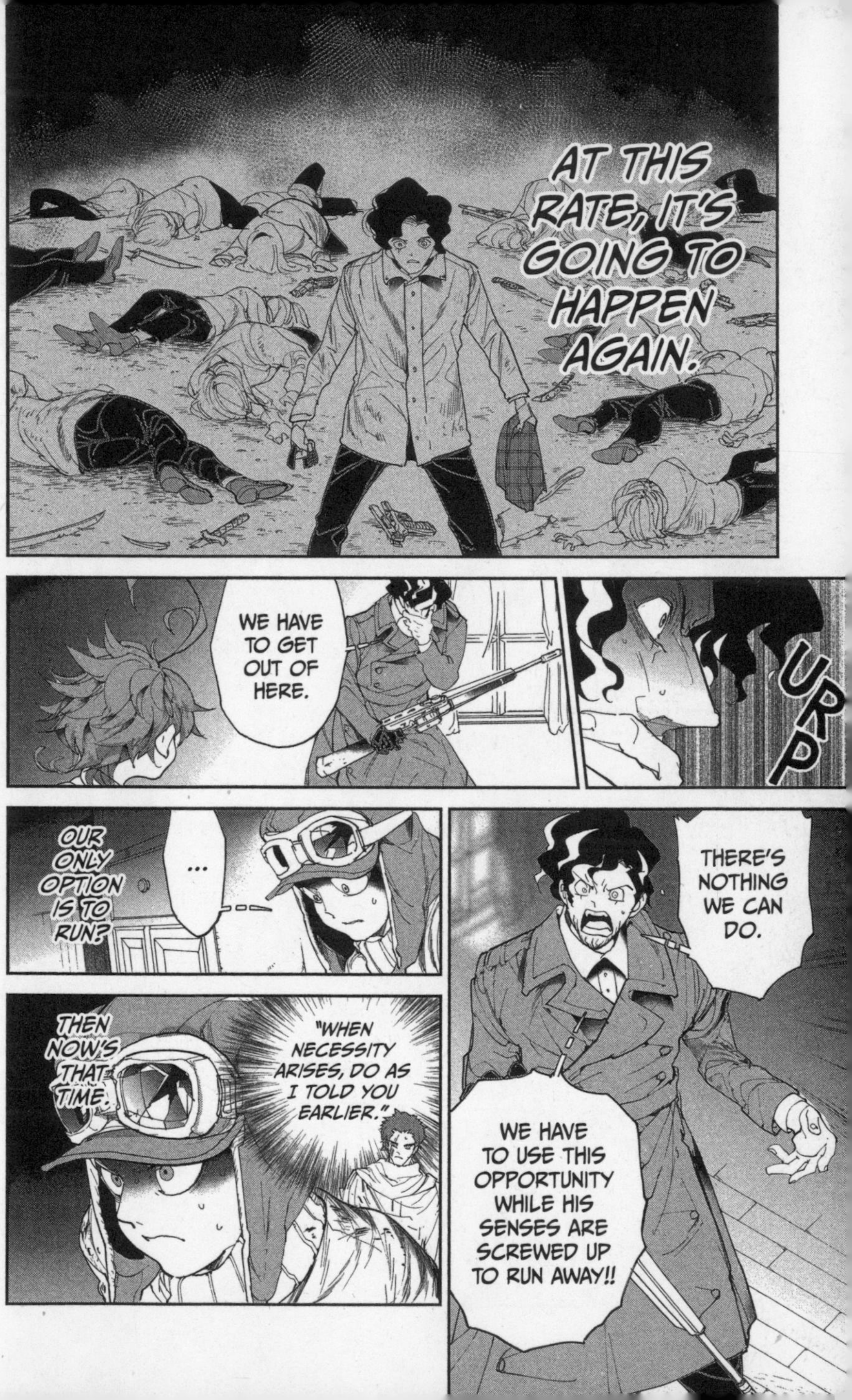
AT THIS RATE, IT'S GOING TO HAPPEN AGAIN.
URP
WE HAVE TO GET OUT OF HERE.
THERE'S NOTHING WE CAN DO.
WE HAVE TO USE THIS OPPORTUNITY WHILE HIS SENSES ARE SCREWED UP TO RUN AWAY!!
...
OUR ONLY OPTION IS TO RUN?
"WHEN NECESSITY ARISES, DO AS I TOLD YOU EARLIER."
THEN NOW'S THAT TIME.

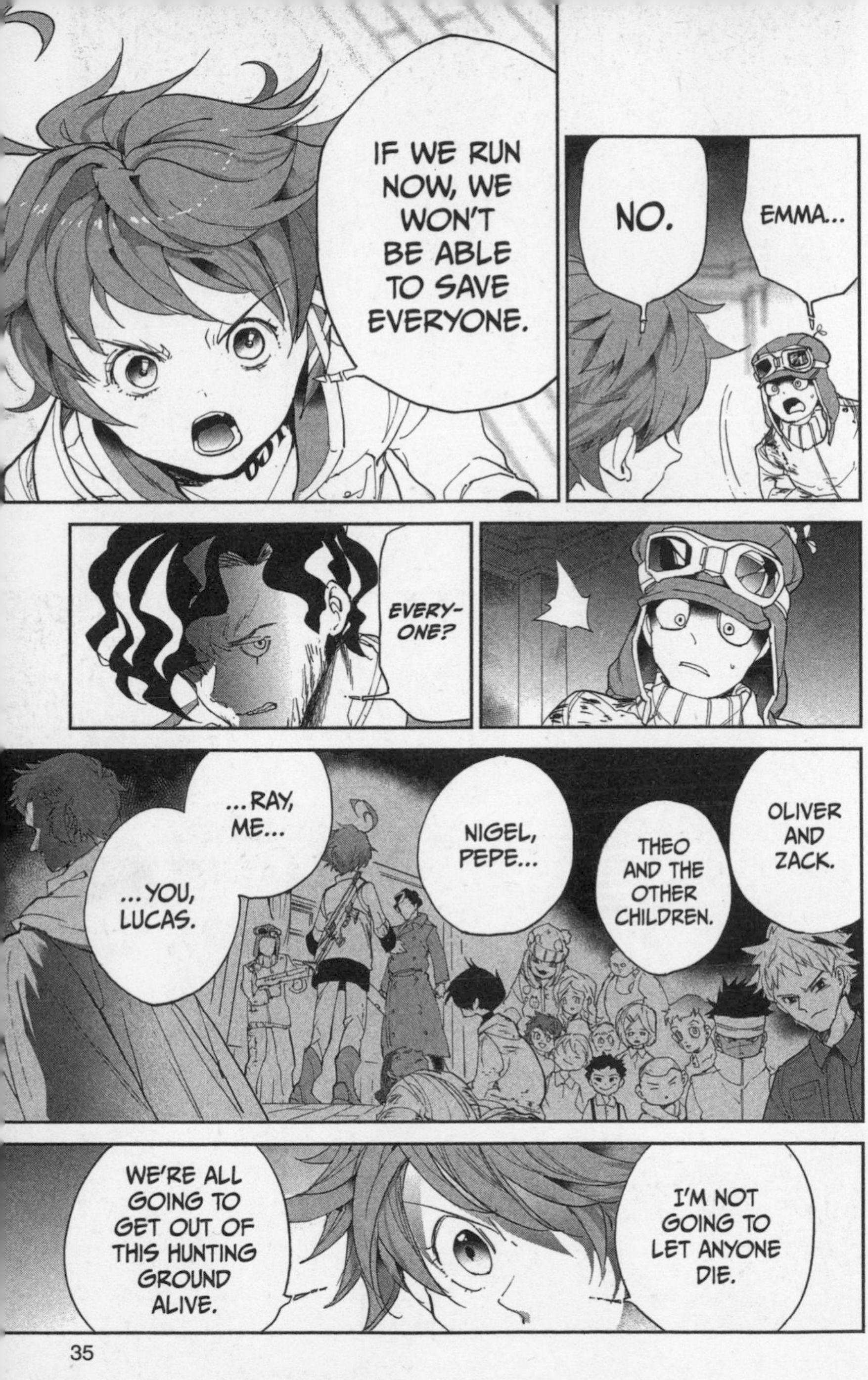
EMMA...
NO.
IF WE RUN NOW, WE WON'T BE ABLE TO SAVE EVERYONE.
EVERY- ONE?
OLIVER AND ZACK.
THEO AND THE OTHER CHILDREN.
NIGEL, PEPE...
...RAY, ME...
...YOU, LUCAS.
I'M NOT GOING TO LET ANYONE DIE.
WE'RE ALL GOING TO GET OUT OF THIS HUNTING GROUND ALIVE.

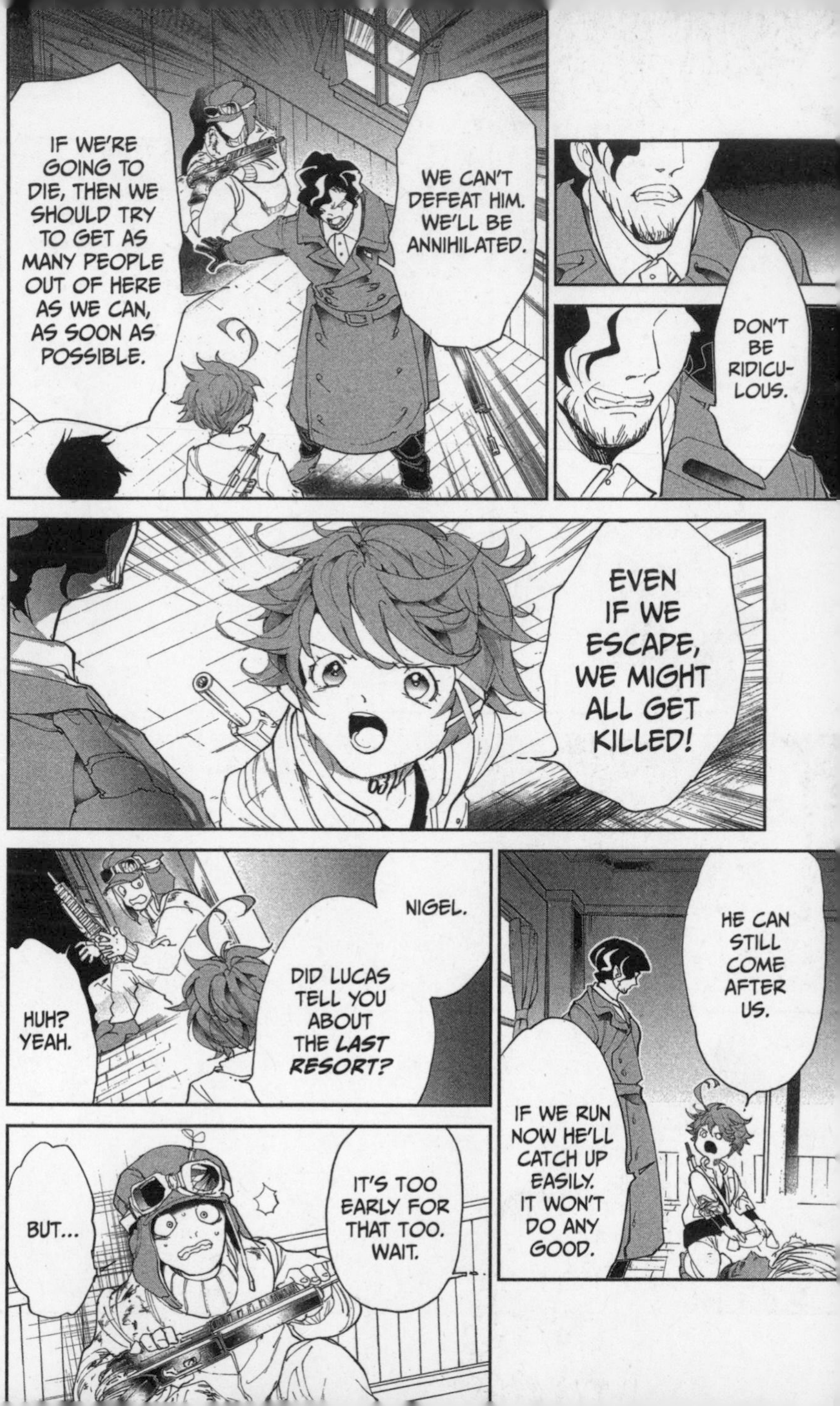
DON'T BE RIDICULOUS.
WE CAN'T DEFEAT HIM. WE'LL BE ANNIHILATED.
IF WE'RE GOING TO DIE, THEN WE SHOULD TRY TO GET AS MANY PEOPLE OUT OF HERE AS WE CAN, AS SOON AS POSSIBLE.
EVEN IF WE ESCAPE, WE MIGHT ALL GET KILLED!
HE CAN STILL COME AFTER US.
IF WE RUN NOW HE'LL CATCH UP EASILY. IT WON'T DO ANY GOOD.
NIGEL.
DID LUCAS TELL YOU ABOUT THE *LAST RESORT?*
HUH? YEAH.
IT'S TOO EARLY FOR THAT TOO. WAIT.
BUT...

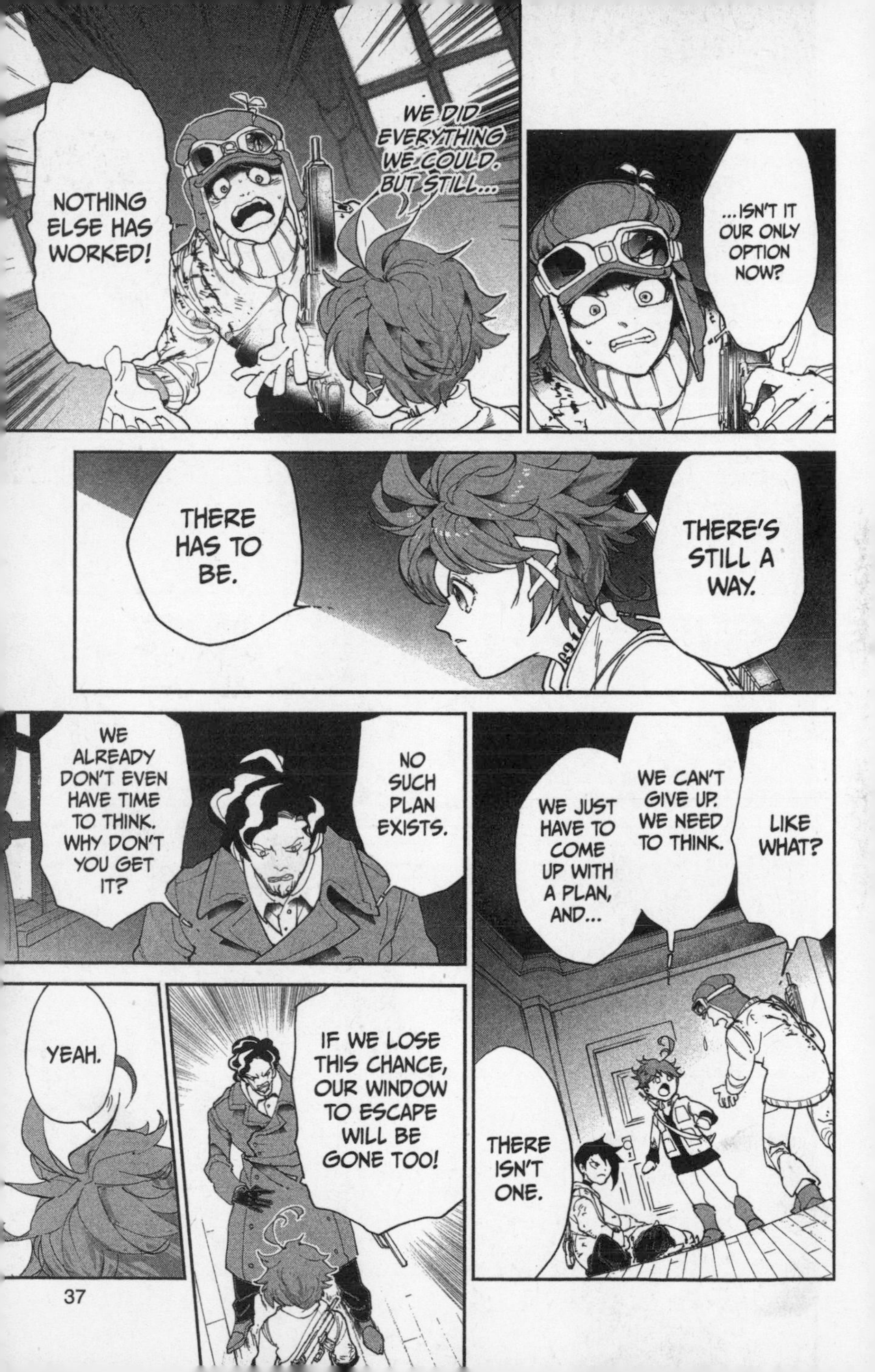
...ISN'T IT OUR ONLY OPTION NOW?
WE DID EVERYTHING WE COULD. BUT STILL...
NOTHING ELSE HAS WORKED!
THERE'S STILL A WAY.
THERE HAS TO BE.
LIKE WHAT?
WE CAN'T GIVE UP. WE NEED TO THINK.
WE JUST HAVE TO COME UP WITH A PLAN, AND...
THERE ISN'T ONE.
NO SUCH PLAN EXISTS.
WE ALREADY DON'T EVEN HAVE TIME TO THINK. WHY DON'T YOU GET IT?
IF WE LOSE THIS CHANCE, OUR WINDOW TO ESCAPE WILL BE GONE TOO!
YEAH.

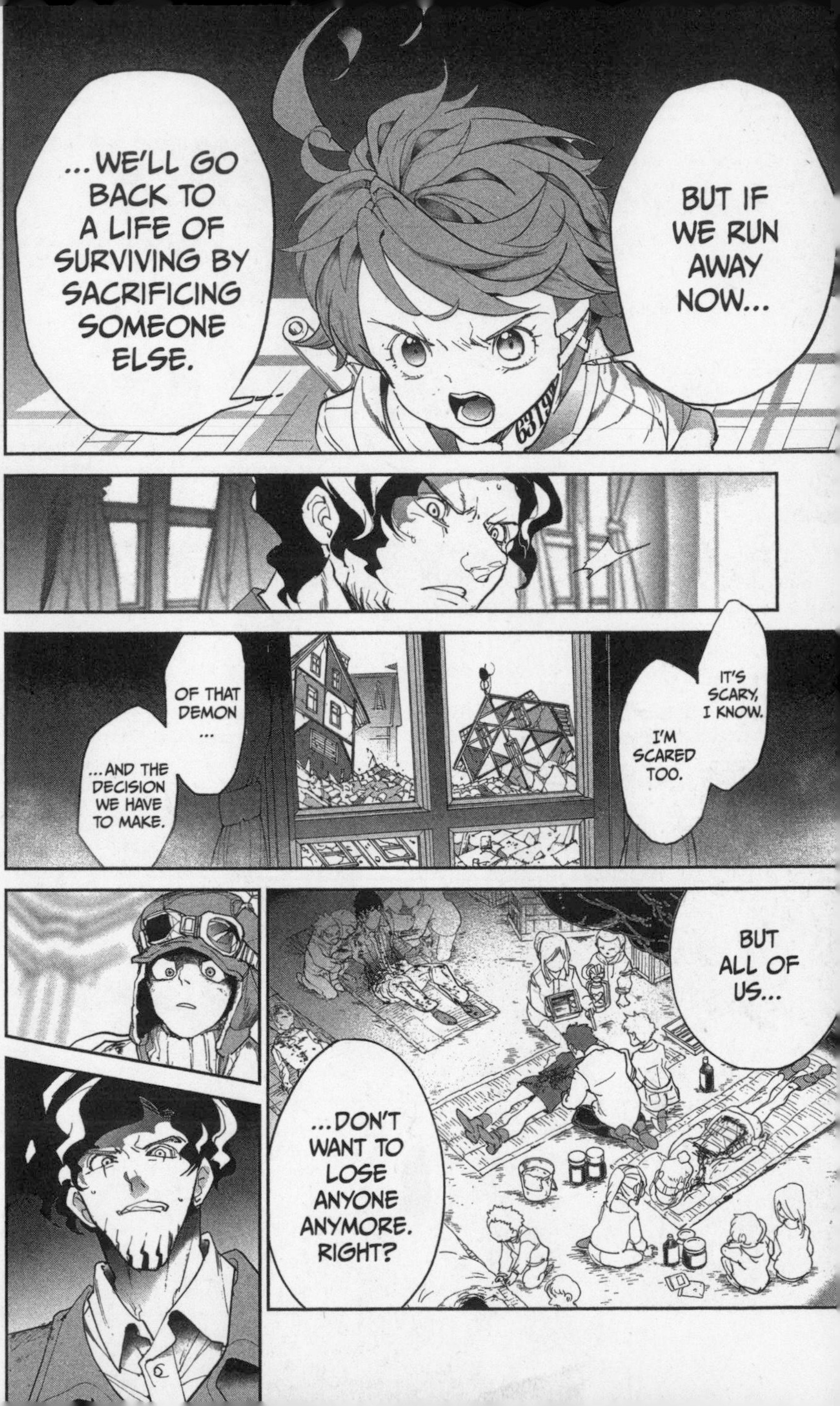
BUT IF WE RUN AWAY NOW...
...WE'LL GO BACK TO A LIFE OF SURVIVING BY SACRIFICING SOMEONE ELSE.
IT'S SCARY, I KNOW.
I'M SCARED TOO.
OF THAT DEMON ...
...AND THE DECISION WE HAVE TO MAKE.
BUT ALL OF US...
...DON'T WANT TO LOSE ANYONE ANYMORE. RIGHT?

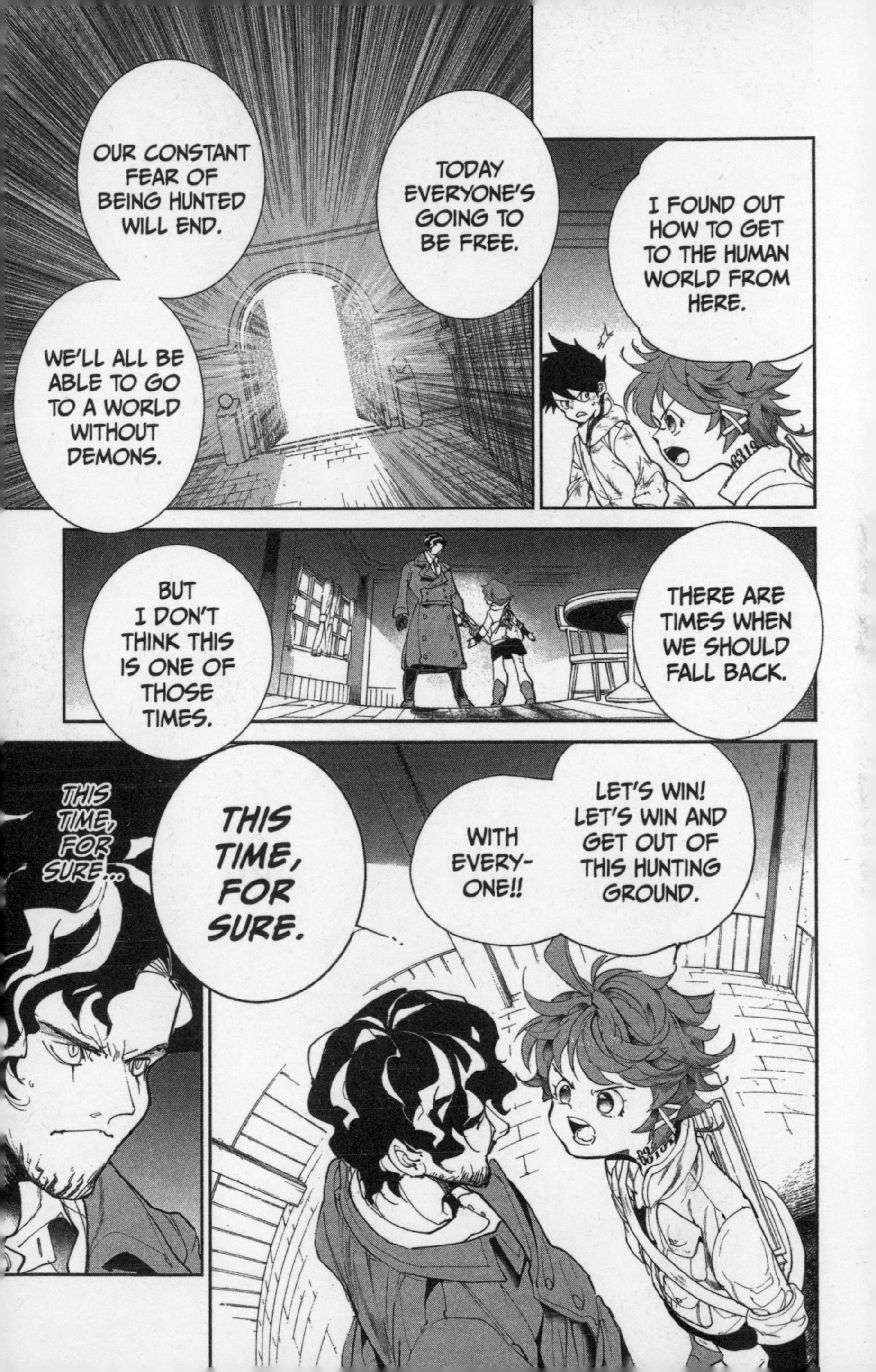
I FOUND OUT HOW TO GET TO THE HUMAN WORLD FROM HERE.
TODAY EVERYONE'S GOING TO BE FREE.
OUR CONSTANT FEAR OF BEING HUNTED WILL END.
WE'LL ALL BE ABLE TO GO TO A WORLD WITHOUT DEMONS.
THERE ARE TIMES WHEN WE SHOULD FALL BACK.
BUT I DON'T THINK THIS IS ONE OF THOSE TIMES.
LET'S WIN! LET'S WIN AND GET OUT OF THIS HUNTING GROUND.
WITH EVERY-ONE!!
THIS TIME, FOR SURE.
THIS TIME, FOR SURE...

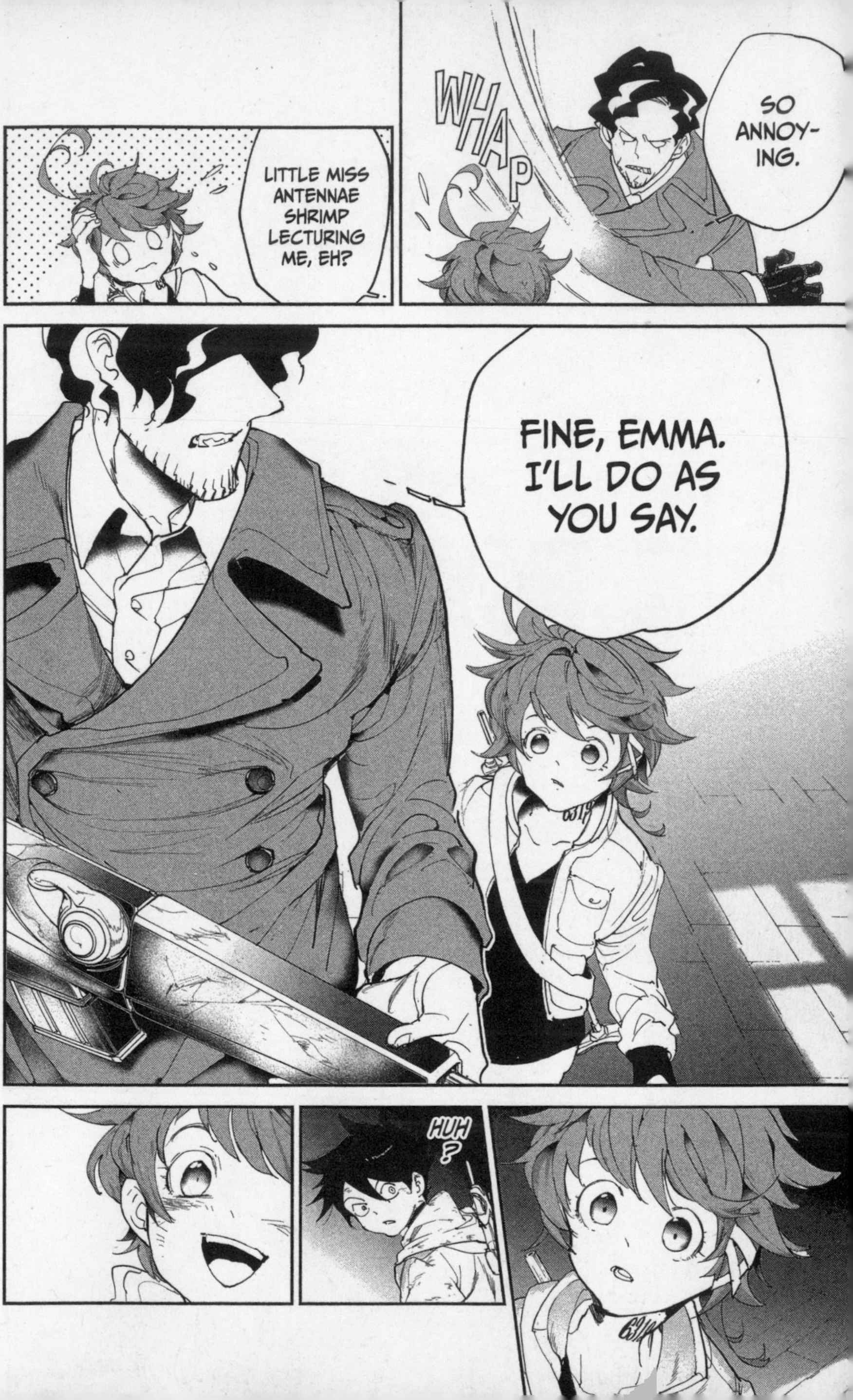
WHAP
SO ANNOY-ING.
LITTLE MISS ANTENNAE SHRIMP LECTURING ME, EH?
FINE, EMMA. I'LL DO AS YOU SAY.
HUH?

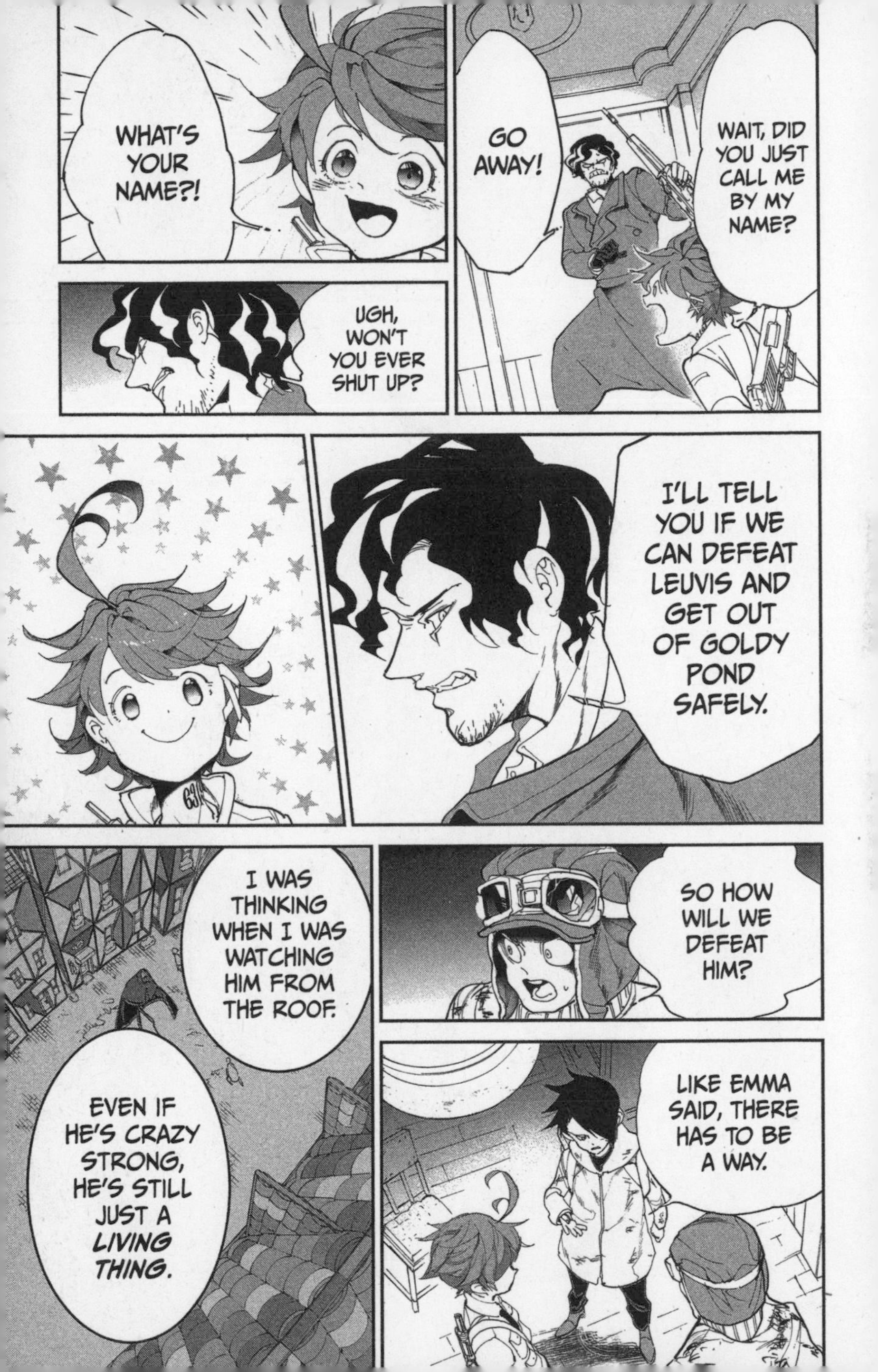
WAIT, DID YOU JUST CALL ME BY MY NAME?
GO AWAY!
WHAT'S YOUR NAME?!
UGH, WON'T YOU EVER SHUT UP?
I'LL TELL YOU IF WE CAN DEFEAT LEUVIS AND GET OUT OF GOLDY POND SAFELY.
SO HOW WILL WE DEFEAT HIM?
LIKE EMMA SAID, THERE HAS TO BE A WAY.
I WAS THINKING WHEN I WAS WATCHING HIM FROM THE ROOF.
EVEN IF HE'S CRAZY STRONG, HE'S STILL JUST A *LIVING THING*.

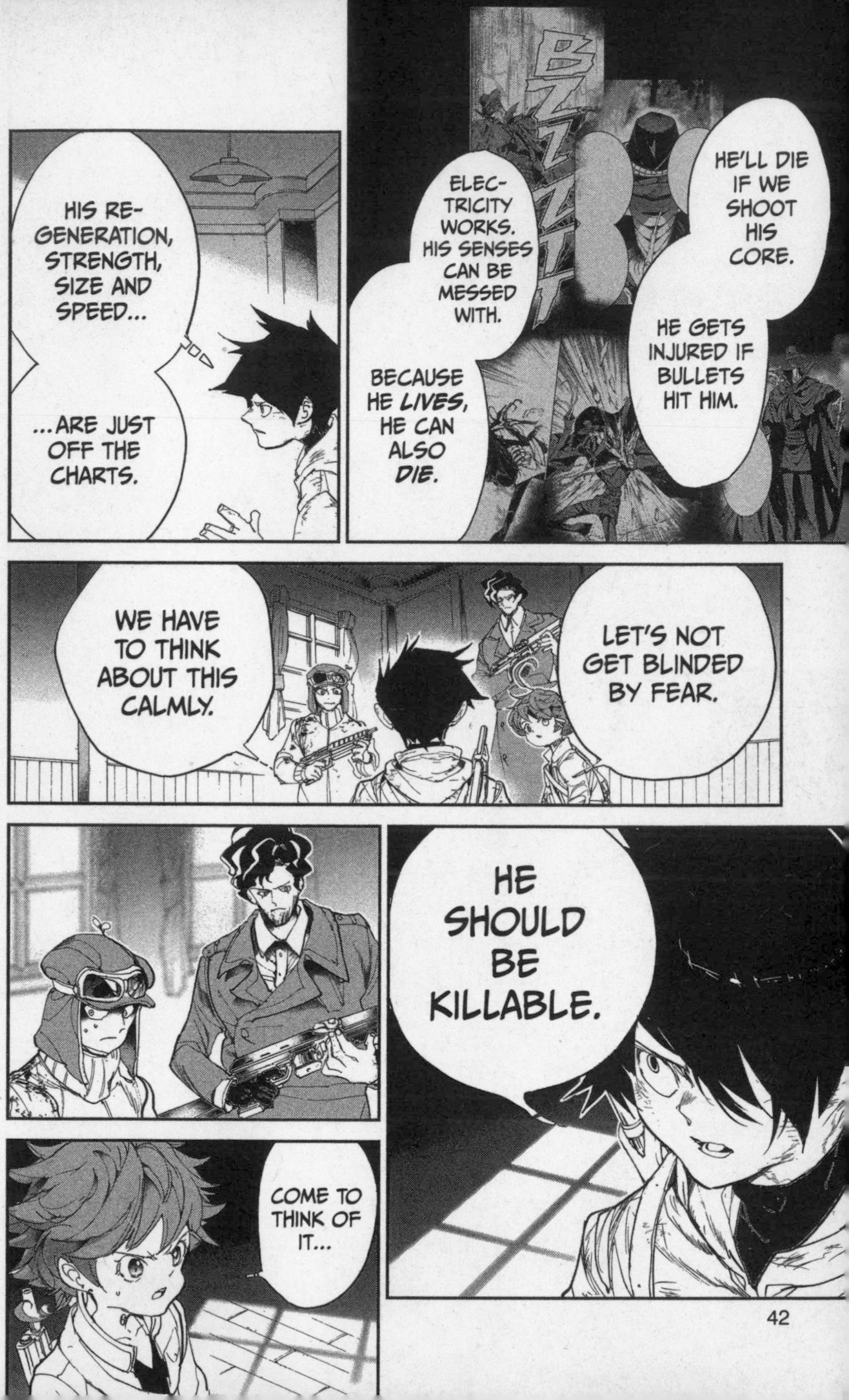
BZZT
HE'LL DIE IF WE SHOOT HIS CORE.
ELEC-TRICITY WORKS. HIS SENSES CAN BE MESSED WITH.
HE GETS INJURED IF BULLETS HIT HIM.
BECAUSE HE *LIVES*, HE CAN ALSO *DIE*.
HIS RE-GENERATION, STRENGTH, SIZE AND SPEED...
...ARE JUST OFF THE CHARTS.
LET'S NOT GET BLINDED BY FEAR.
WE HAVE TO THINK ABOUT THIS CALMLY.
HE SHOULD BE KILLABLE.
COME TO THINK OF IT...

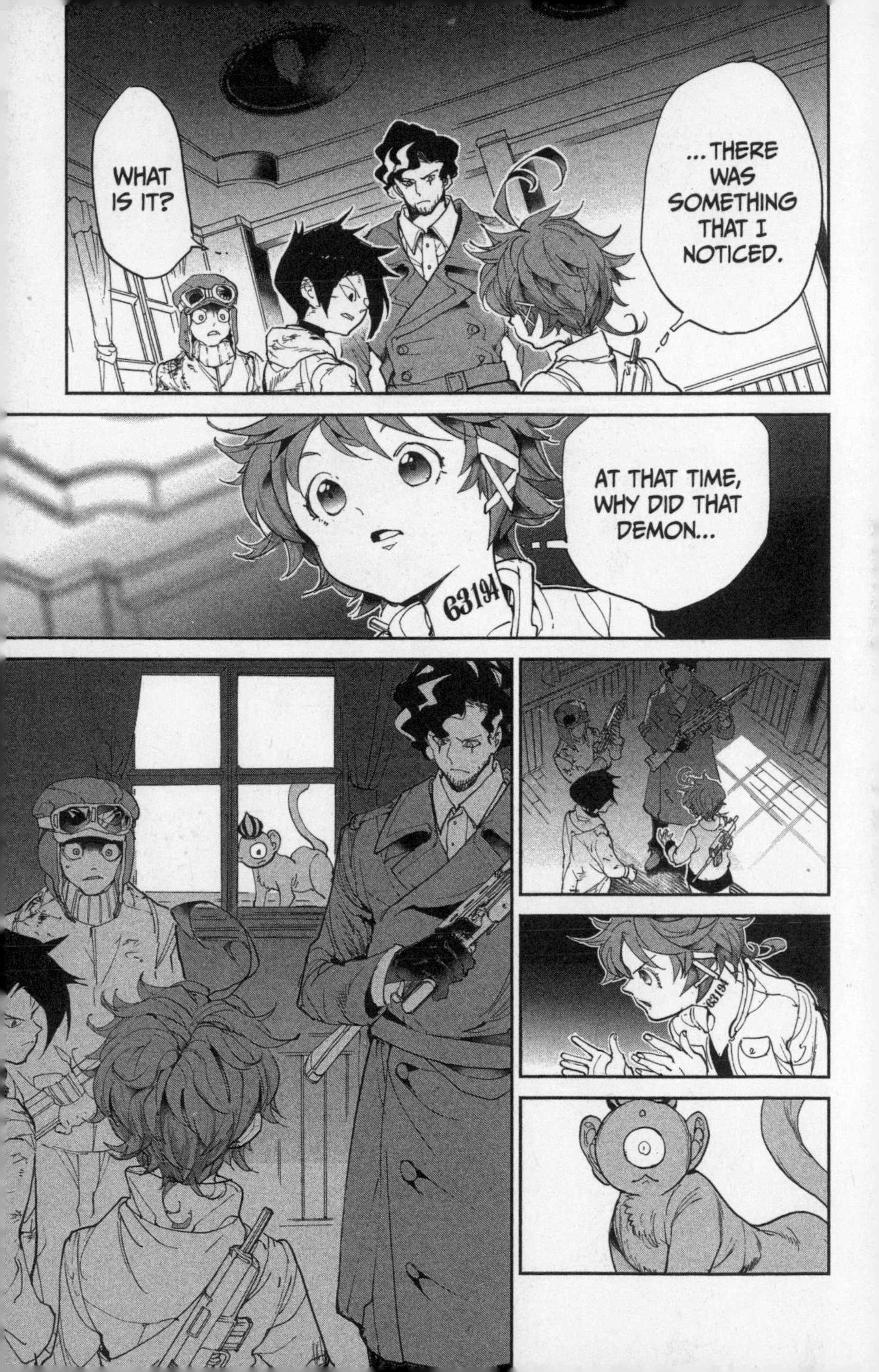
...THERE WAS SOMETHING THAT I NOTICED.
WHAT IS IT?
AT THAT TIME, WHY DID THAT DEMON...
63194

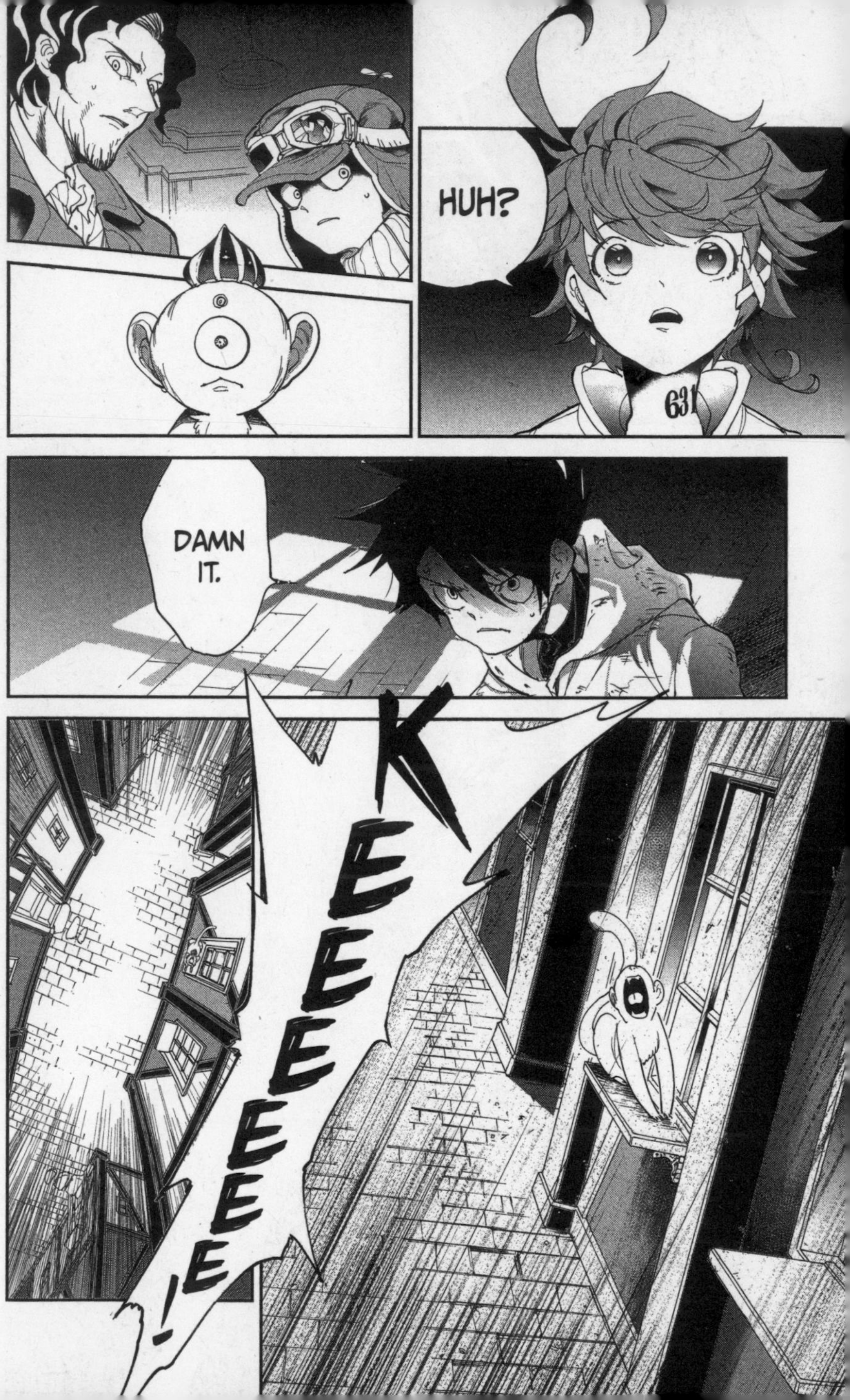
HUH?
631
DAMN IT.
KEEEEEEEEEE!

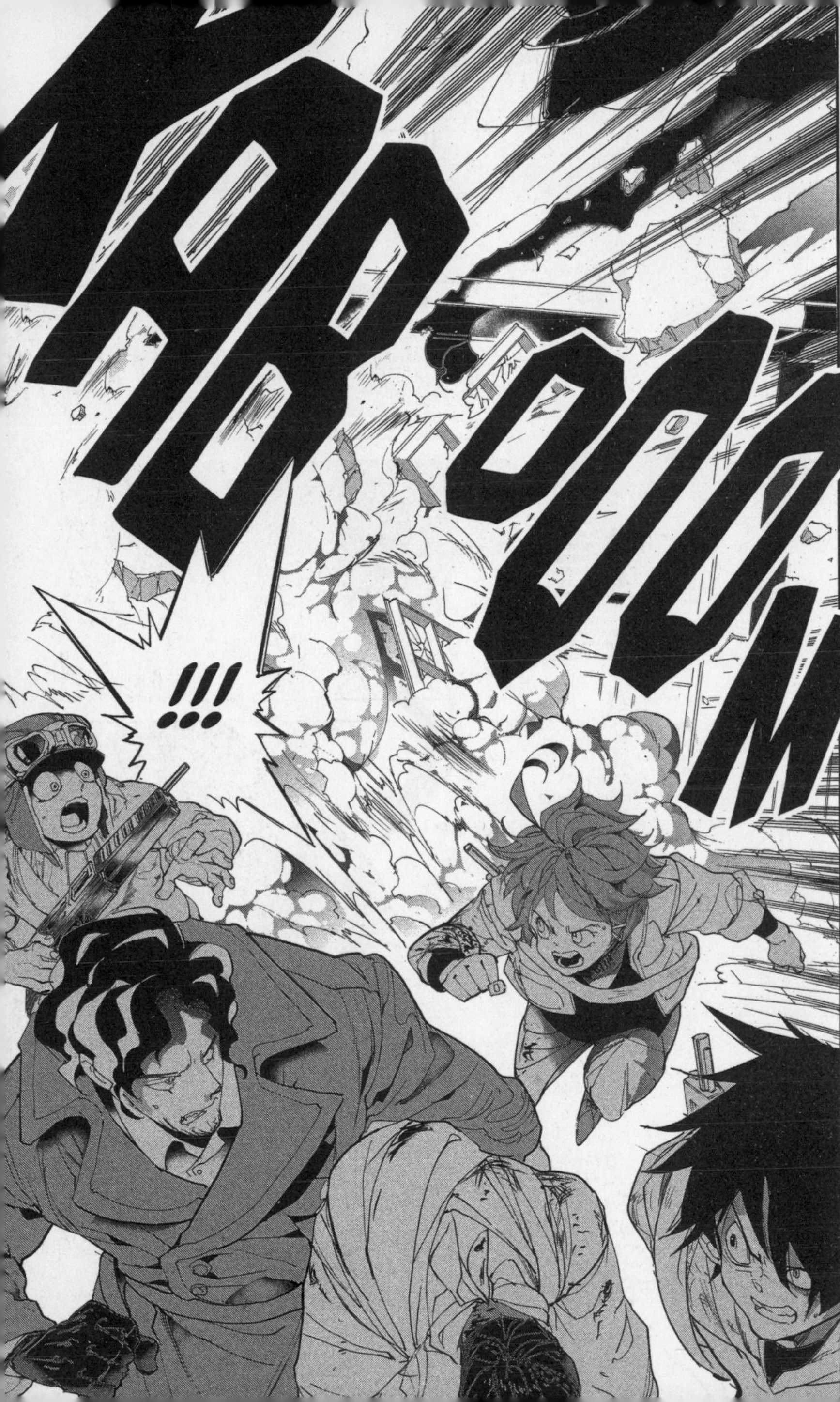
KA-BOOOM
!!!

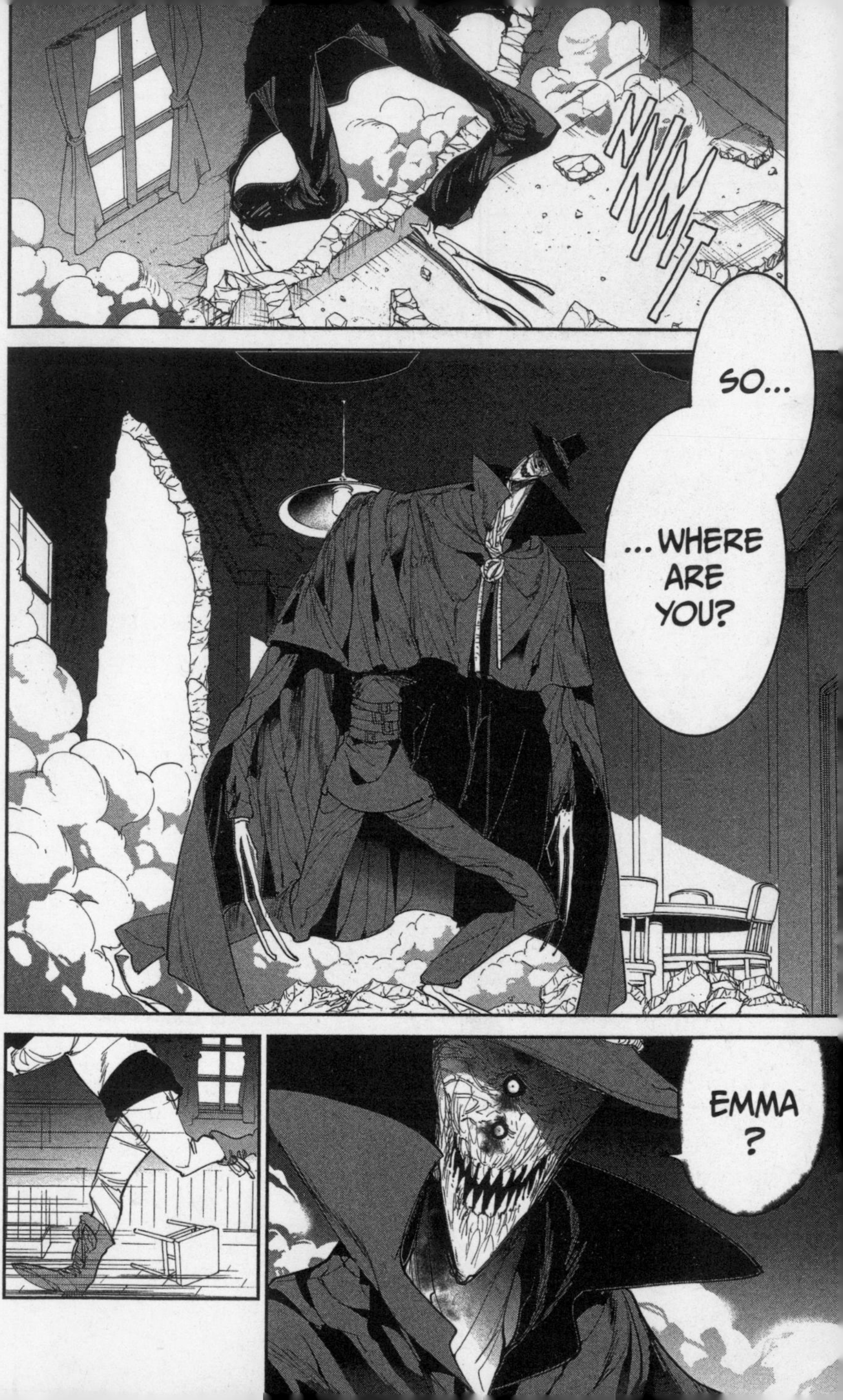
NNMMT
SO...
...WHERE ARE YOU?
EMMA?

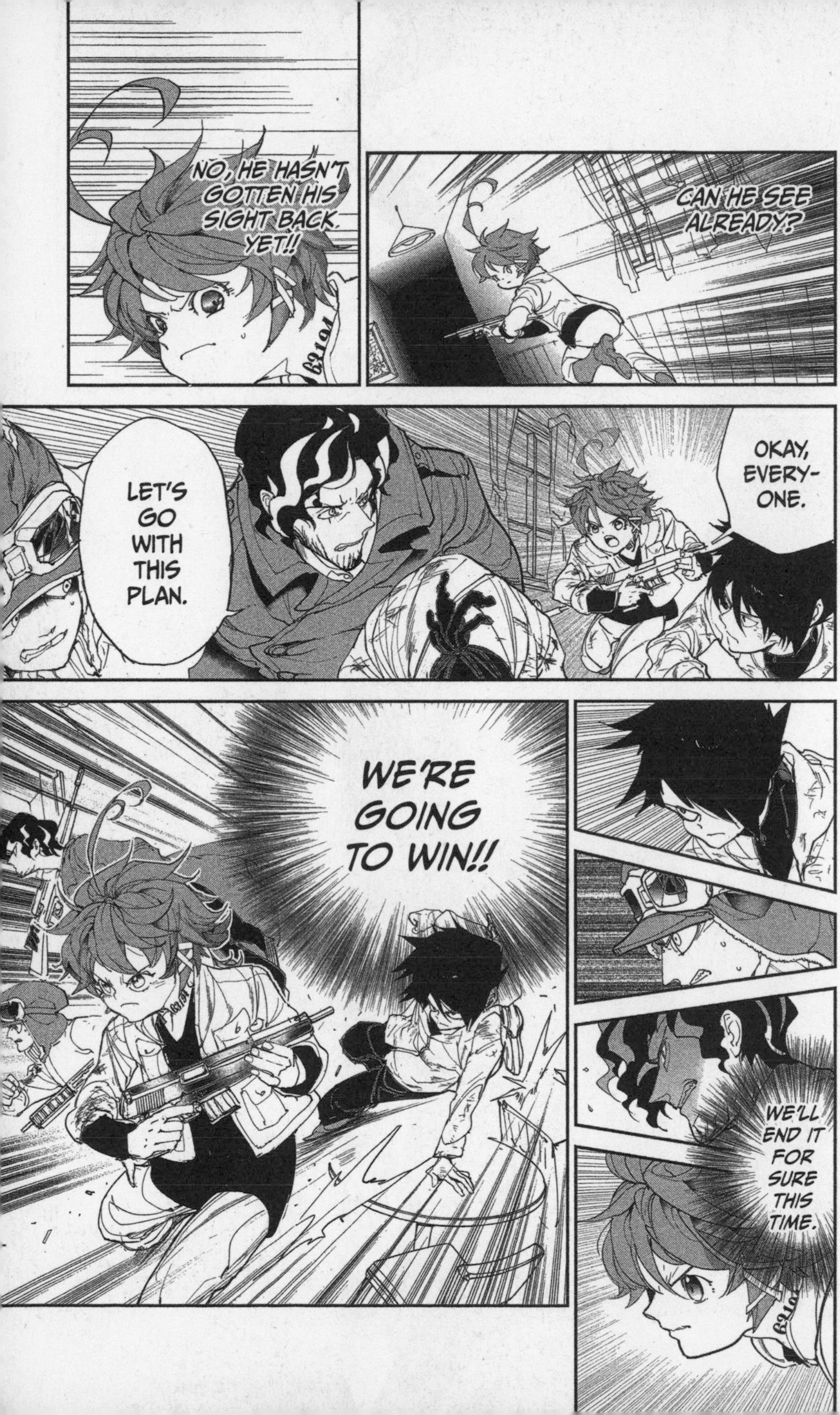
CAN HE SEE ALREADY?
NO, HE HASN'T GOTTEN HIS SIGHT BACK YET!!
OKAY, EVERYONE.
LET'S GO WITH THIS PLAN.
WE'LL END IT FOR SURE THIS TIME.
WE'RE GOING TO WIN!!

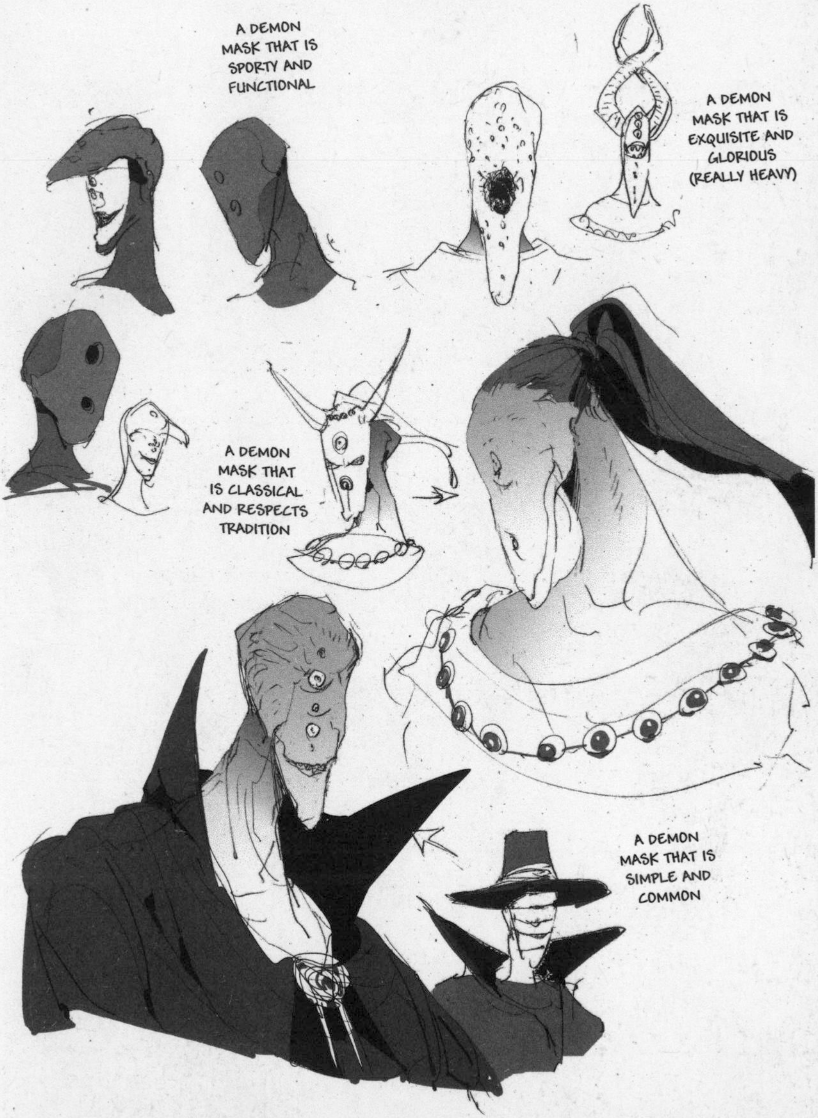
A DEMON MASK THAT IS EXQUISITE AND GLORIOUS (REALLY HEAVY)
A DEMON MASK THAT IS SPORTY AND FUNCTIONAL
A DEMON MASK THAT IS CLASSICAL AND RESPECTS TRADITION
A DEMON MASK THAT IS SIMPLE AND COMMON

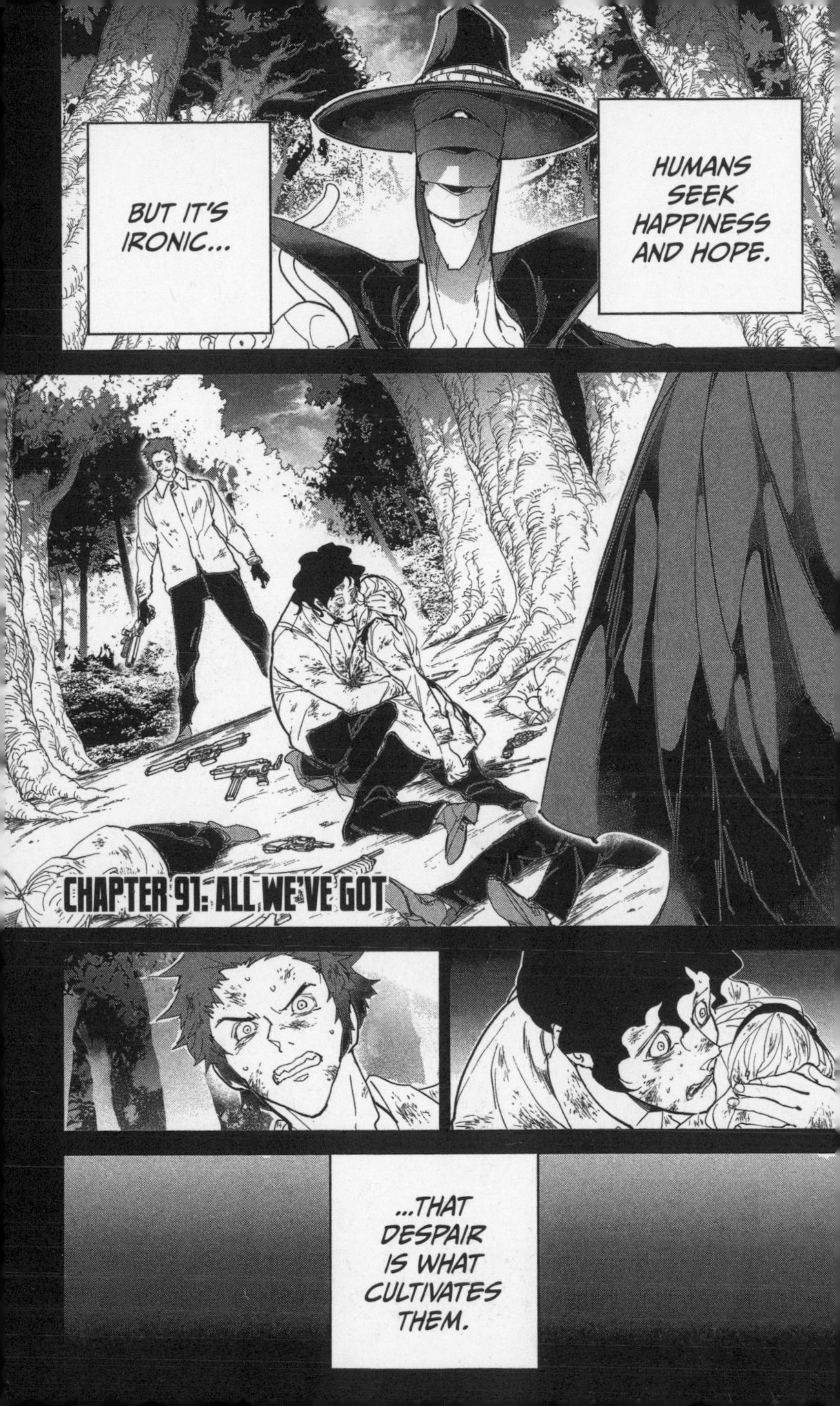
HUMANS SEEK HAPPINESS AND HOPE.
BUT IT'S IRONIC...
CHAPTER 91: ALL WE'VE GOT
...THAT DESPAIR IS WHAT CULTIVATES THEM.

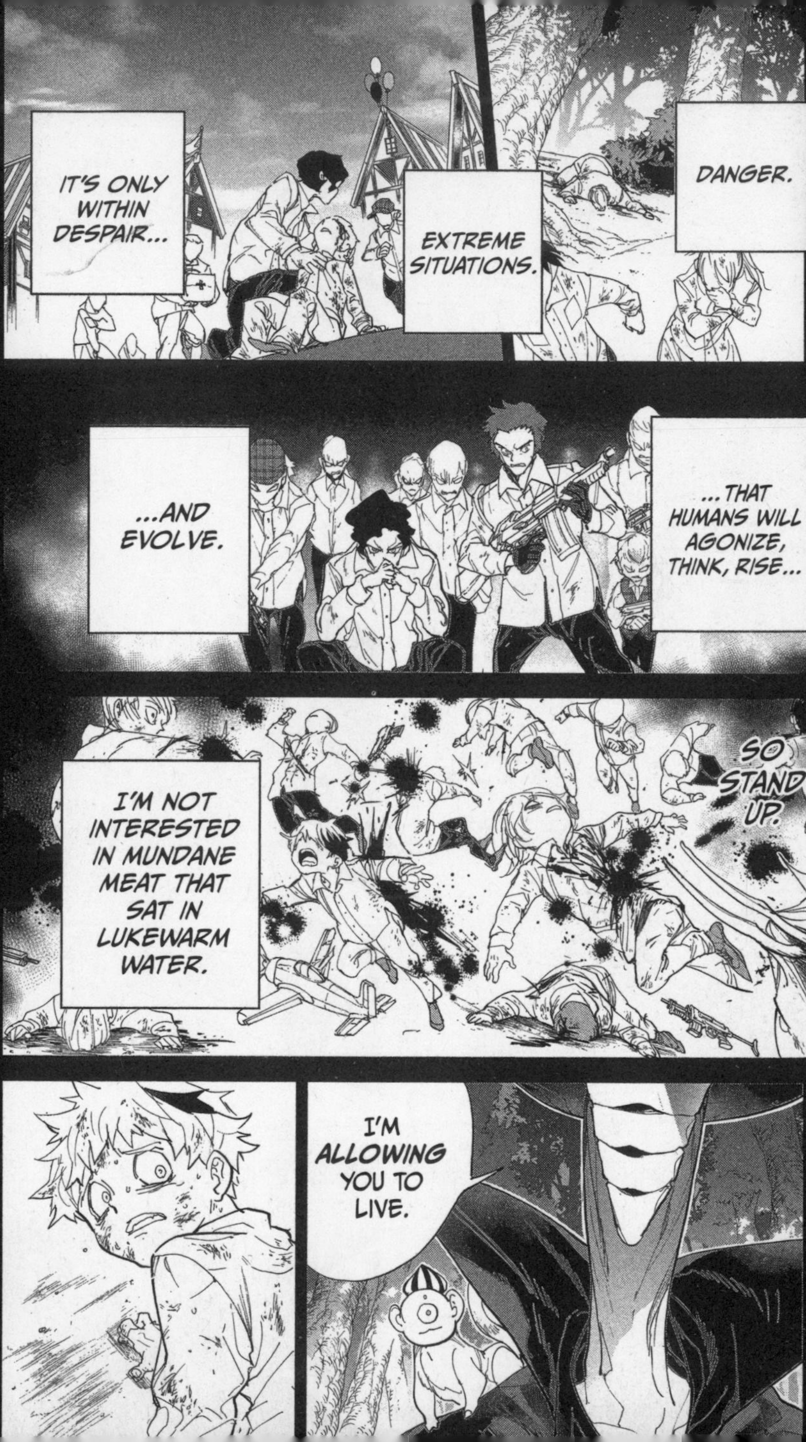
DANGER.
EXTREME SITUATIONS.
IT'S ONLY WITHIN DESPAIR...
...THAT HUMANS WILL AGONIZE, THINK, RISE...
...AND EVOLVE.
I'M NOT INTERESTED IN MUNDANE MEAT THAT SAT IN LUKEWARM WATER.
SO STAND UP.
I'M ALLOWING YOU TO LIVE.

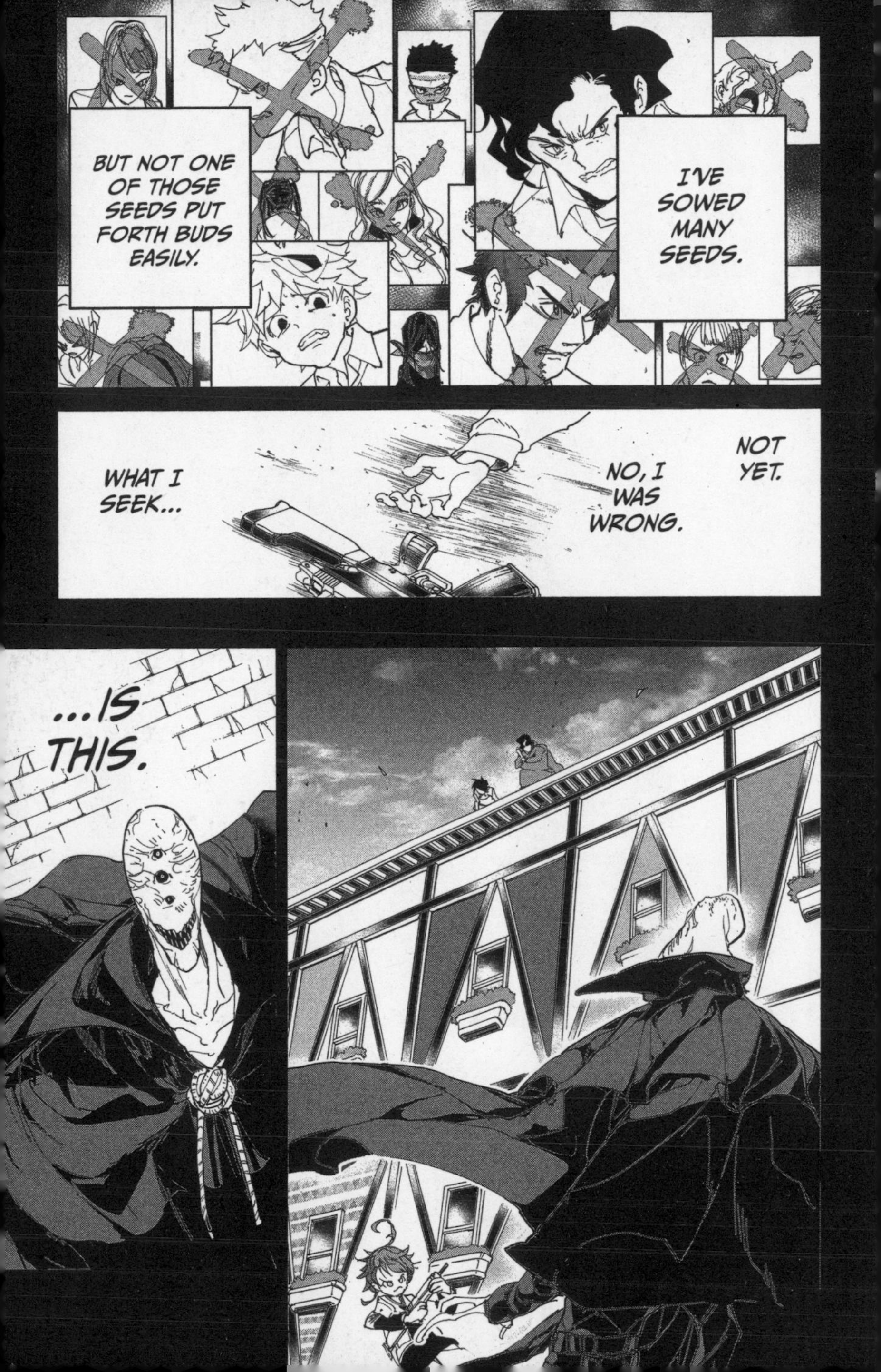
I'VE SOWED MANY SEEDS.
BUT NOT ONE OF THOSE SEEDS PUT FORTH BUDS EASILY.
NOT YET.
NO, I WAS WRONG.
WHAT I SEEK...
...IS THIS.

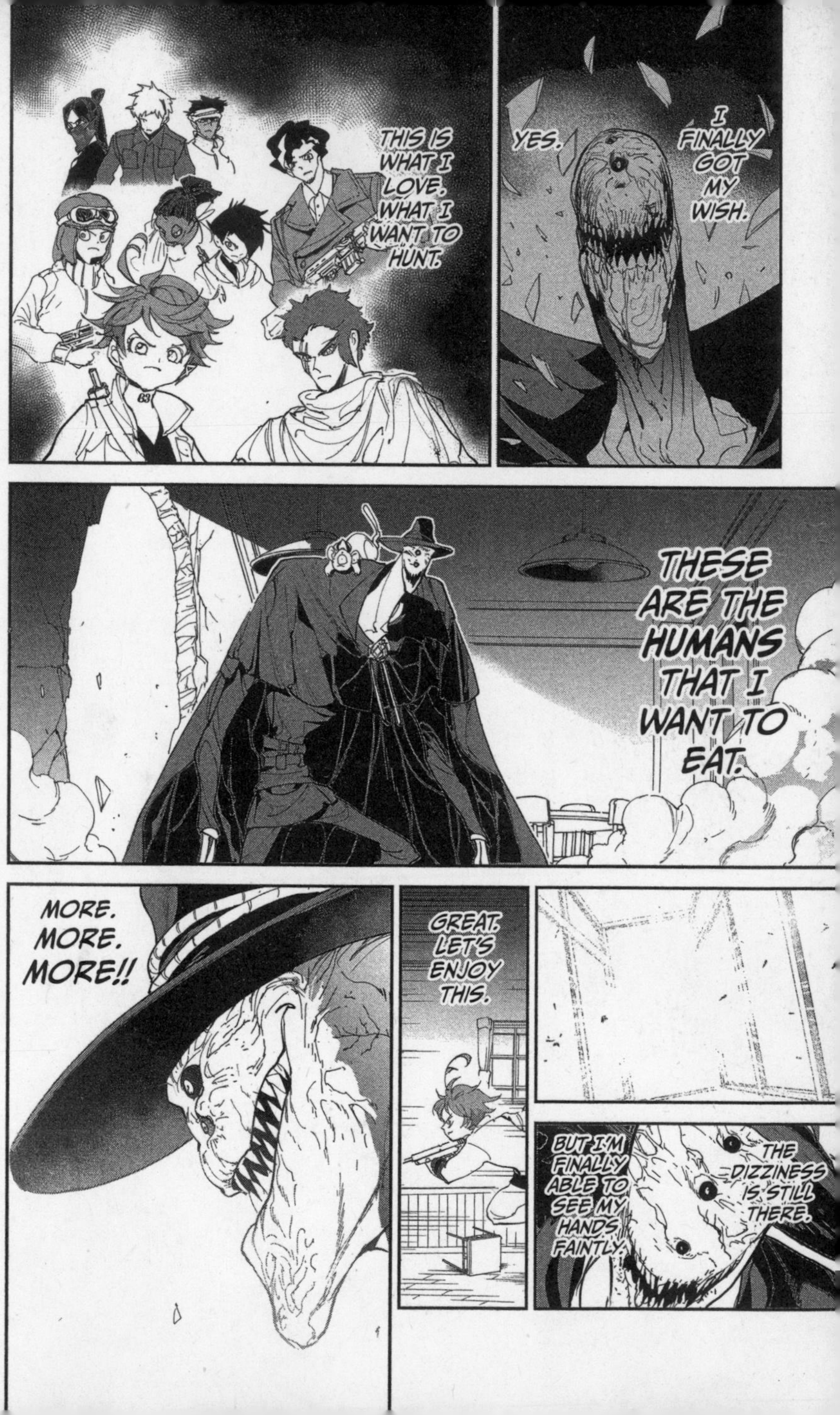
I FINALLY GOT MY WISH.
YES.
THIS IS WHAT I LOVE. WHAT I WANT TO HUNT.
THESE ARE THE HUMANS THAT I WANT TO EAT.
THE DIZZINESS IS STILL THERE.
BUT I'M FINALLY ABLE TO SEE MY HANDS FAINTLY.
GREAT. LET'S ENJOY THIS.
MORE. MORE. MORE!!

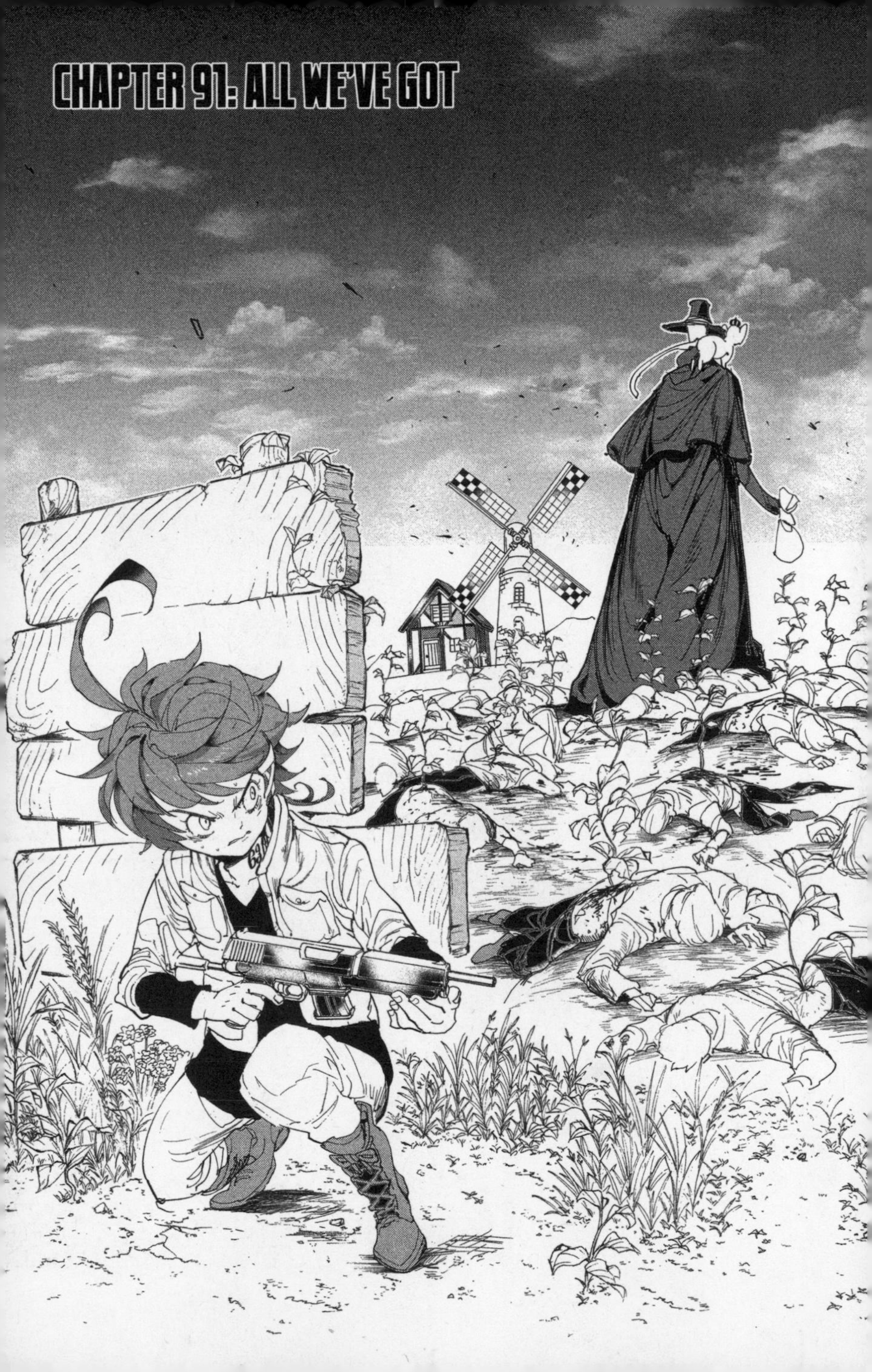
CHAPTER 91: ALL WE'VE GOT

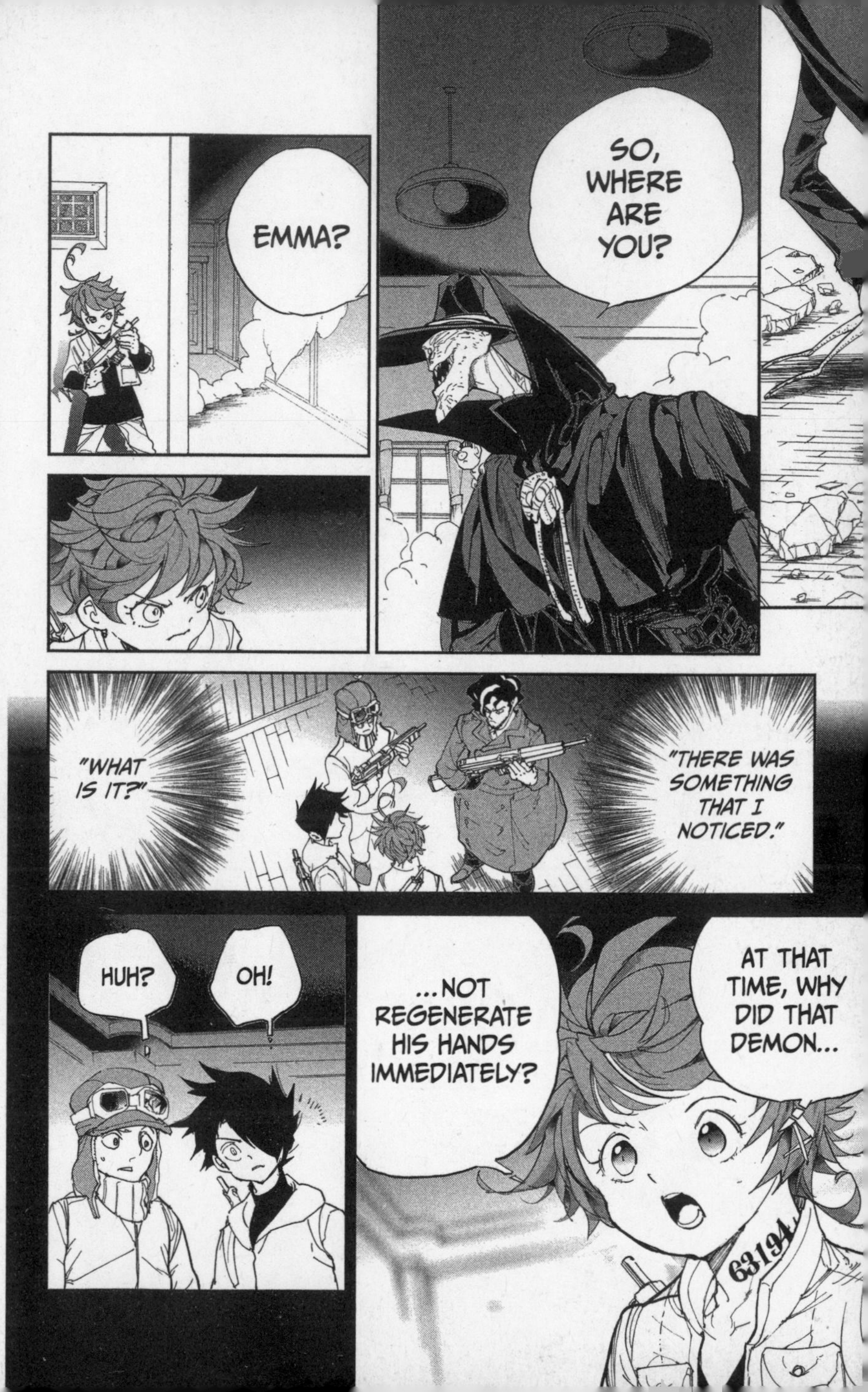
SO, WHERE ARE YOU?
EMMA?
"THERE WAS SOMETHING THAT I NOTICED."
"WHAT IS IT?"
AT THAT TIME, WHY DID THAT DEMON...
...NOT REGENERATE HIS HANDS IMMEDIATELY?
63194
OH!
HUH?

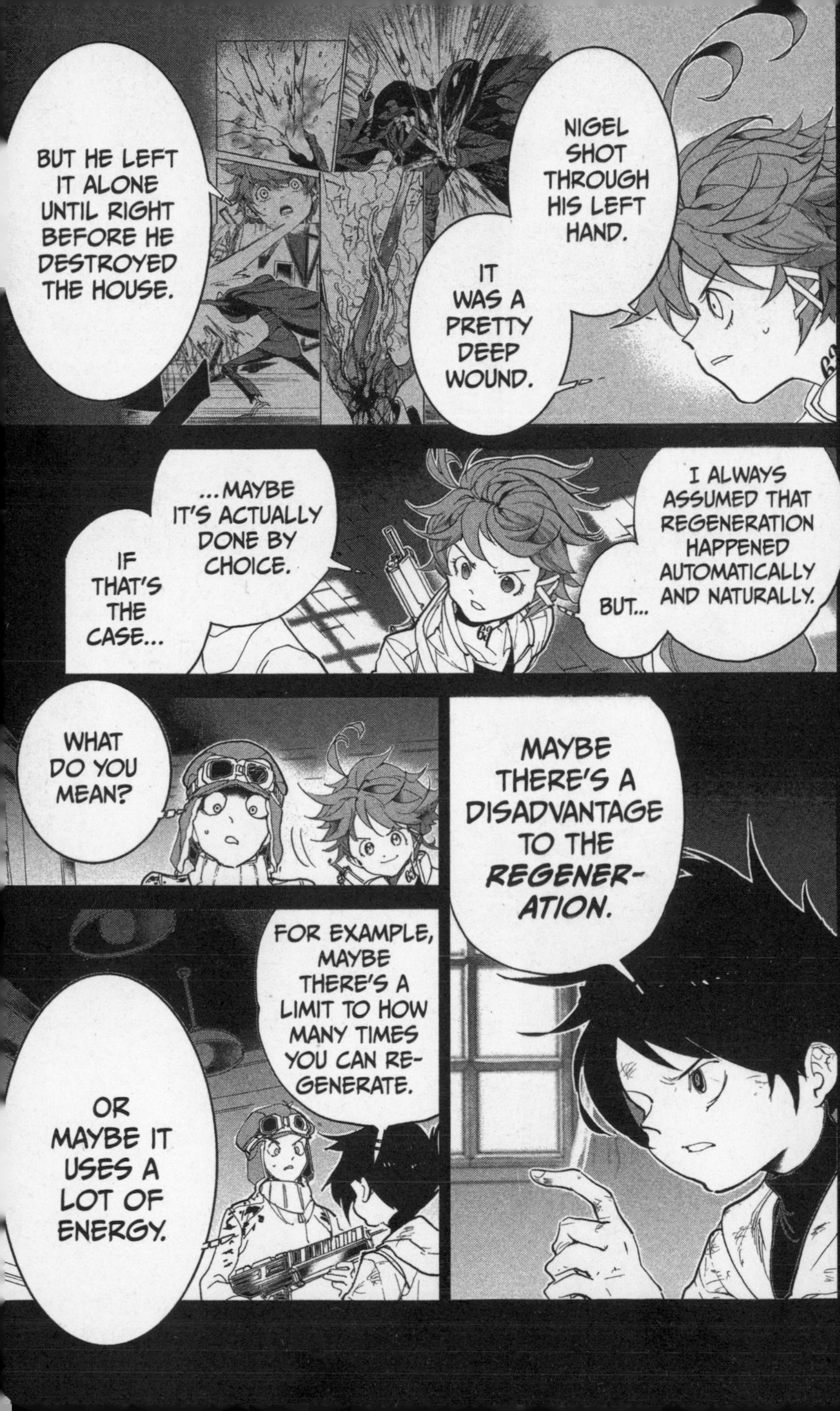
NIGEL SHOT THROUGH HIS LEFT HAND.
IT WAS A PRETTY DEEP WOUND.
BUT HE LEFT IT ALONE UNTIL RIGHT BEFORE HE DESTROYED THE HOUSE.
I ALWAYS ASSUMED THAT REGENERATION HAPPENED AUTOMATICALLY AND NATURALLY.
BUT...
...MAYBE IT'S ACTUALLY DONE BY CHOICE.
IF THAT'S THE CASE...
MAYBE THERE'S A DISADVANTAGE TO THE *REGENER-ATION.*
WHAT DO YOU MEAN?
FOR EXAMPLE, MAYBE THERE'S A LIMIT TO HOW MANY TIMES YOU CAN RE-GENERATE.
OR MAYBE IT USES A LOT OF ENERGY.

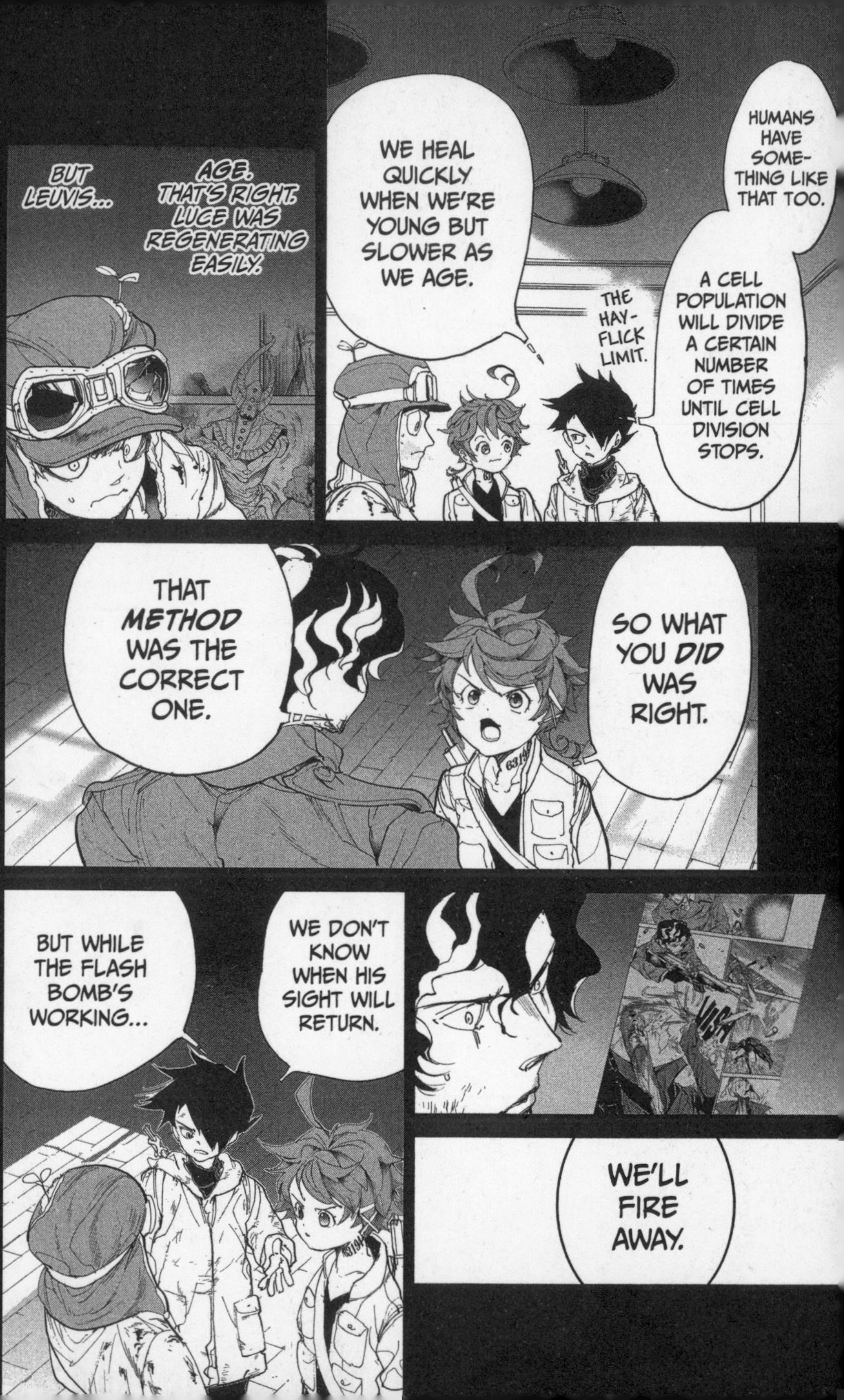
HUMANS HAVE SOME-THING LIKE THAT TOO.
A CELL POPULATION WILL DIVIDE A CERTAIN NUMBER OF TIMES UNTIL CELL DIVISION STOPS.
THE HAY-FLICK LIMIT.
WE HEAL QUICKLY WHEN WE'RE YOUNG BUT SLOWER AS WE AGE.
AGE. THAT'S RIGHT. LUCE WAS REGENERATING EASILY.
BUT LEUVIS...
SO WHAT YOU *DID* WAS RIGHT.
THAT *METHOD* WAS THE CORRECT ONE.
WE'LL FIRE AWAY.
WE DON'T KNOW WHEN HIS SIGHT WILL RETURN.
BUT WHILE THE FLASH BOMB'S WORKING...

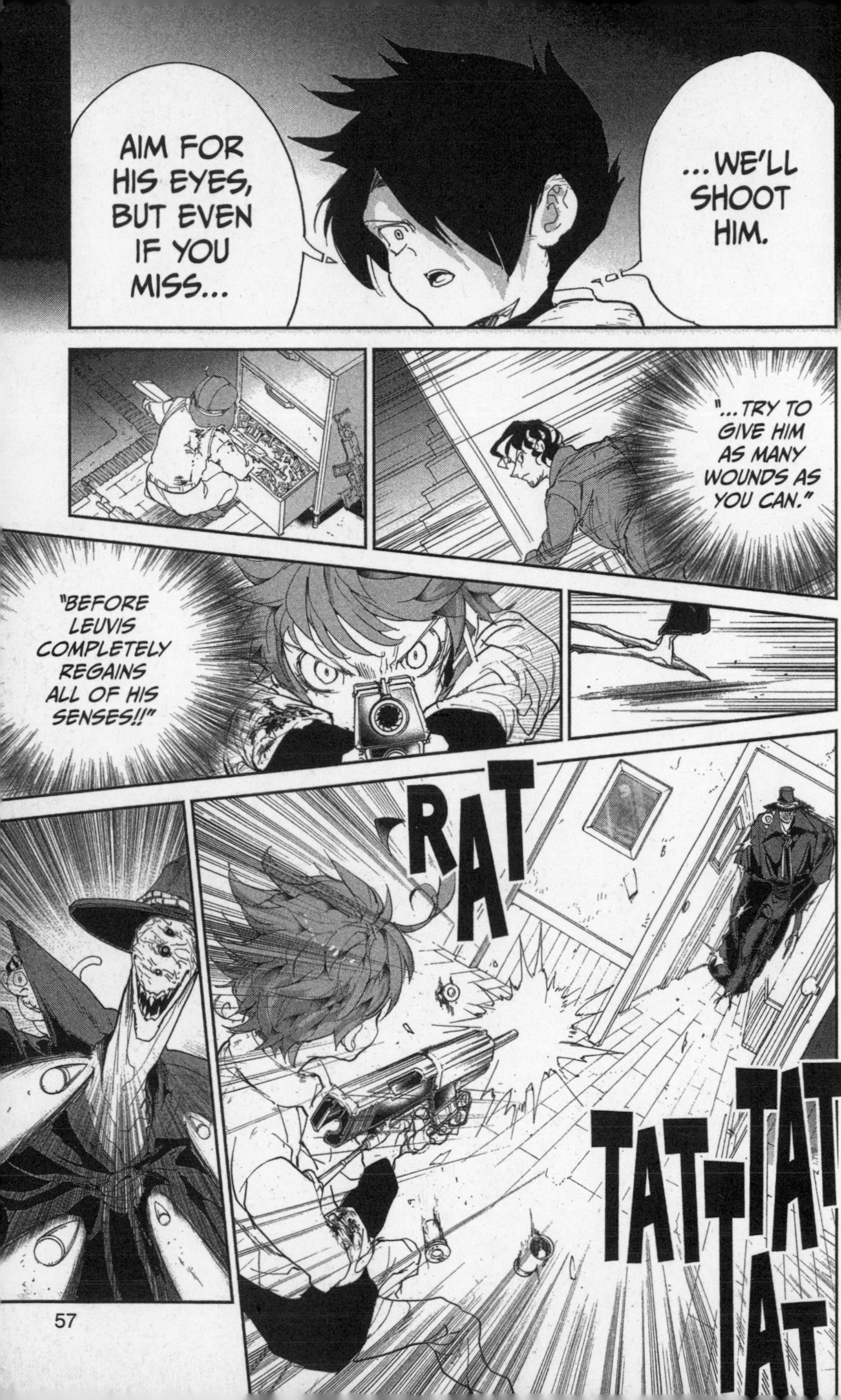
AIM FOR HIS EYES, BUT EVEN IF YOU MISS...
...WE'LL SHOOT HIM.
"...TRY TO GIVE HIM AS MANY WOUNDS AS YOU CAN."
"BEFORE LEUVIS COMPLETELY REGAINS ALL OF HIS SENSES!!"
RAT
TAT-TAT
TAT

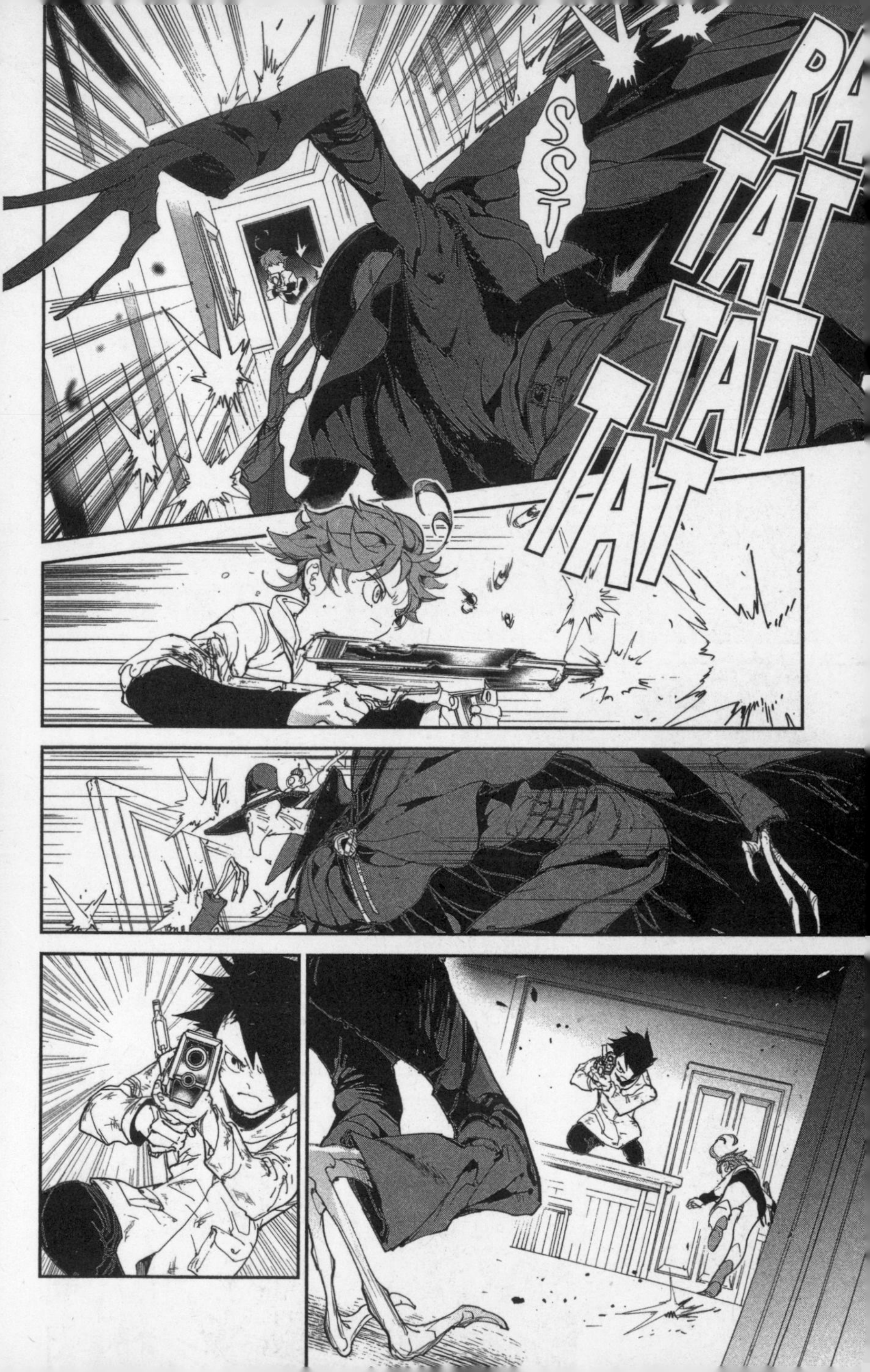
RA TAT TAT TAT TAT
SSST

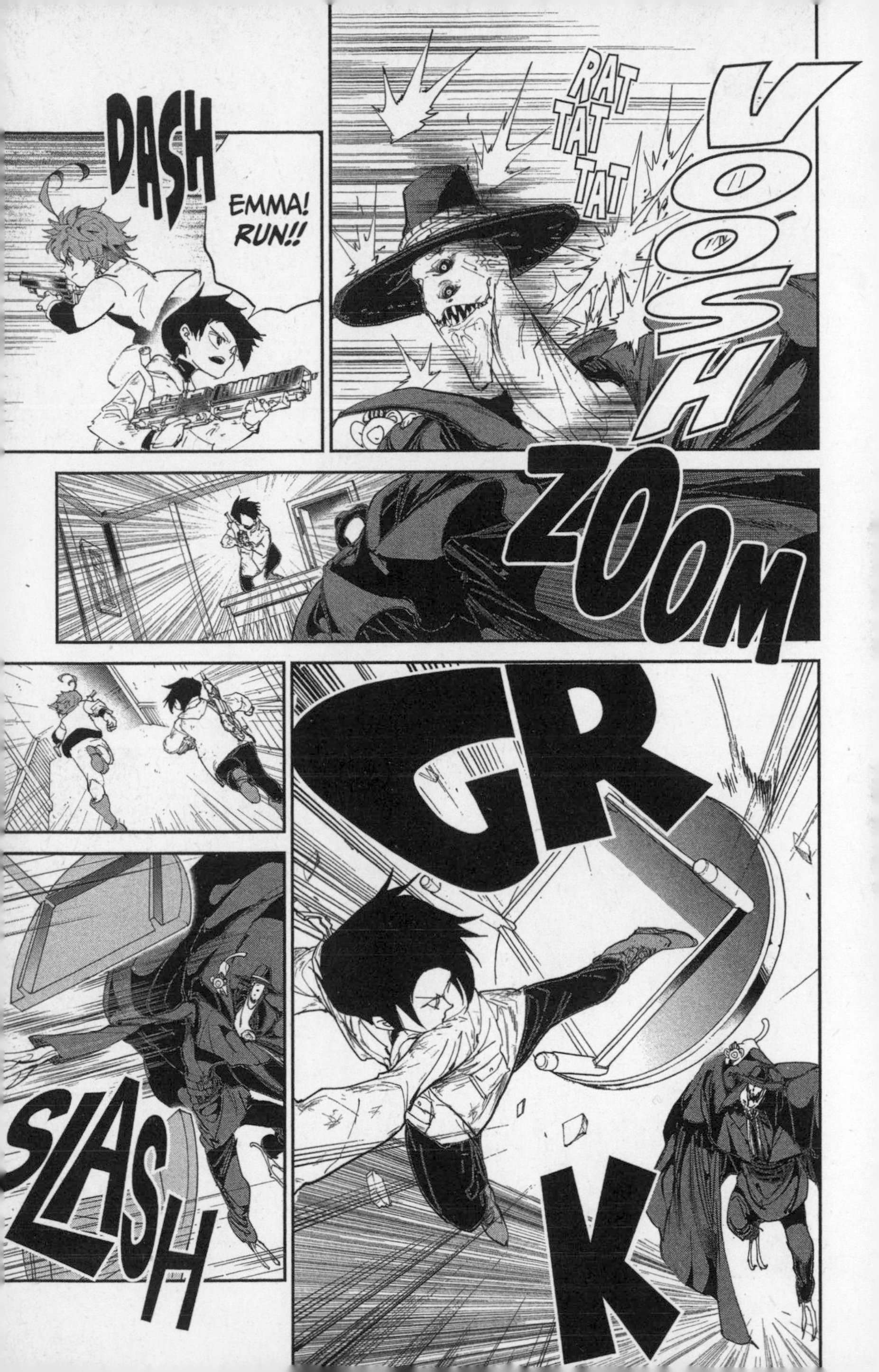
VOOSH
RAT TAT TAT
DASH
EMMA! RUN!!
ZOOM
GRK
SLASH

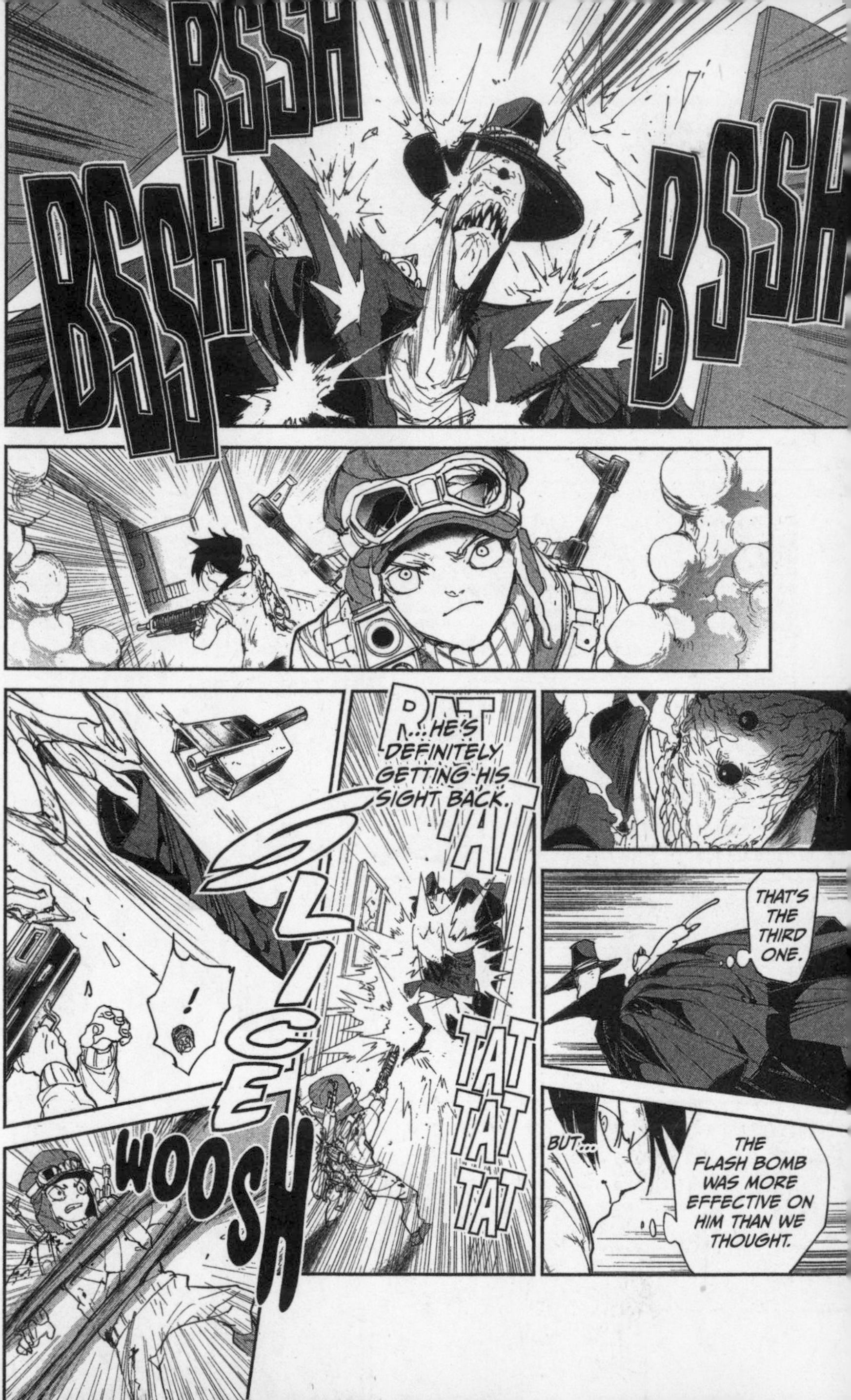
BSSH
BSSH
BSSH
THAT'S THE THIRD ONE.
BUT...
THE FLASH BOMB WAS MORE EFFECTIVE ON HIM THAN WE THOUGHT.
...HE'S DEFINITELY GETTING HIS SIGHT BACK.
RAT TAT
TAT TAT TAT TAT
SLICE
!
WOOSH

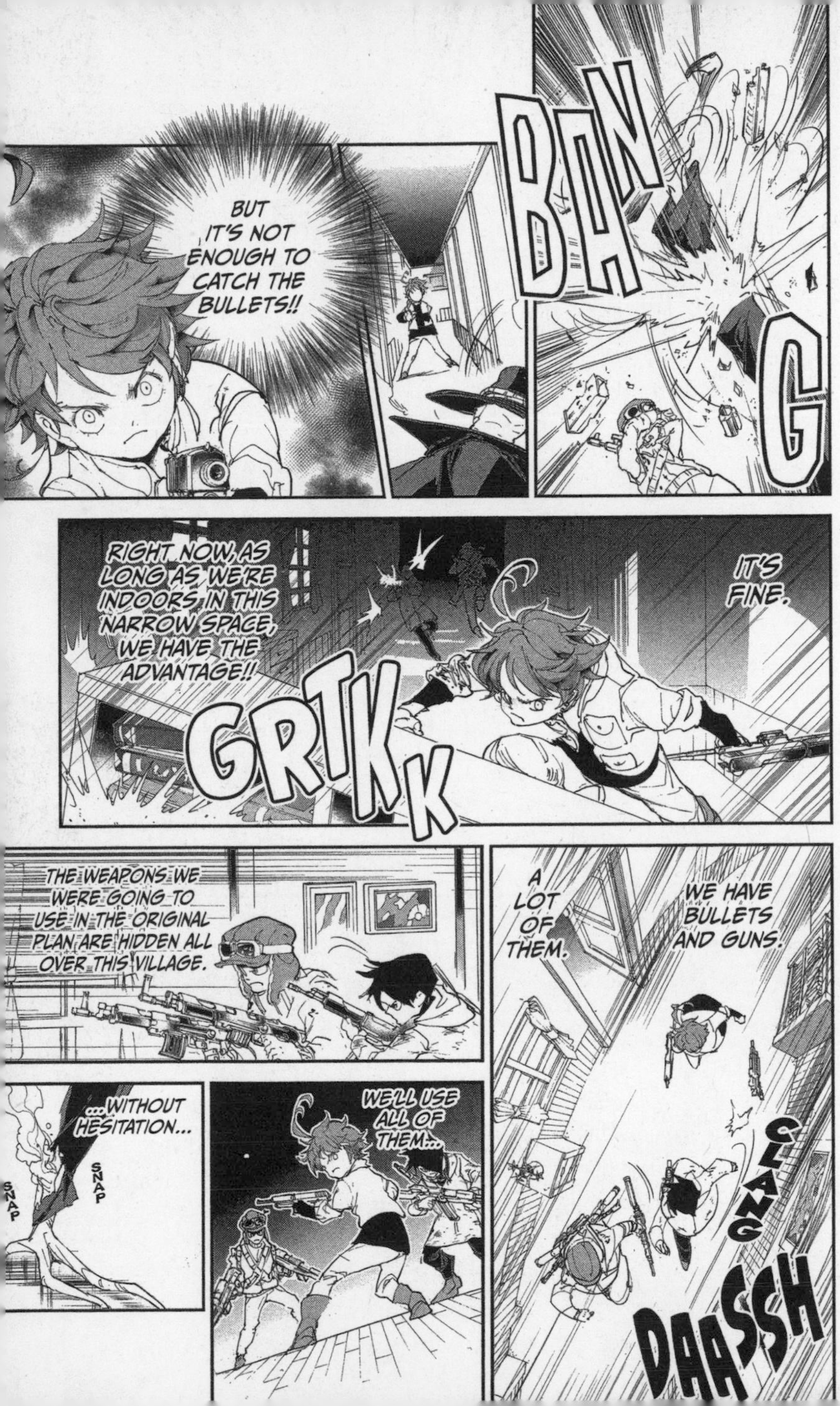
BANG
BUT IT'S NOT ENOUGH TO CATCH THE BULLETS!!
IT'S FINE.
RIGHT NOW, AS LONG AS WE'RE INDOORS IN THIS NARROW SPACE, WE HAVE THE ADVANTAGE!!
GRTKK
WE HAVE BULLETS AND GUNS.
A LOT OF THEM.
CLANG
DAASSH
THE WEAPONS WE WERE GOING TO USE IN THE ORIGINAL PLAN ARE HIDDEN ALL OVER THIS VILLAGE.
WE'LL USE ALL OF THEM...
...WITHOUT HESITATION...
SNAP
SNAP

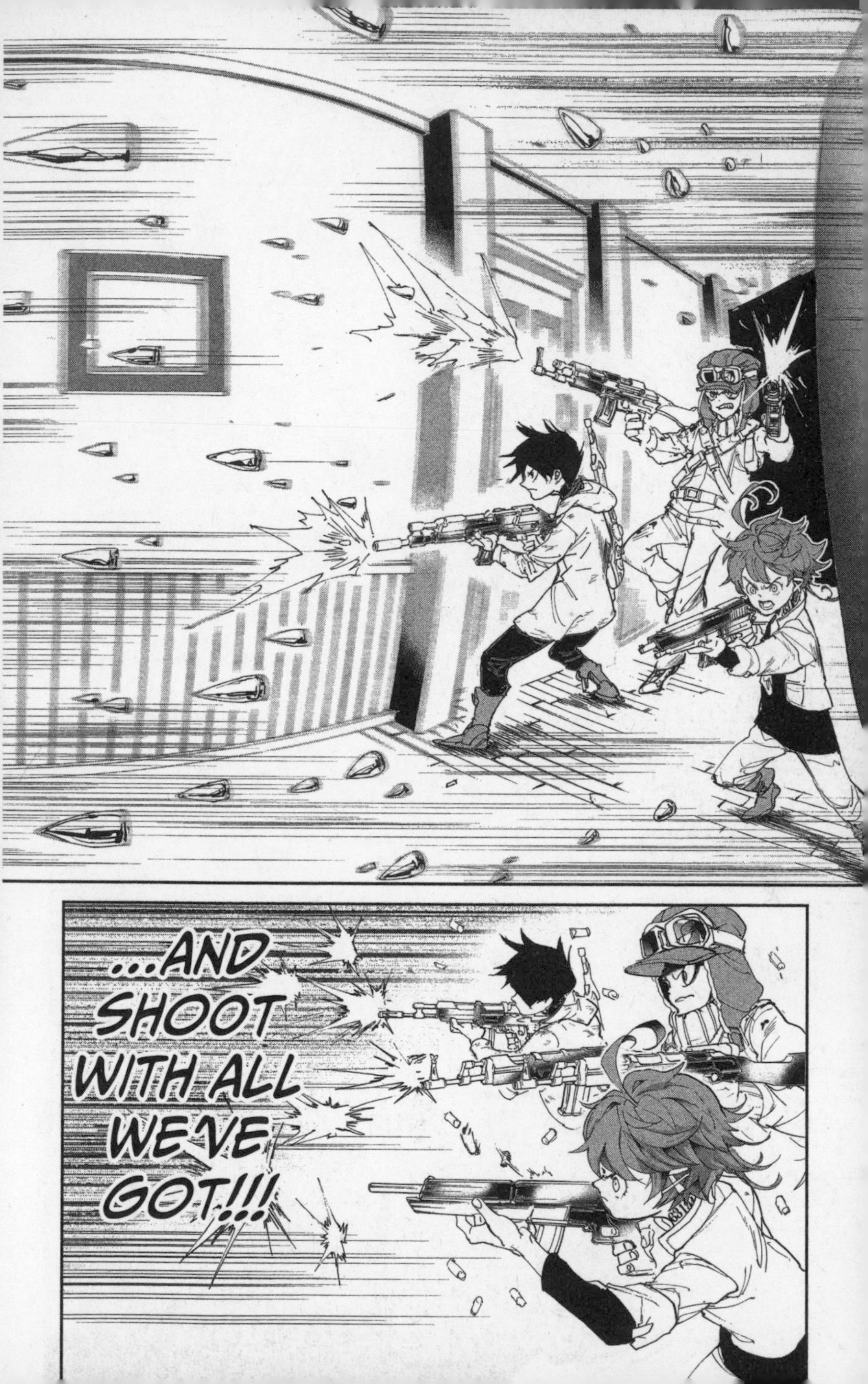
...AND SHOOT WITH ALL WE'VE GOT!!!

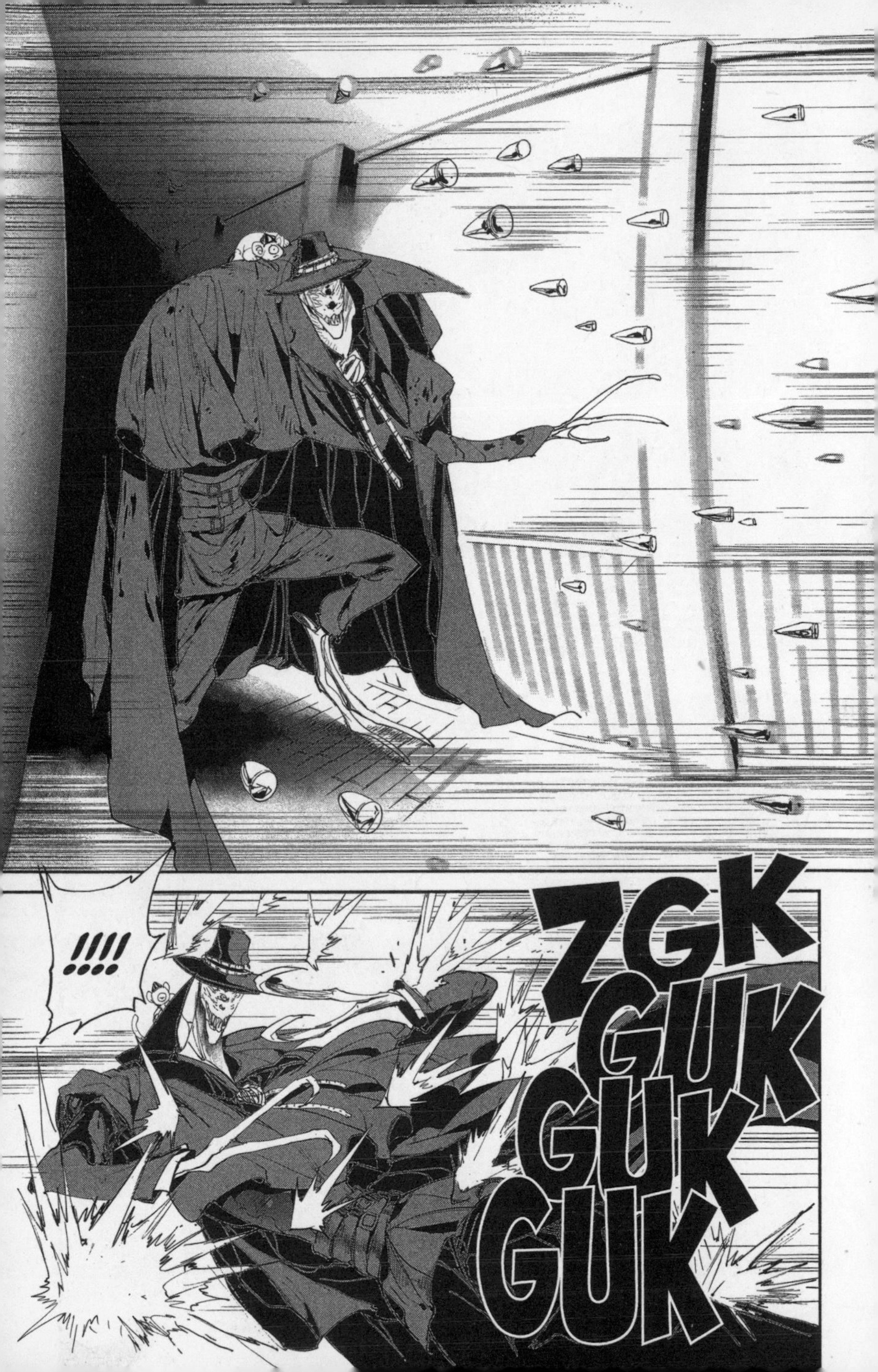
ZGK
GUK
GUK
GUK
!!!!

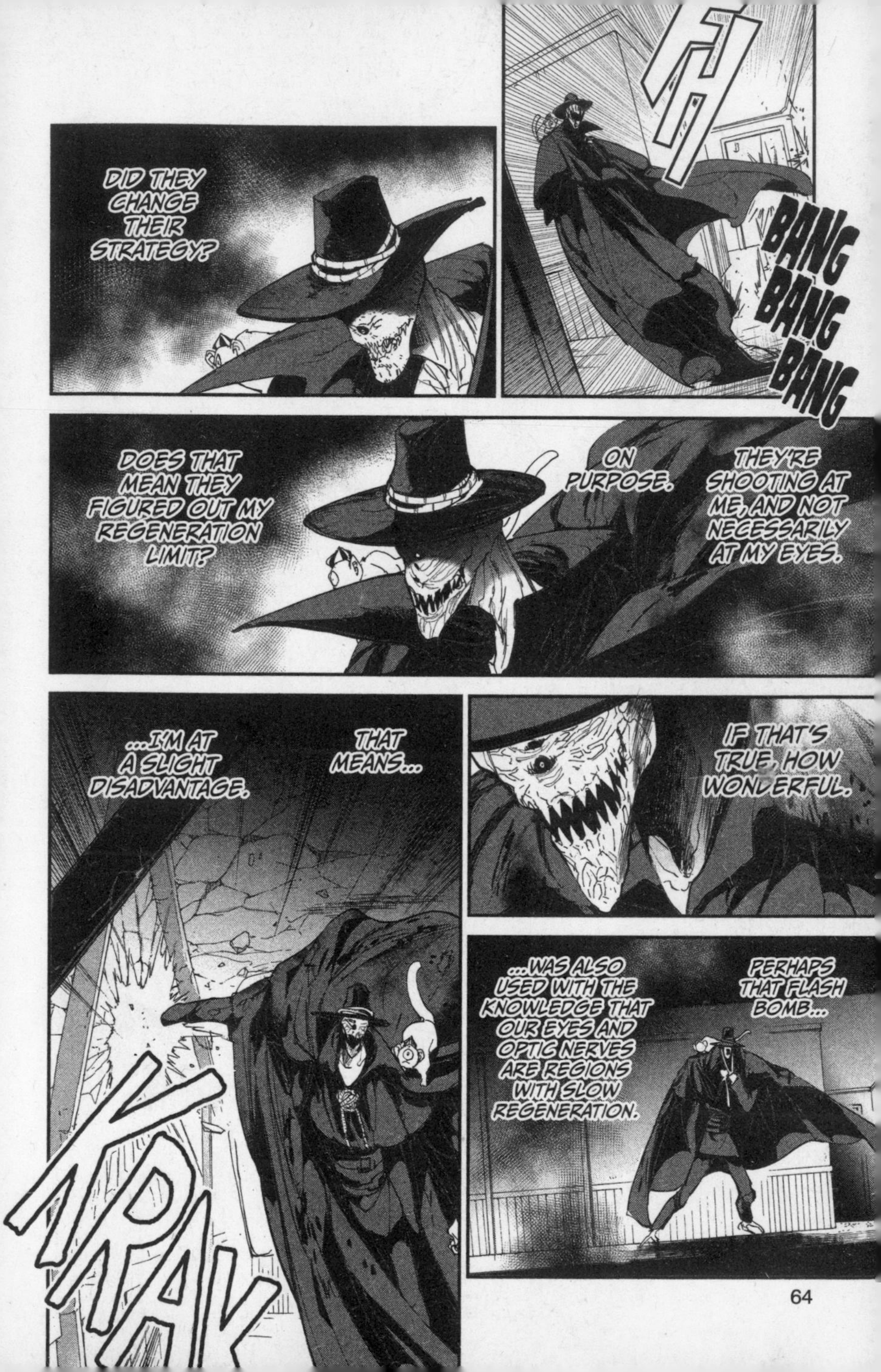
FH
BANG BANG BANG
DID THEY CHANGE THEIR STRATEGY?
THEY'RE SHOOTING AT ME, AND NOT NECESSARILY AT MY EYES.
ON PURPOSE.
DOES THAT MEAN THEY FIGURED OUT MY REGENERATION LIMIT?
IF THAT'S TRUE, HOW WONDERFUL.
PERHAPS THAT FLASH BOMB...
...WAS ALSO USED WITH THE KNOWLEDGE THAT OUR EYES AND OPTIC NERVES ARE REGIONS WITH SLOW REGENERATION.
THAT MEANS...
...I'M AT A SLIGHT DISADVANTAGE.
KRAK

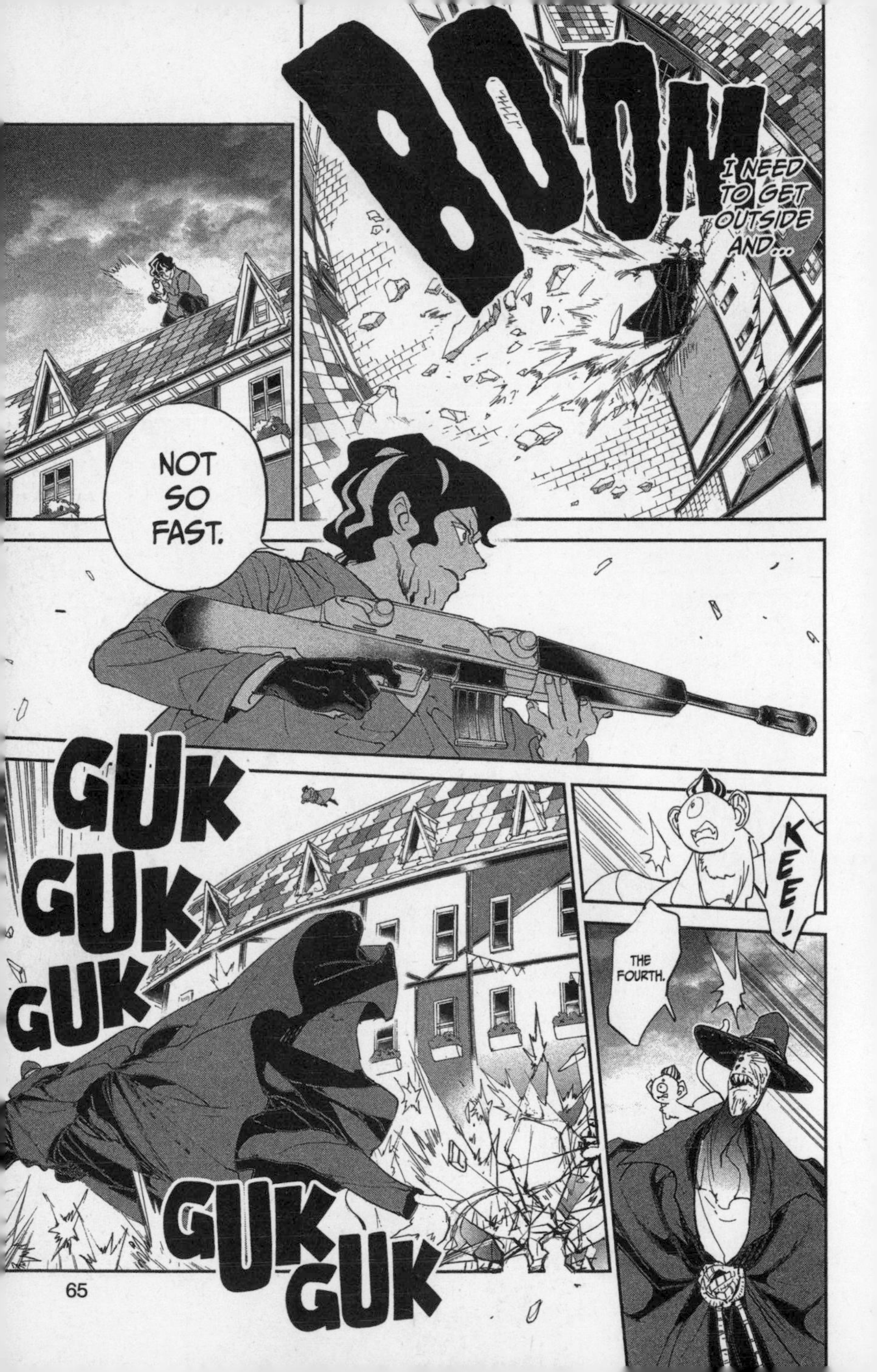
BOOM
I NEED TO GET OUTSIDE AND...
NOT SO FAST.
KEE!
THE FOURTH.
GUK GUK GUK
GUK GUK

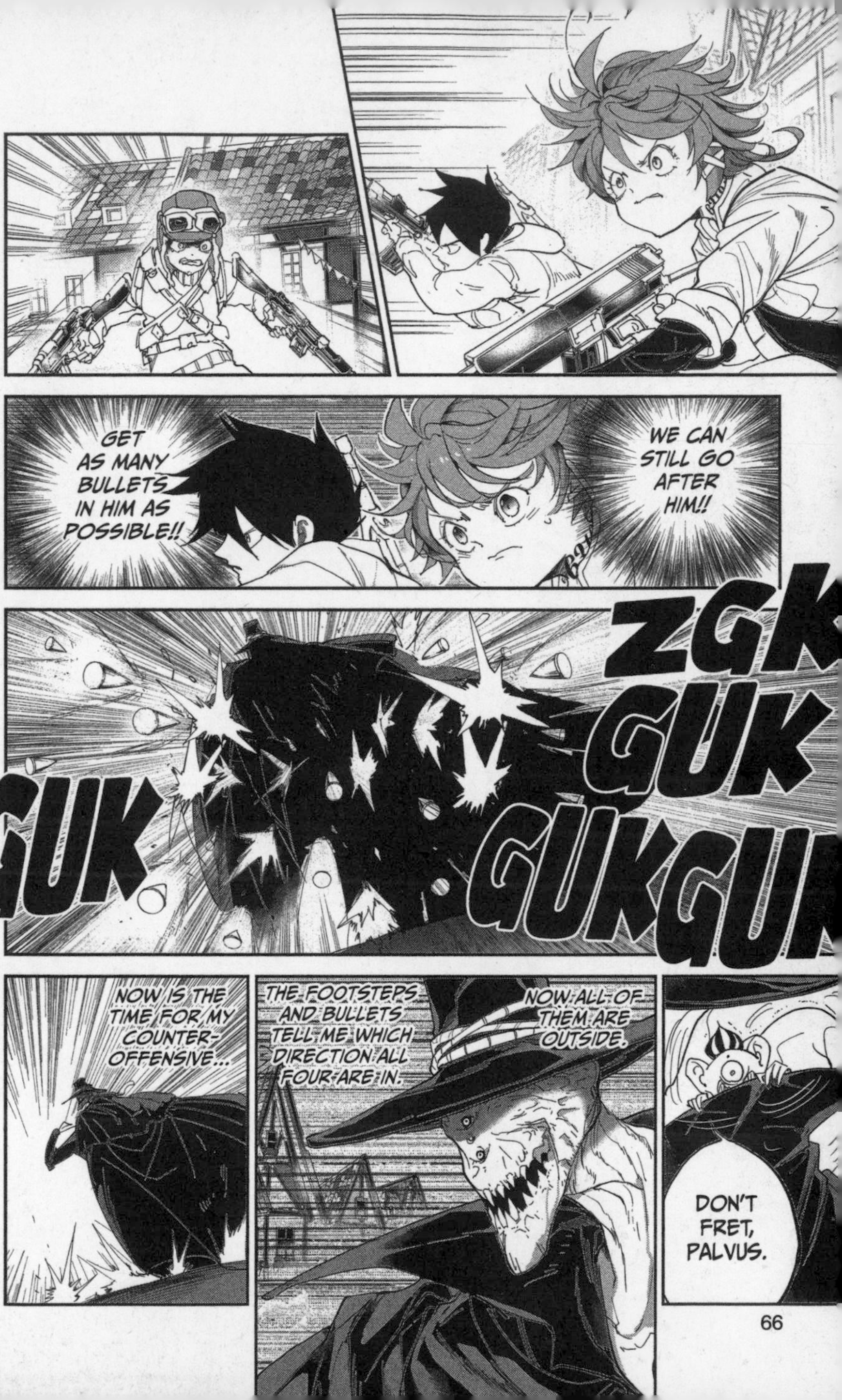
WE CAN STILL GO AFTER HIM!!
GET AS MANY BULLETS IN HIM AS POSSIBLE!!
ZGK
GUK
GUKGU
GUK
DON'T FRET, PALVUS.
NOW ALL OF THEM ARE OUTSIDE.
THE FOOTSTEPS AND BULLETS TELL ME WHICH DIRECTION ALL FOUR ARE IN.
NOW IS THE TIME FOR MY COUNTER-OFFENSIVE...

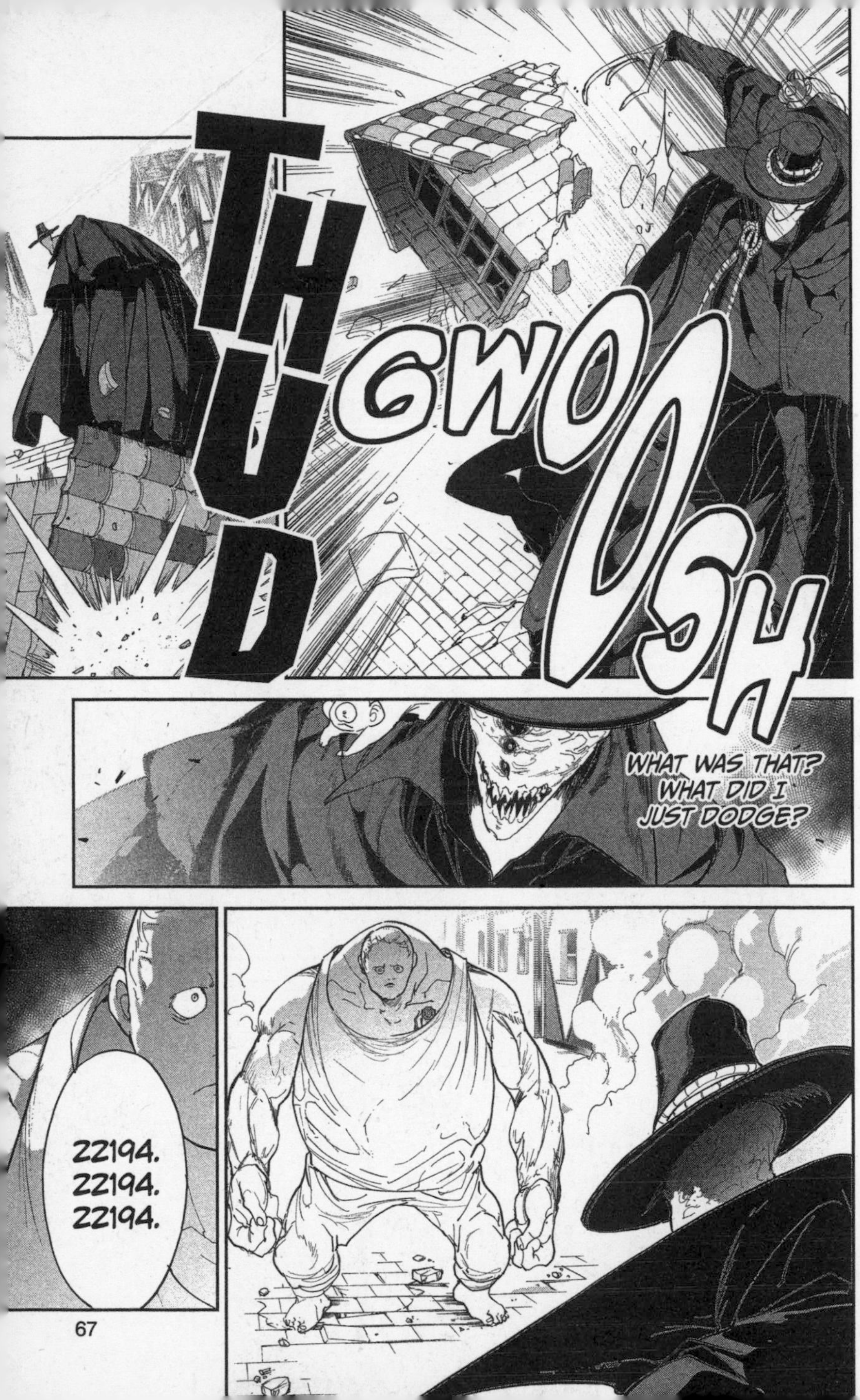
THUD
GWOOSH
WHAT WAS THAT? WHAT DID I JUST DODGE?
22194. 22194. 22194.

DIDN'T UNDERSTAND

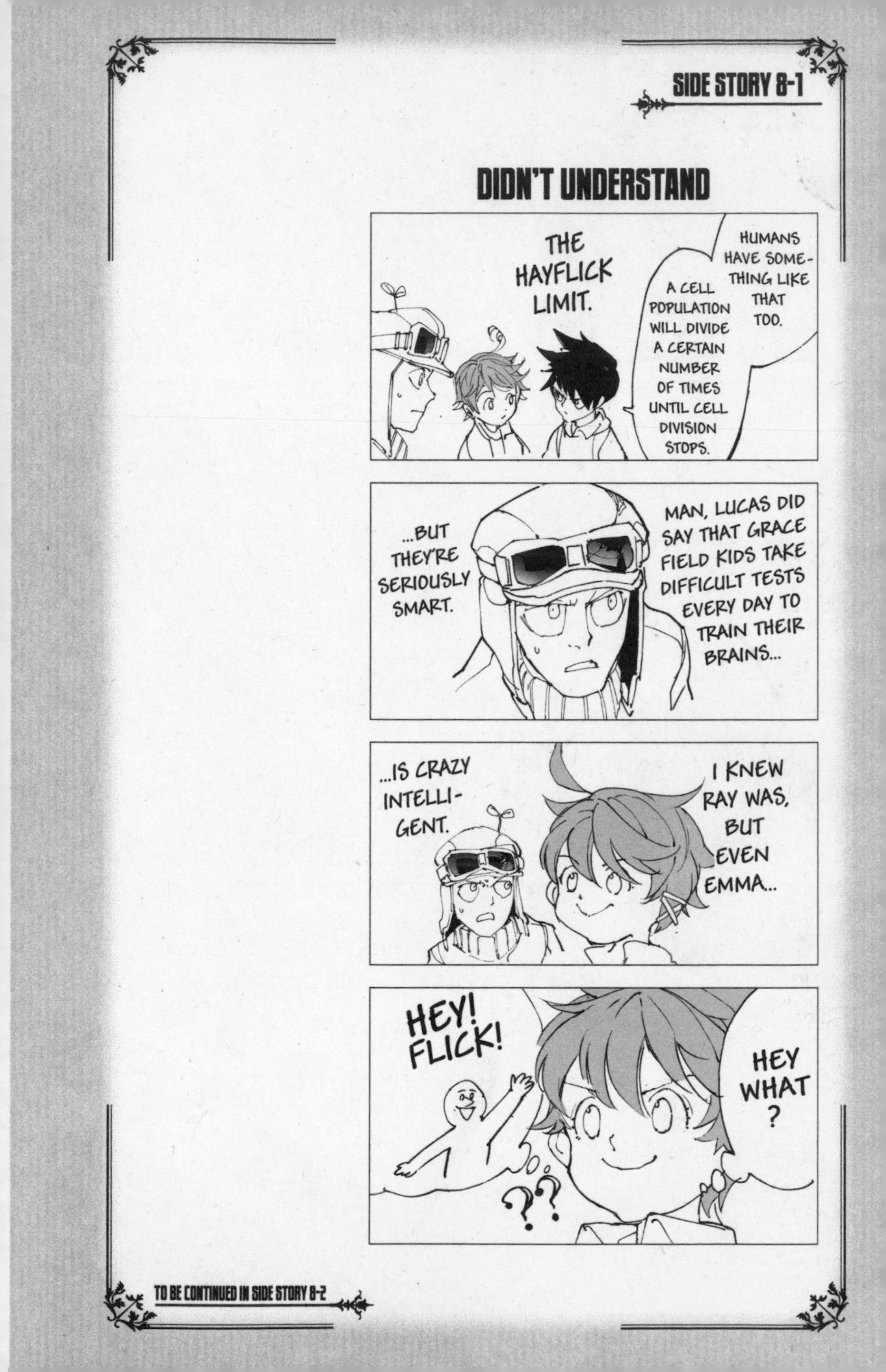
HUMANS HAVE SOME-THING LIKE THAT TOO.
A CELL POPULATION WILL DIVIDE A CERTAIN NUMBER OF TIMES UNTIL CELL DIVISION STOPS.
THE HAYFLICK LIMIT.
MAN, LUCAS DID SAY THAT GRACE FIELD KIDS TAKE DIFFICULT TESTS EVERY DAY TO TRAIN THEIR BRAINS...
...BUT THEY'RE SERIOUSLY SMART.
I KNEW RAY WAS, BUT EVEN EMMA...
...IS CRAZY INTELLI-GENT.
HEY WHAT ?
HEY! FLICK!
??

TO BE CONTINUED IN SIDE STORY 8-2

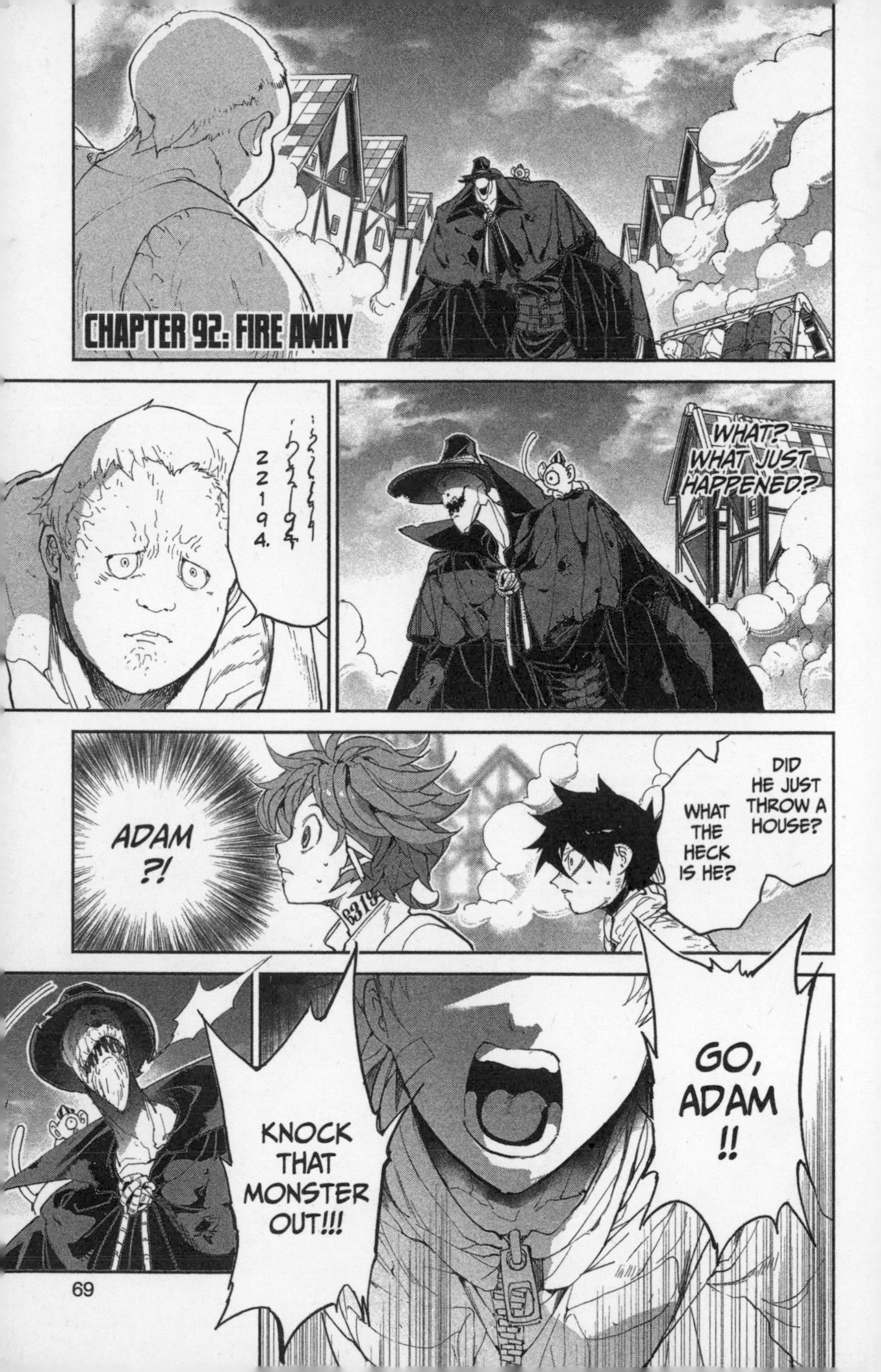

CHAPTER 92: FIRE AWAY
WHAT? WHAT JUST HAPPENED?
22194.
DID HE JUST THROW A HOUSE?
WHAT THE HECK IS HE?
ADAM ?!
GO, ADAM !!
KNOCK THAT MONSTER OUT!!!

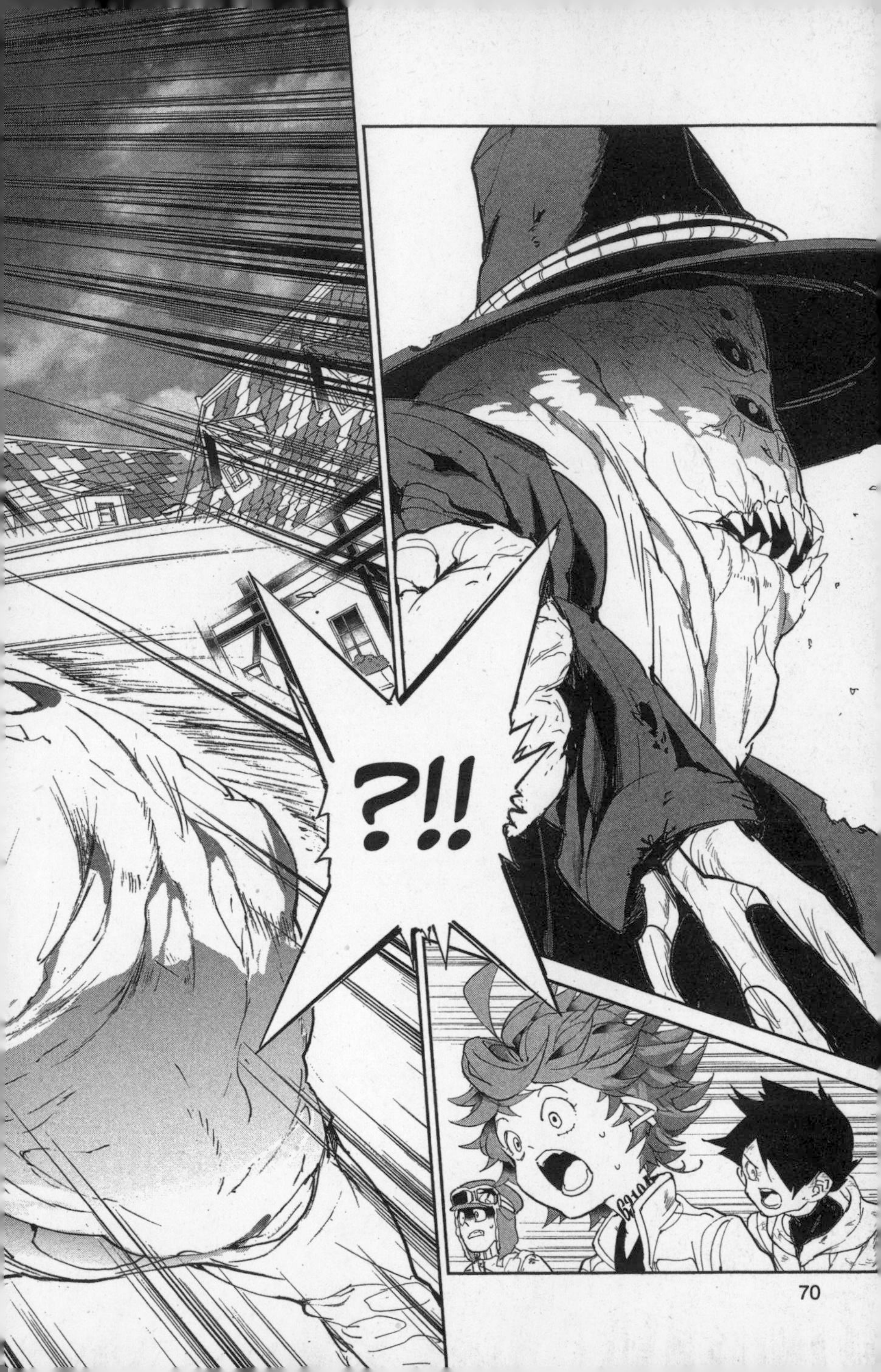
?!!

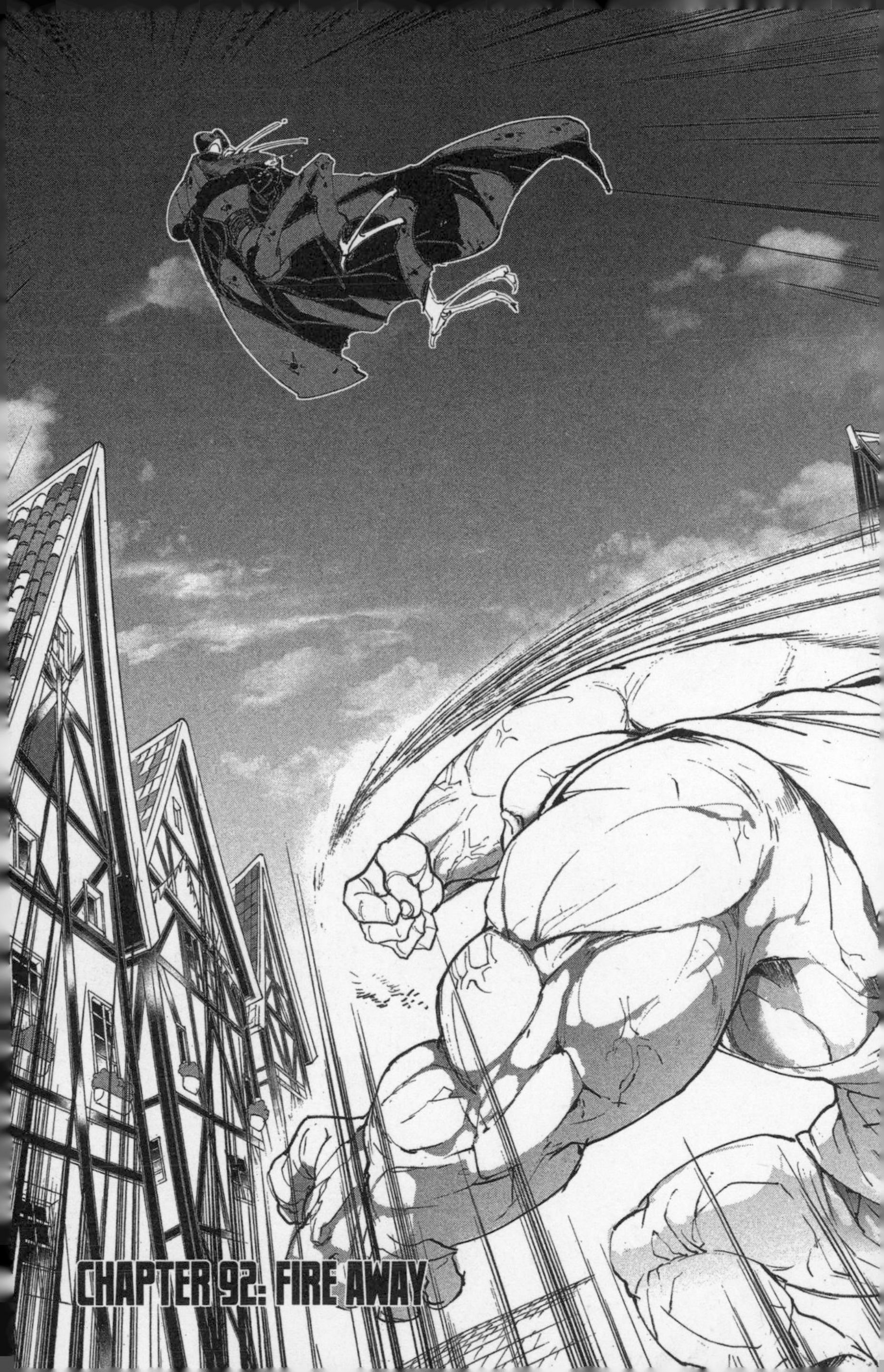
CHAPTER 92: FIRE AWAY

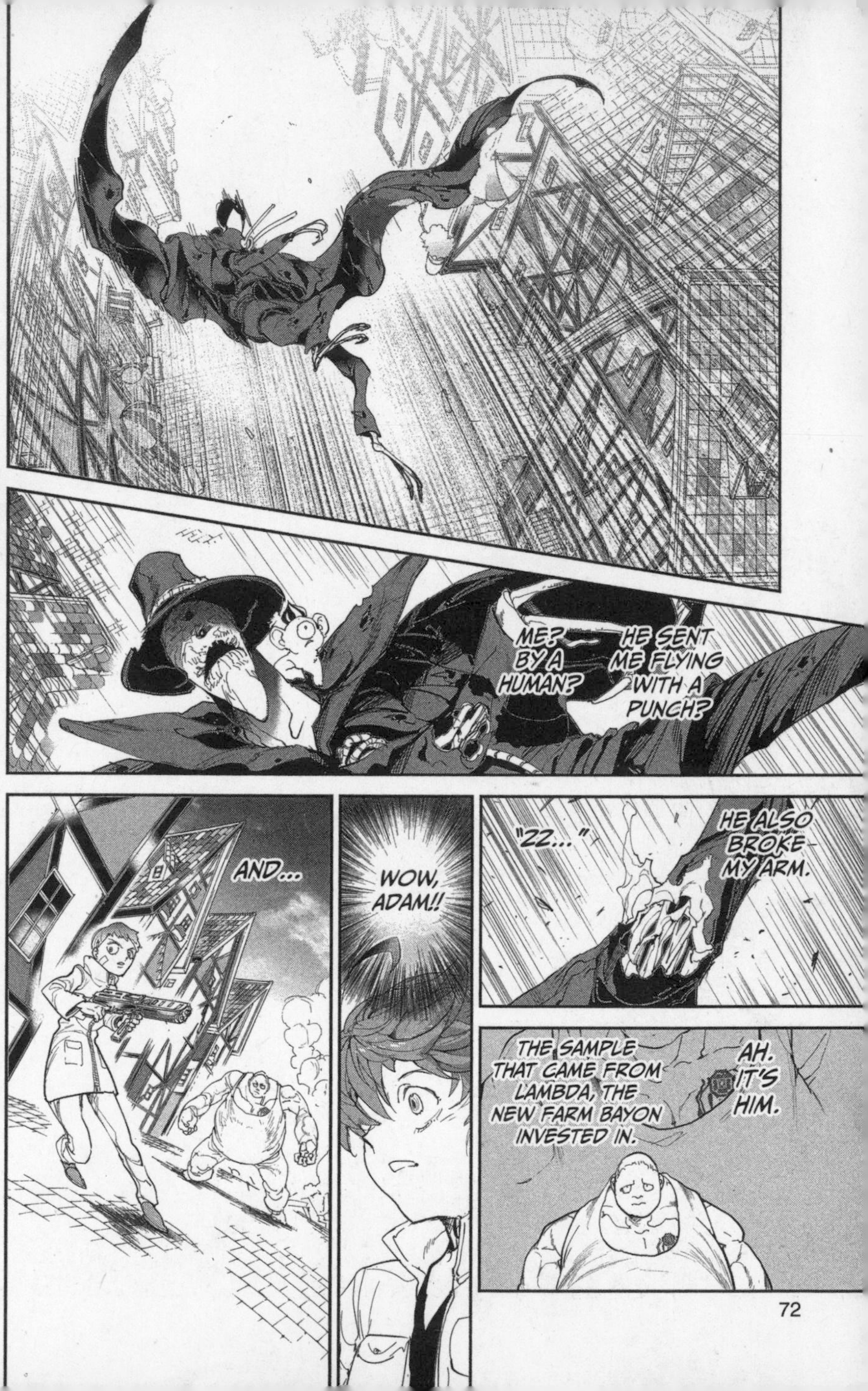
HE SENT ME FLYING WITH A PUNCH?
ME? BY A HUMAN?
HE ALSO BROKE MY ARM.
"ZZ..."
AH. IT'S HIM.
THE SAMPLE THAT CAME FROM LAMBDA, THE NEW FARM BAYON INVESTED IN.
WOW, ADAM!!
AND...

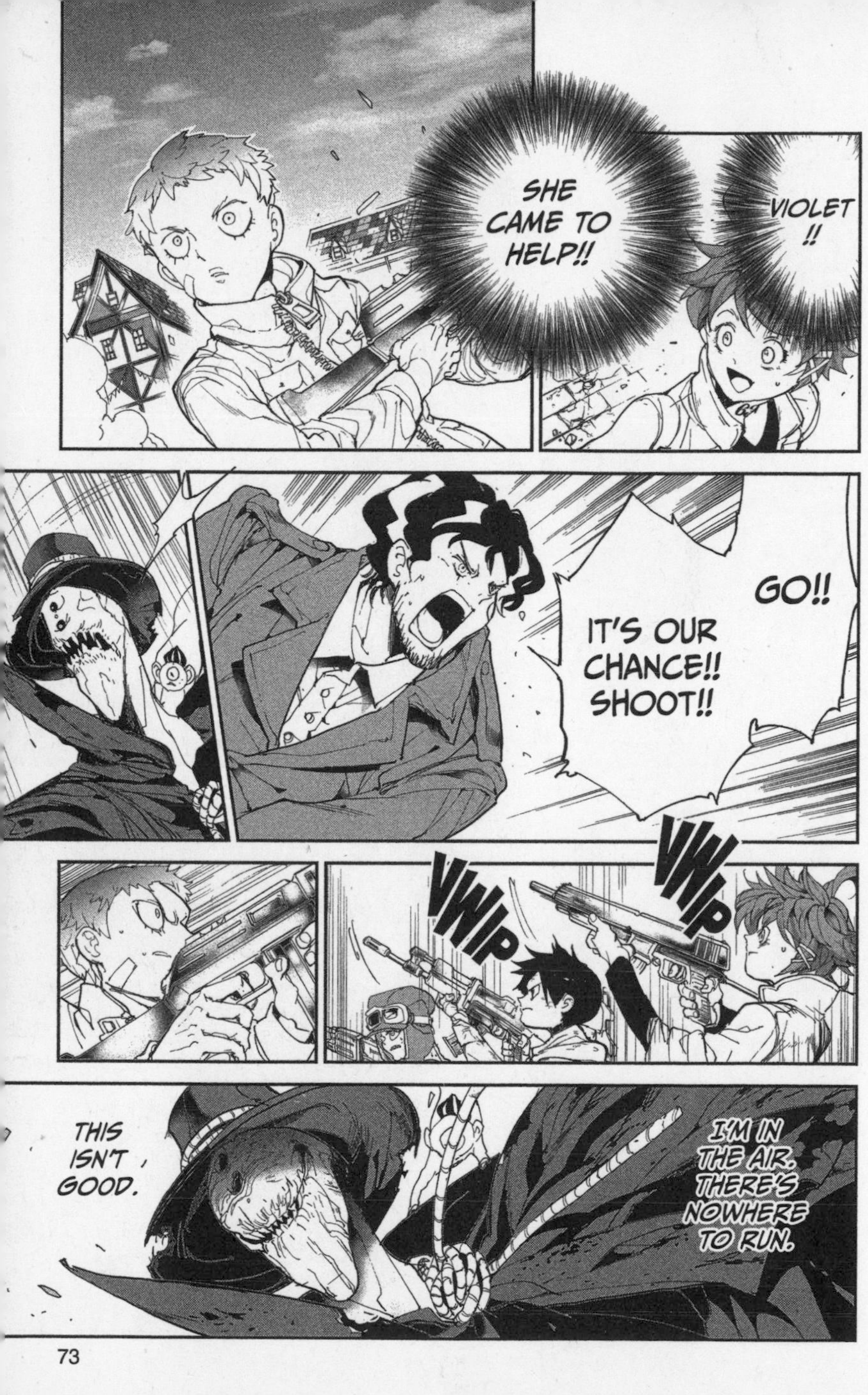
VIOLET !!
SHE CAME TO HELP!!
GO!! IT'S OUR CHANCE!! SHOOT!!
VWIP
VWIP
I'M IN THE AIR. THERE'S NOWHERE TO RUN.
THIS ISN'T GOOD.

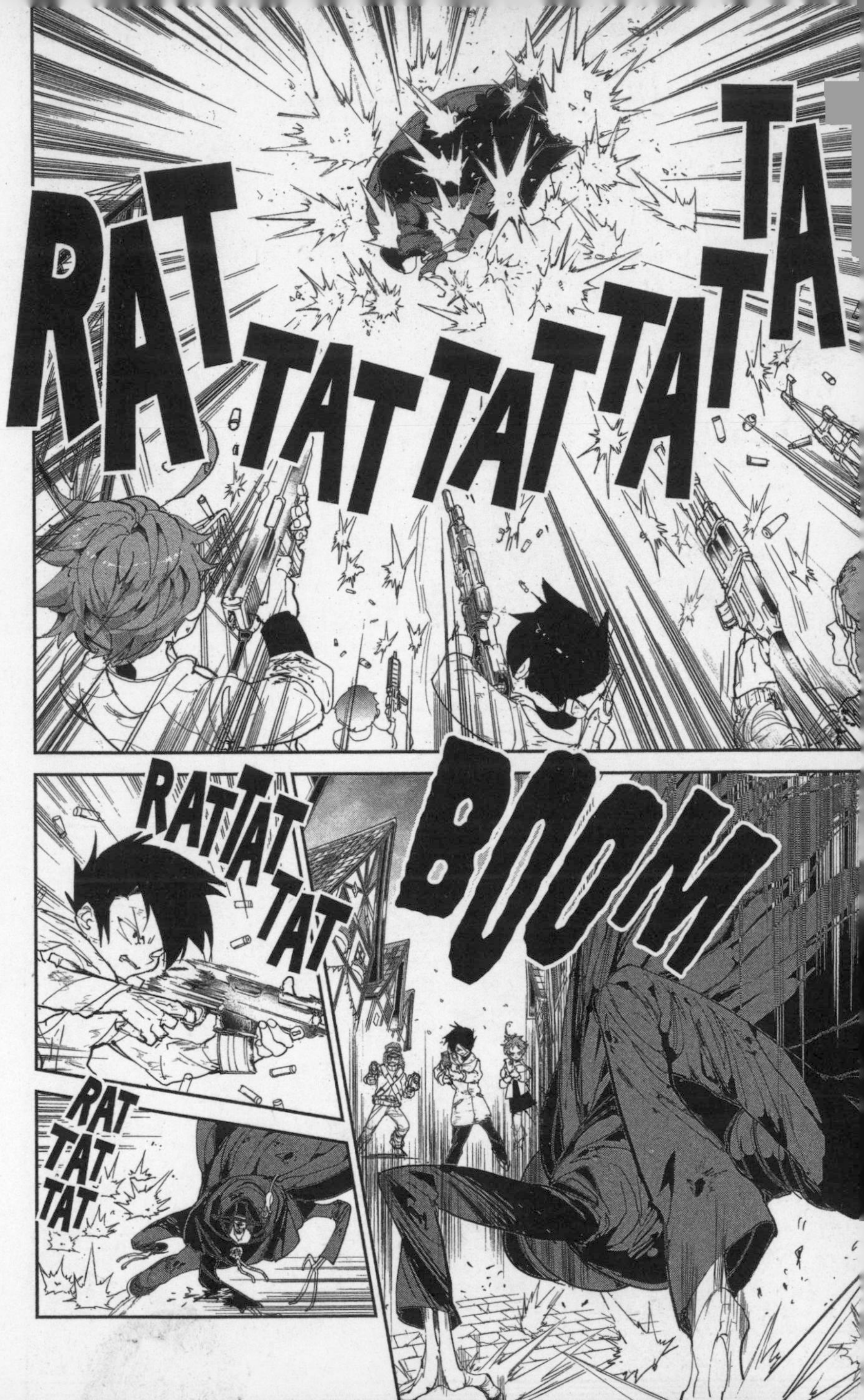
RAT TAT TAT TAT TA TA
BOOM
RAT TAT TAT TAT
RAT TAT TAT

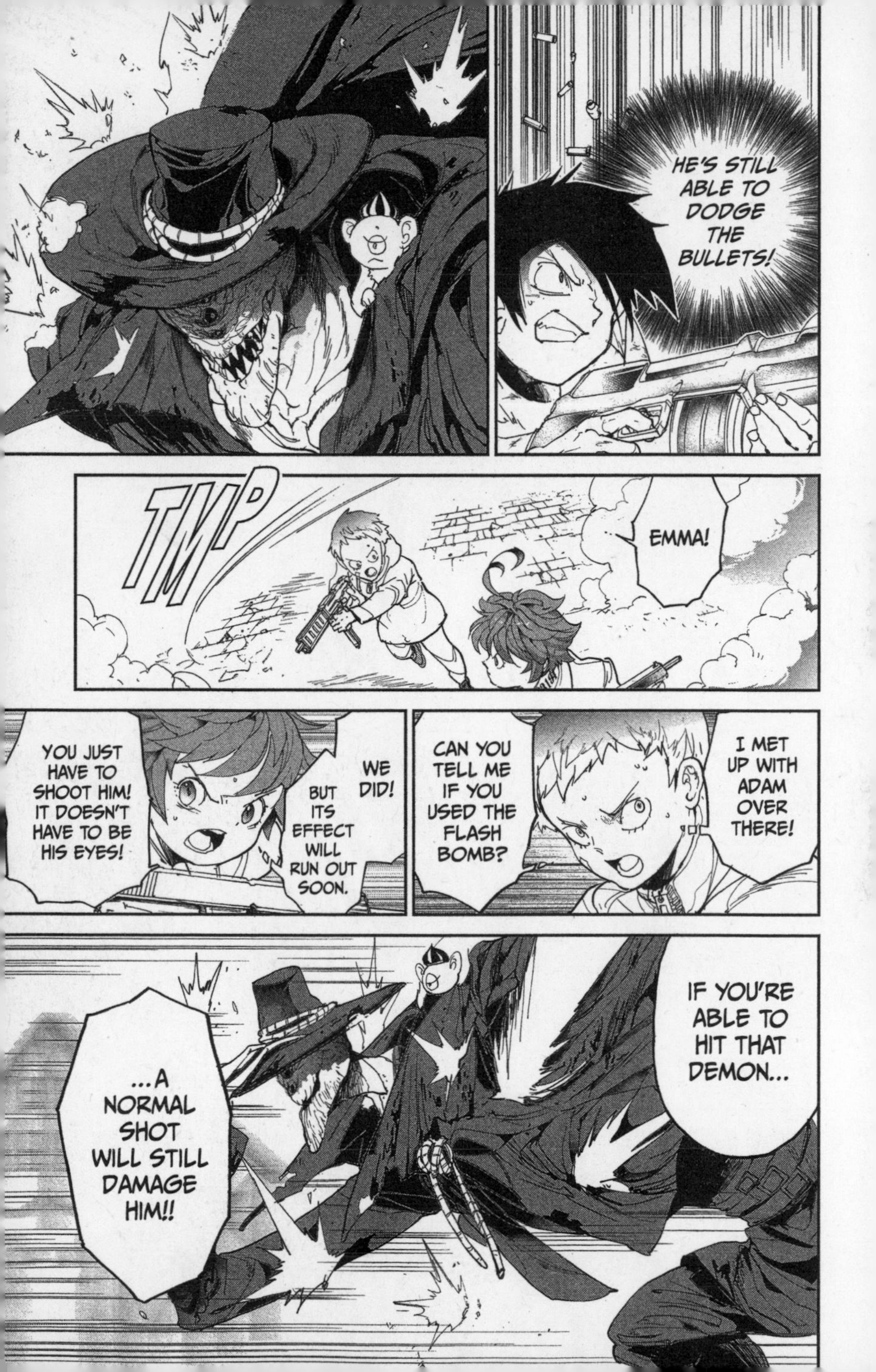
HE'S STILL ABLE TO DODGE THE BULLETS!
EMMA!
TMP
I MET UP WITH ADAM OVER THERE!
CAN YOU TELL ME IF YOU USED THE FLASH BOMB?
WE DID!
BUT ITS EFFECT WILL RUN OUT SOON.
YOU JUST HAVE TO SHOOT HIM! IT DOESN'T HAVE TO BE HIS EYES!
IF YOU'RE ABLE TO HIT THAT DEMON...
...A NORMAL SHOT WILL STILL DAMAGE HIM!!

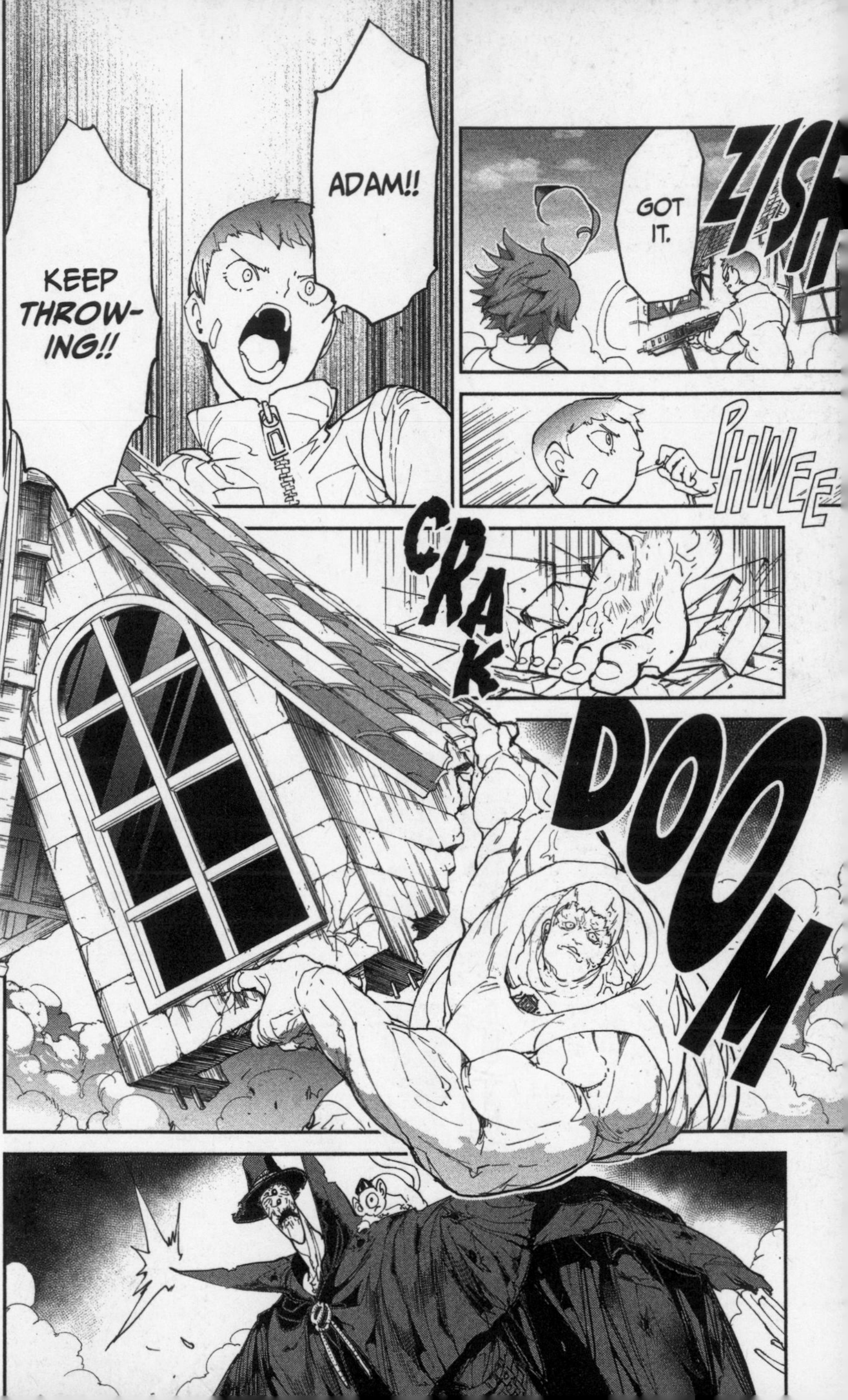
GOT IT.
ZISH
PHWEEE
ADAM!!
KEEP THROWING!!
CRAK
DOOOM

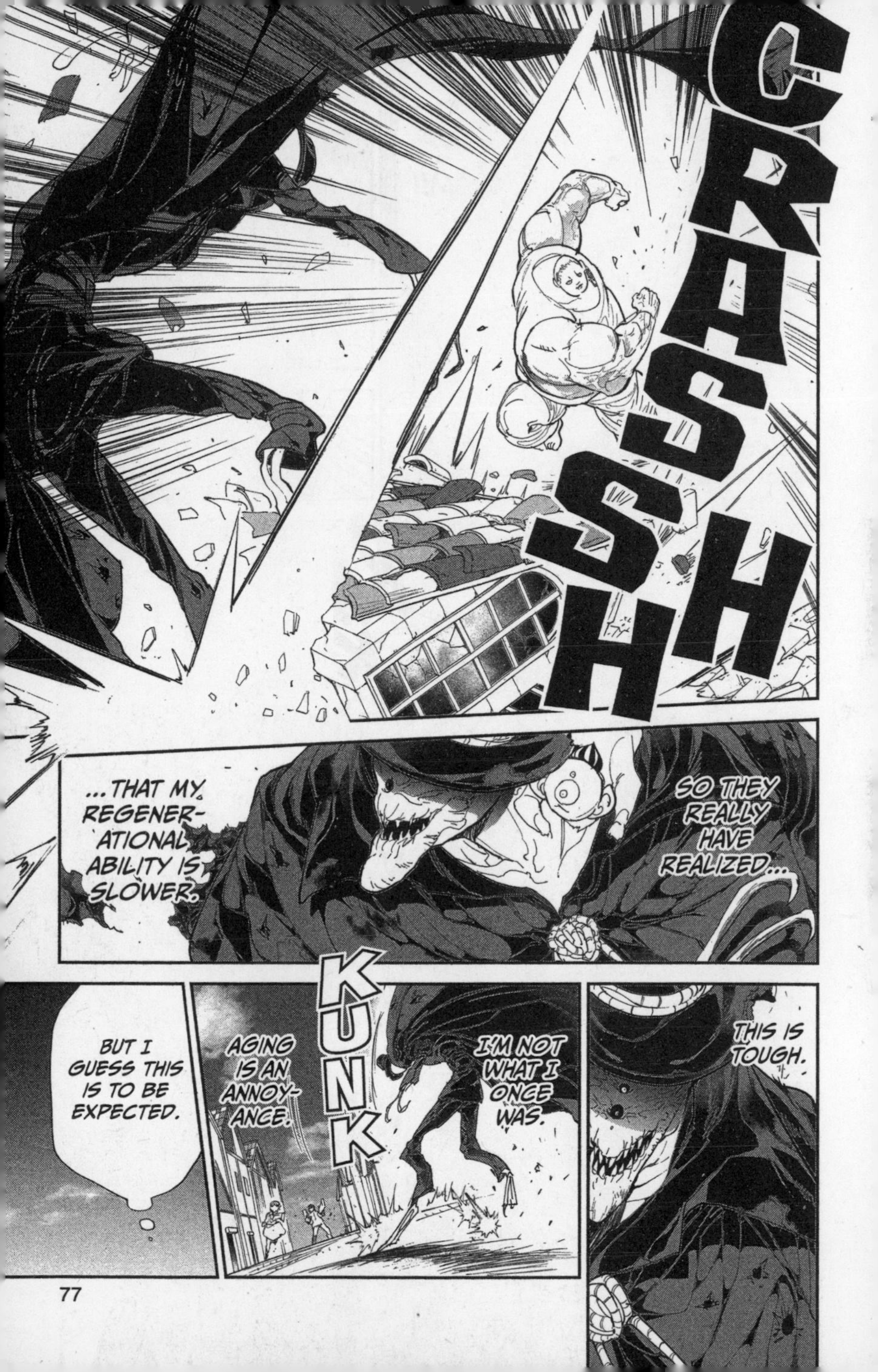
CRASSHH
SO THEY REALLY HAVE REALIZED...
...THAT MY REGENER-ATIONAL ABILITY IS SLOWER.
THIS IS TOUGH.
I'M NOT WHAT I ONCE WAS.
KUNK
AGING IS AN ANNOY-ANCE.
BUT I GUESS THIS IS TO BE EXPECTED.

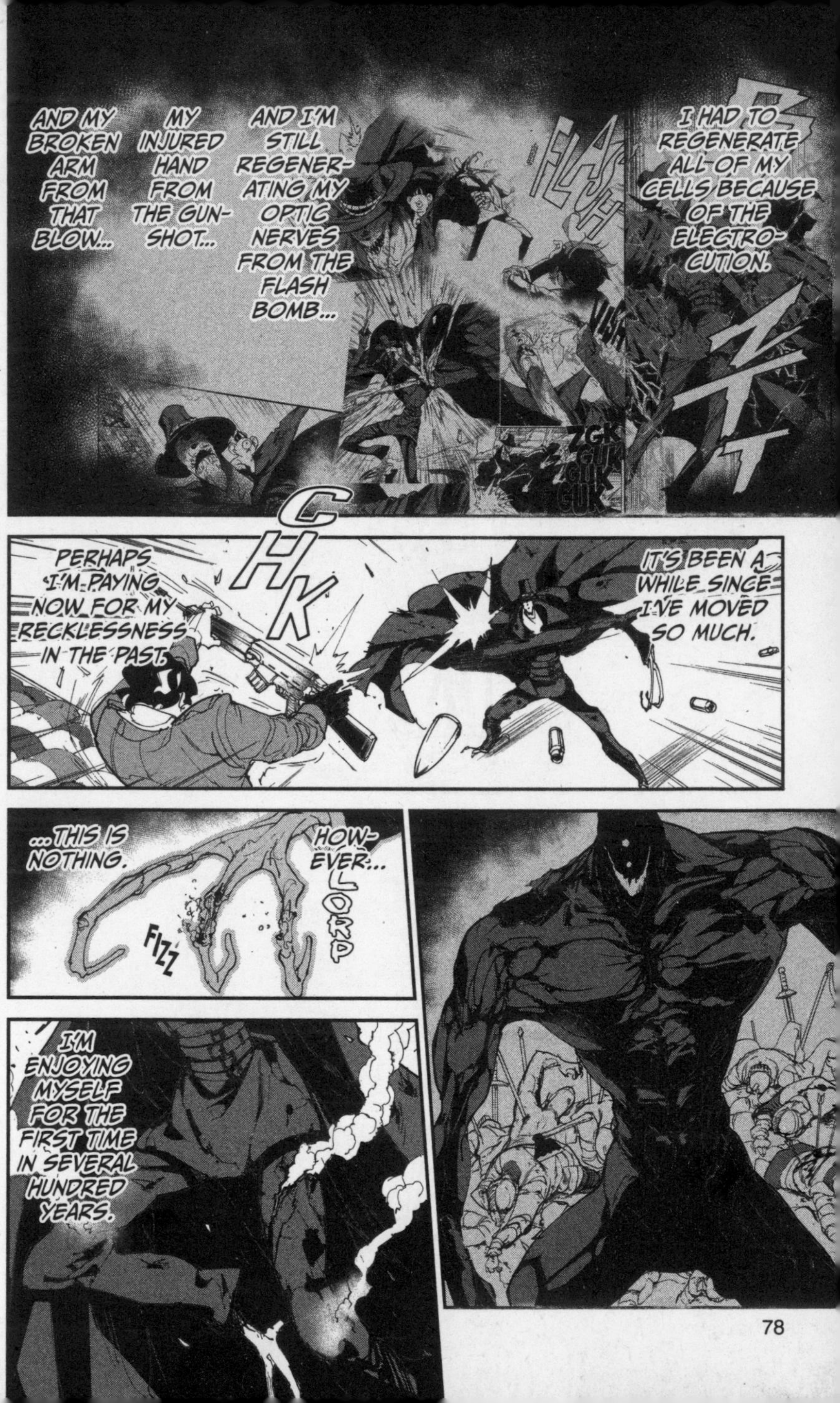
I HAD TO REGENERATE ALL OF MY CELLS BECAUSE OF THE ELECTROCUTION.
FLASH
AND I'M STILL REGENERATING MY OPTIC NERVES FROM THE FLASH BOMB...
MY INJURED HAND FROM THE GUNSHOT...
AND MY BROKEN ARM FROM THAT BLOW...
ZGK GUK GUK GUK
IT'S BEEN A WHILE SINCE I'VE MOVED SO MUCH.
CHK
PERHAPS I'M PAYING NOW FOR MY RECKLESSNESS IN THE PAST.
HOWEVER...
LORP
FIZZ
...THIS IS NOTHING.
I'M ENJOYING MYSELF FOR THE FIRST TIME IN SEVERAL HUNDRED YEARS.

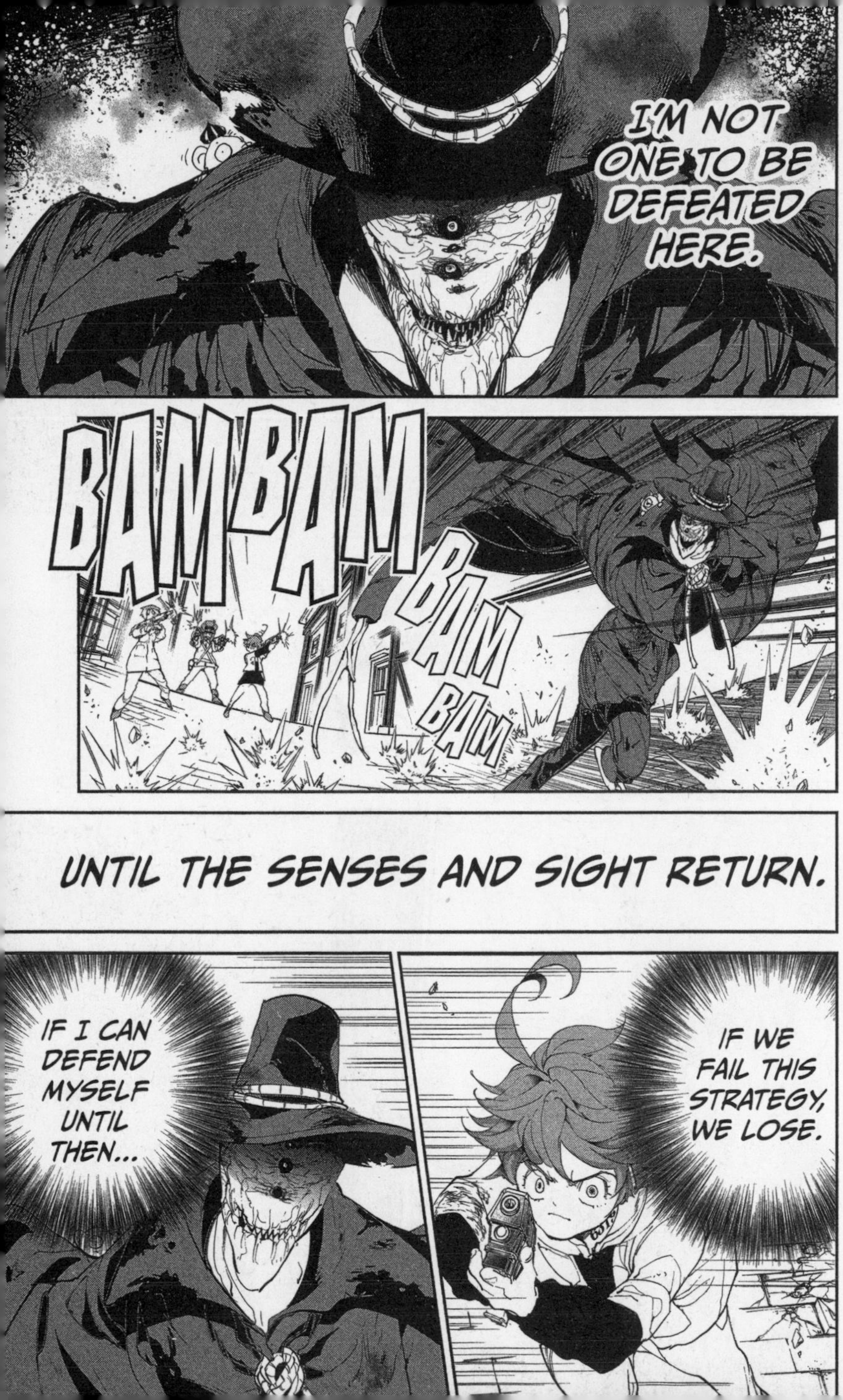
I'M NOT ONE TO BE DEFEATED HERE.
BAM BAM BAM
BAM BAM
UNTIL THE SENSES AND SIGHT RETURN.
IF WE FAIL THIS STRATEGY, WE LOSE.
IF I CAN DEFEND MYSELF UNTIL THEN...

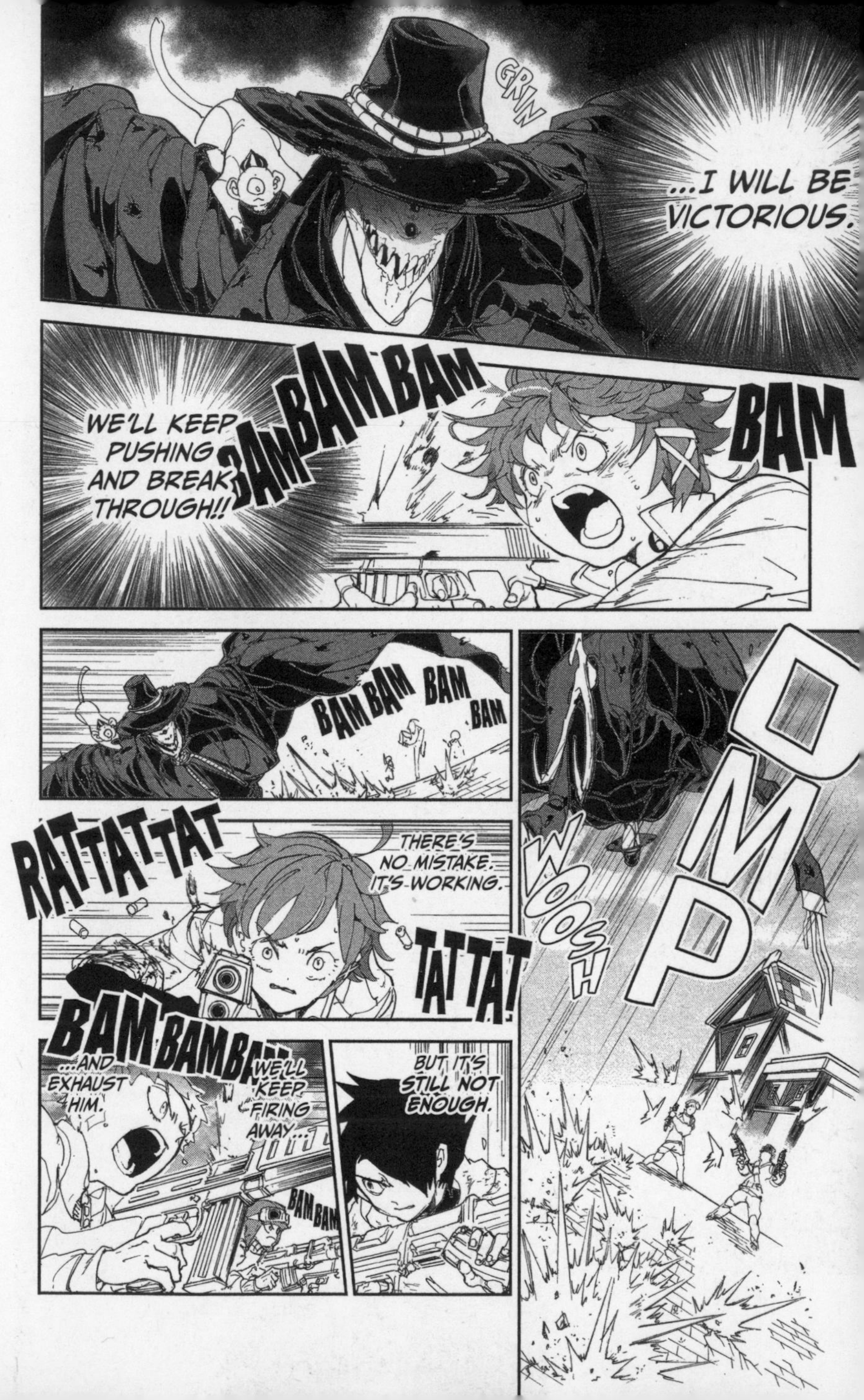
GRIN
...I WILL BE VICTORIOUS.
BAM
BAM BAM BAM
WE'LL KEEP PUSHING AND BREAK THROUGH!!
WOOSH
BAM BAM BAM BAM
RATTATTAT
THERE'S NO MISTAKE. IT'S WORKING.
TATTAT!
BUT IT'S STILL NOT ENOUGH.
BAMBAMBAM
WE'LL KEEP FIRING AWAY...
...AND EXHAUST HIM.
BAM BAM

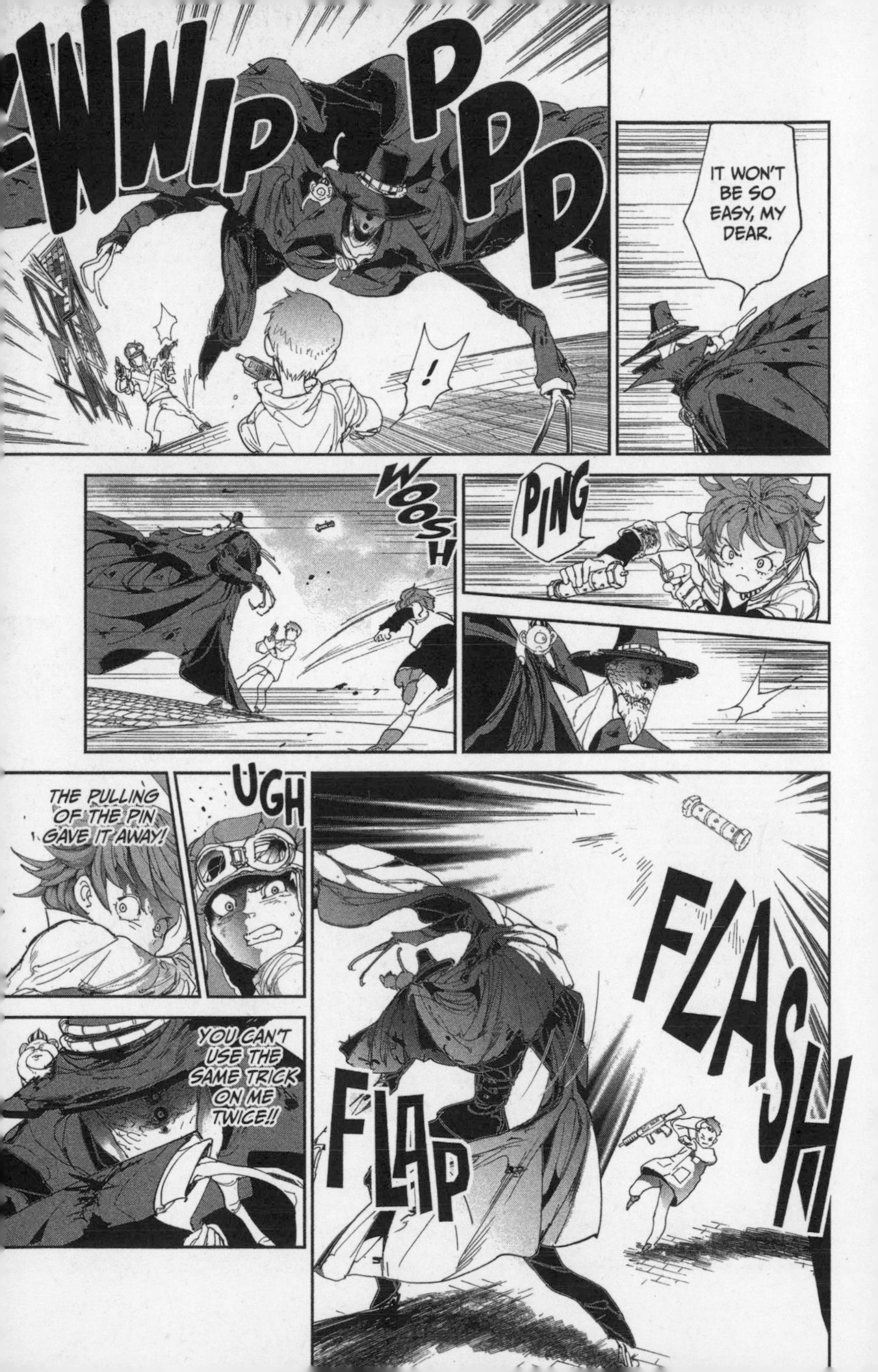
IT WON'T BE SO EASY, MY DEAR.
WWIPPPP
!
PING
WOOSH
FLASH
FLAP
UGH
THE PULLING OF THE PIN GAVE IT AWAY!
YOU CAN'T USE THE SAME TRICK ON ME TWICE!!

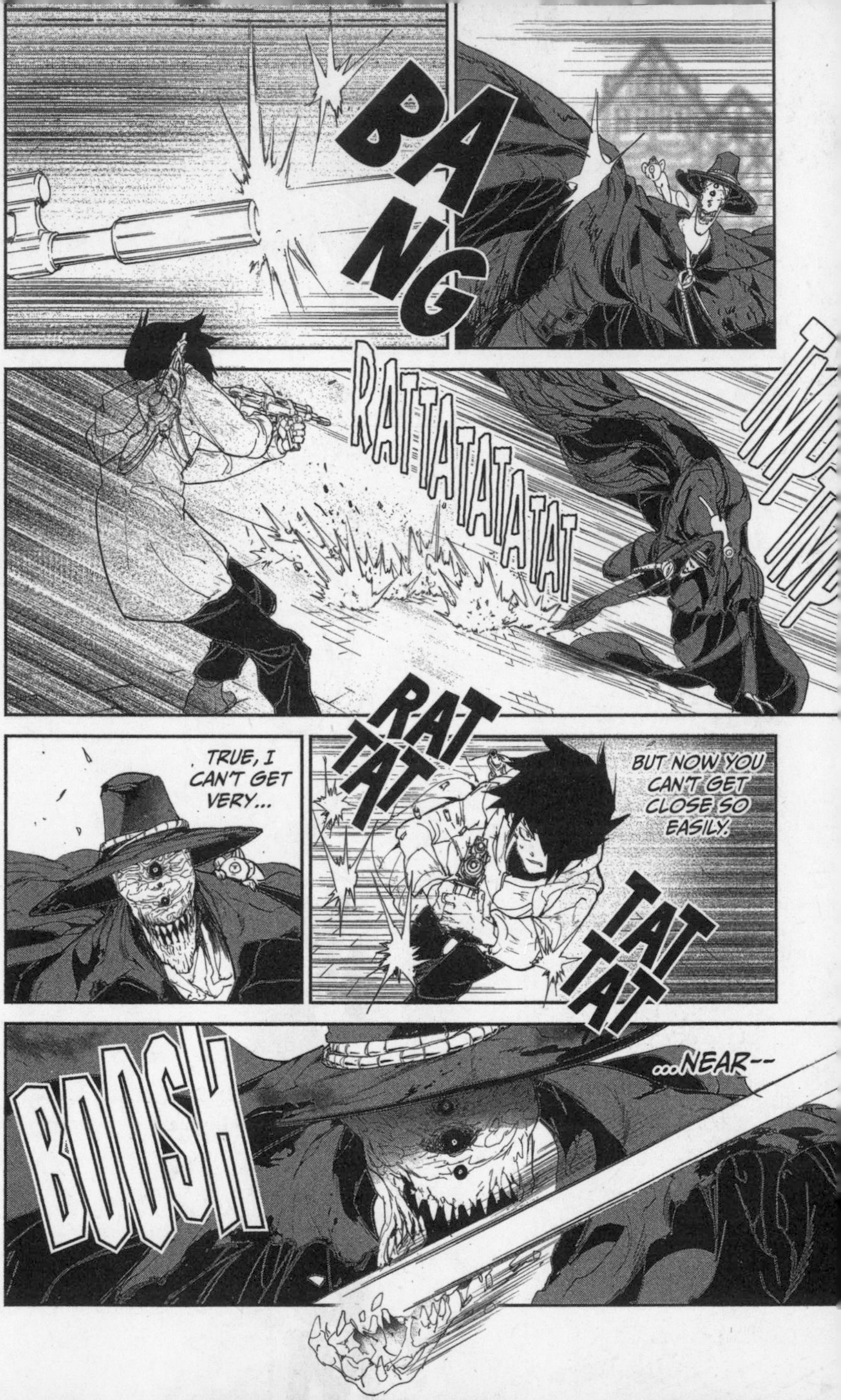
BANG
TMP TMP
RATTATATATATAT
RAT TAT
BUT NOW YOU CAN'T GET CLOSE SO EASILY.
TAT TAT
TRUE, I CAN'T GET VERY...
...NEAR--
BOOSH

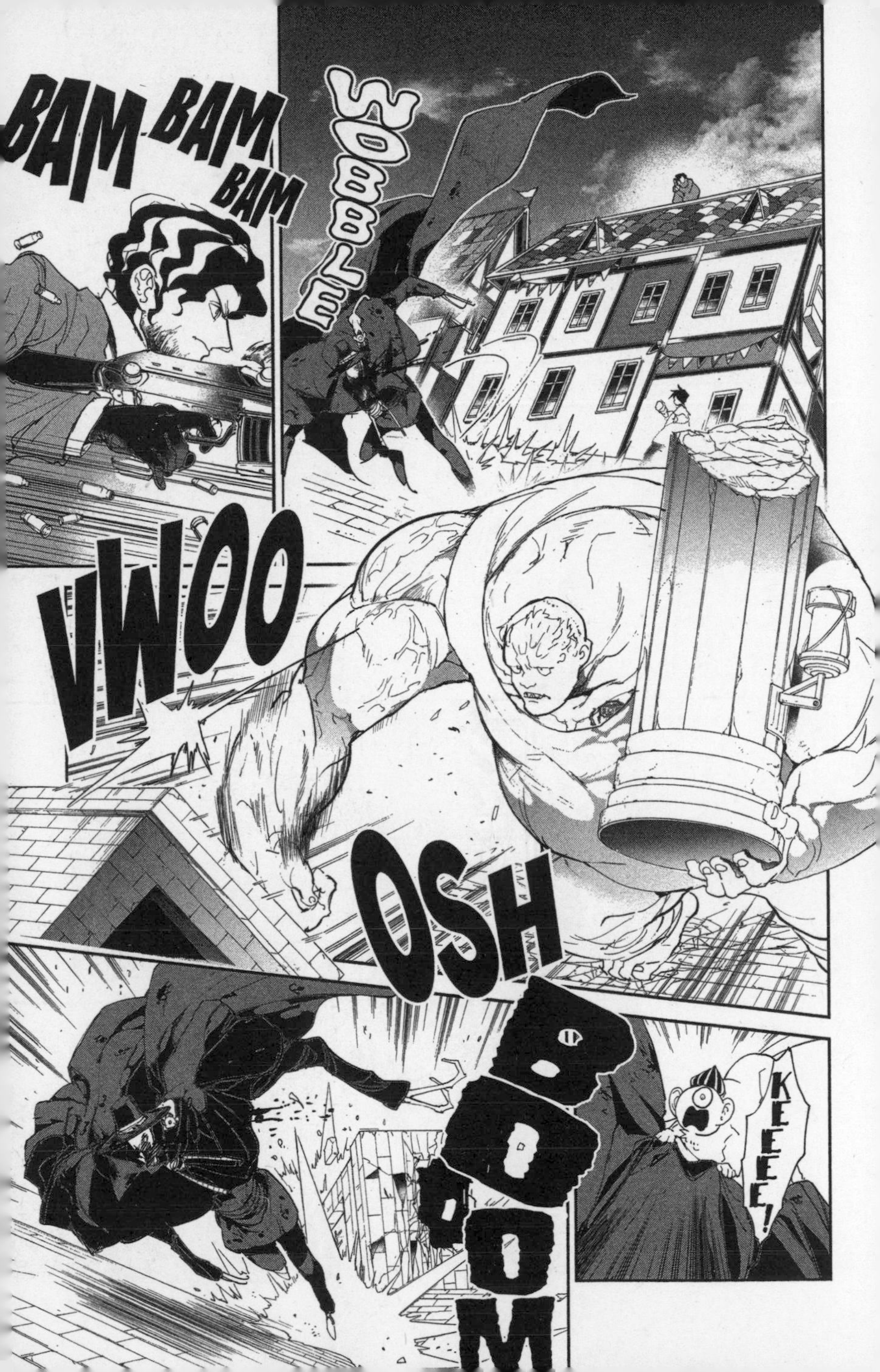
WOBBLE
BAM BAM BAM
VWOOOSH
KEEEEE!
BOOM

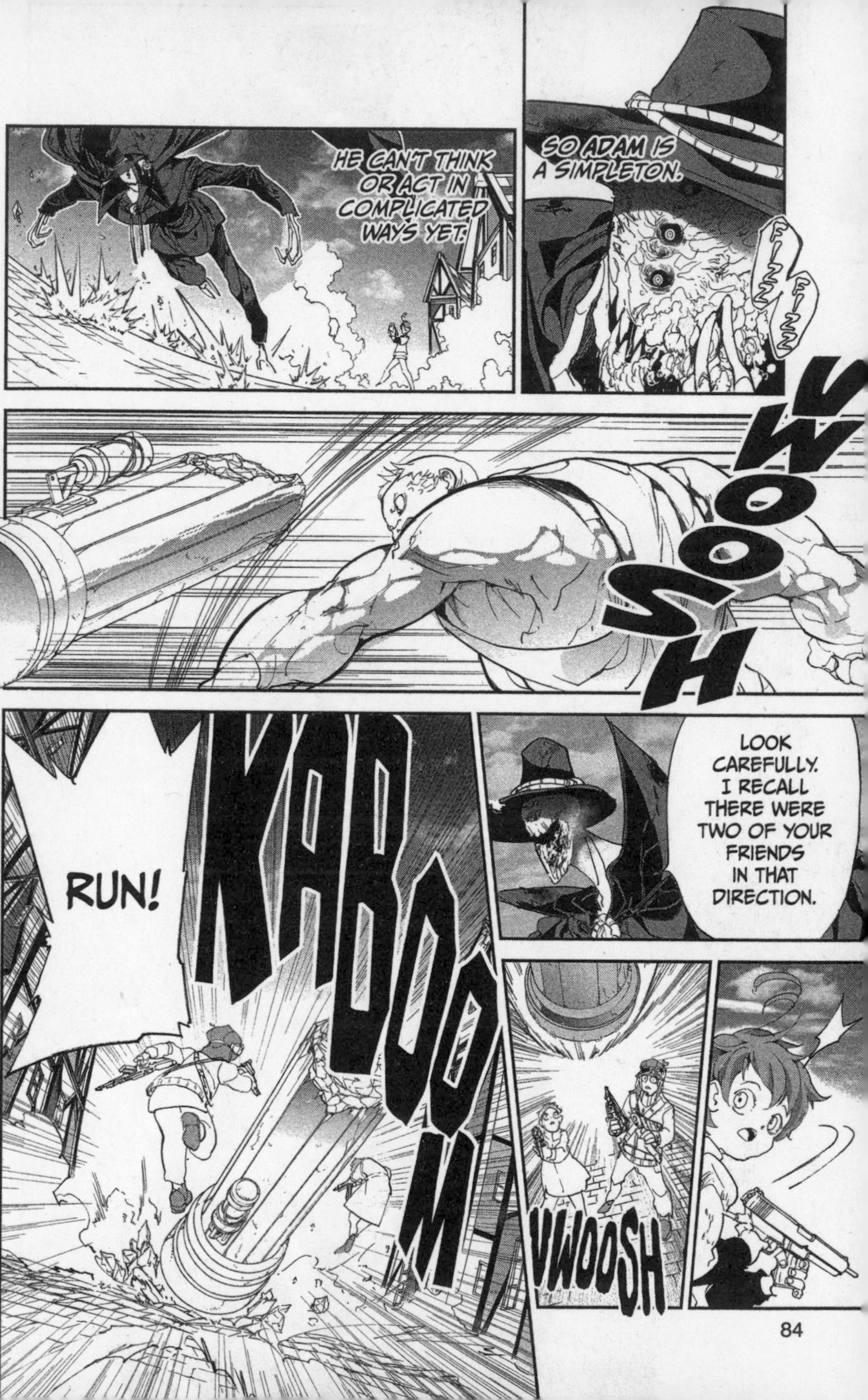
SO ADAM IS A SIMPLETON.
FIZZ FIZZ
HE CAN'T THINK OR ACT IN COMPLICATED WAYS YET.
VWOOSH
LOOK CAREFULLY. I RECALL THERE WERE TWO OF YOUR FRIENDS IN THAT DIRECTION.
VWOOSH
KABOOM
RUN!

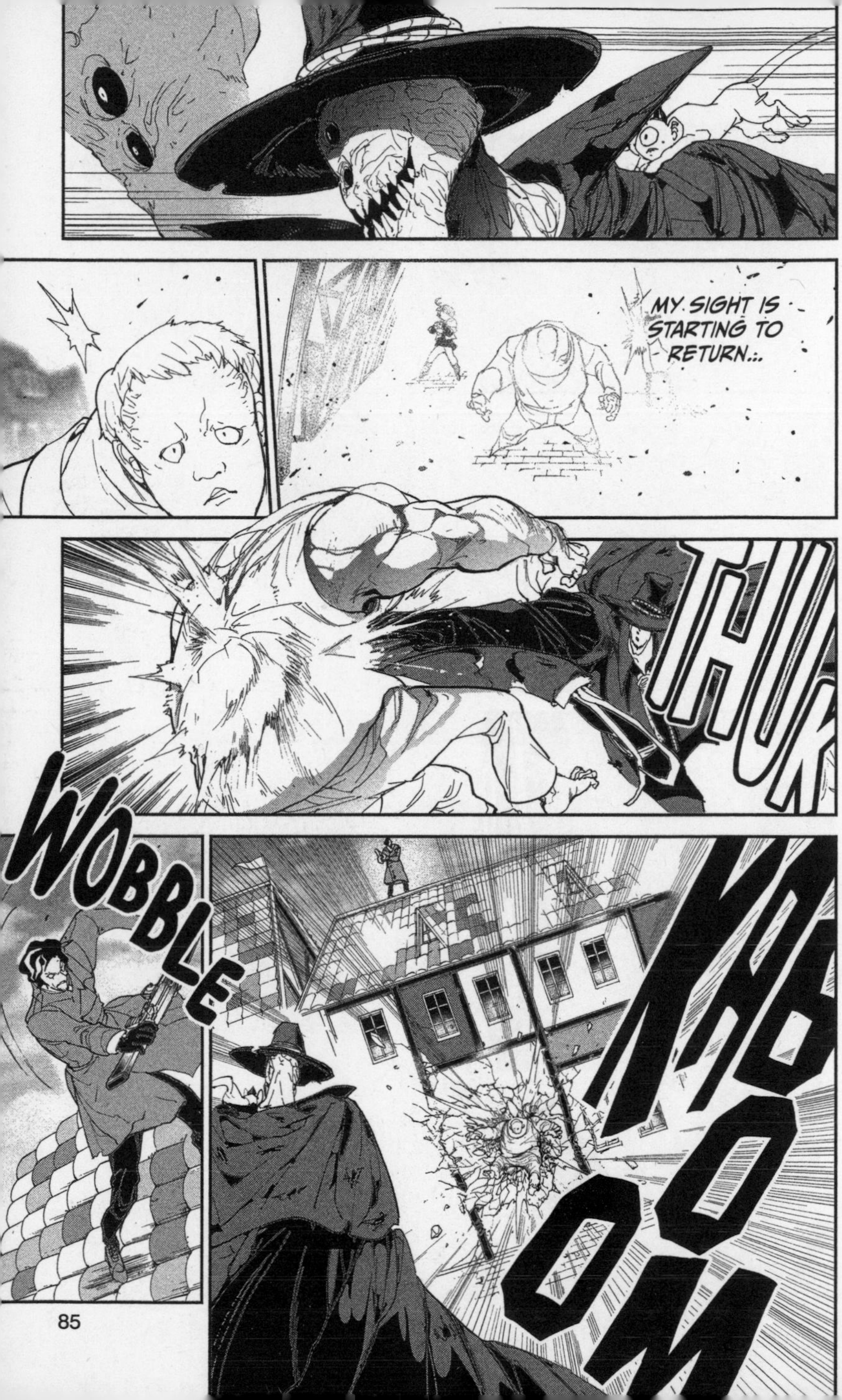
MY SIGHT IS STARTING TO RETURN...
THUK
KABOOM
WOBBLE

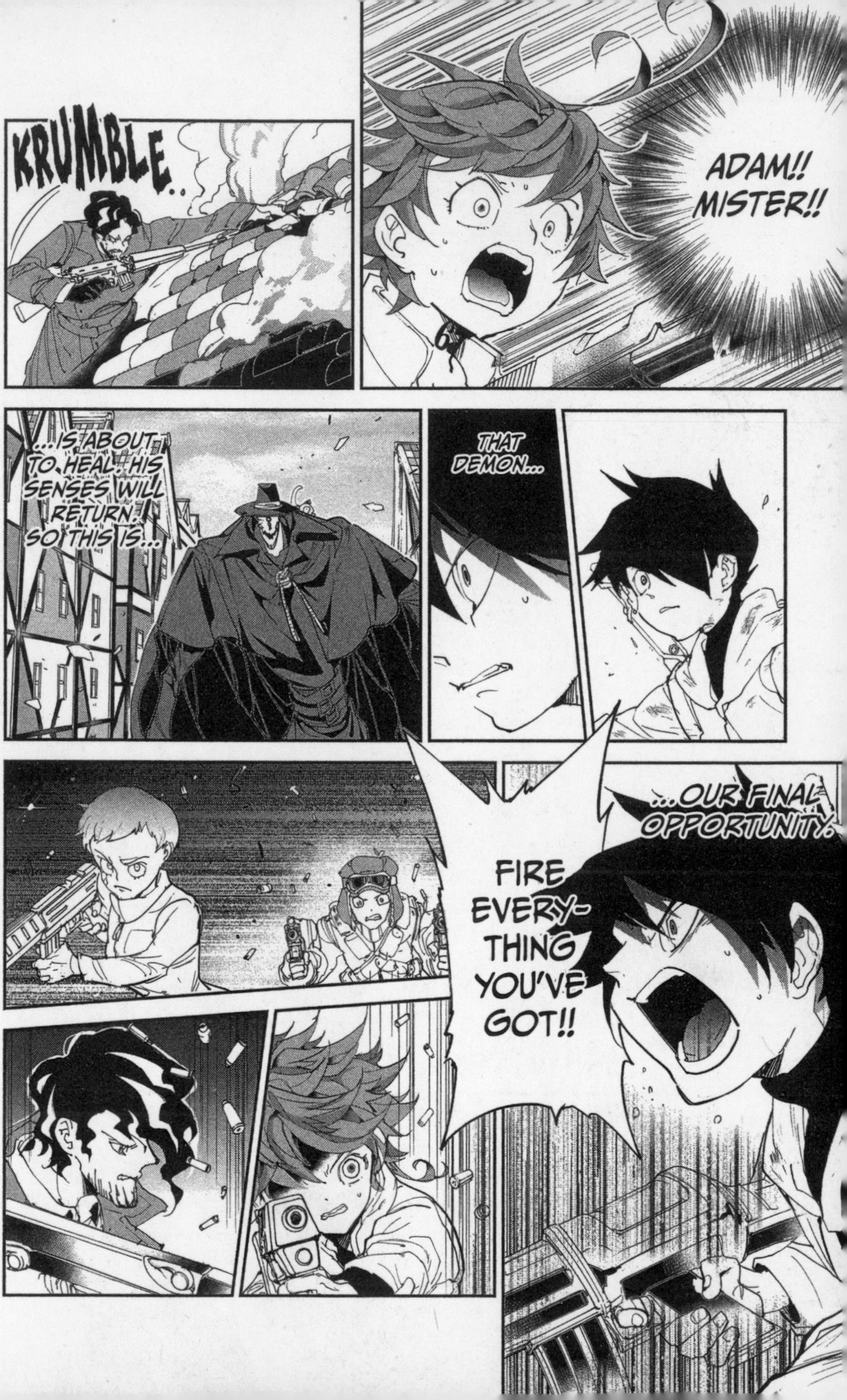
ADAM!! MISTER!!
KRUMBLE..
THAT DEMON...
...IS ABOUT TO HEAL. HIS SENSES WILL RETURN. SO THIS IS...
...OUR FINAL OPPORTUNITY.
FIRE EVERY-THING YOU'VE GOT!!

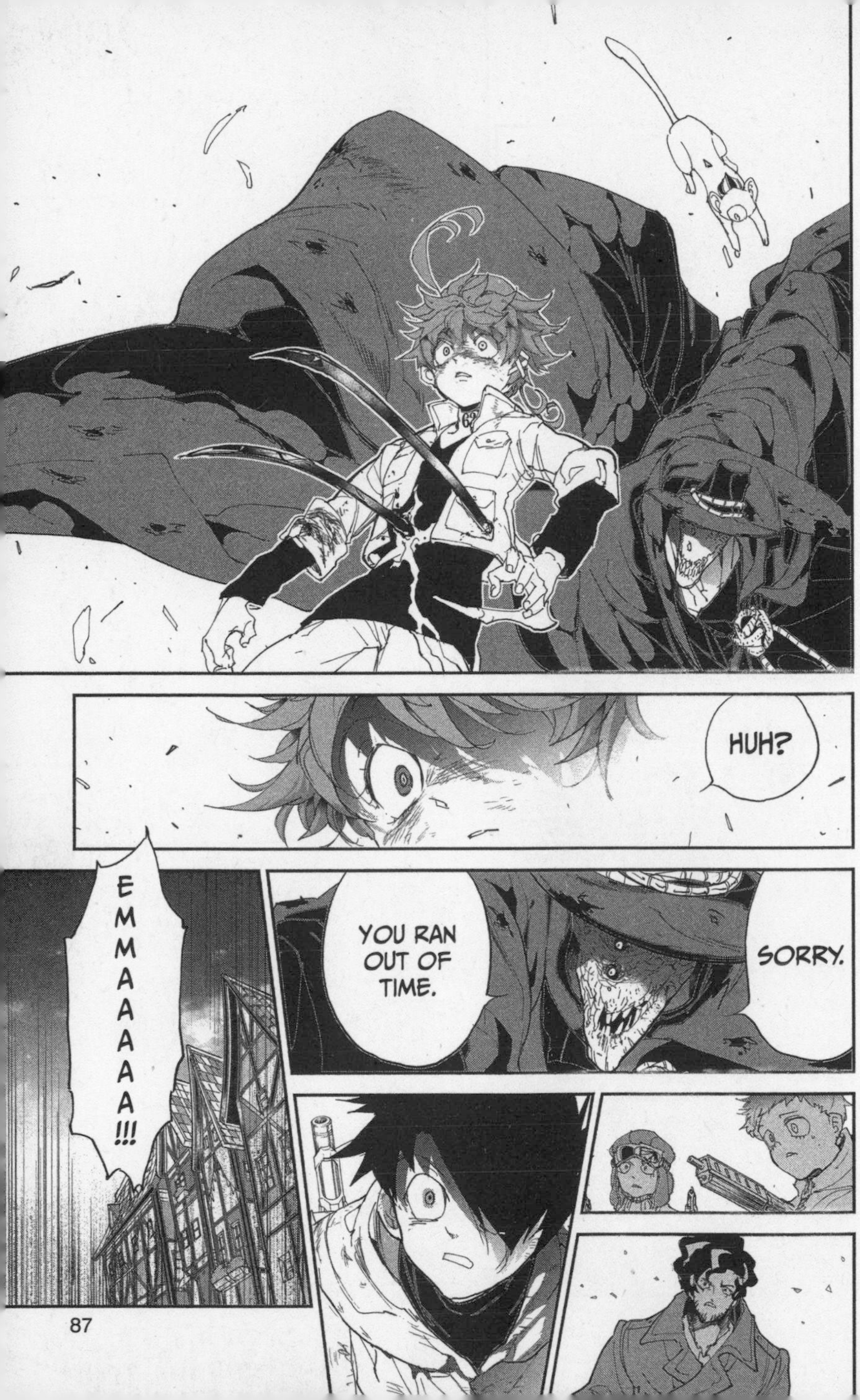
HUH?
SORRY.
YOU RAN OUT OF TIME.
EMMAAAAA!!!

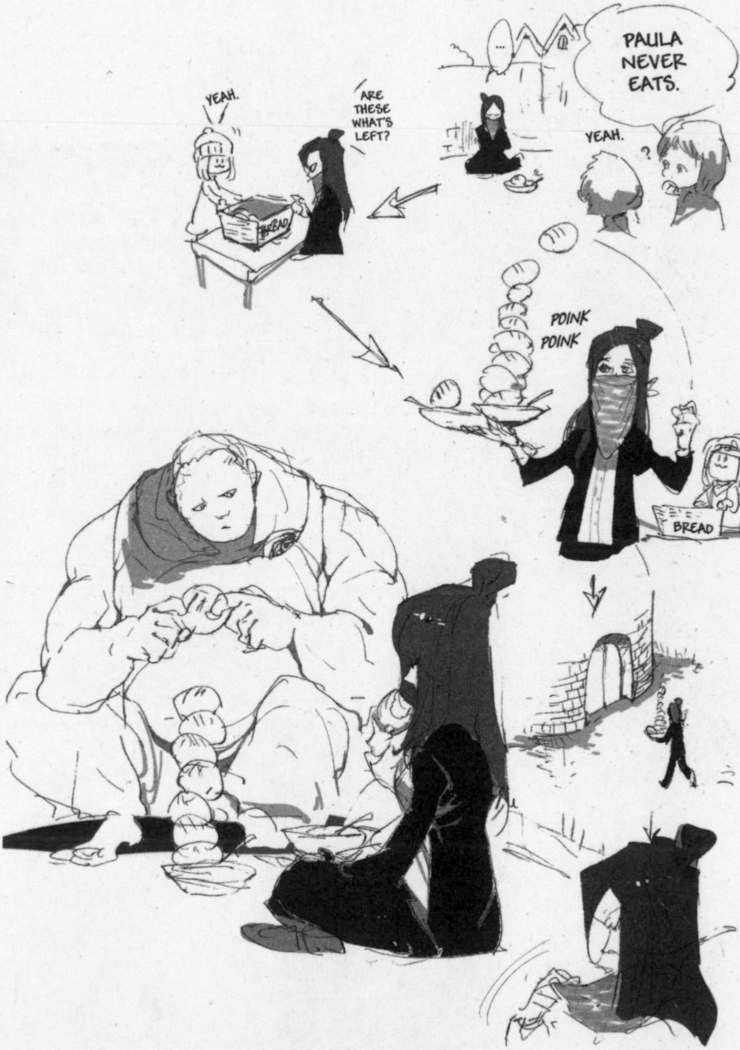
PAULA NEVER EATS.
YEAH.
...
ARE THESE WHAT'S LEFT?
YEAH.
BREAD
POINK POINK
BREAD

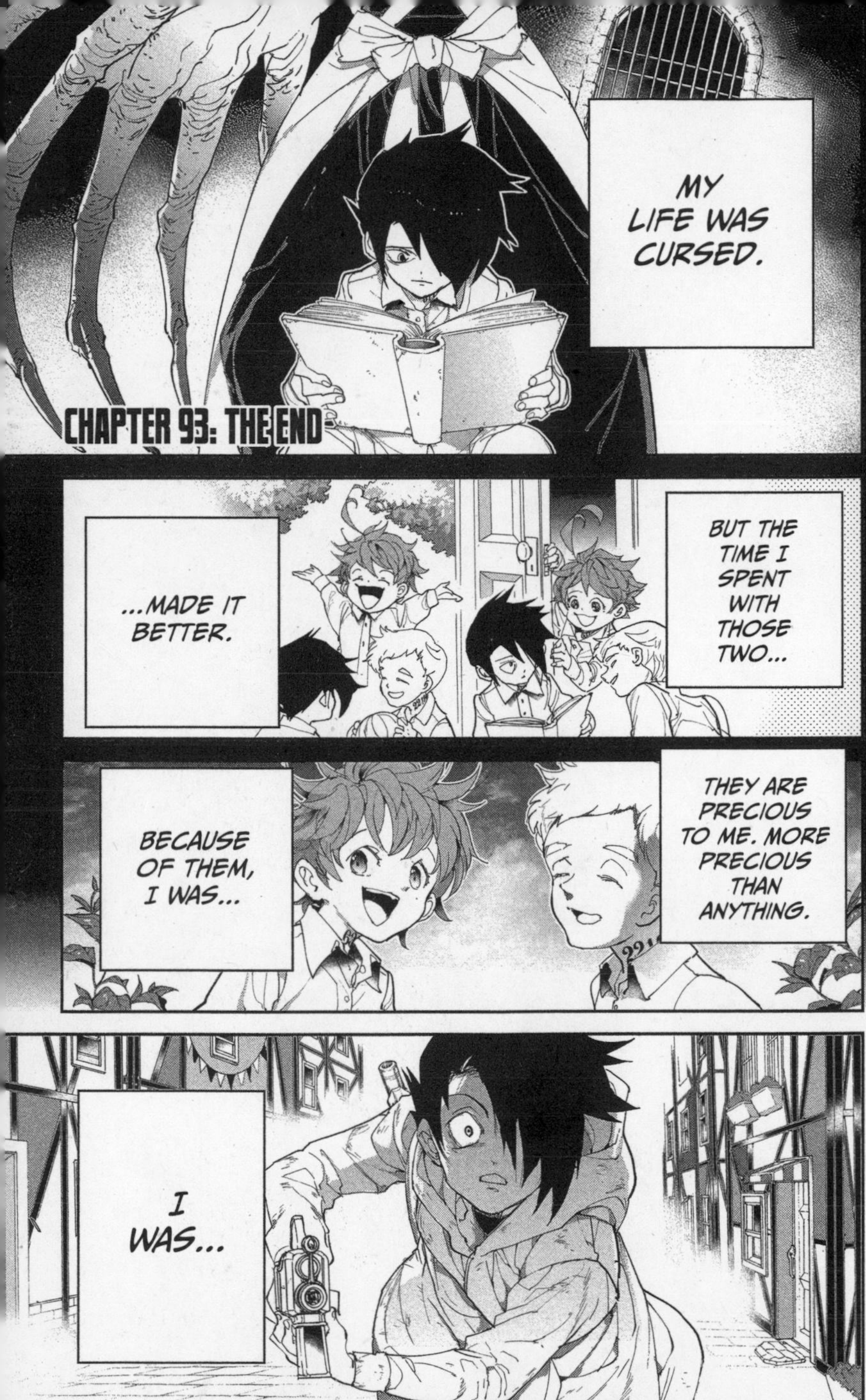
MY LIFE WAS CURSED.
CHAPTER 93: THE END
BUT THE TIME I SPENT WITH THOSE TWO...
...MADE IT BETTER.
THEY ARE PRECIOUS TO ME. MORE PRECIOUS THAN ANYTHING.
BECAUSE OF THEM, I WAS...
I WAS...

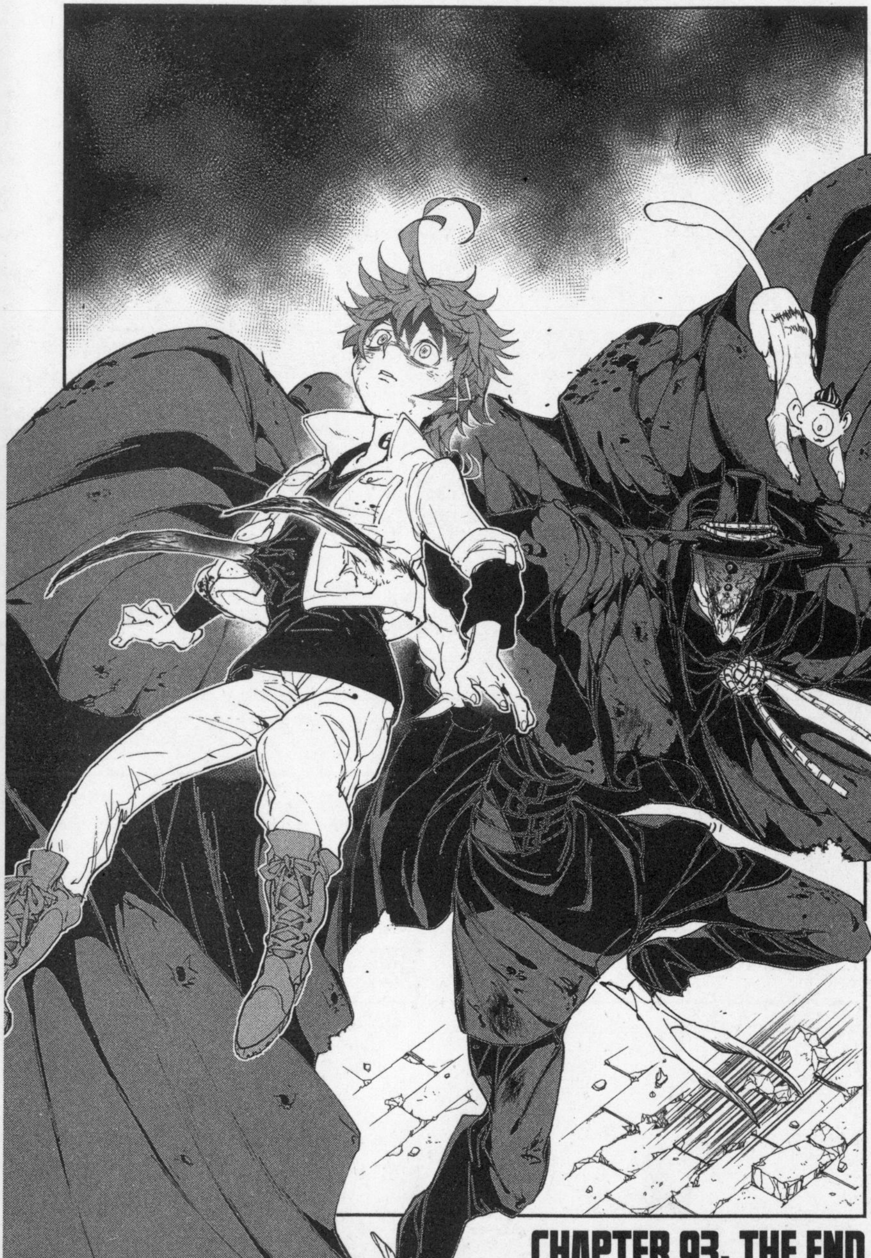
CHAPTER 93: THE END

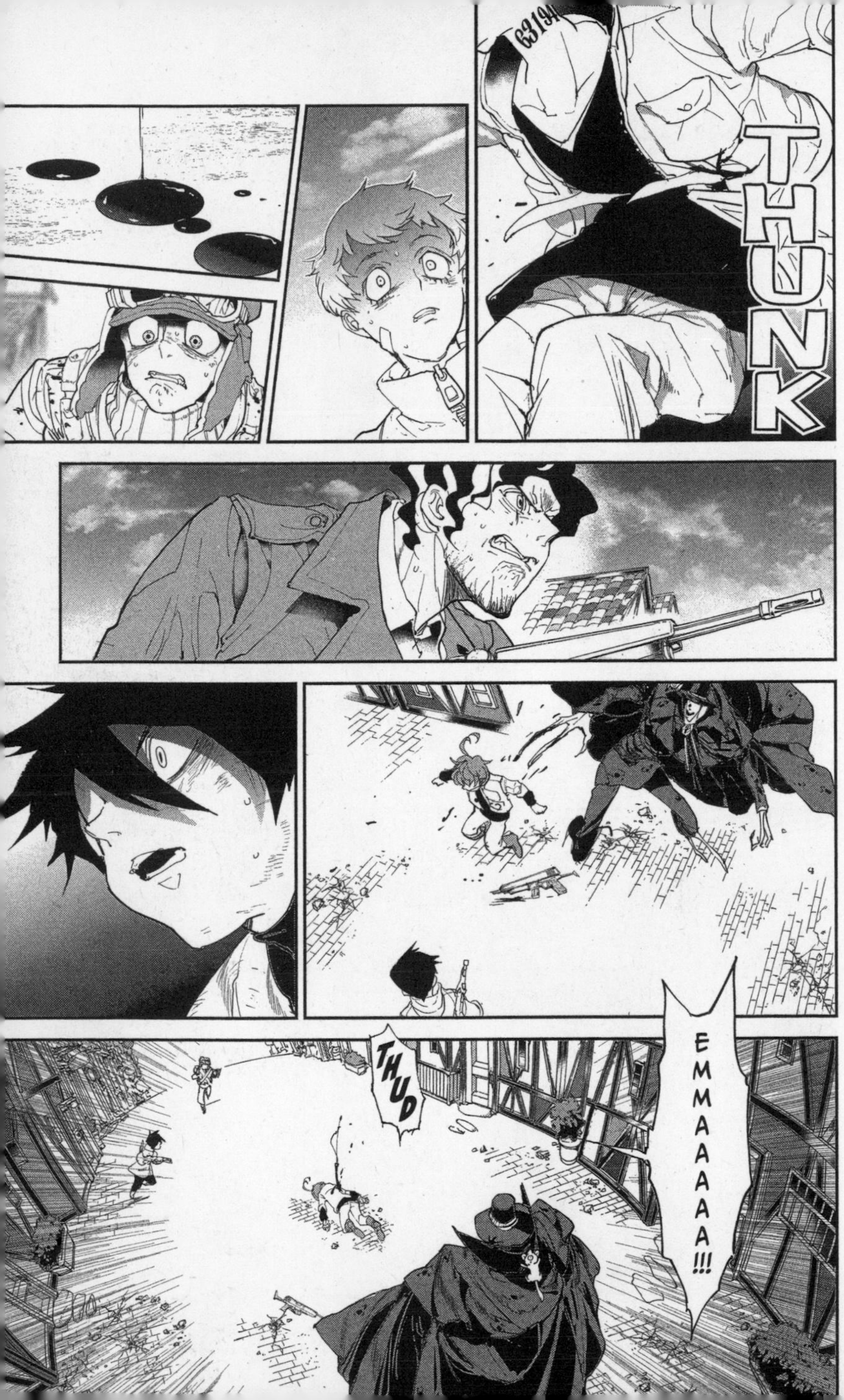
63194
THUNK
EMMAAAAAAA!!!
THUD

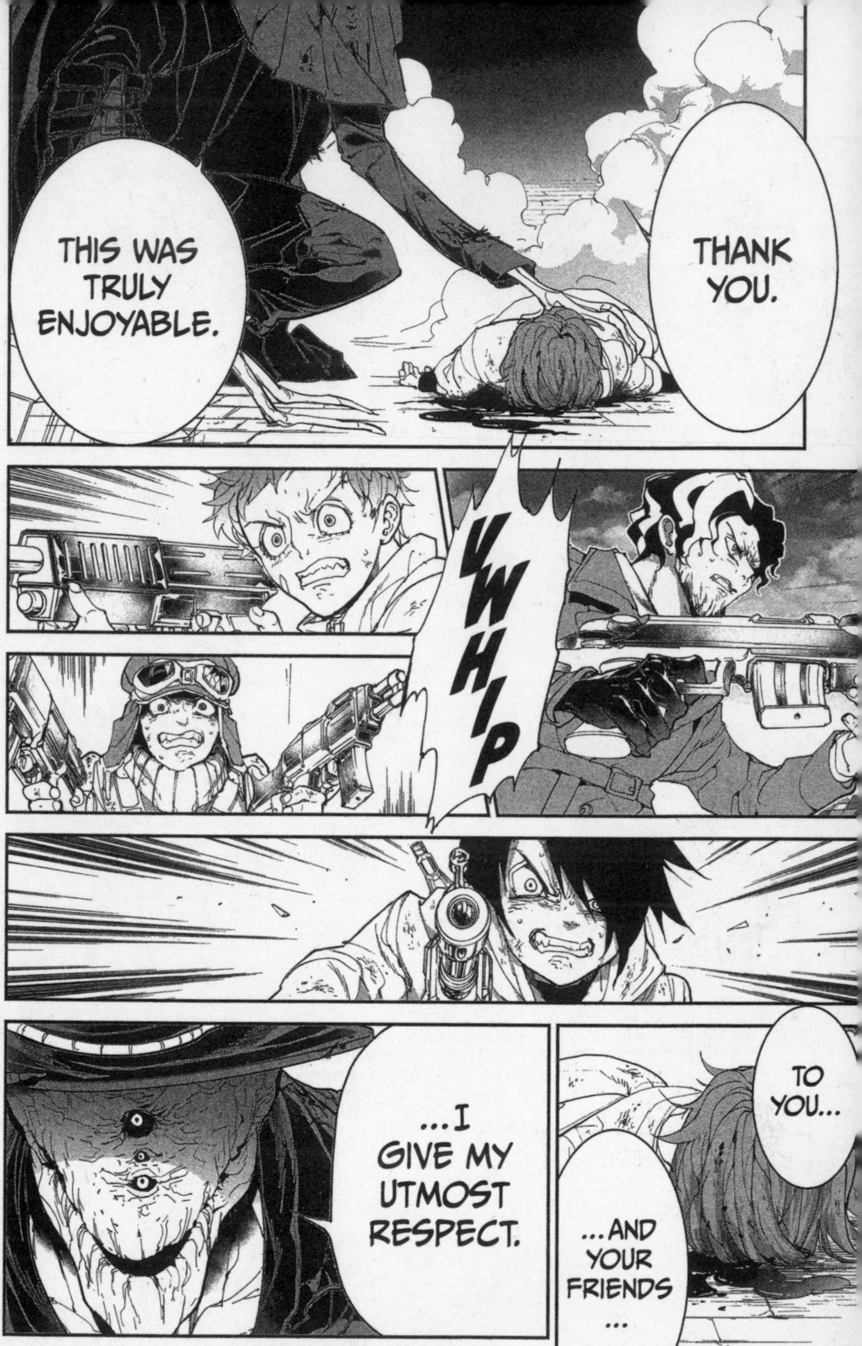
THANK YOU.
THIS WAS TRULY ENJOYABLE.
WHIP
TO YOU...
...AND YOUR FRIENDS ...
...I GIVE MY UTMOST RESPECT.

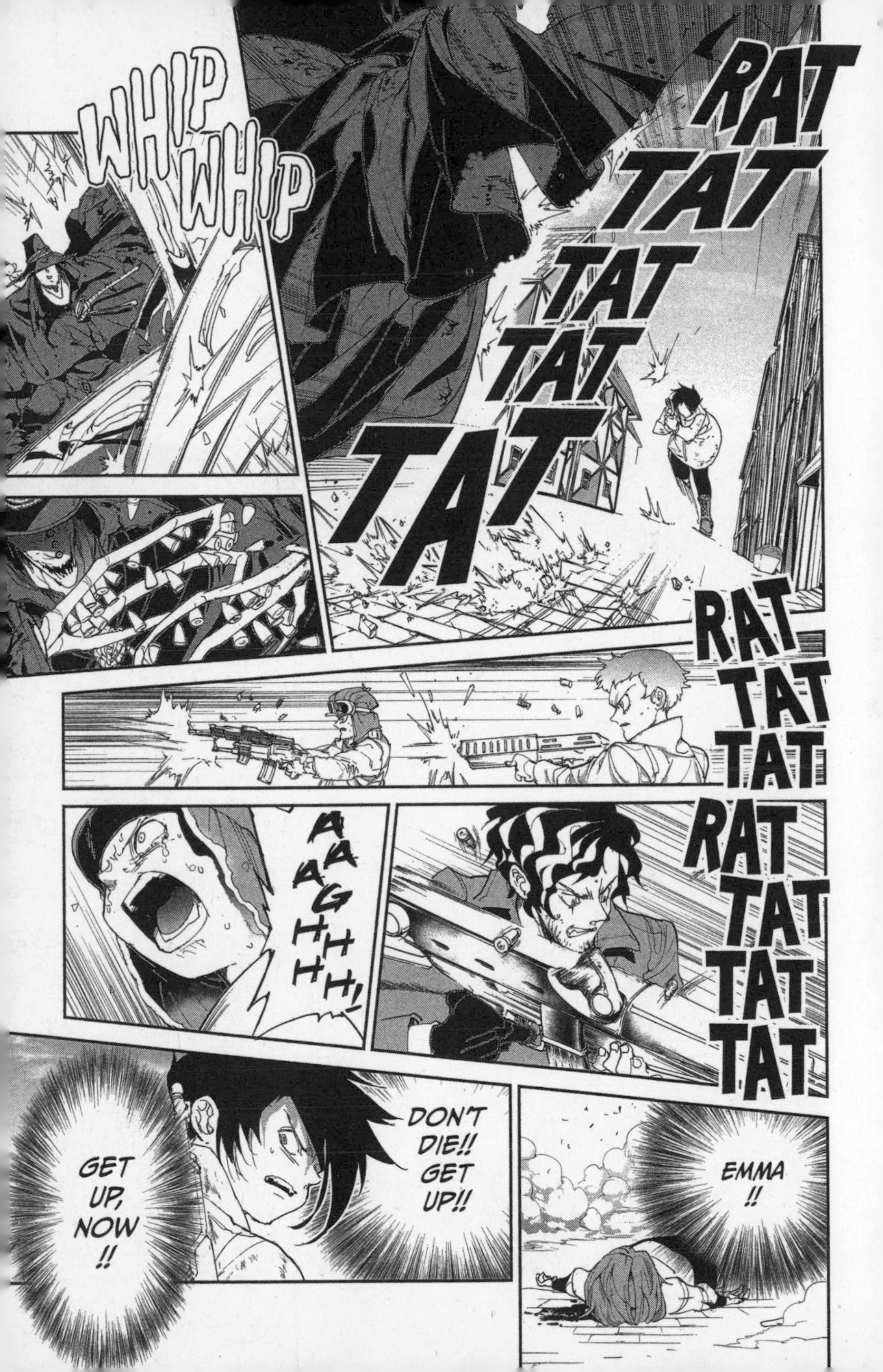
RAT TAT TAT TAT TAT
WHIP WHIP
RAT TAT TAT
RAT TAT TAT TAT
AAAGHHH!!
EMMA!!
DON'T DIE!! GET UP!!
GET UP, NOW!!

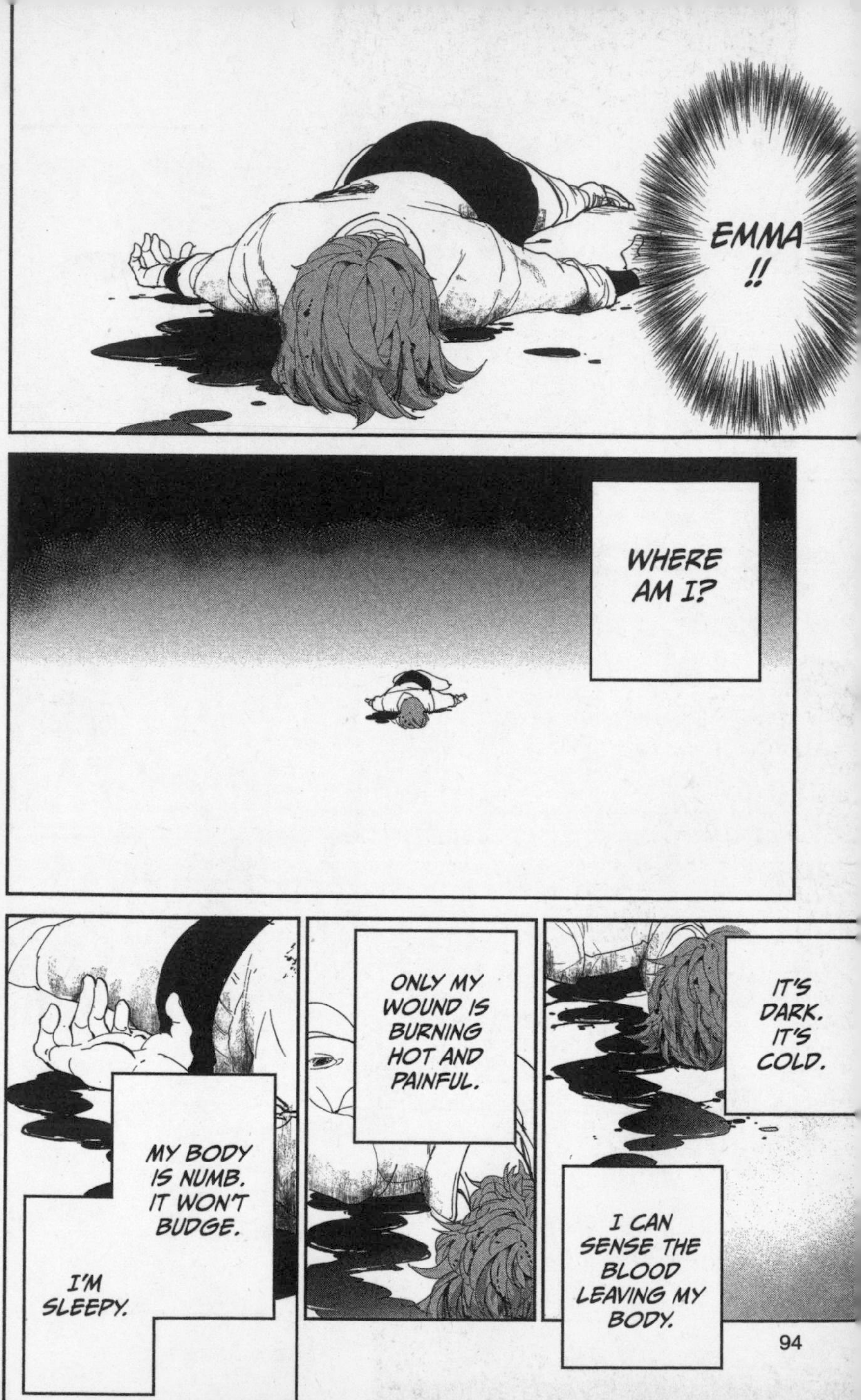
EMMA !!
WHERE AM I?
IT'S DARK. IT'S COLD.
I CAN SENSE THE BLOOD LEAVING MY BODY.
ONLY MY WOUND IS BURNING HOT AND PAINFUL.
MY BODY IS NUMB. IT WON'T BUDGE.
I'M SLEEPY.

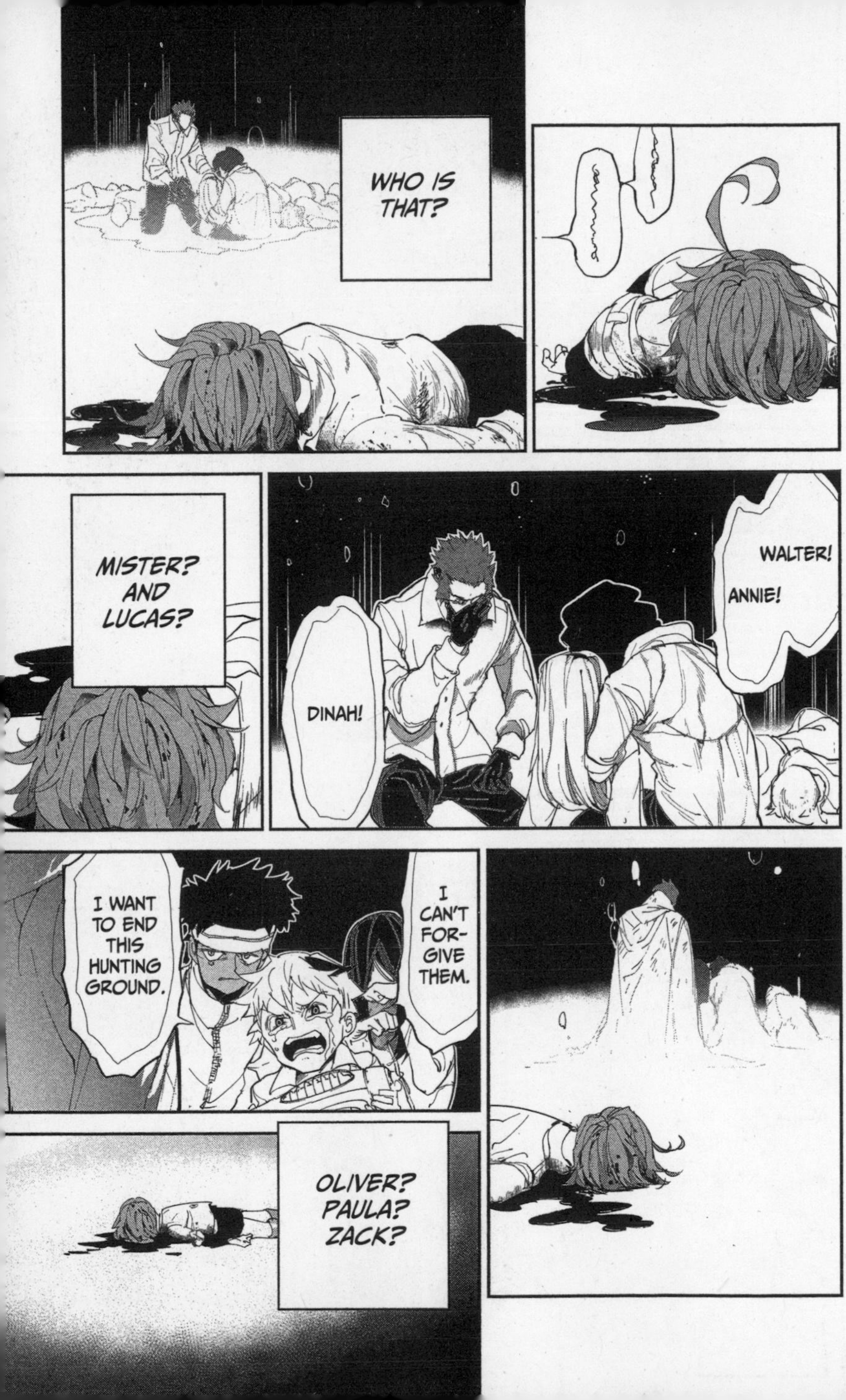
WHO IS THAT?
WALTER!
ANNIE!
DINAH!
MISTER? AND LUCAS?
I CAN'T FOR-GIVE THEM.
I WANT TO END THIS HUNTING GROUND.
OLIVER? PAULA? ZACK?

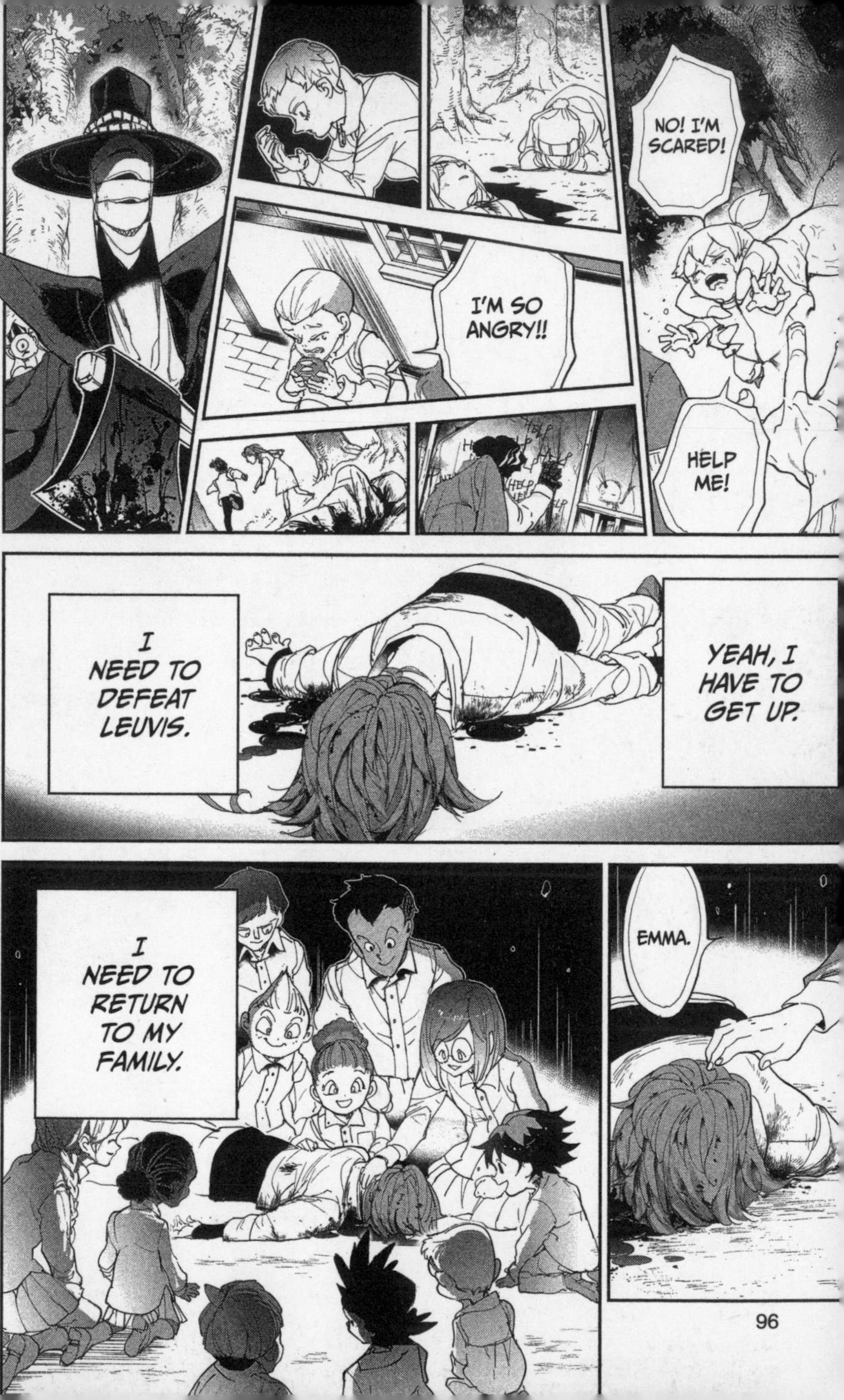

NO! I'M SCARED!
HELP ME!
I'M SO ANGRY!!
YEAH, I HAVE TO GET UP.
I NEED TO DEFEAT LEUVIS.
EMMA.
I NEED TO RETURN TO MY FAMILY.

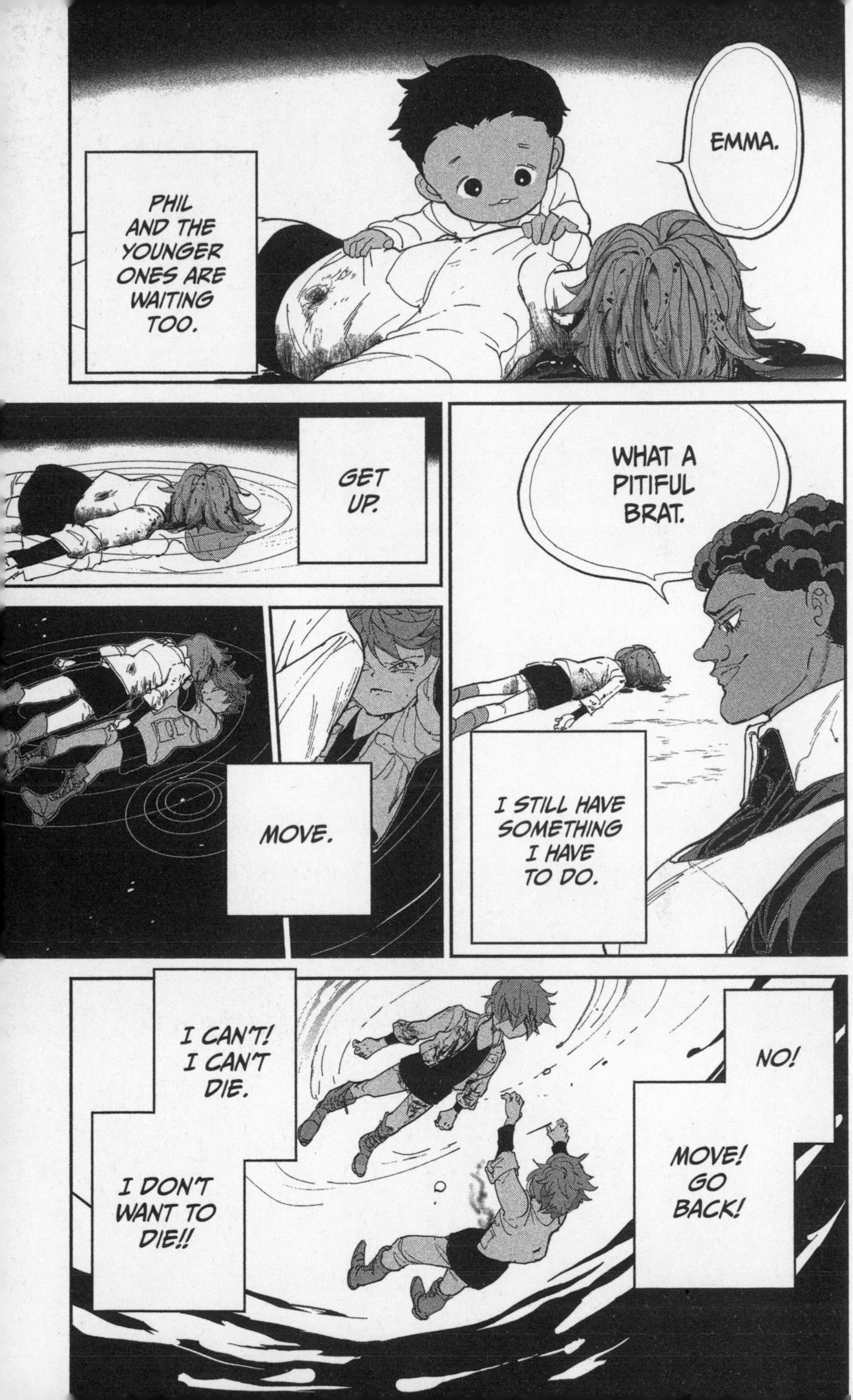
EMMA.
PHIL AND THE YOUNGER ONES ARE WAITING TOO.
WHAT A PITIFUL BRAT.
I STILL HAVE SOMETHING I HAVE TO DO.
GET UP.
MOVE.
NO!
MOVE! GO BACK!
I CAN'T! I CAN'T DIE.
I DON'T WANT TO DIE!!

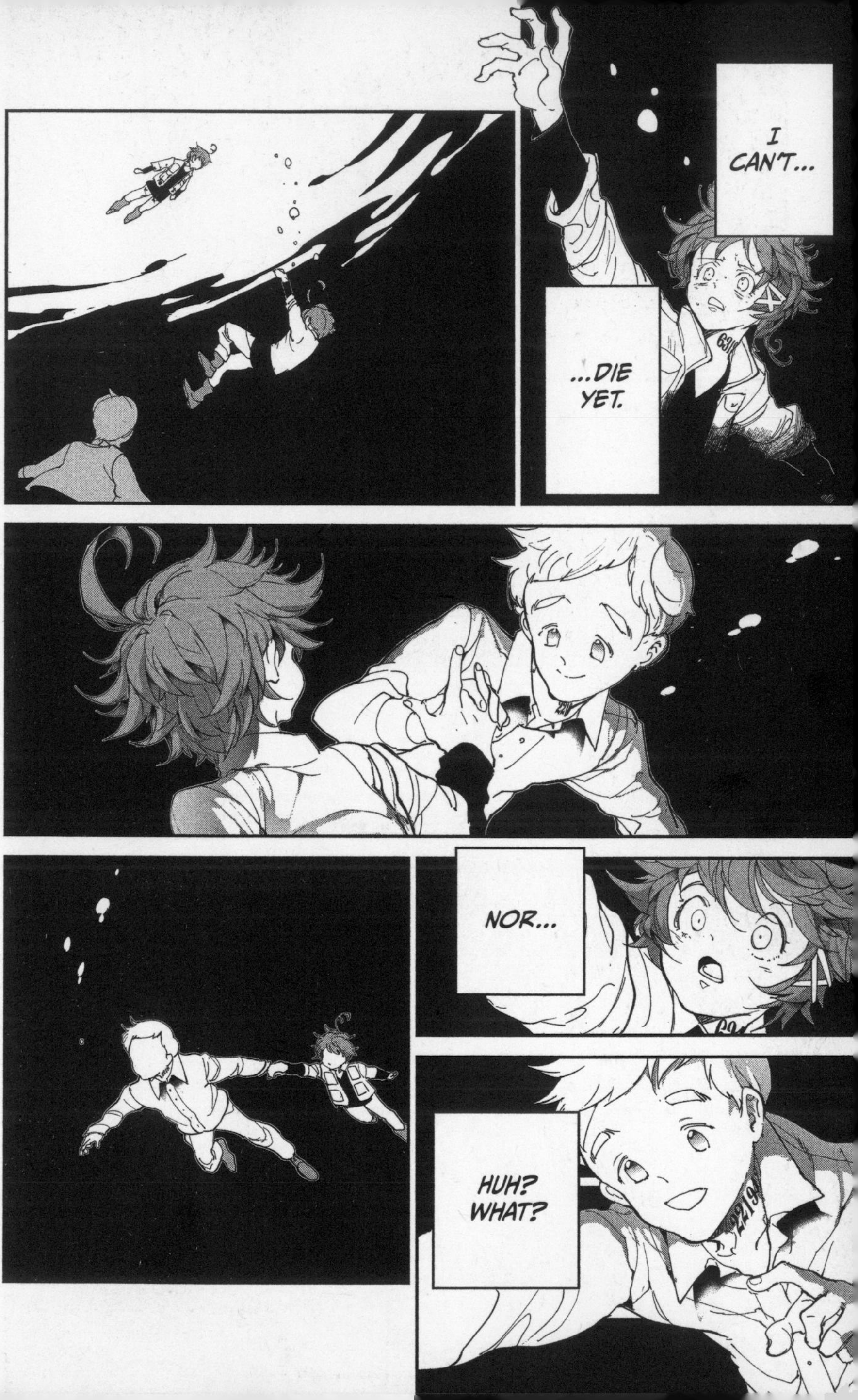
I CAN'T...
...DIE YET.
NOR...
HUH? WHAT?

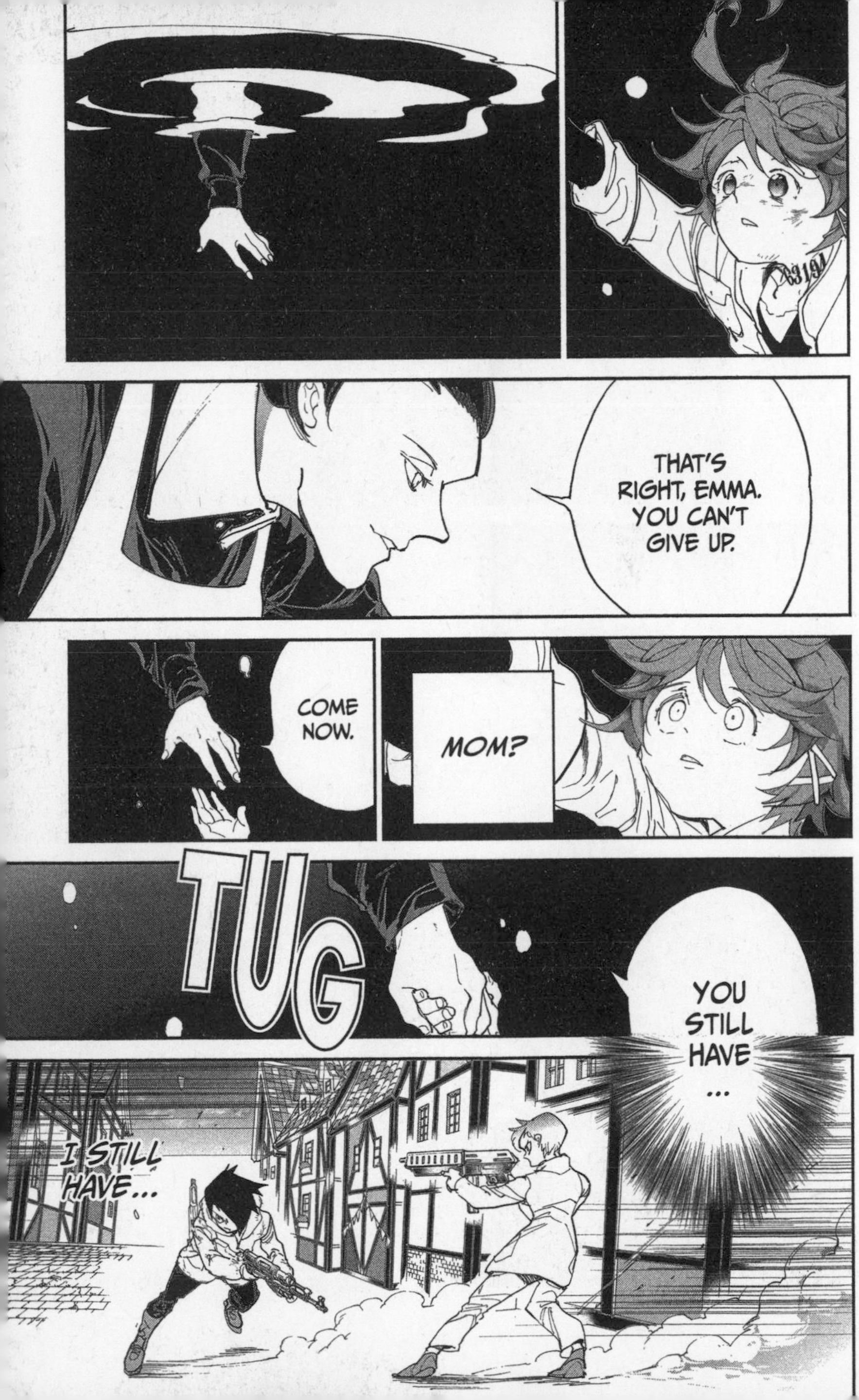
THAT'S RIGHT, EMMA. YOU CAN'T GIVE UP.
MOM?
COME NOW.
YOU STILL HAVE ...
TUG
I STILL HAVE...

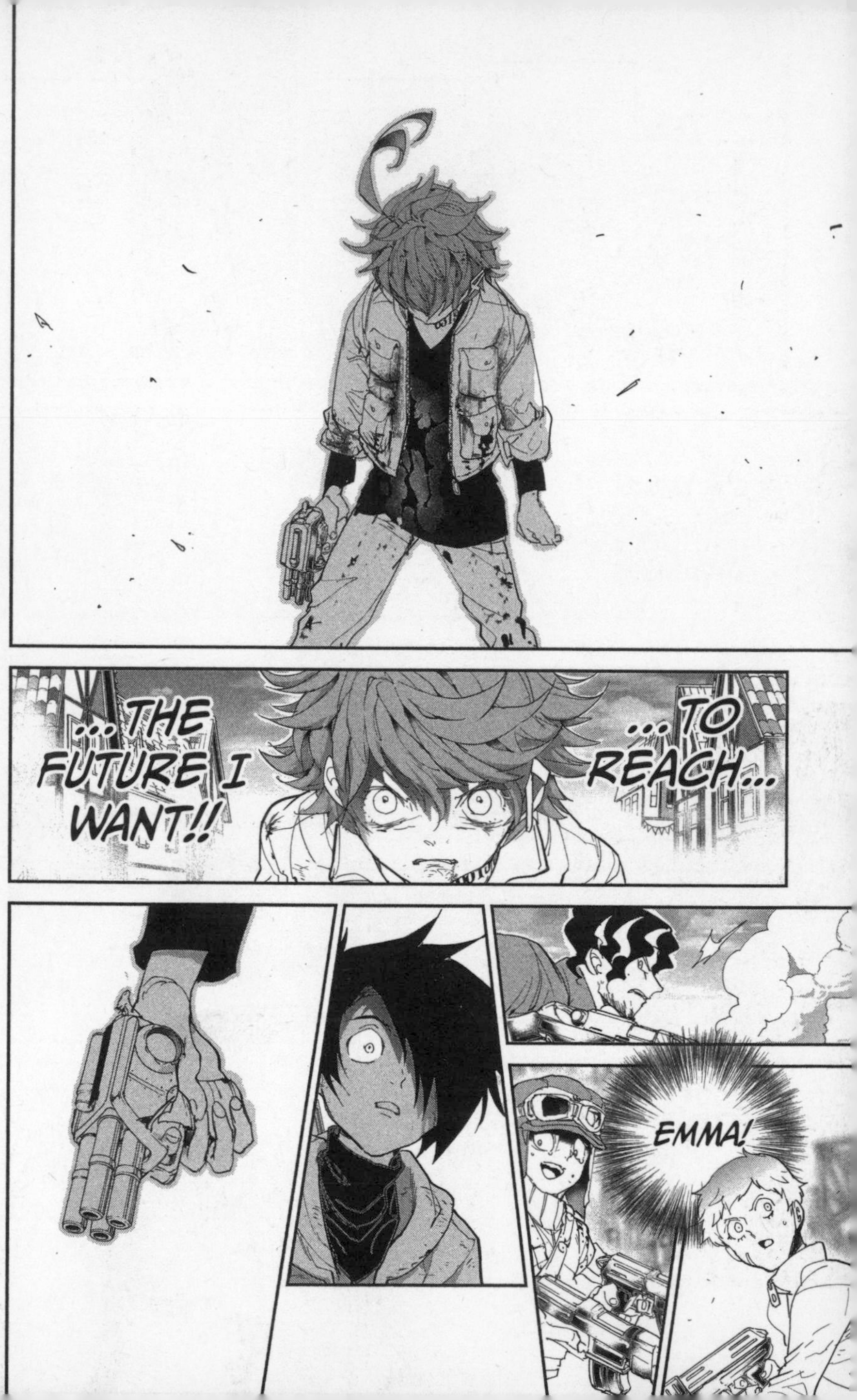
...TO REACH...
...THE FUTURE I WANT!!
EMMA!

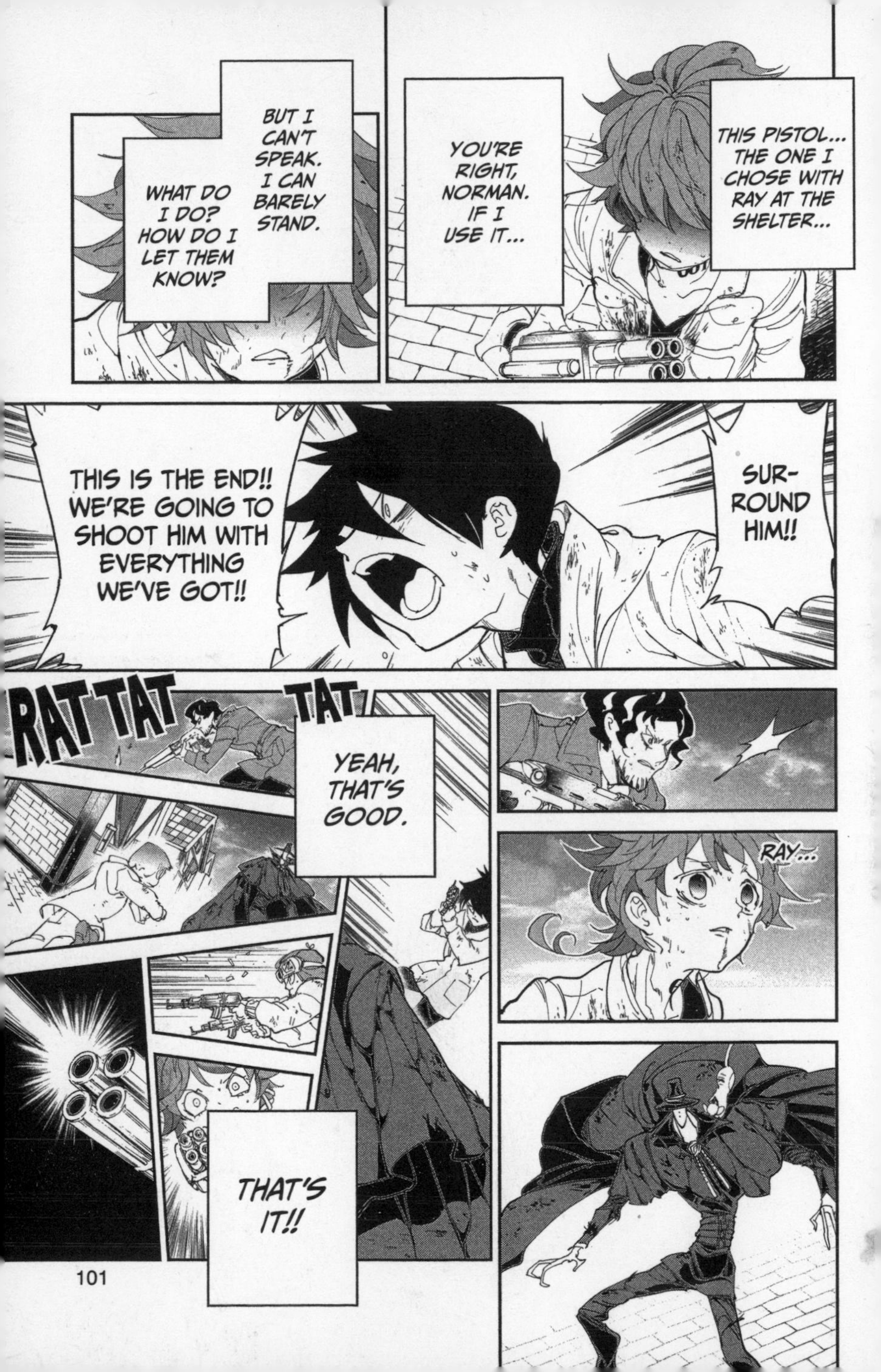
THIS PISTOL... THE ONE I CHOSE WITH RAY AT THE SHELTER...
YOU'RE RIGHT, NORMAN. IF I USE IT...
BUT I CAN'T SPEAK. I CAN BARELY STAND.
WHAT DO I DO? HOW DO I LET THEM KNOW?
SUR-ROUND HIM!!
THIS IS THE END!! WE'RE GOING TO SHOOT HIM WITH EVERYTHING WE'VE GOT!!
RAY...
RAT TAT TAT
YEAH, THAT'S GOOD.
THAT'S IT!!

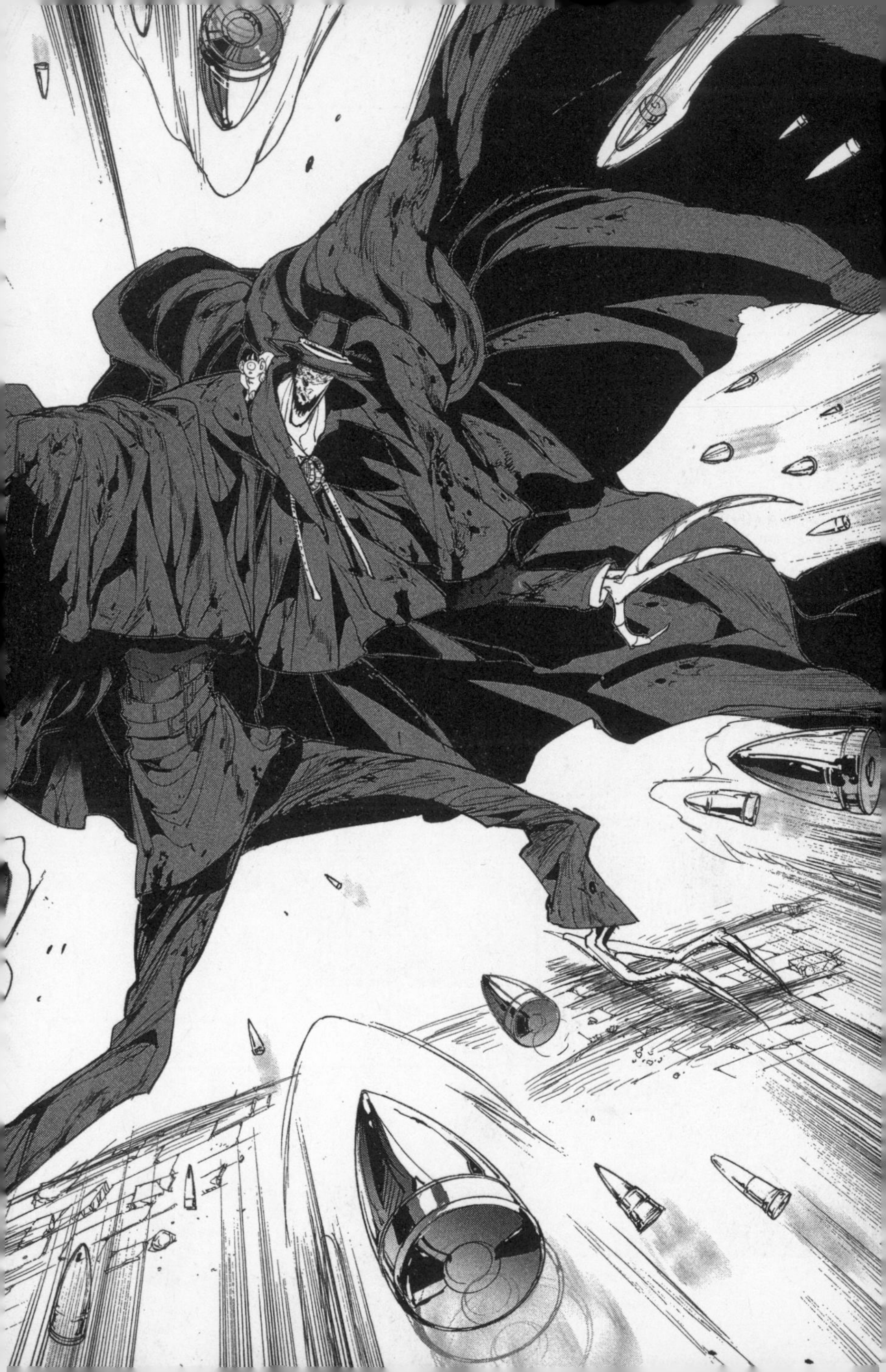

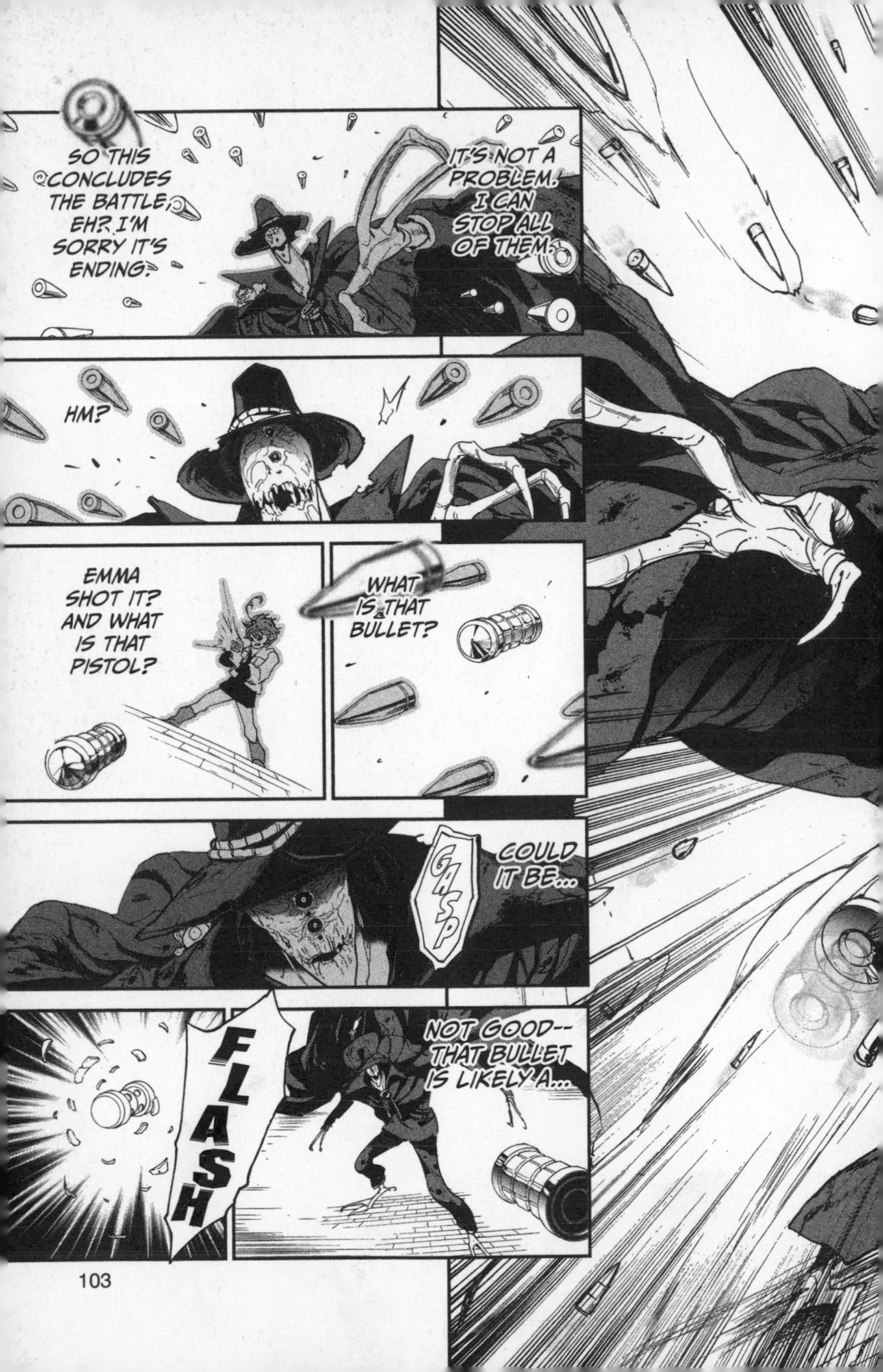
IT'S NOT A PROBLEM. I CAN STOP ALL OF THEM.
SO THIS CONCLUDES THE BATTLE, EH? I'M SORRY IT'S ENDING.
HM?
WHAT IS THAT BULLET?
EMMA SHOT IT? AND WHAT IS THAT PISTOL?
COULD IT BE...
GASP
NOT GOOD-- THAT BULLET IS LIKELY A...
FLASH

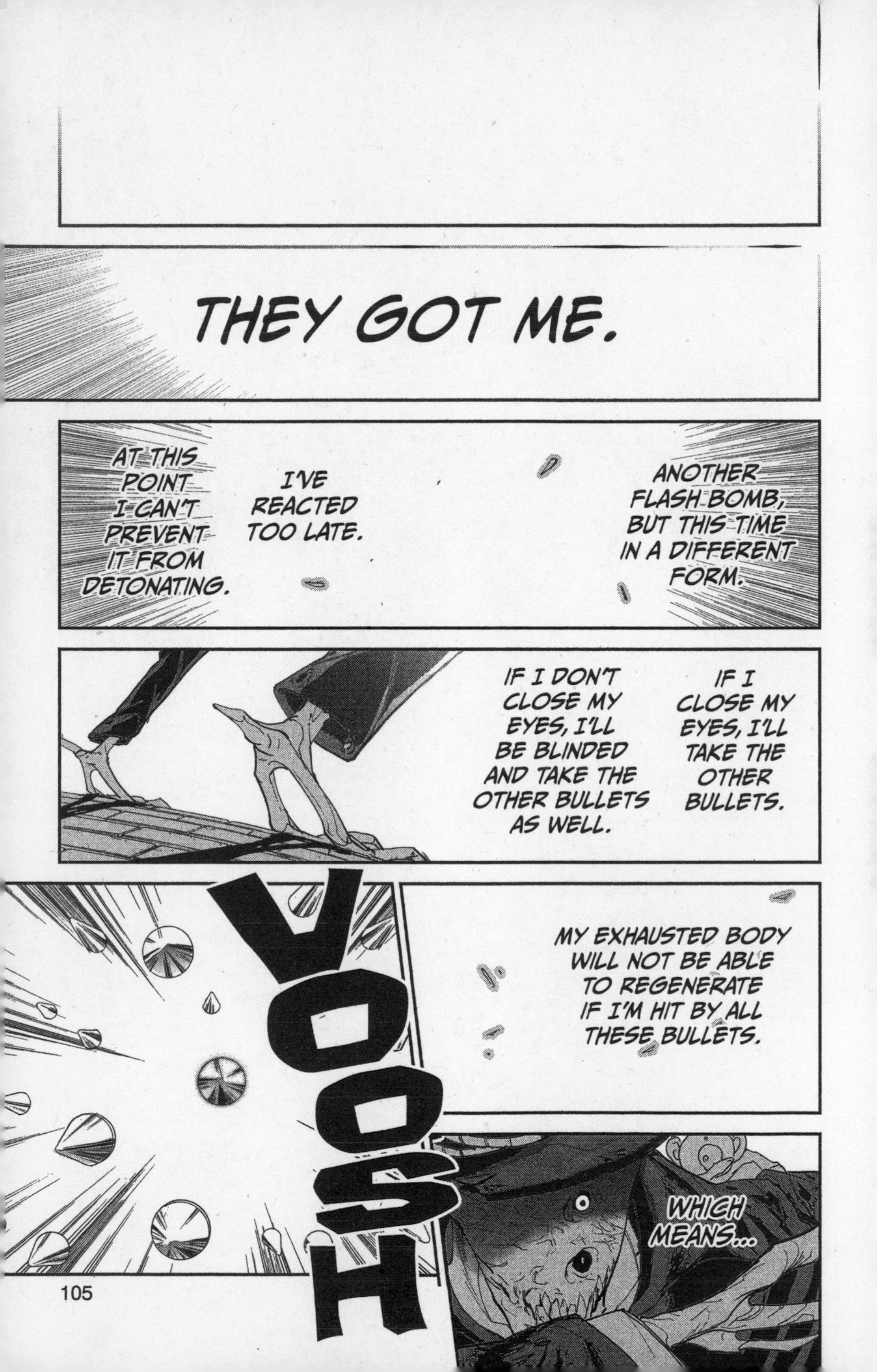
THEY GOT ME.
ANOTHER FLASH BOMB, BUT THIS TIME IN A DIFFERENT FORM.
I'VE REACTED TOO LATE.
AT THIS POINT I CAN'T PREVENT IT FROM DETONATING.
IF I CLOSE MY EYES, I'LL TAKE THE OTHER BULLETS.
IF I DON'T CLOSE MY EYES, I'LL BE BLINDED AND TAKE THE OTHER BULLETS AS WELL.
MY EXHAUSTED BODY WILL NOT BE ABLE TO REGENERATE IF I'M HIT BY ALL THESE BULLETS.
WHICH MEANS...
VOOSH

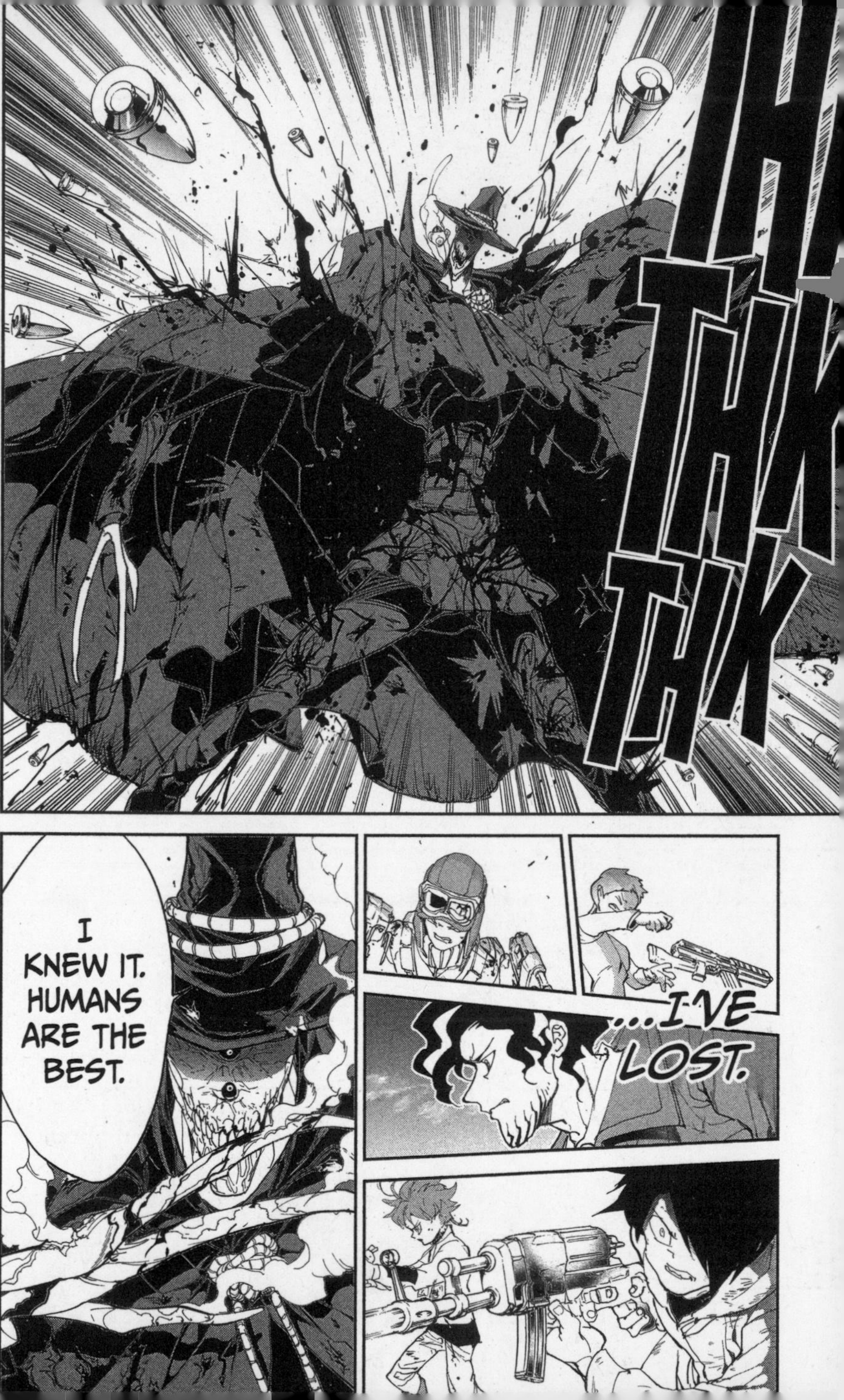
THK
THK
...I'VE LOST.
I KNEW IT. HUMANS ARE THE BEST.

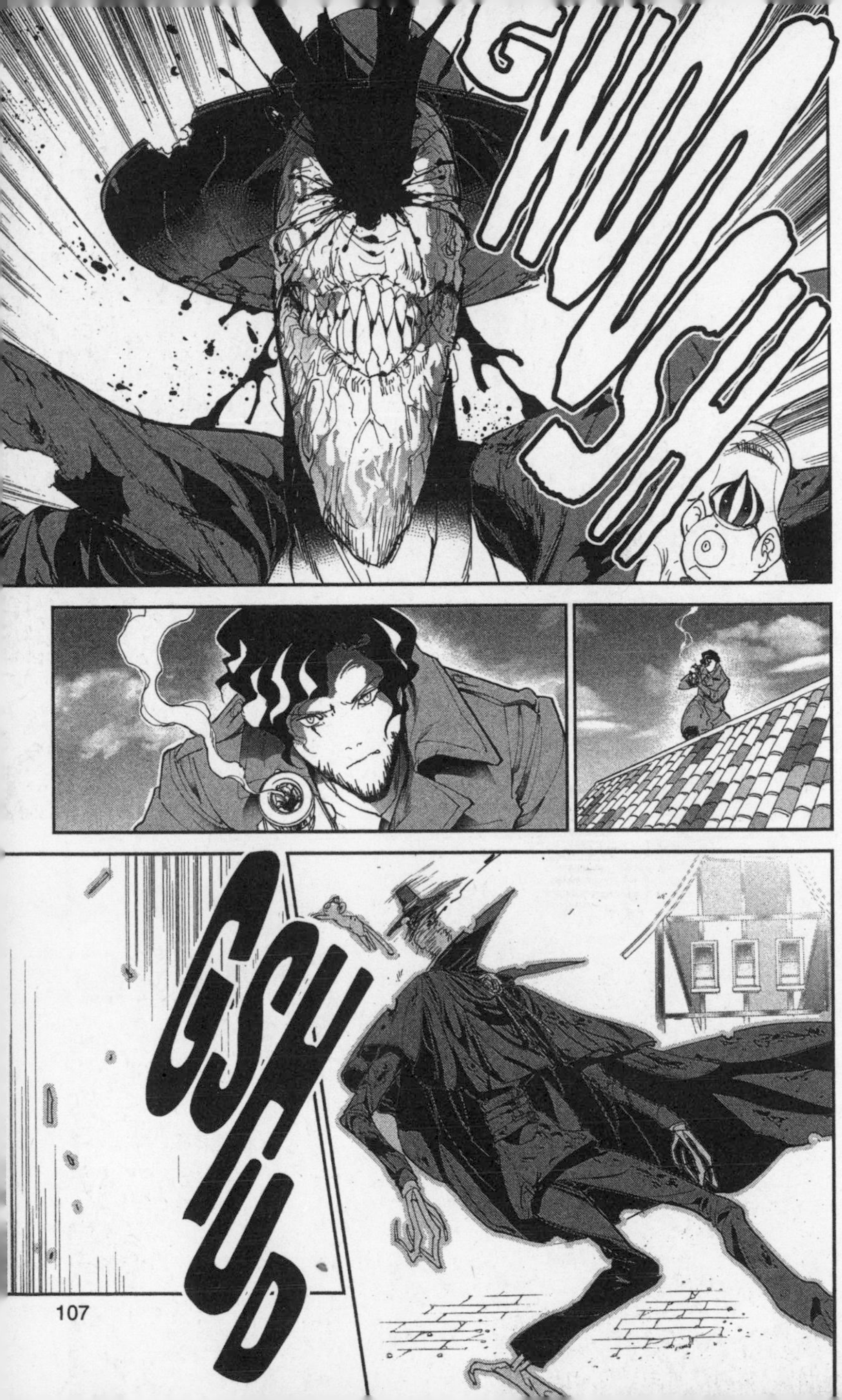
GWHOOSH
GSHUD

GRAND VALLEY KIDS

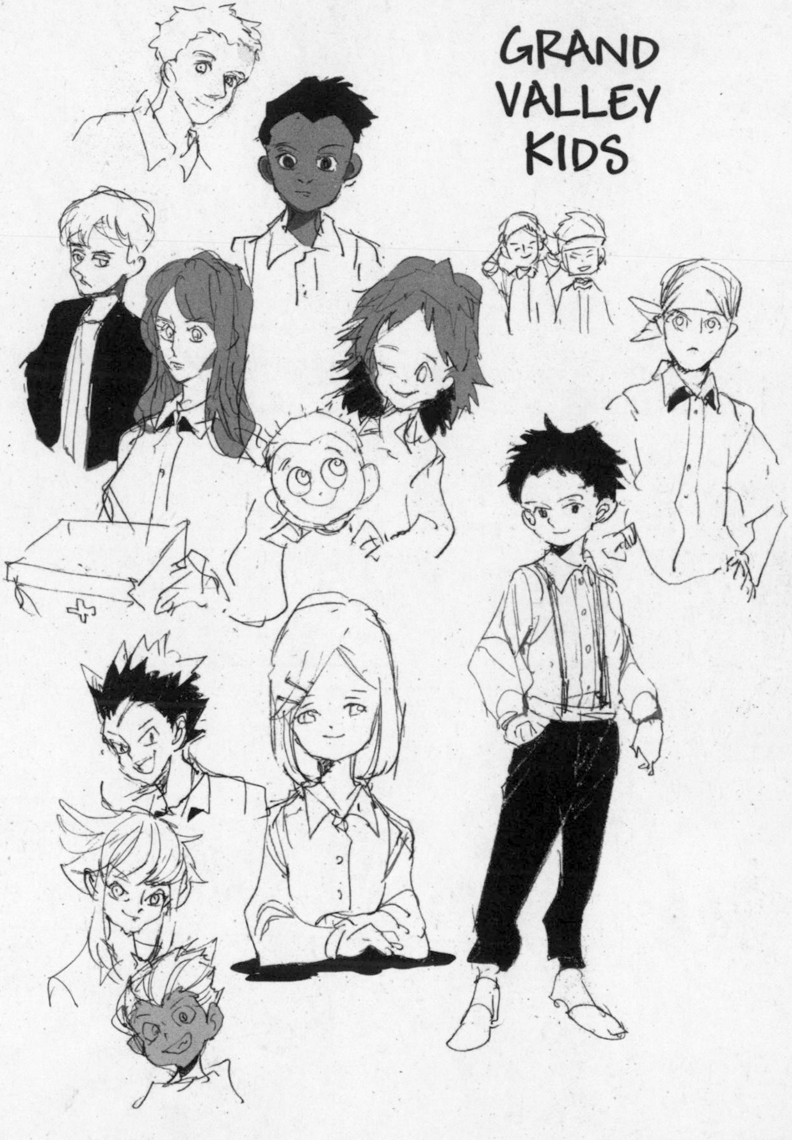

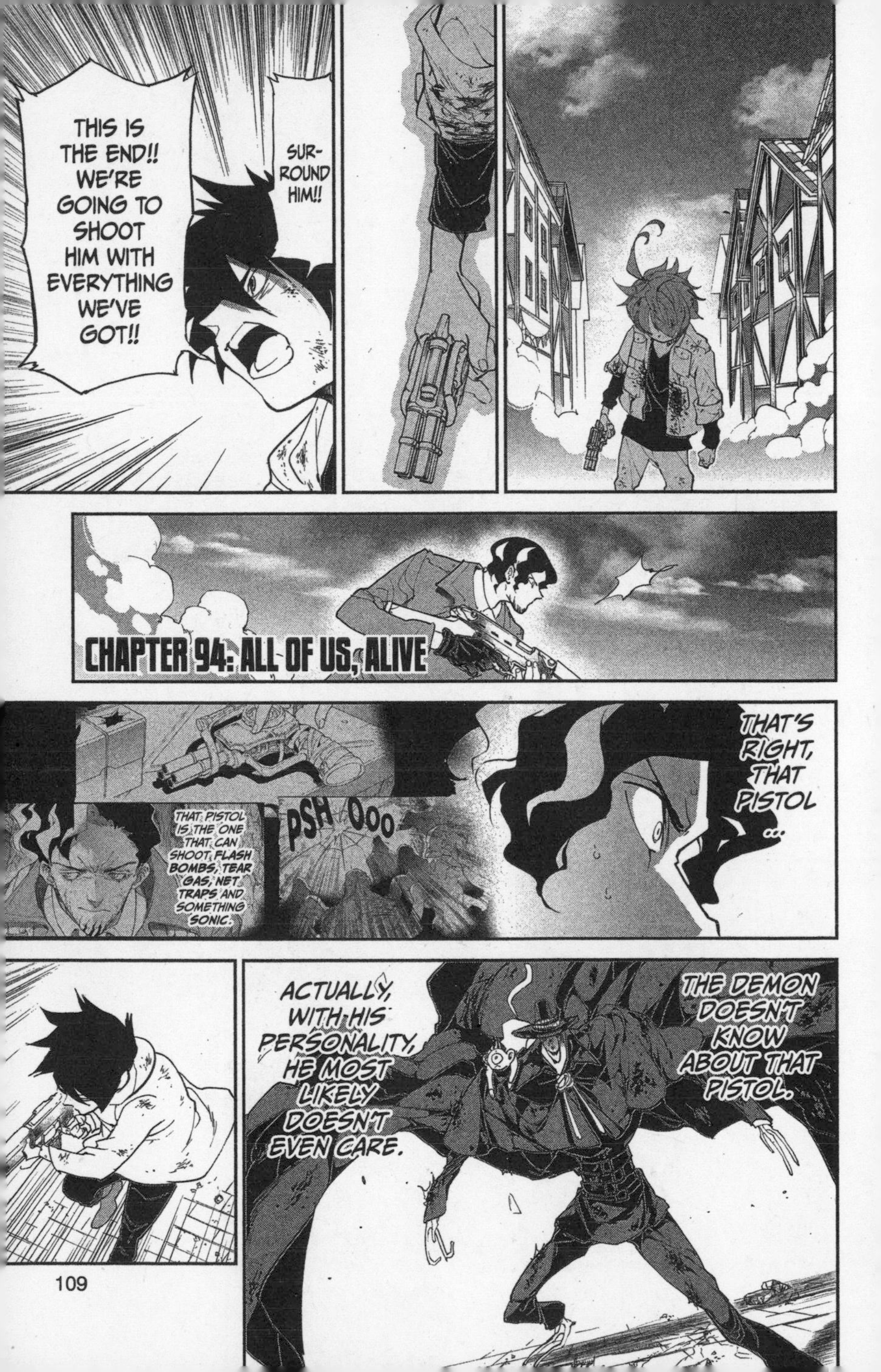
SUR-ROUND HIM!!
THIS IS THE END!! WE'RE GOING TO SHOOT HIM WITH EVERYTHING WE'VE GOT!!
CHAPTER 94: ALL OF US, ALIVE
THAT'S RIGHT, THAT PISTOL...
PSH OOO
THAT PISTOL IS THE ONE THAT CAN SHOOT FLASH BOMBS, TEAR GAS, NET TRAPS AND SOMETHING SONIC.
THE DEMON DOESN'T KNOW ABOUT THAT PISTOL.
ACTUALLY, WITH HIS PERSONALITY, HE MOST LIKELY DOESN'T EVEN CARE.

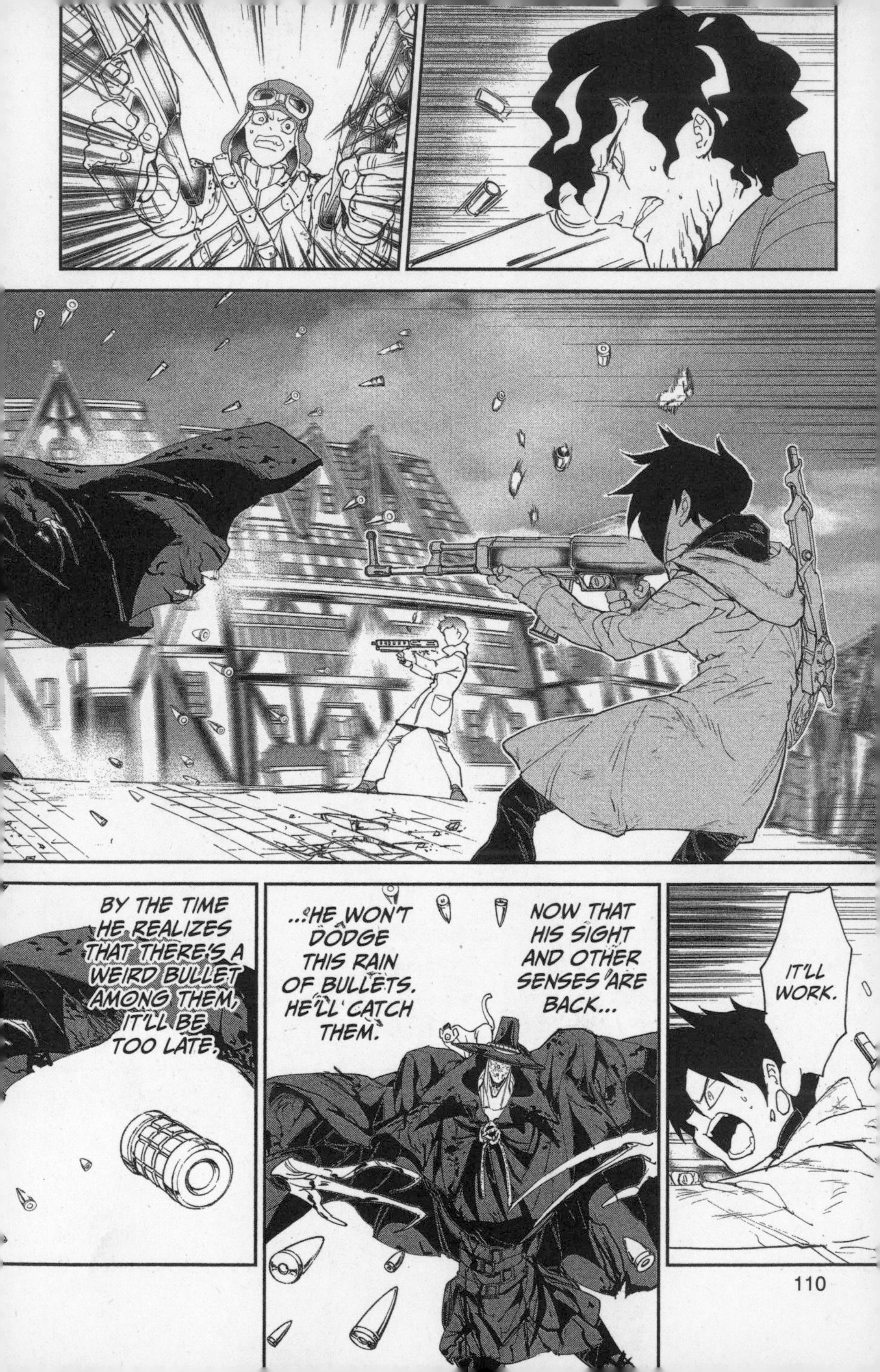
IT'LL WORK.
NOW THAT HIS SIGHT AND OTHER SENSES ARE BACK...
...HE WON'T DODGE THIS RAIN OF BULLETS. HE'LL CATCH THEM.
BY THE TIME HE REALIZES THAT THERE'S A WEIRD BULLET AMONG THEM, IT'LL BE TOO LATE.

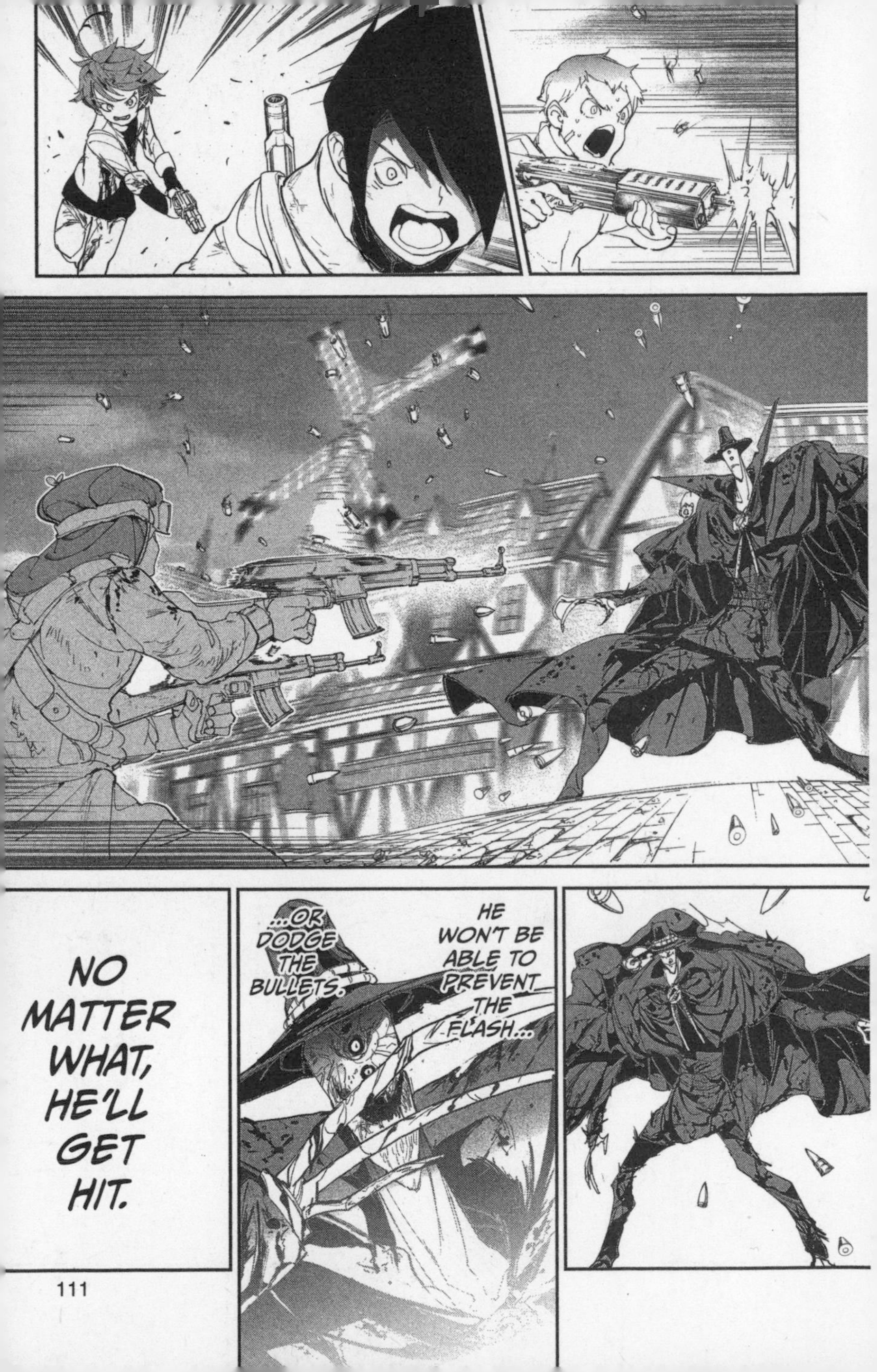
HE WON'T BE ABLE TO PREVENT THE FLASH...
...OR DODGE THE BULLETS.
NO MATTER WHAT, HE'LL GET HIT.

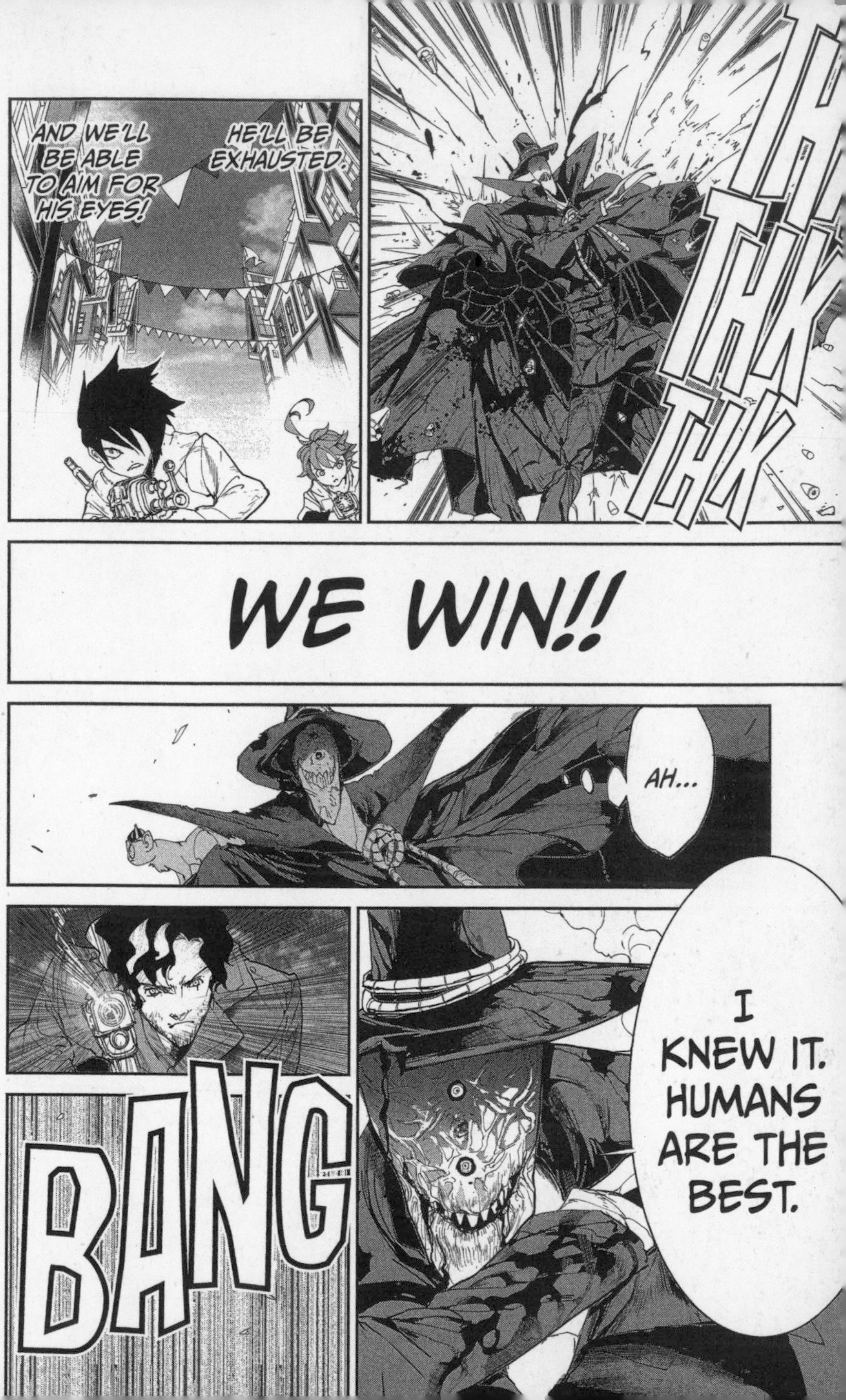
THK
THK
HE'LL BE EXHAUSTED.
AND WE'LL BE ABLE TO AIM FOR HIS EYES!
WE WIN!!
AH...
I KNEW IT. HUMANS ARE THE BEST.
BANG

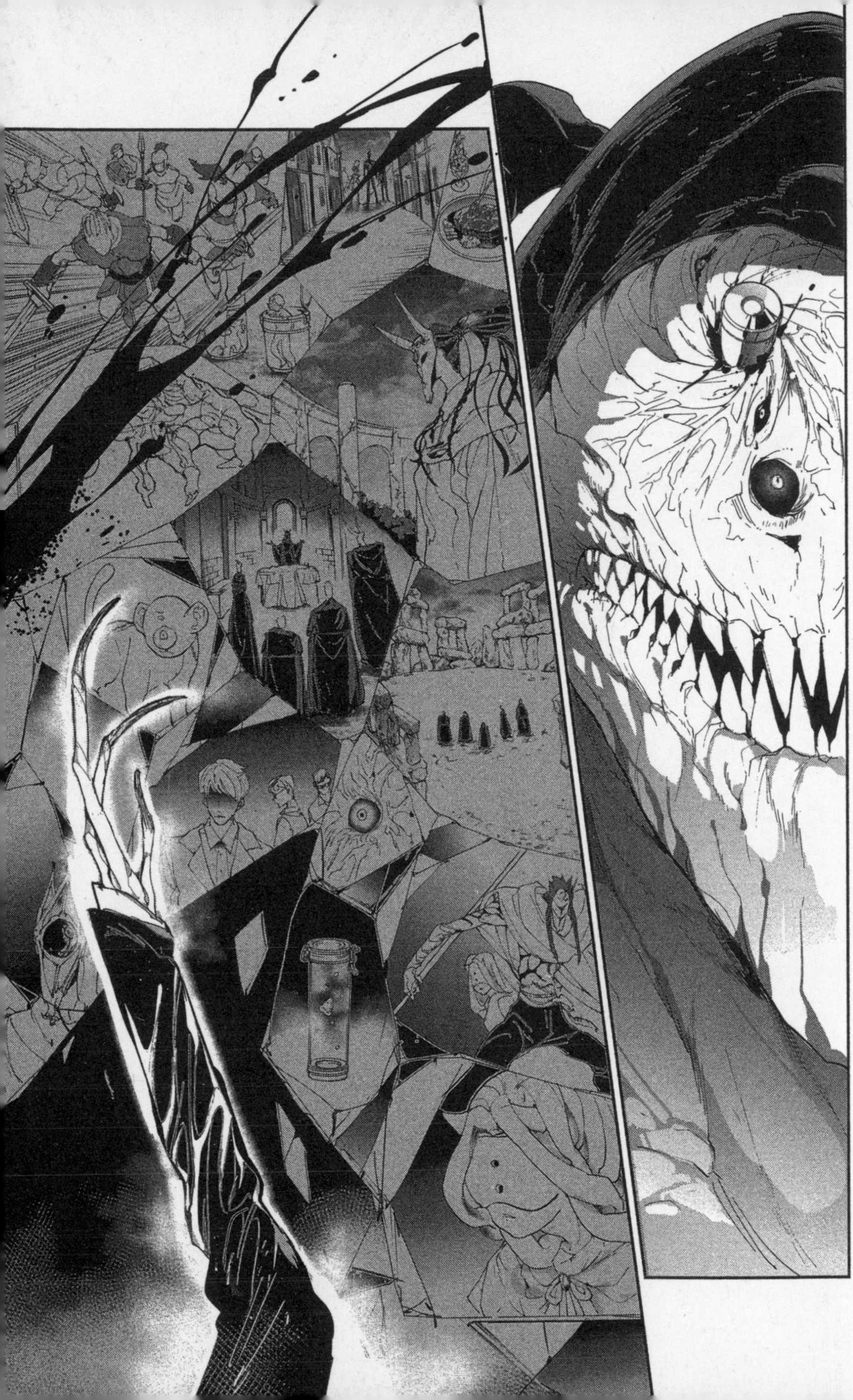

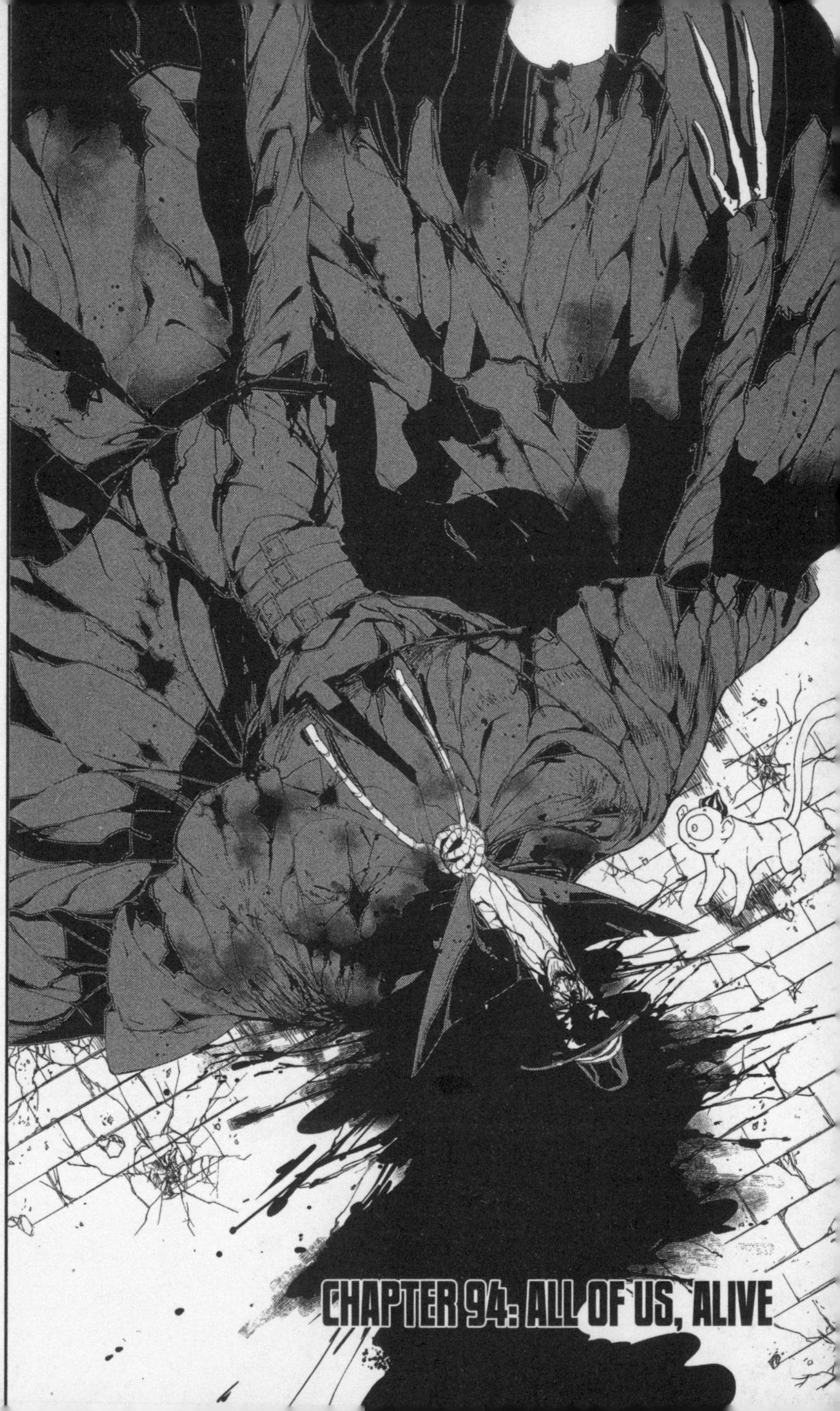
CHAPTER 94: ALL OF US, ALIVE

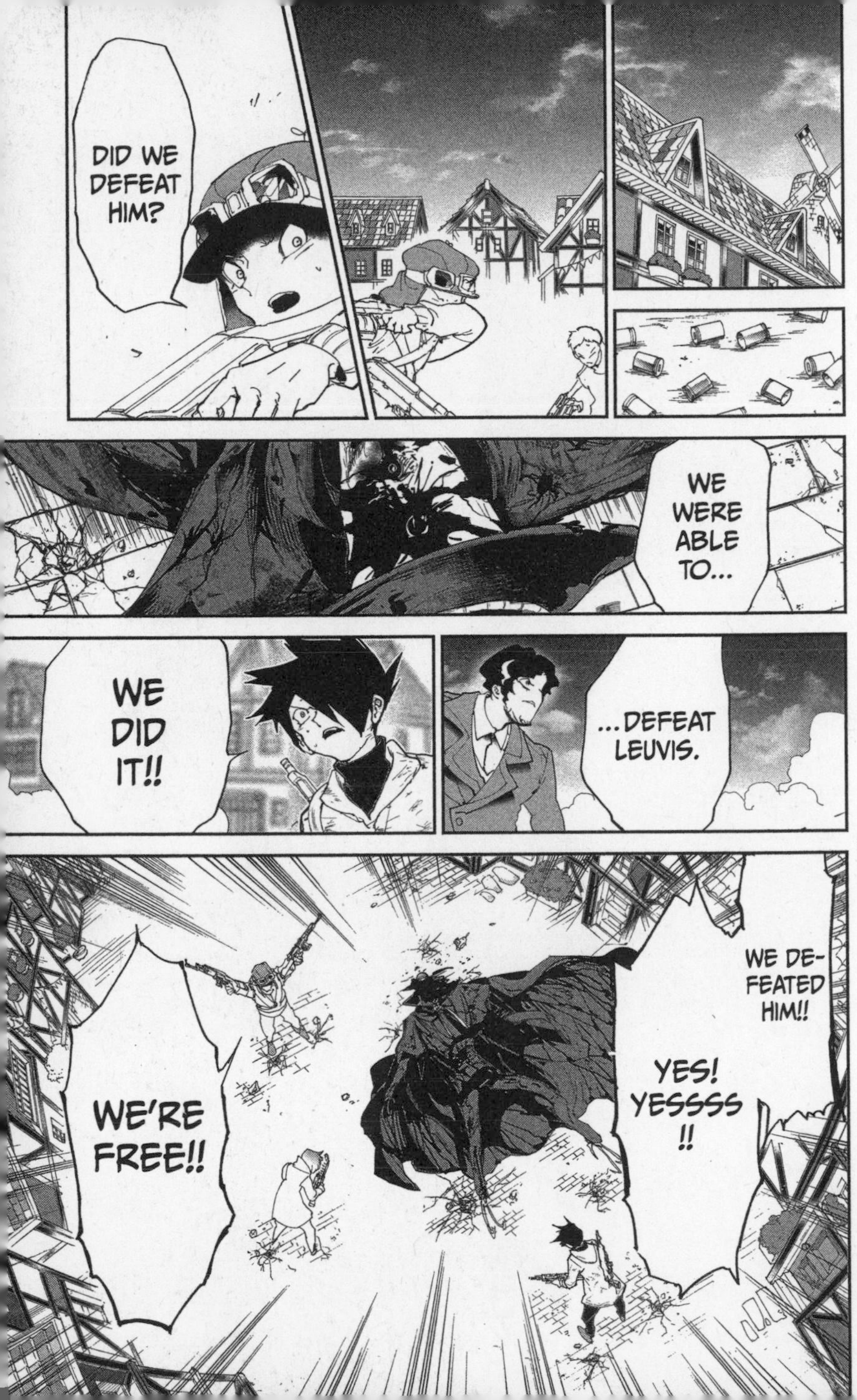
DID WE DEFEAT HIM?
WE WERE ABLE TO...
...DEFEAT LEUVIS.
WE DID IT!!
WE DE-FEATED HIM!!
YES! YESSSS!!
WE'RE FREE!!

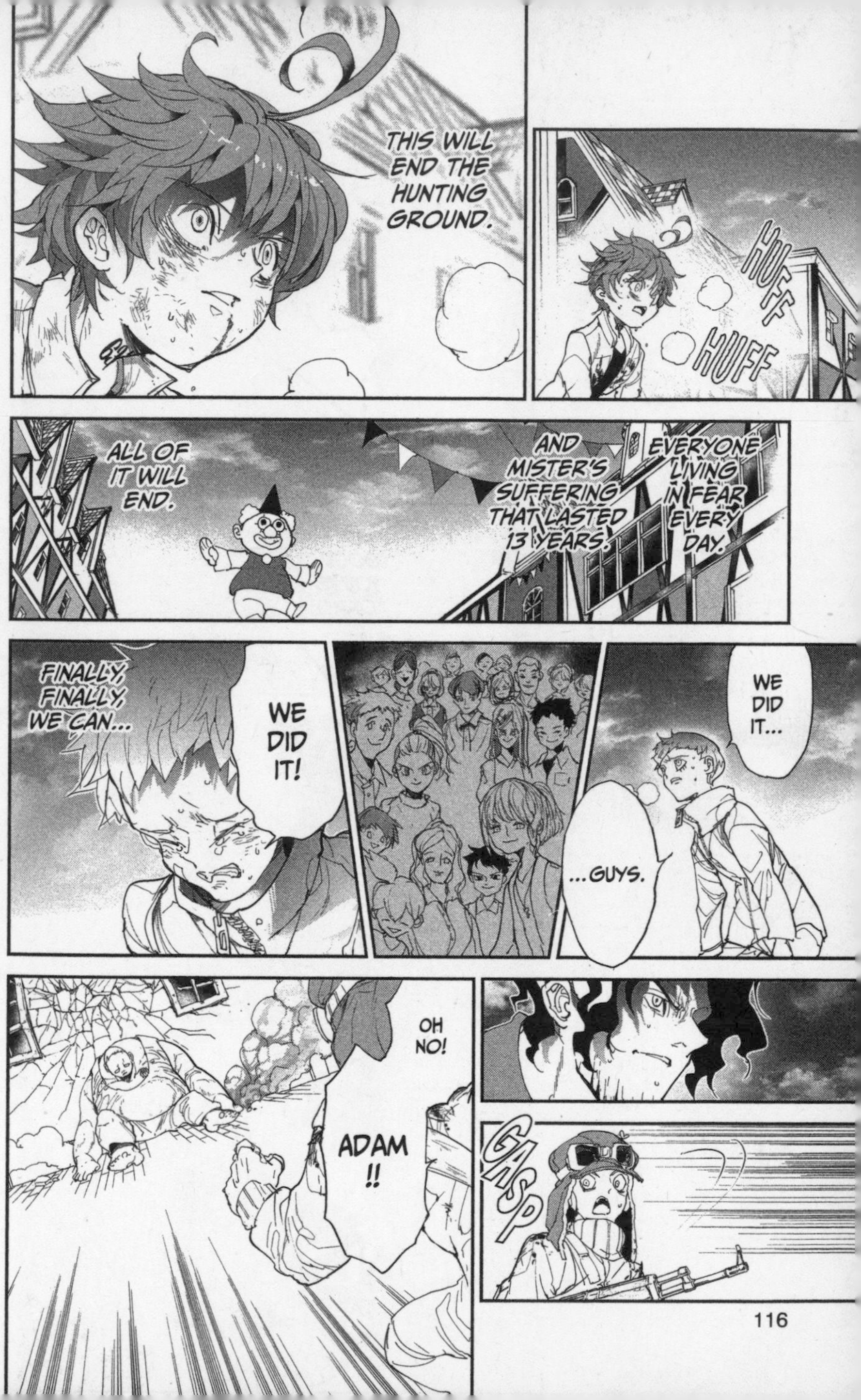
HUFF
HUFF
THIS WILL END THE HUNTING GROUND.
EVERYONE LIVING IN FEAR EVERY DAY.
AND MISTER'S SUFFERING THAT LASTED 13 YEARS.
ALL OF IT WILL END.
WE DID IT...
...GUYS.
WE DID IT!
FINALLY, FINALLY, WE CAN...
GASP
OH NO!
ADAM !!

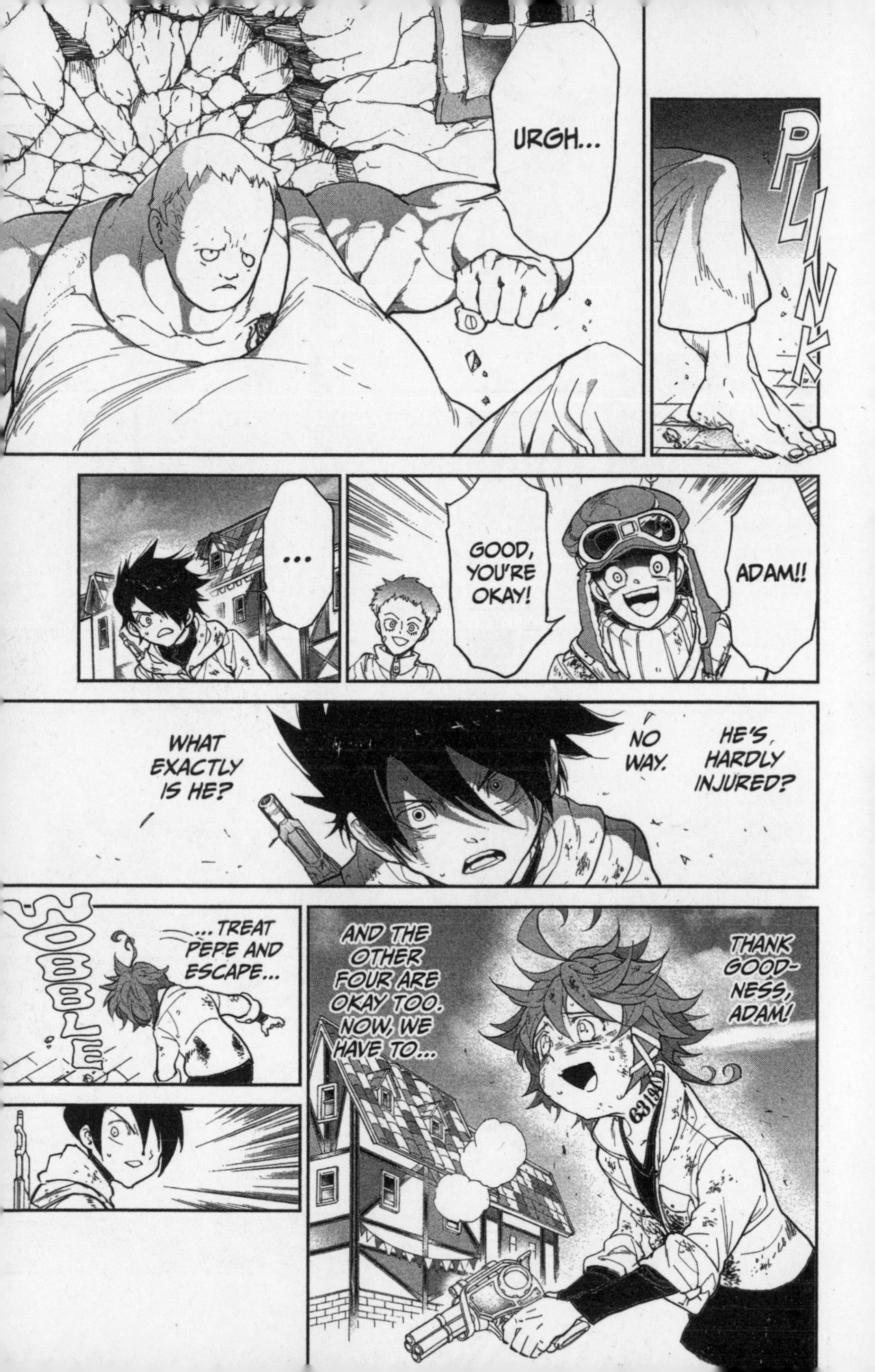
PLINK
URGH...
ADAM!!
GOOD, YOU'RE OKAY!
...
HE'S, HARDLY INJURED?
NO WAY.
WHAT EXACTLY IS HE?
THANK GOOD-NESS, ADAM!
AND THE OTHER FOUR ARE OKAY TOO. NOW, WE HAVE TO...
...TREAT PEPE AND ESCAPE...
WOBBLE

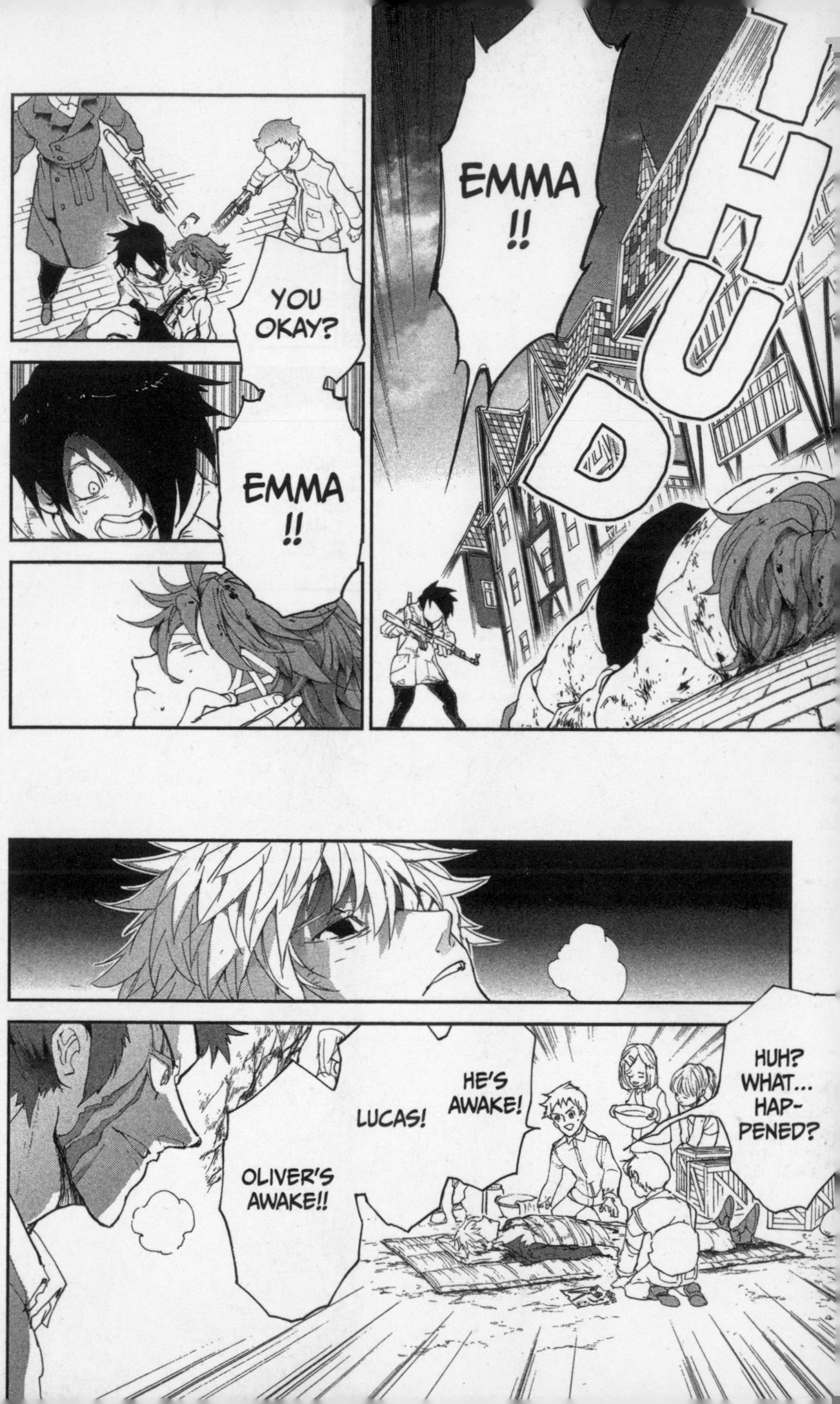
EMMA !!
YOU OKAY?
EMMA !!
HUH? WHAT... HAP-PENED?
HE'S AWAKE!
LUCAS!
OLIVER'S AWAKE!!

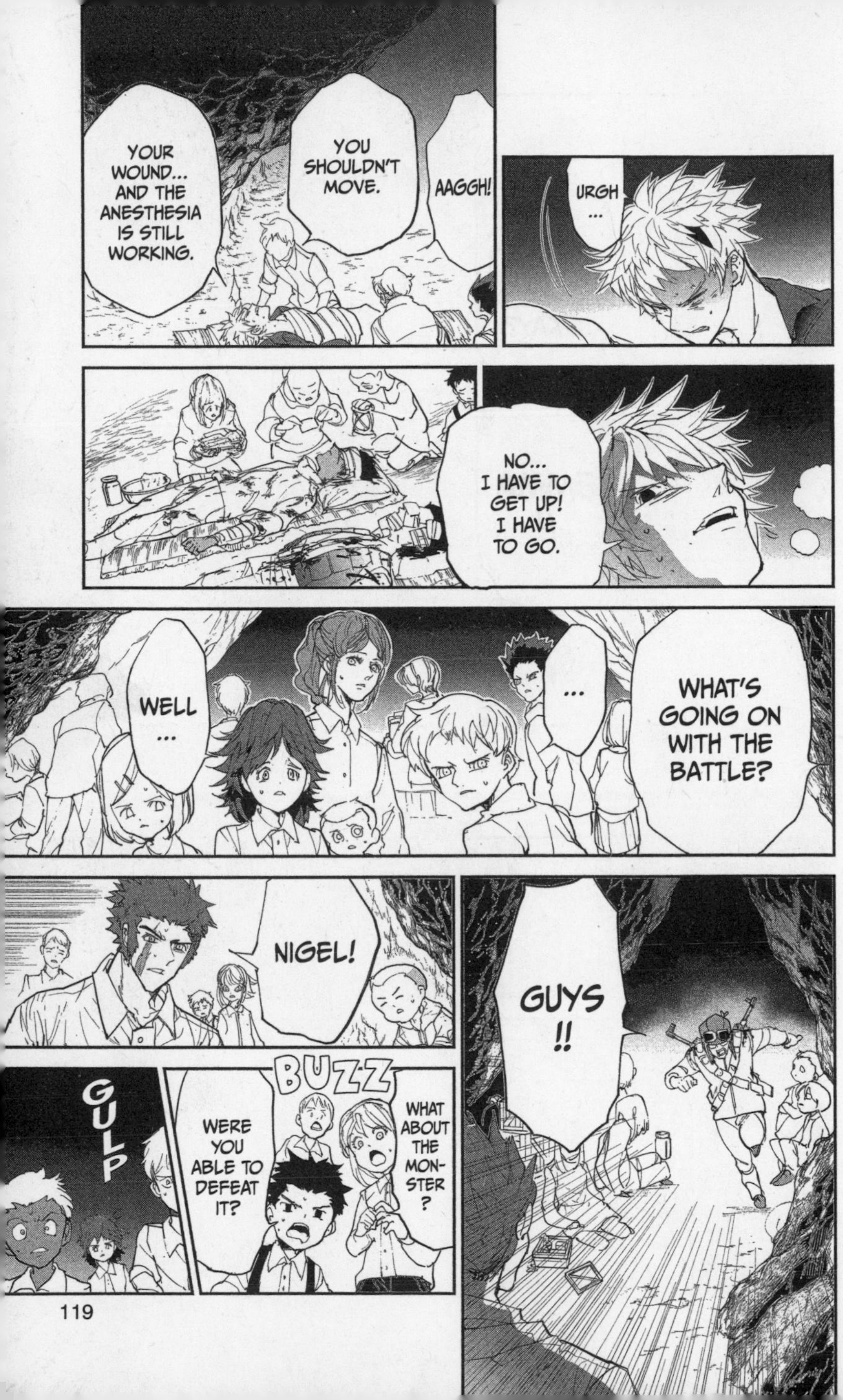
URGH ...
AAGGH!
YOU SHOULDN'T MOVE.
YOUR WOUND... AND THE ANESTHESIA IS STILL WORKING.
NO... I HAVE TO GET UP! I HAVE TO GO.
WHAT'S GOING ON WITH THE BATTLE?
...
WELL ...
GUYS !!
NIGEL!
BUZZ
WHAT ABOUT THE MON-STER ?
WERE YOU ABLE TO DEFEAT IT?
GULP

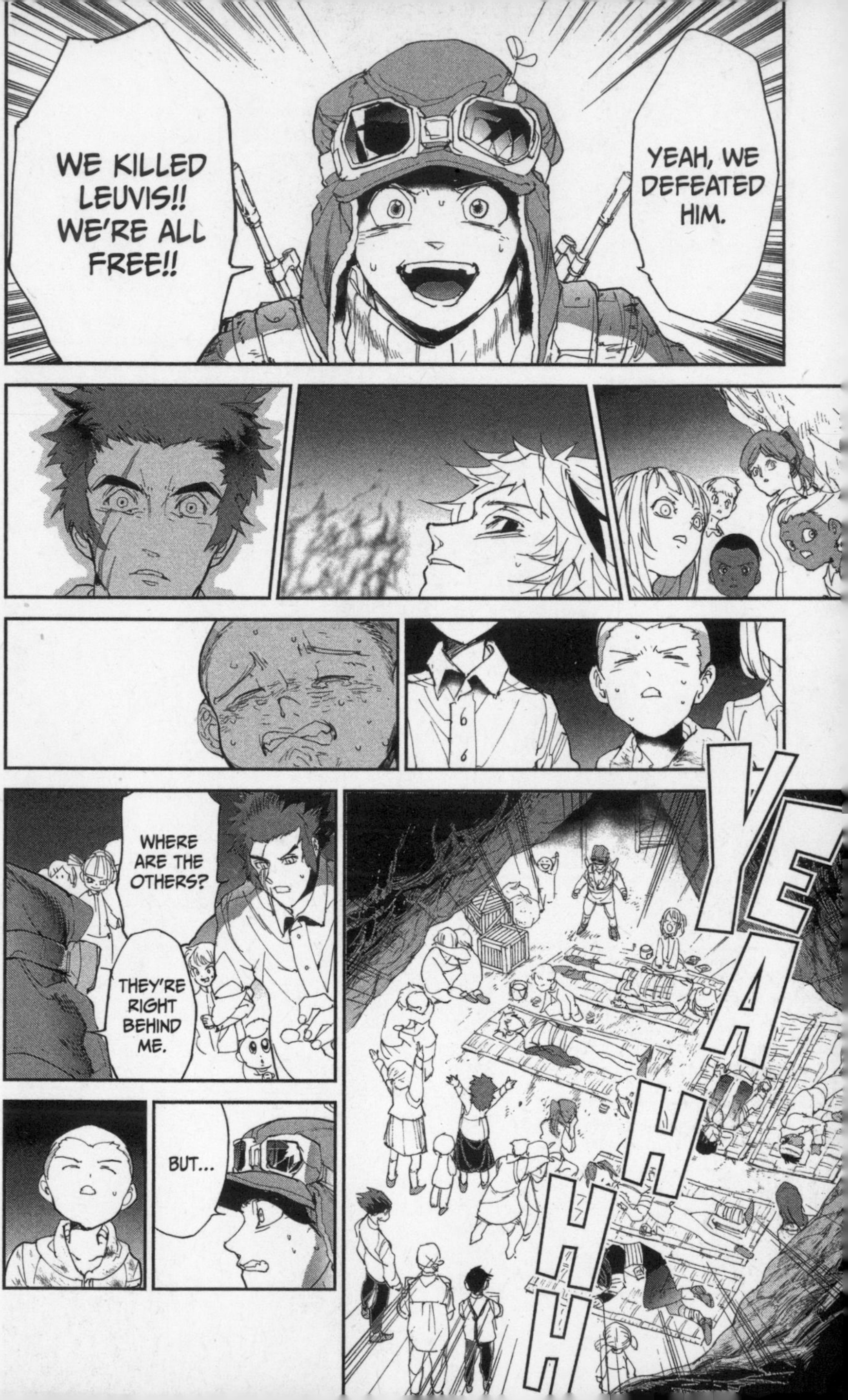
WE KILLED LEUVIS!! WE'RE ALL FREE!!
YEAH, WE DEFEATED HIM.
YEAHHHHH
WHERE ARE THE OTHERS?
THEY'RE RIGHT BEHIND ME.
BUT...

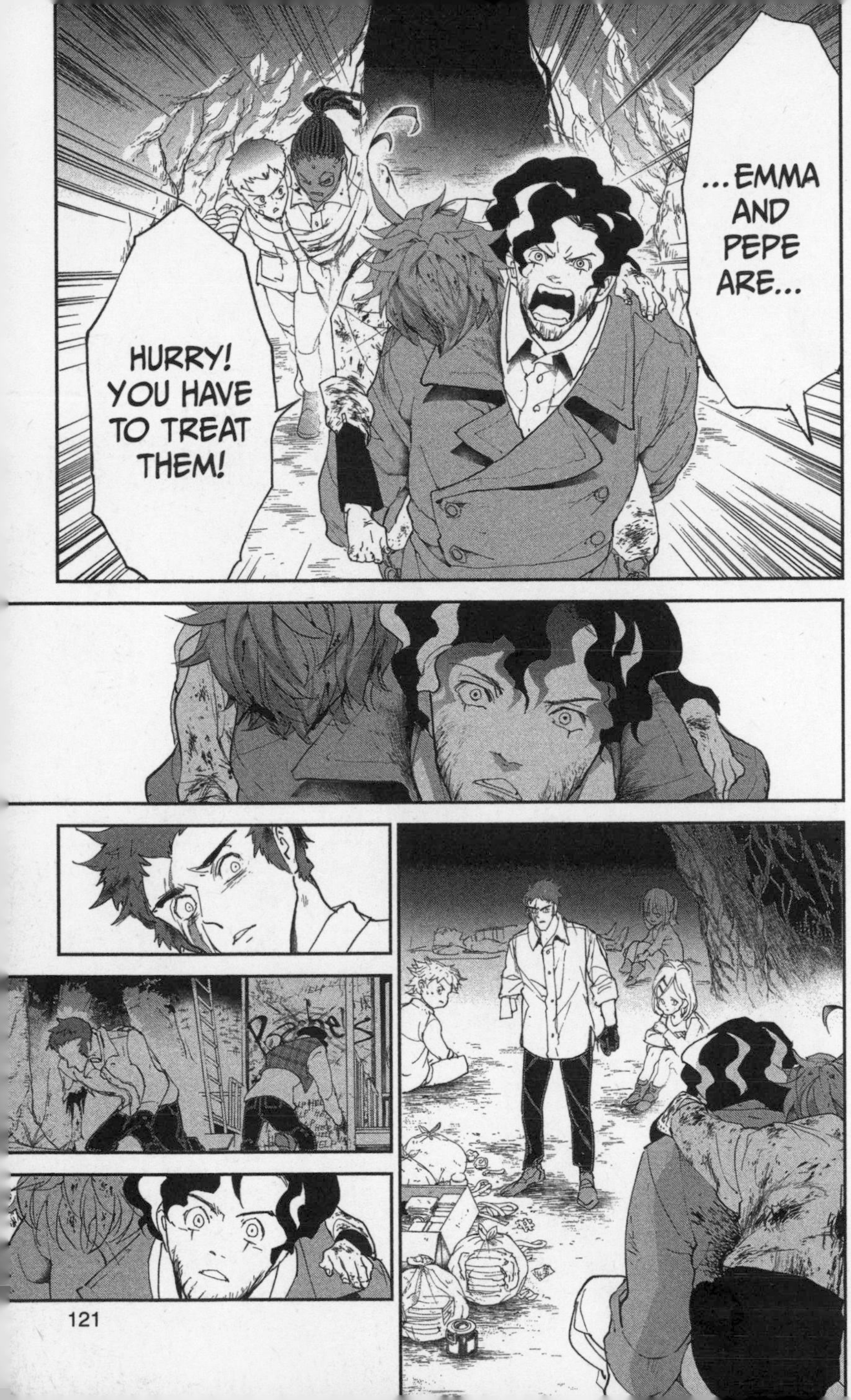
...EMMA AND PEPE ARE...
HURRY! YOU HAVE TO TREAT THEM!

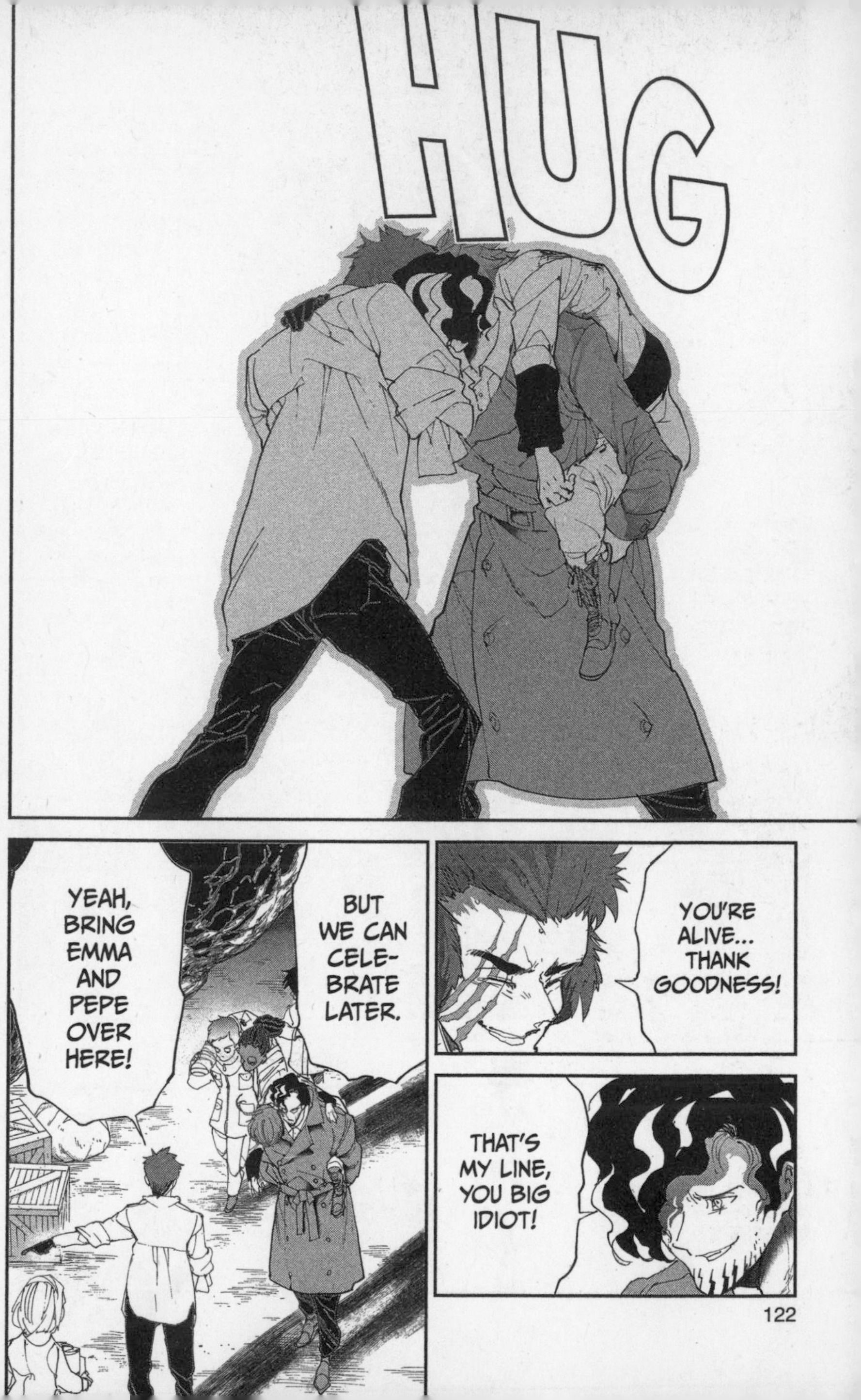
HUG
YOU'RE ALIVE... THANK GOODNESS!
THAT'S MY LINE, YOU BIG IDIOT!
BUT WE CAN CELE-BRATE LATER.
YEAH, BRING EMMA AND PEPE OVER HERE!

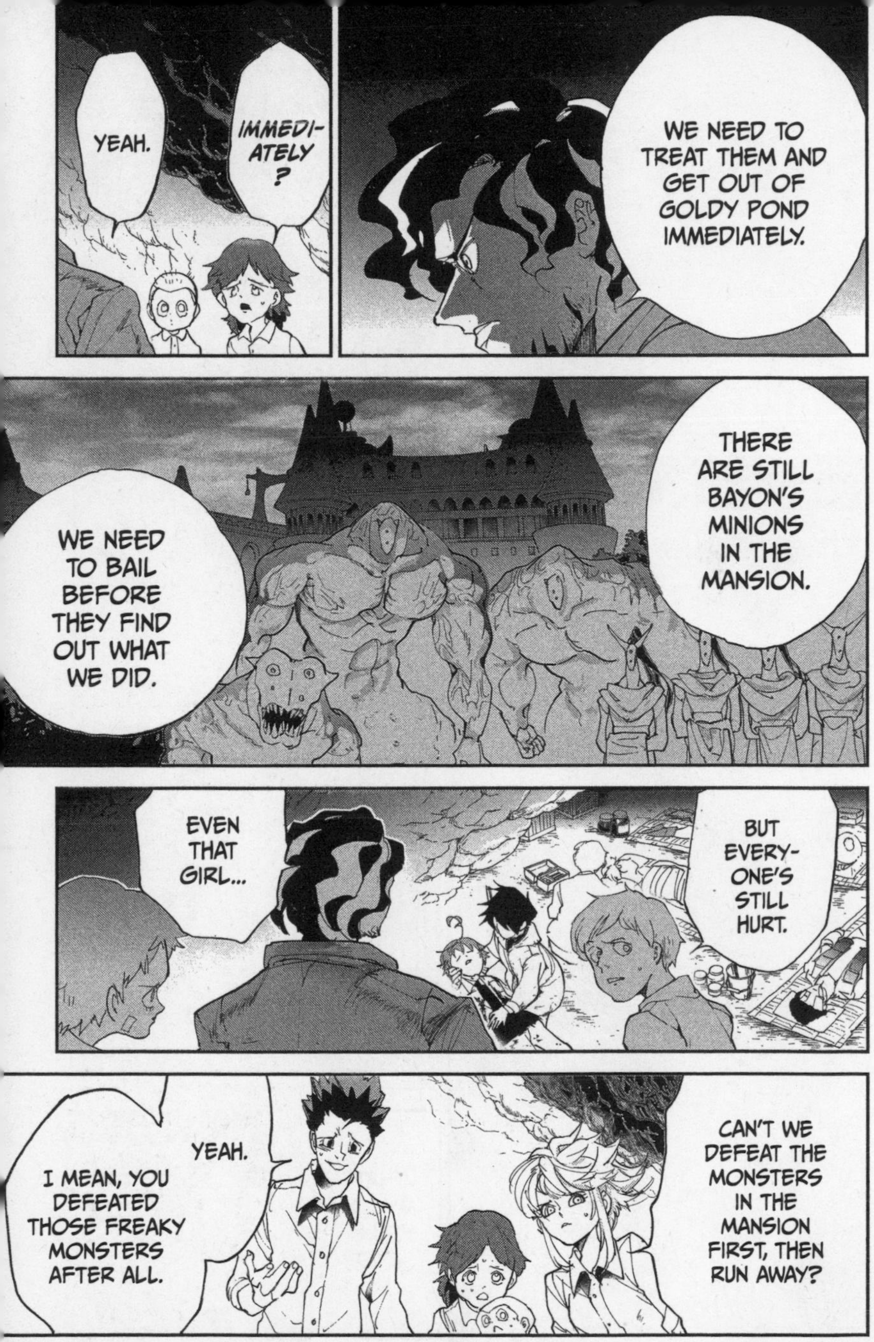
WE NEED TO TREAT THEM AND GET OUT OF GOLDY POND IMMEDIATELY.
IMMEDI-ATELY?
YEAH.
THERE ARE STILL BAYON'S MINIONS IN THE MANSION.
WE NEED TO BAIL BEFORE THEY FIND OUT WHAT WE DID.
BUT EVERY-ONE'S STILL HURT.
EVEN THAT GIRL...
CAN'T WE DEFEAT THE MONSTERS IN THE MANSION FIRST, THEN RUN AWAY?
YEAH.
I MEAN, YOU DEFEATED THOSE FREAKY MONSTERS AFTER ALL.

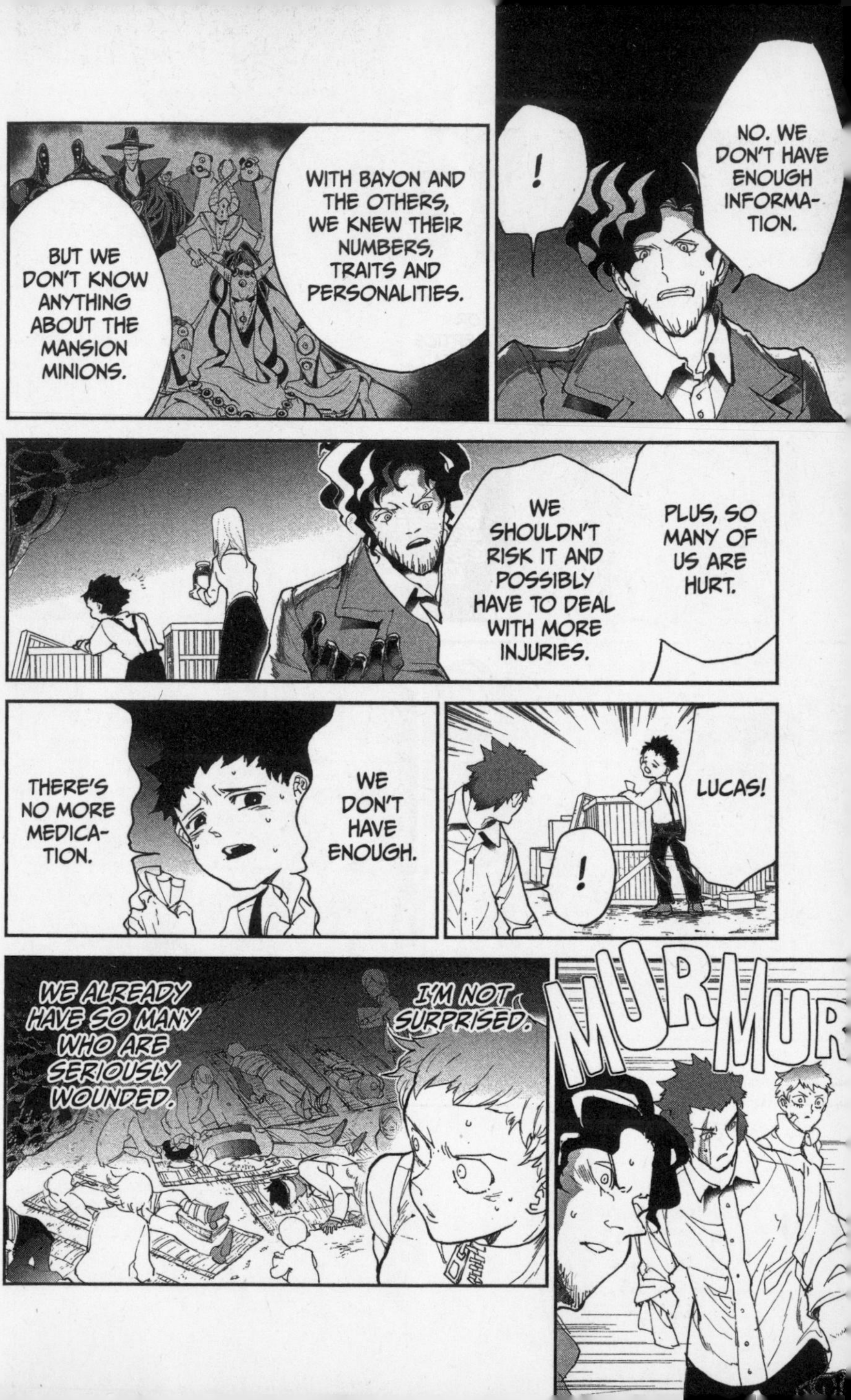
NO. WE DON'T HAVE ENOUGH INFORMATION.
!
WITH BAYON AND THE OTHERS, WE KNEW THEIR NUMBERS, TRAITS AND PERSONALITIES.
BUT WE DON'T KNOW ANYTHING ABOUT THE MANSION MINIONS.
PLUS, SO MANY OF US ARE HURT.
WE SHOULDN'T RISK IT AND POSSIBLY HAVE TO DEAL WITH MORE INJURIES.
LUCAS!
!
WE DON'T HAVE ENOUGH.
THERE'S NO MORE MEDICATION.
MURMUR
I'M NOT SURPRISED.
WE ALREADY HAVE SO MANY WHO ARE SERIOUSLY WOUNDED.

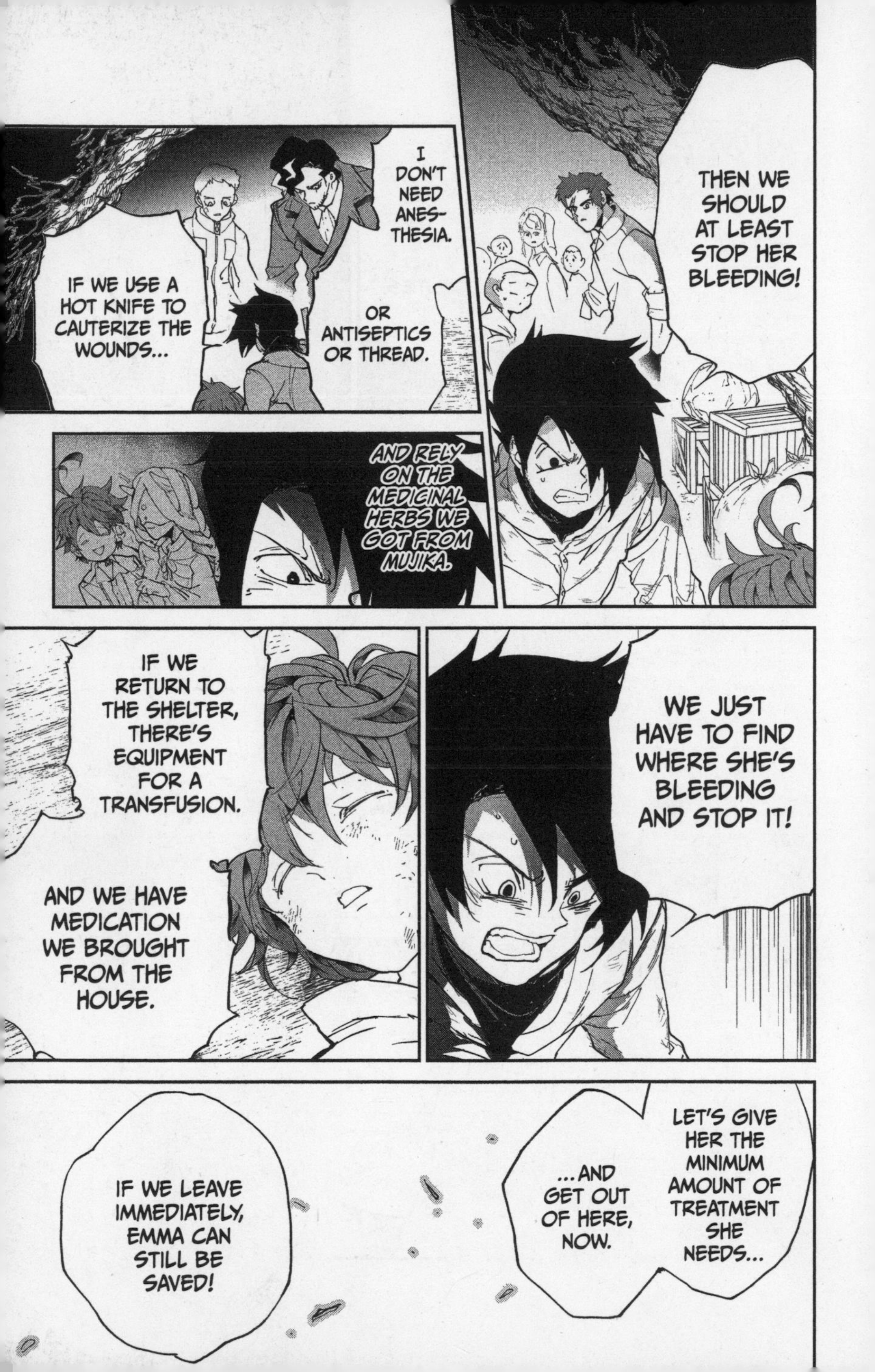
THEN WE SHOULD AT LEAST STOP HER BLEEDING!
I DON'T NEED ANES-THESIA.
OR ANTISEPTICS OR THREAD.
IF WE USE A HOT KNIFE TO CAUTERIZE THE WOUNDS...
AND RELY ON THE MEDICINAL HERBS WE GOT FROM MUJIKA.
WE JUST HAVE TO FIND WHERE SHE'S BLEEDING AND STOP IT!
IF WE RETURN TO THE SHELTER, THERE'S EQUIPMENT FOR A TRANSFUSION.
AND WE HAVE MEDICATION WE BROUGHT FROM THE HOUSE.
LET'S GIVE HER THE MINIMUM AMOUNT OF TREATMENT SHE NEEDS...
...AND GET OUT OF HERE, NOW.
IF WE LEAVE IMMEDIATELY, EMMA CAN STILL BE SAVED!

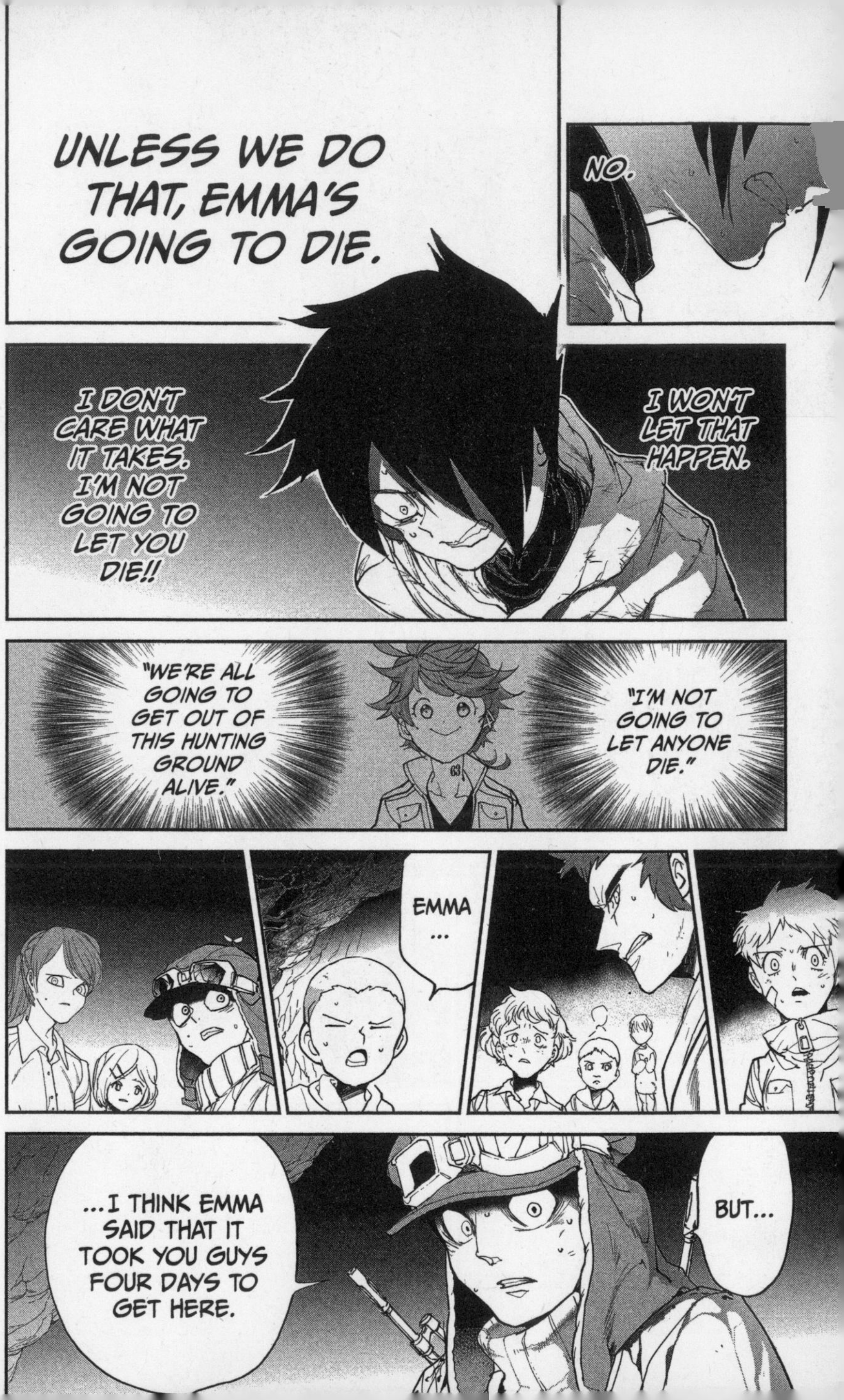
NO.
UNLESS WE DO THAT, EMMA'S GOING TO DIE.
I WON'T LET THAT HAPPEN.
I DON'T CARE WHAT IT TAKES. I'M NOT GOING TO LET YOU DIE!!
"I'M NOT GOING TO LET ANYONE DIE."
"WE'RE ALL GOING TO GET OUT OF THIS HUNTING GROUND ALIVE."
EMMA...
BUT...
...I THINK EMMA SAID THAT IT TOOK YOU GUYS FOUR DAYS TO GET HERE.

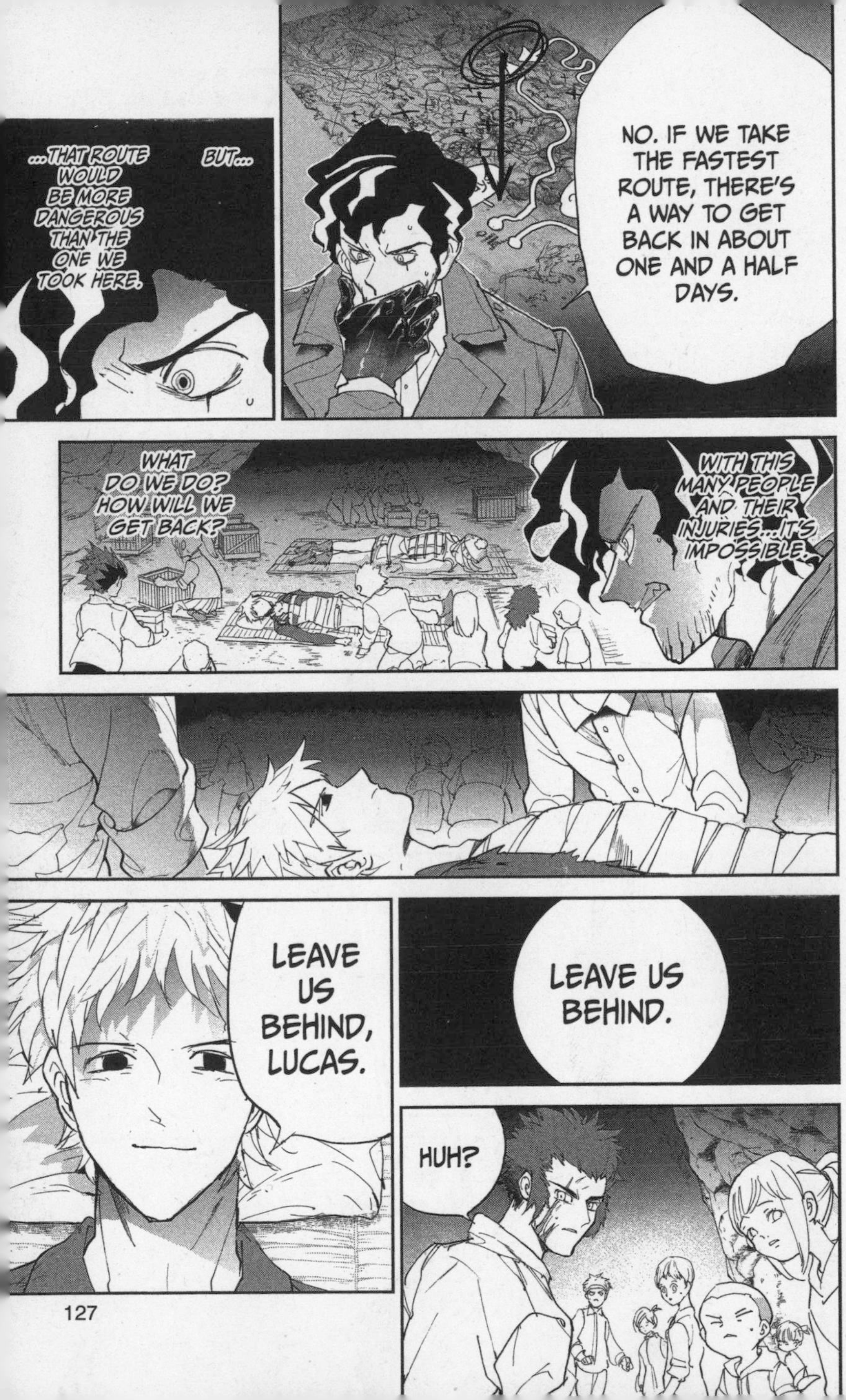
NO. IF WE TAKE THE FASTEST ROUTE, THERE'S A WAY TO GET BACK IN ABOUT ONE AND A HALF DAYS.
BUT...
...THAT ROUTE WOULD BE MORE DANGEROUS THAN THE ONE WE TOOK HERE.
WITH THIS MANY PEOPLE AND THEIR INJURIES...IT'S IMPOSSIBLE.
WHAT DO WE DO? HOW WILL WE GET BACK?
LEAVE US BEHIND.
HUH?
LEAVE US BEHIND, LUCAS.

THE PROMISED NEVERLAND DELETED SCENE

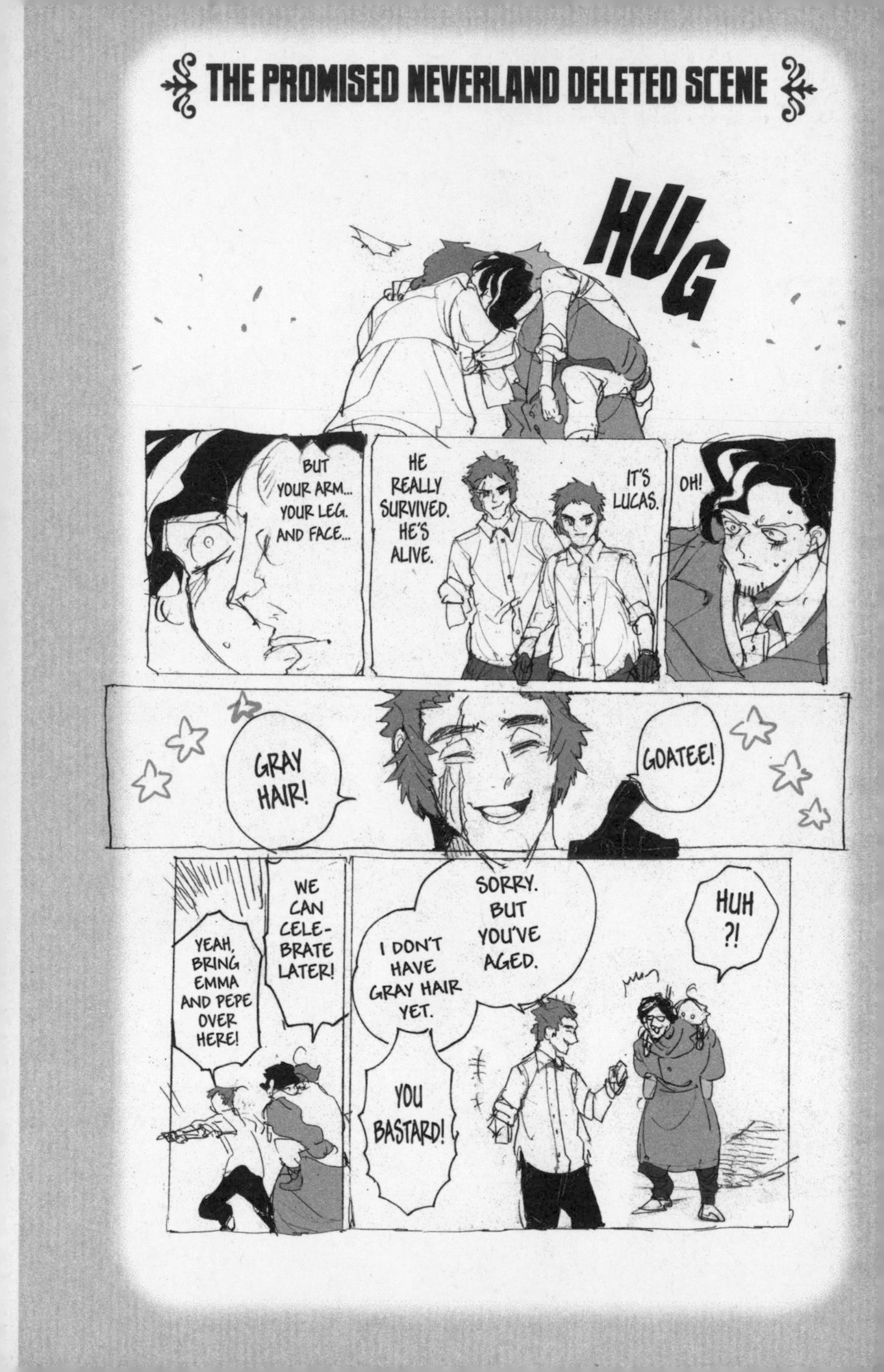
HUG
OH!
IT'S LUCAS.
HE REALLY SURVIVED. HE'S ALIVE.
BUT YOUR ARM... YOUR LEG. AND FACE...
GOATEE!
GRAY HAIR!
HUH ?!
SORRY. BUT YOU'VE AGED.
I DON'T HAVE GRAY HAIR YET.
YOU BASTARD!
WE CAN CELE-BRATE LATER!
YEAH, BRING EMMA AND PEPE OVER HERE!

CHAPTER 95: LET'S GO HOME

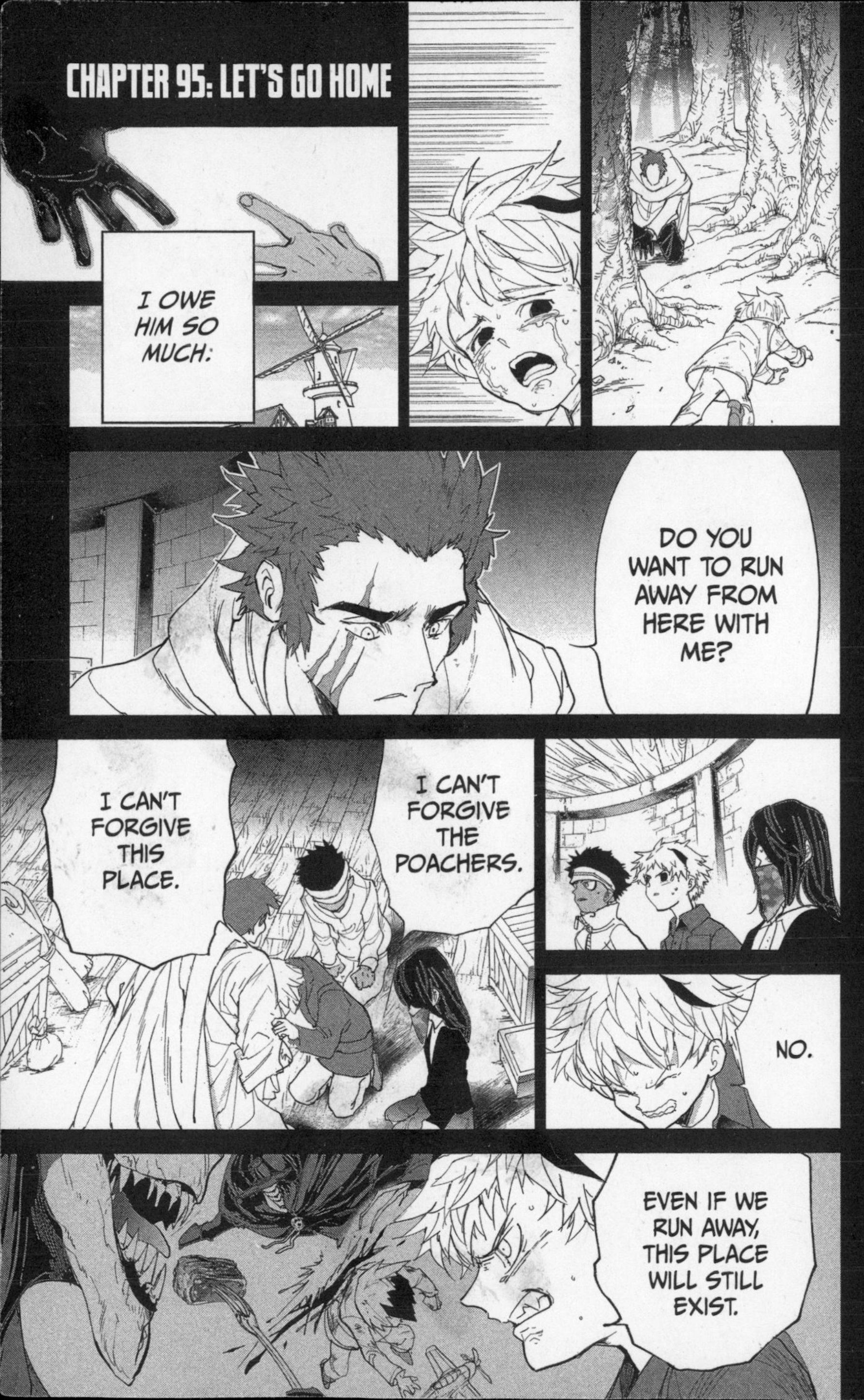
I OWE HIM SO MUCH:
DO YOU WANT TO RUN AWAY FROM HERE WITH ME?
NO.
I CAN'T FORGIVE THE POACHERS.
I CAN'T FORGIVE THIS PLACE.
EVEN IF WE RUN AWAY, THIS PLACE WILL STILL EXIST.

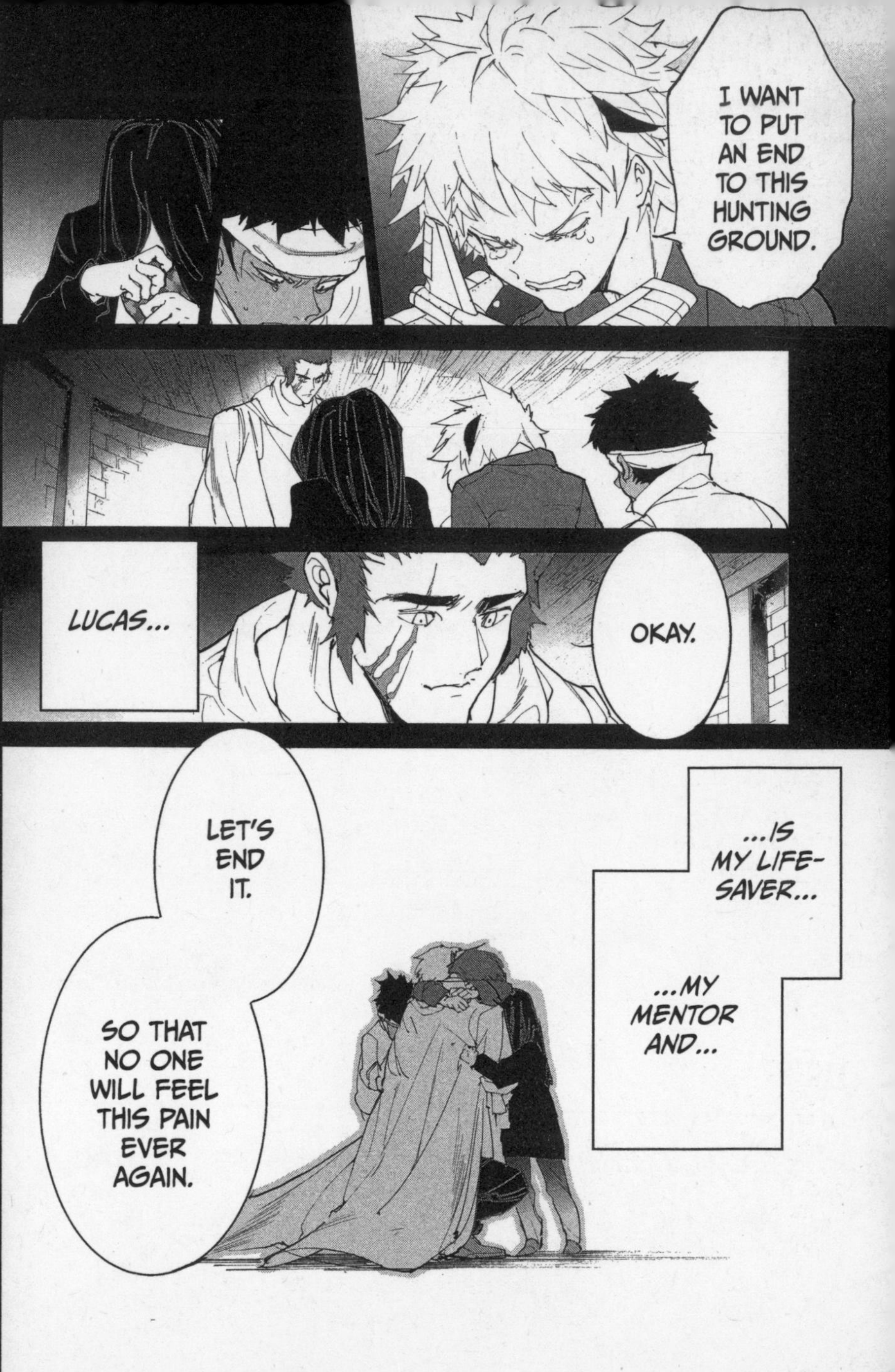
I WANT TO PUT AN END TO THIS HUNTING GROUND.
OKAY.
LUCAS...
...IS MY LIFE-SAVER...
...MY MENTOR AND...
LET'S END IT.
SO THAT NO ONE WILL FEEL THIS PAIN EVER AGAIN.

CHAPTER 95: LET'S GO HOME

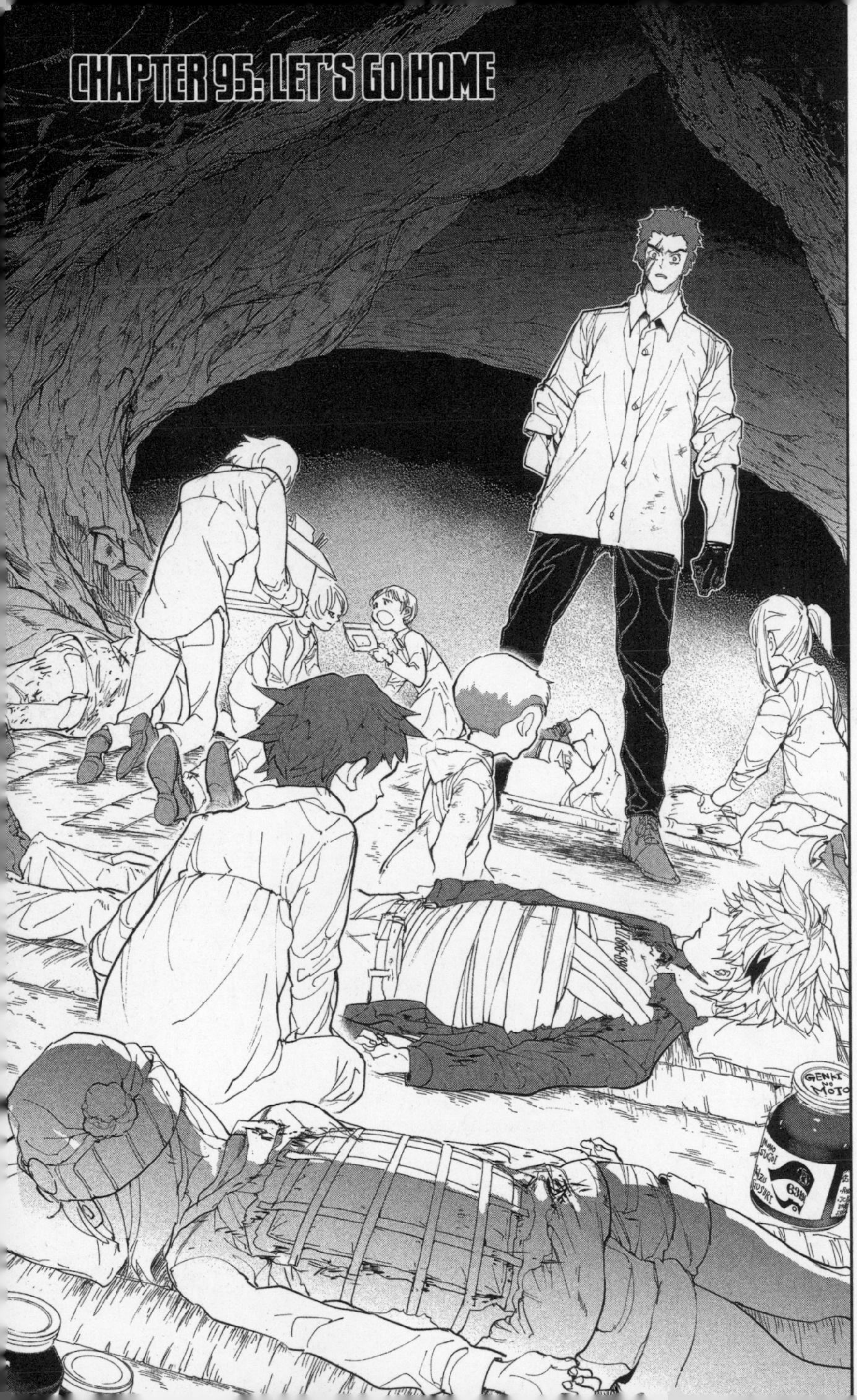
GENKI NO MOTO

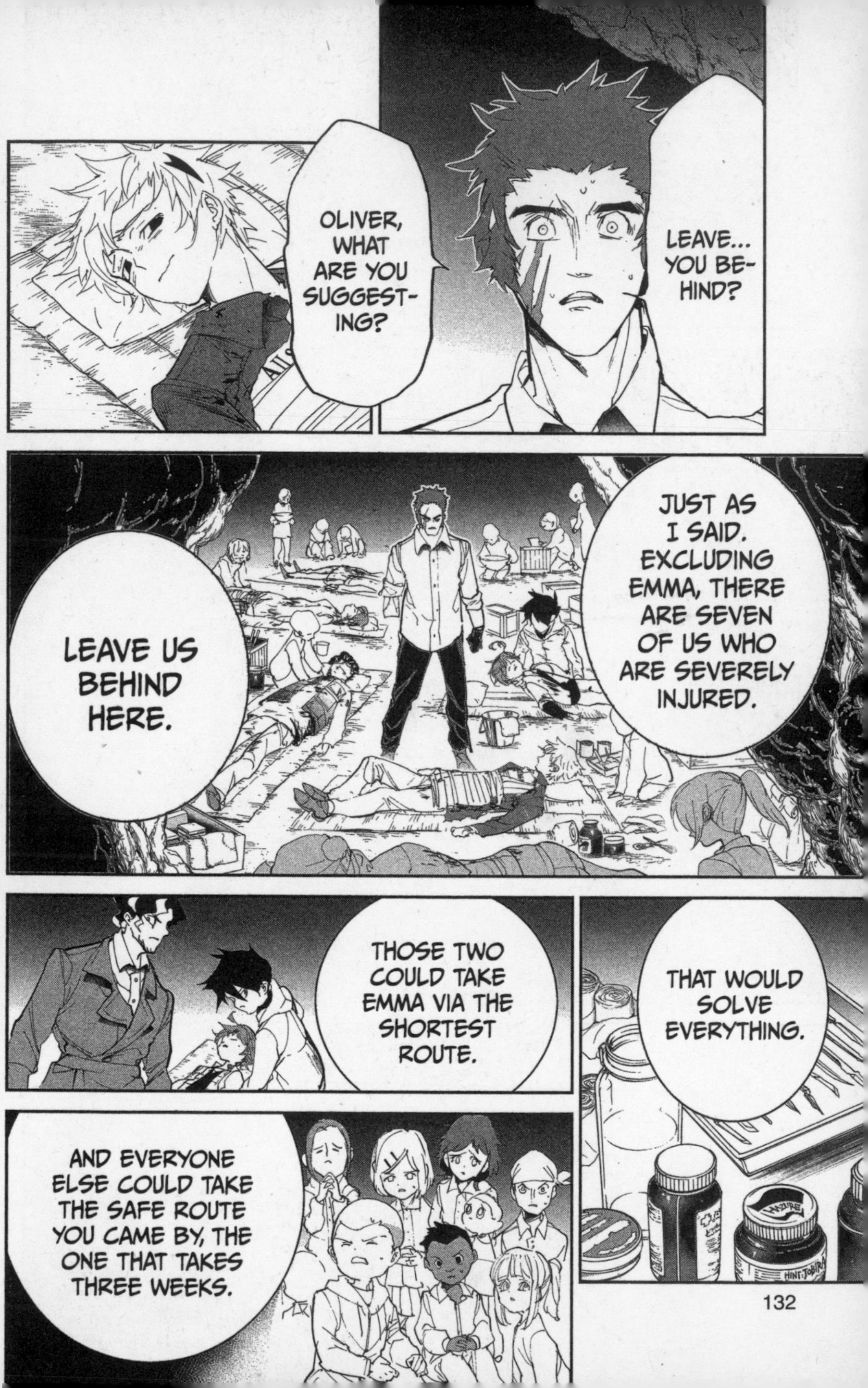
LEAVE... YOU BE-HIND?
OLIVER, WHAT ARE YOU SUGGEST-ING?
JUST AS I SAID. EXCLUDING EMMA, THERE ARE SEVEN OF US WHO ARE SEVERELY INJURED.
LEAVE US BEHIND HERE.
THAT WOULD SOLVE EVERYTHING.
THOSE TWO COULD TAKE EMMA VIA THE SHORTEST ROUTE.
AND EVERYONE ELSE COULD TAKE THE SAFE ROUTE YOU CAME BY, THE ONE THAT TAKES THREE WEEKS.

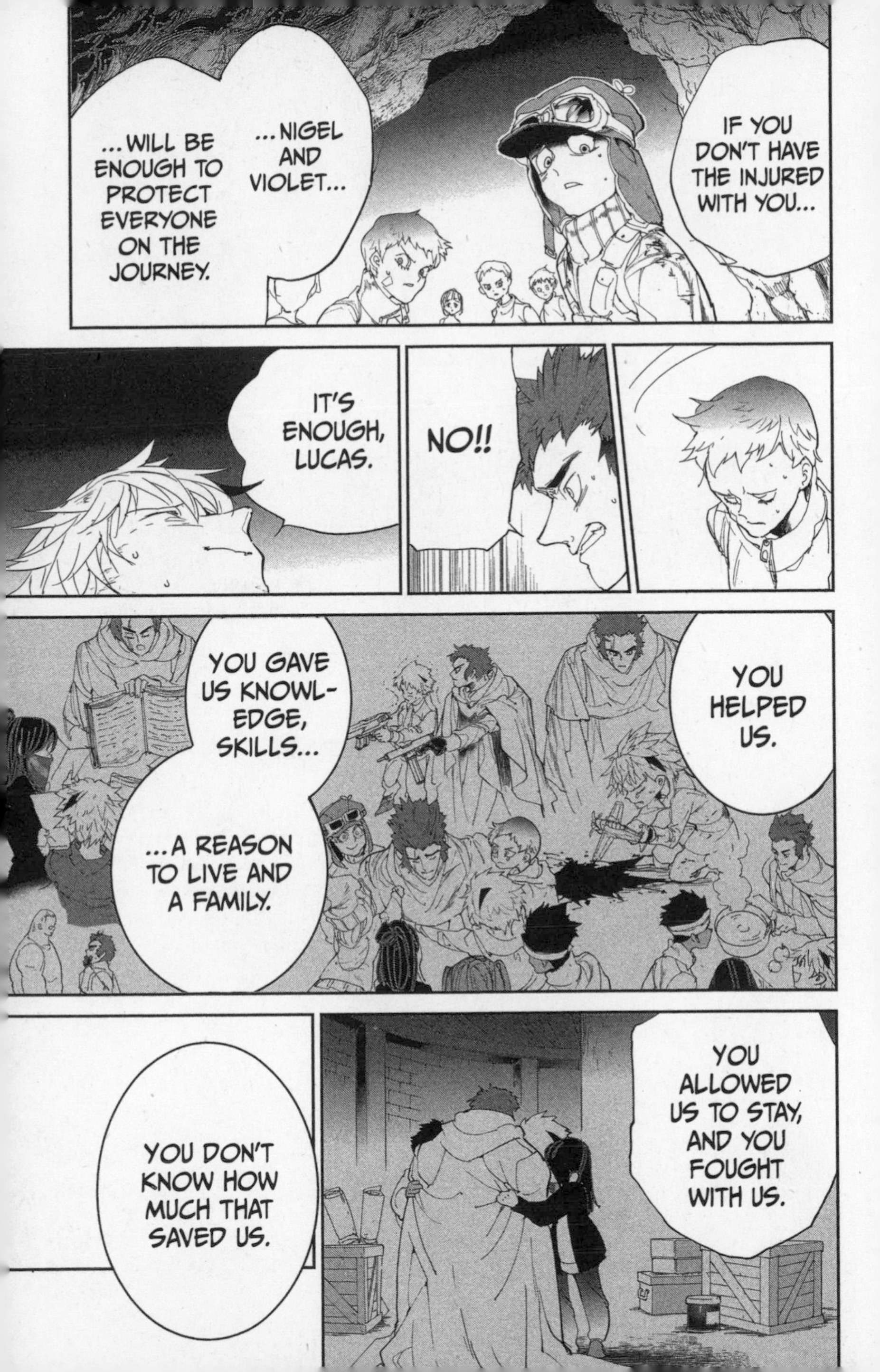
IF YOU DON'T HAVE THE INJURED WITH YOU...
...NIGEL AND VIOLET...
...WILL BE ENOUGH TO PROTECT EVERYONE ON THE JOURNEY.
NO!!
IT'S ENOUGH, LUCAS.
YOU HELPED US.
YOU GAVE US KNOWL-EDGE, SKILLS...
...A REASON TO LIVE AND A FAMILY.
YOU ALLOWED US TO STAY, AND YOU FOUGHT WITH US.
YOU DON'T KNOW HOW MUCH THAT SAVED US.

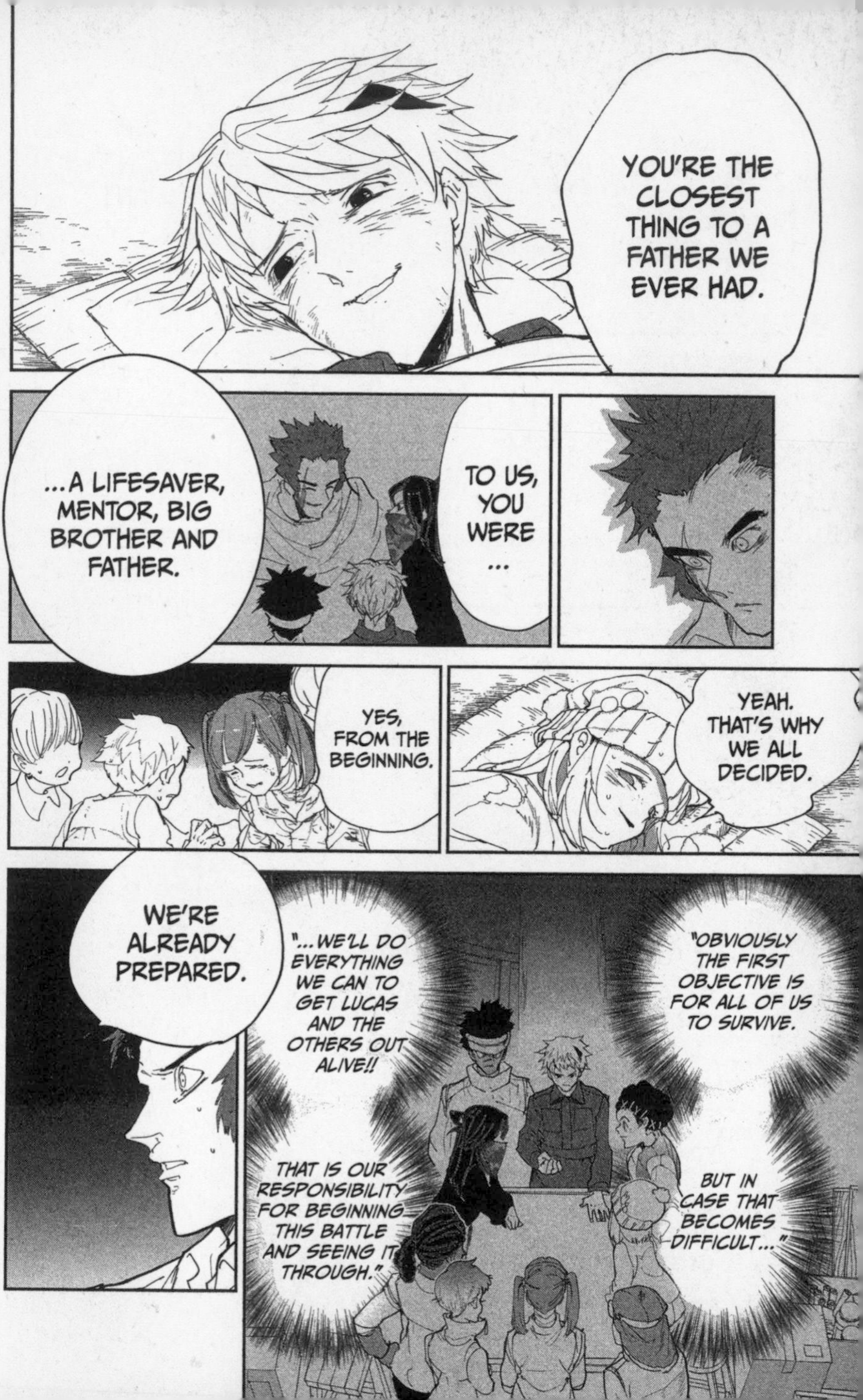
YOU'RE THE CLOSEST THING TO A FATHER WE EVER HAD.
TO US, YOU WERE ...
...A LIFESAVER, MENTOR, BIG BROTHER AND FATHER.
YEAH. THAT'S WHY WE ALL DECIDED.
YES, FROM THE BEGINNING.
"OBVIOUSLY THE FIRST OBJECTIVE IS FOR ALL OF US TO SURVIVE.
BUT IN CASE THAT BECOMES DIFFICULT..."
"...WE'LL DO EVERYTHING WE CAN TO GET LUCAS AND THE OTHERS OUT ALIVE!!
THAT IS OUR RESPONSIBILITY FOR BEGINNING THIS BATTLE AND SEEING IT THROUGH."
WE'RE ALREADY PREPARED.

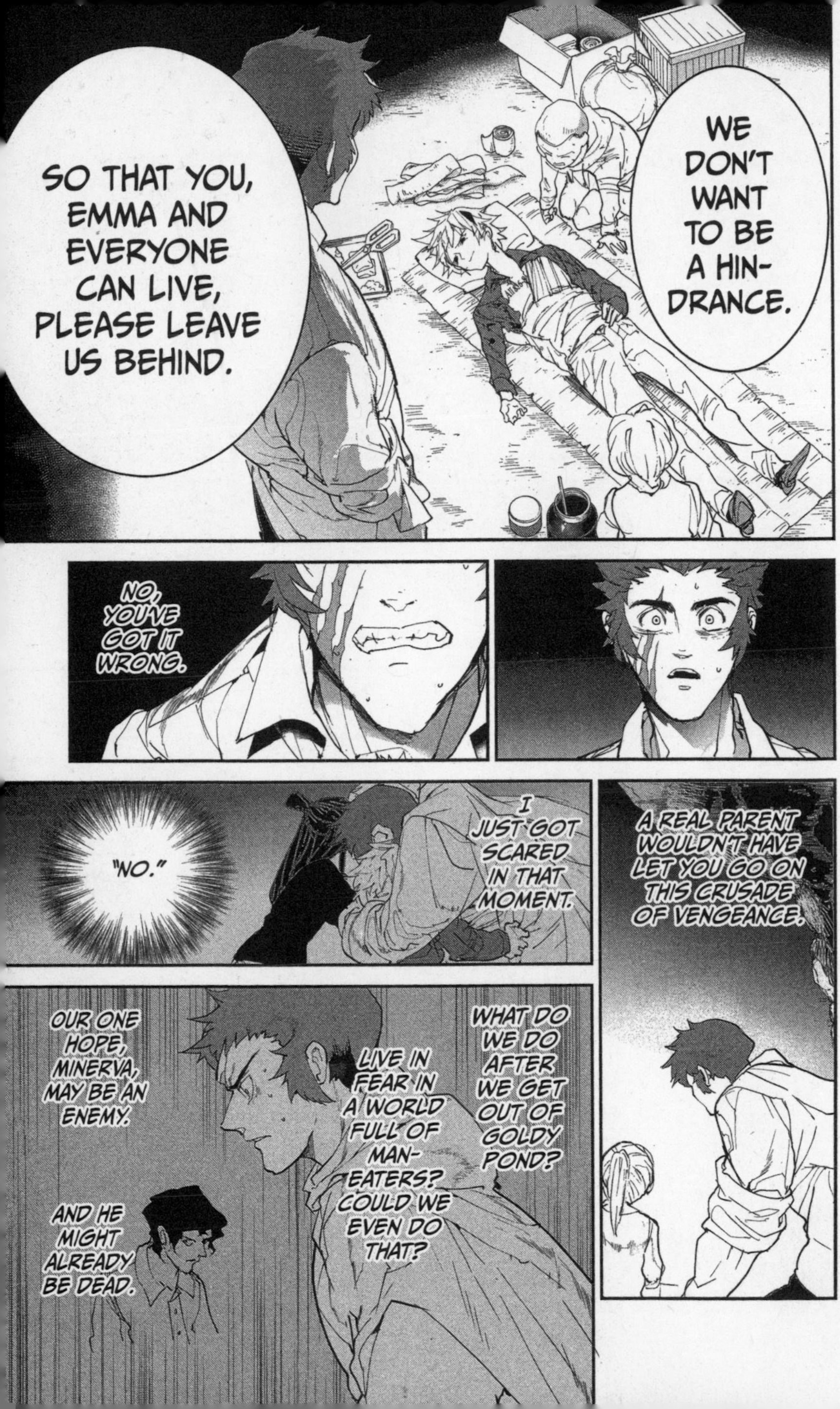
WE DON'T WANT TO BE A HIN-DRANCE.
SO THAT YOU, EMMA AND EVERYONE CAN LIVE, PLEASE LEAVE US BEHIND.
NO, YOU'VE GOT IT WRONG.
A REAL PARENT WOULDN'T HAVE LET YOU GO ON THIS CRUSADE OF VENGEANCE.
I JUST GOT SCARED IN THAT MOMENT.
"NO."
WHAT DO WE DO AFTER WE GET OUT OF GOLDY POND?
LIVE IN FEAR IN A WORLD FULL OF MAN-EATERS? COULD WE EVEN DO THAT?
OUR ONE HOPE, MINERVA, MAY BE AN ENEMY.
AND HE MIGHT ALREADY BE DEAD.

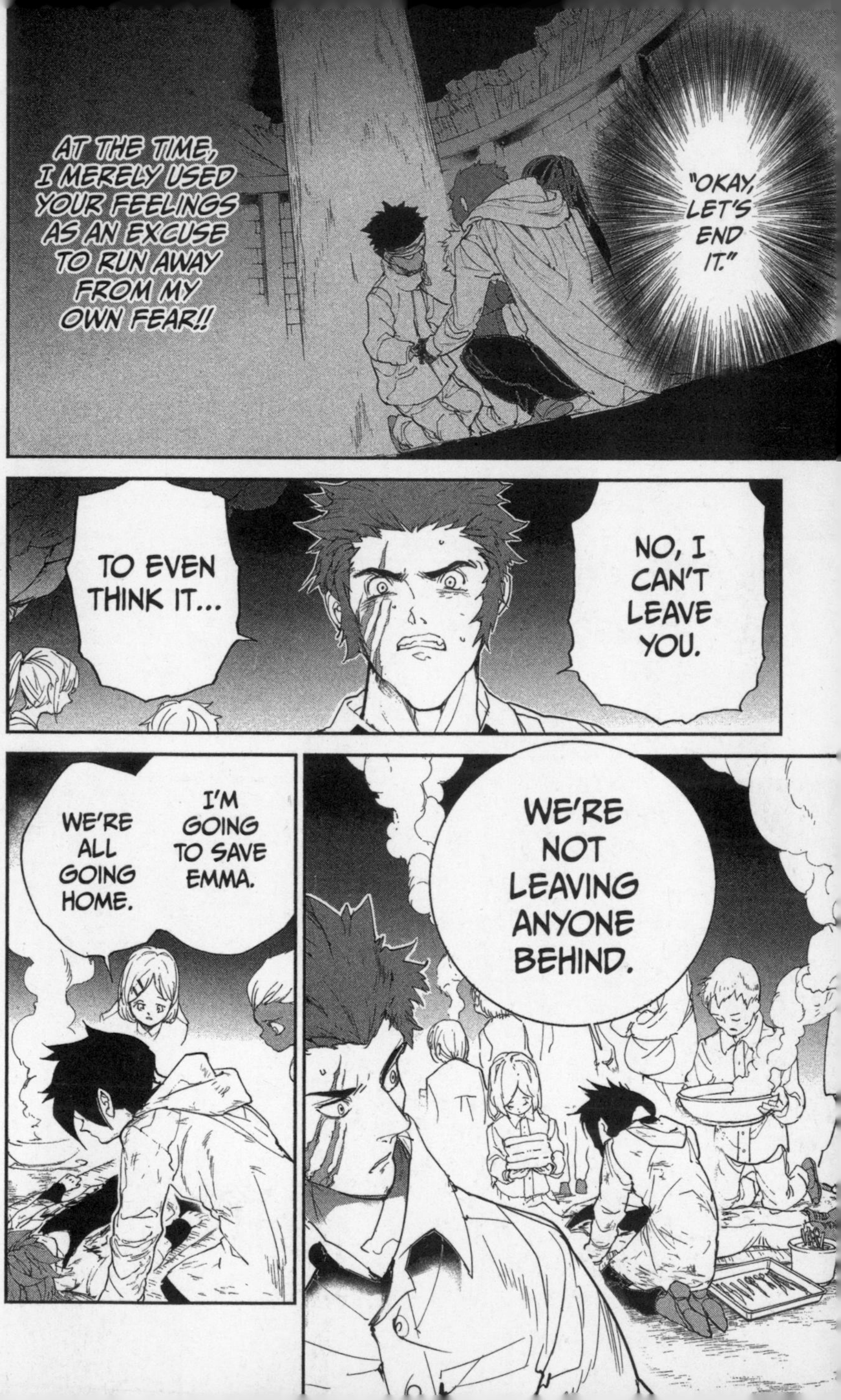
"OKAY, LET'S END IT."
AT THE TIME, I MERELY USED YOUR FEELINGS AS AN EXCUSE TO RUN AWAY FROM MY OWN FEAR!!
NO, I CAN'T LEAVE YOU.
TO EVEN THINK IT...
WE'RE NOT LEAVING ANYONE BEHIND.
I'M GOING TO SAVE EMMA.
WE'RE ALL GOING HOME.

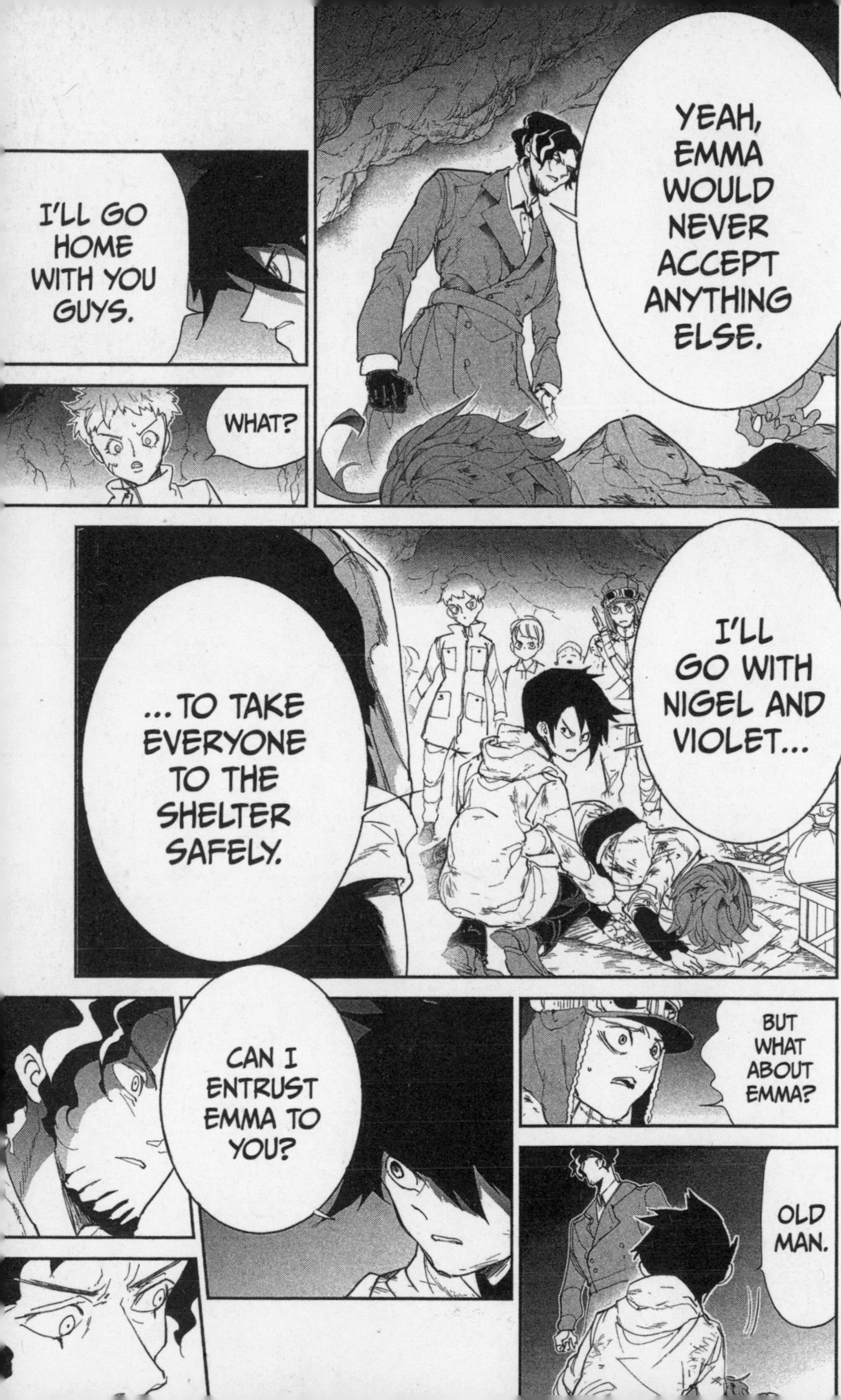
YEAH, EMMA WOULD NEVER ACCEPT ANYTHING ELSE.
I'LL GO HOME WITH YOU GUYS.
WHAT?
I'LL GO WITH NIGEL AND VIOLET...
...TO TAKE EVERYONE TO THE SHELTER SAFELY.
BUT WHAT ABOUT EMMA?
OLD MAN.
CAN I ENTRUST EMMA TO YOU?

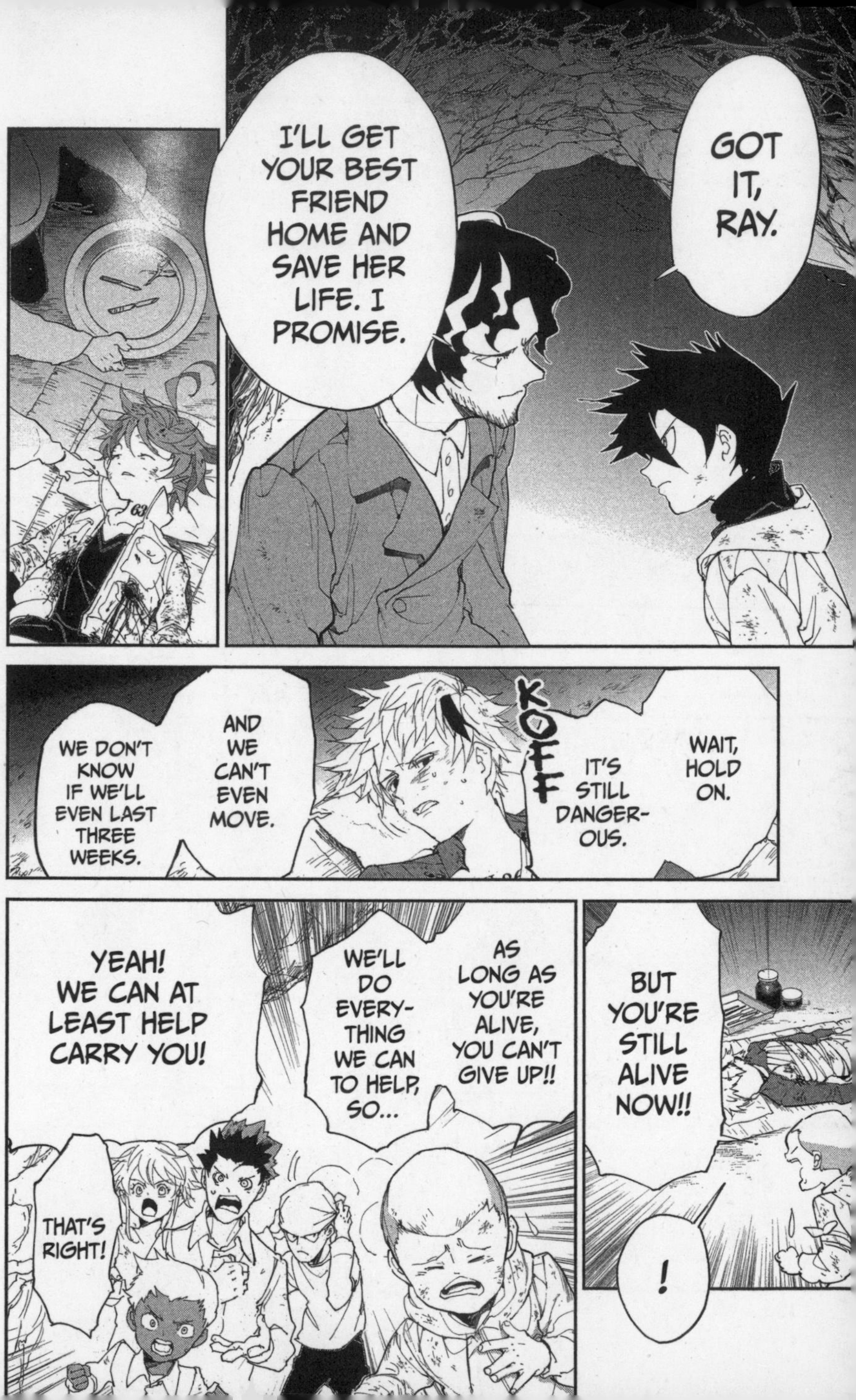
GOT IT, RAY.
I'LL GET YOUR BEST FRIEND HOME AND SAVE HER LIFE. I PROMISE.
WAIT, HOLD ON.
IT'S STILL DANGER-OUS.
KOFF
AND WE CAN'T EVEN MOVE.
WE DON'T KNOW IF WE'LL EVEN LAST THREE WEEKS.
BUT YOU'RE STILL ALIVE NOW!!
!
AS LONG AS YOU'RE ALIVE, YOU CAN'T GIVE UP!!
WE'LL DO EVERY-THING WE CAN TO HELP, SO...
YEAH! WE CAN AT LEAST HELP CARRY YOU!
THAT'S RIGHT!

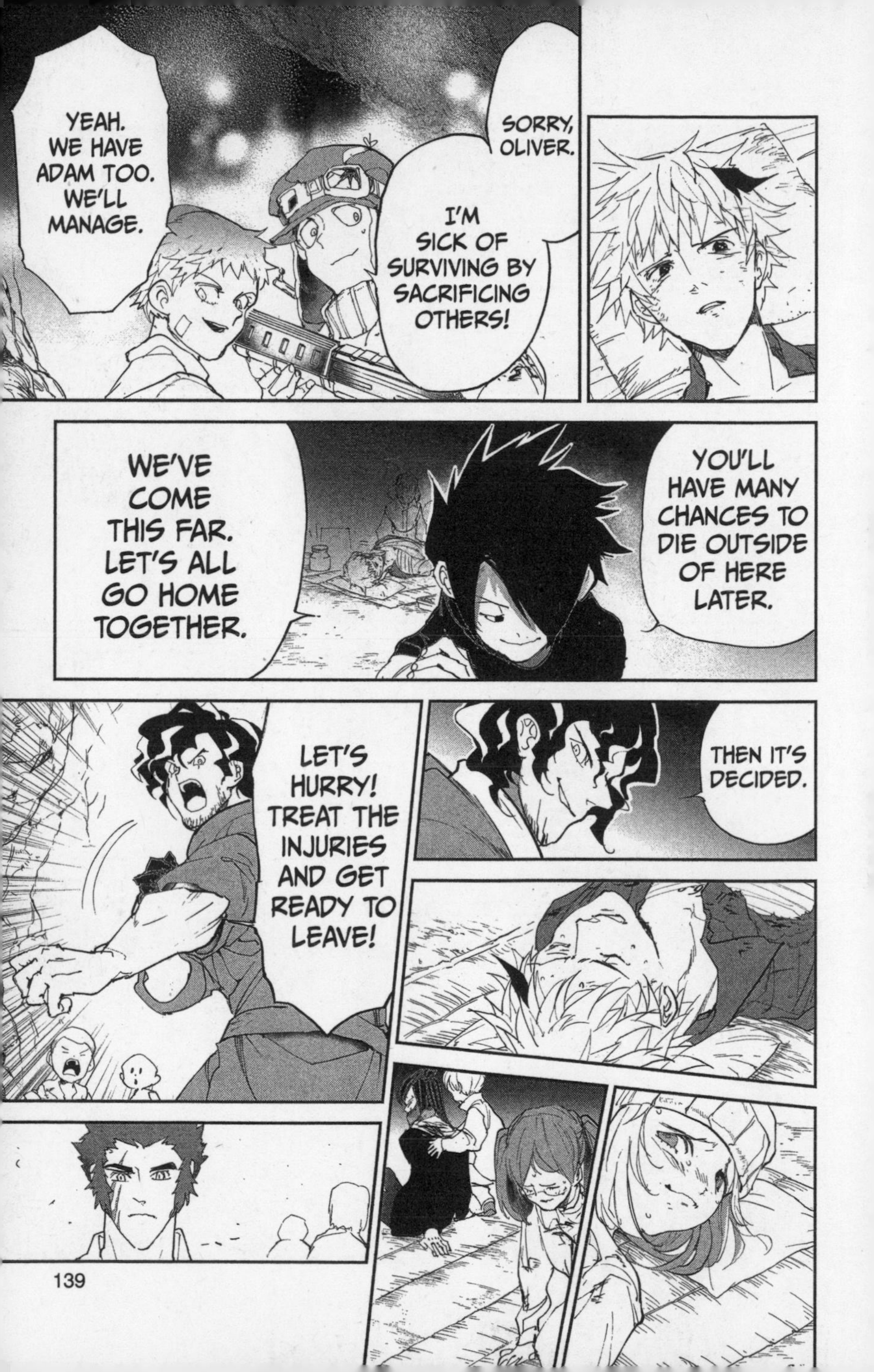
SORRY, OLIVER.
I'M SICK OF SURVIVING BY SACRIFICING OTHERS!
YEAH. WE HAVE ADAM TOO. WE'LL MANAGE.
YOU'LL HAVE MANY CHANCES TO DIE OUTSIDE OF HERE LATER.
WE'VE COME THIS FAR. LET'S ALL GO HOME TOGETHER.
THEN IT'S DECIDED.
LET'S HURRY! TREAT THE INJURIES AND GET READY TO LEAVE!

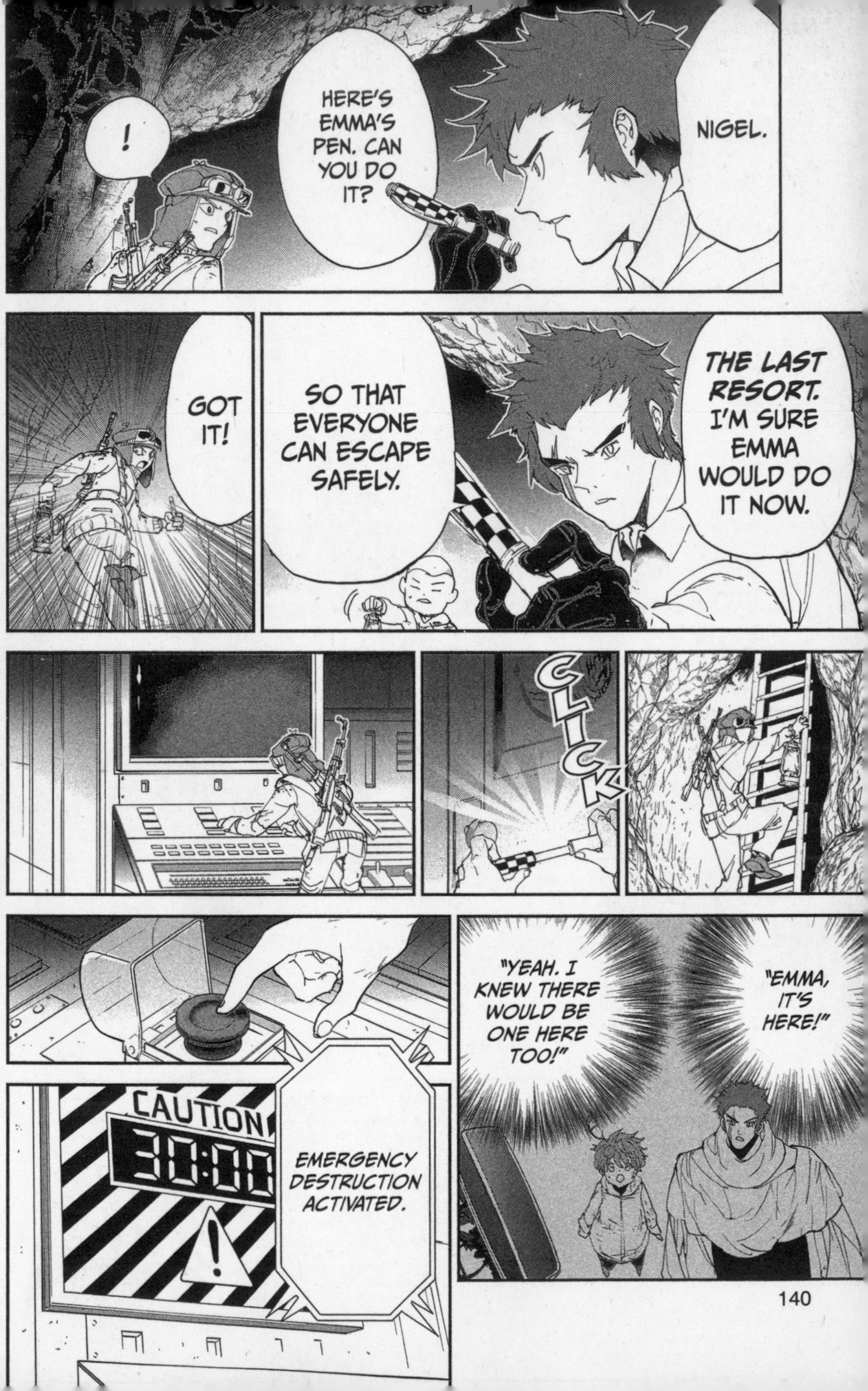
NIGEL.
HERE'S EMMA'S PEN. CAN YOU DO IT?
!
THE LAST RESORT. I'M SURE EMMA WOULD DO IT NOW.
SO THAT EVERYONE CAN ESCAPE SAFELY.
GOT IT!
CLICK
"EMMA, IT'S HERE!"
"YEAH. I KNEW THERE WOULD BE ONE HERE TOO!"
CAUTION
30:00
EMERGENCY DESTRUCTION ACTIVATED.

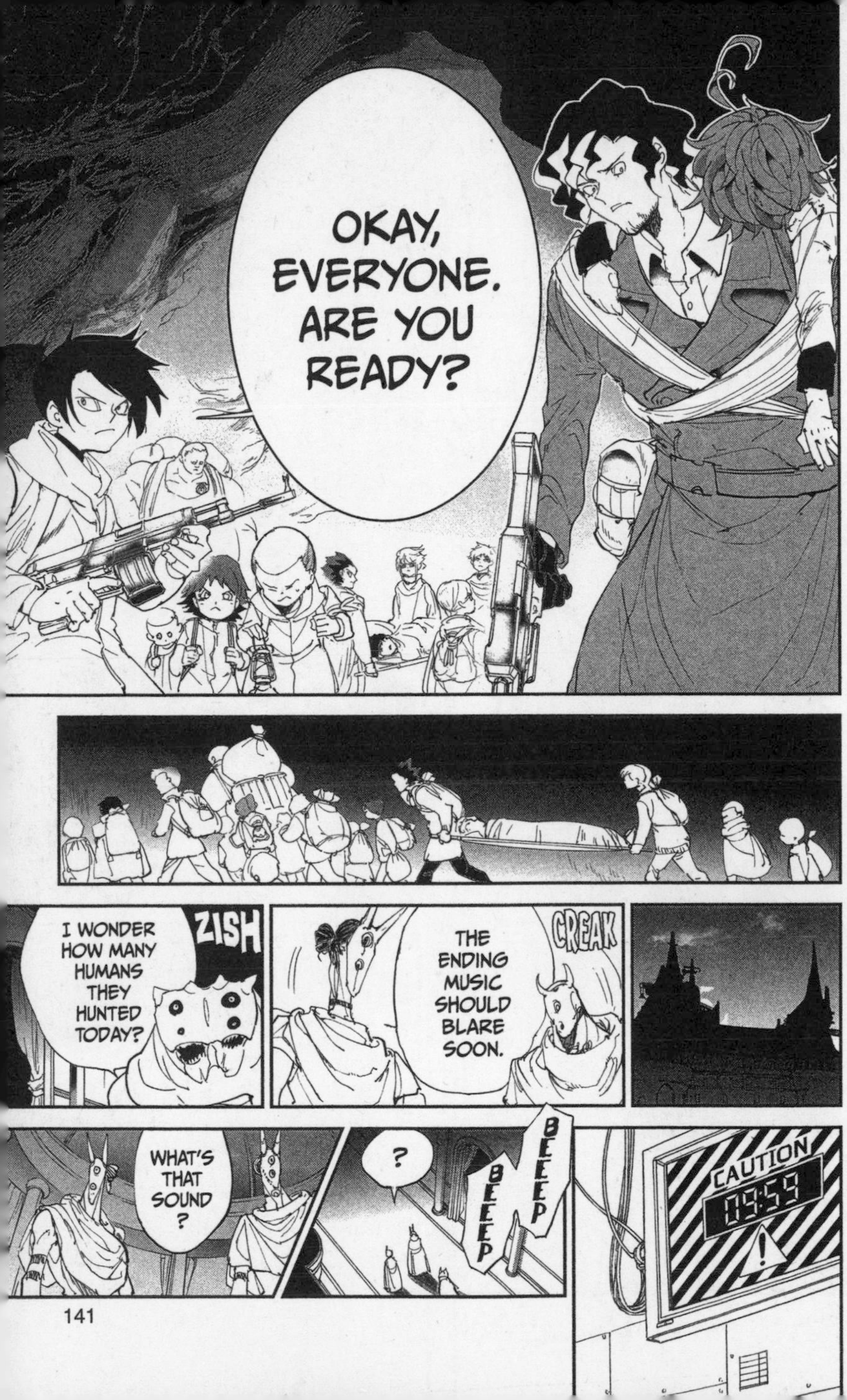
OKAY, EVERYONE. ARE YOU READY?
CREAK
THE ENDING MUSIC SHOULD BLARE SOON.
ZISH
I WONDER HOW MANY HUMANS THEY HUNTED TODAY?
CAUTION
09:59
BEEEP
BEEEP
?
WHAT'S THAT SOUND?

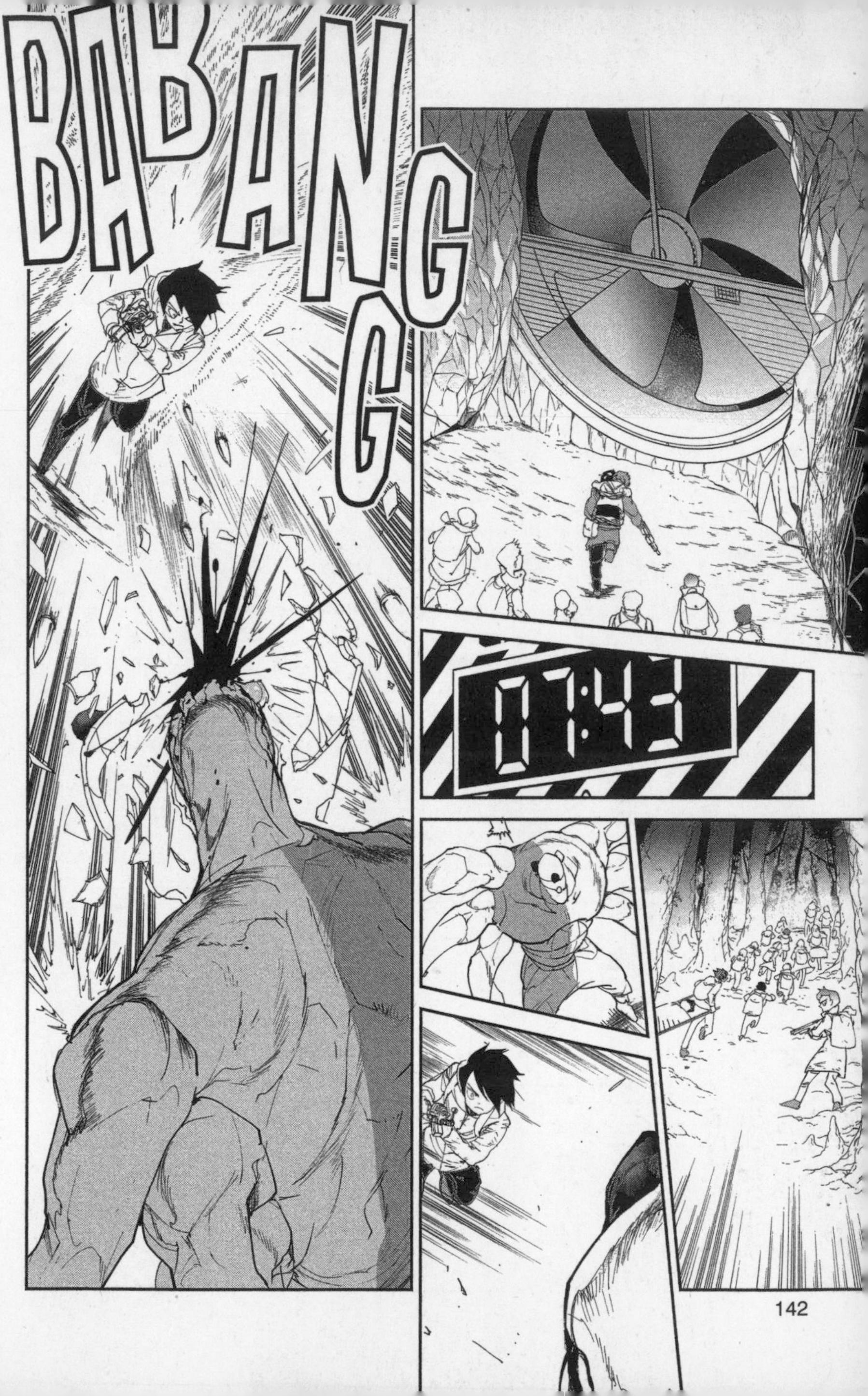

BABANG
07:43

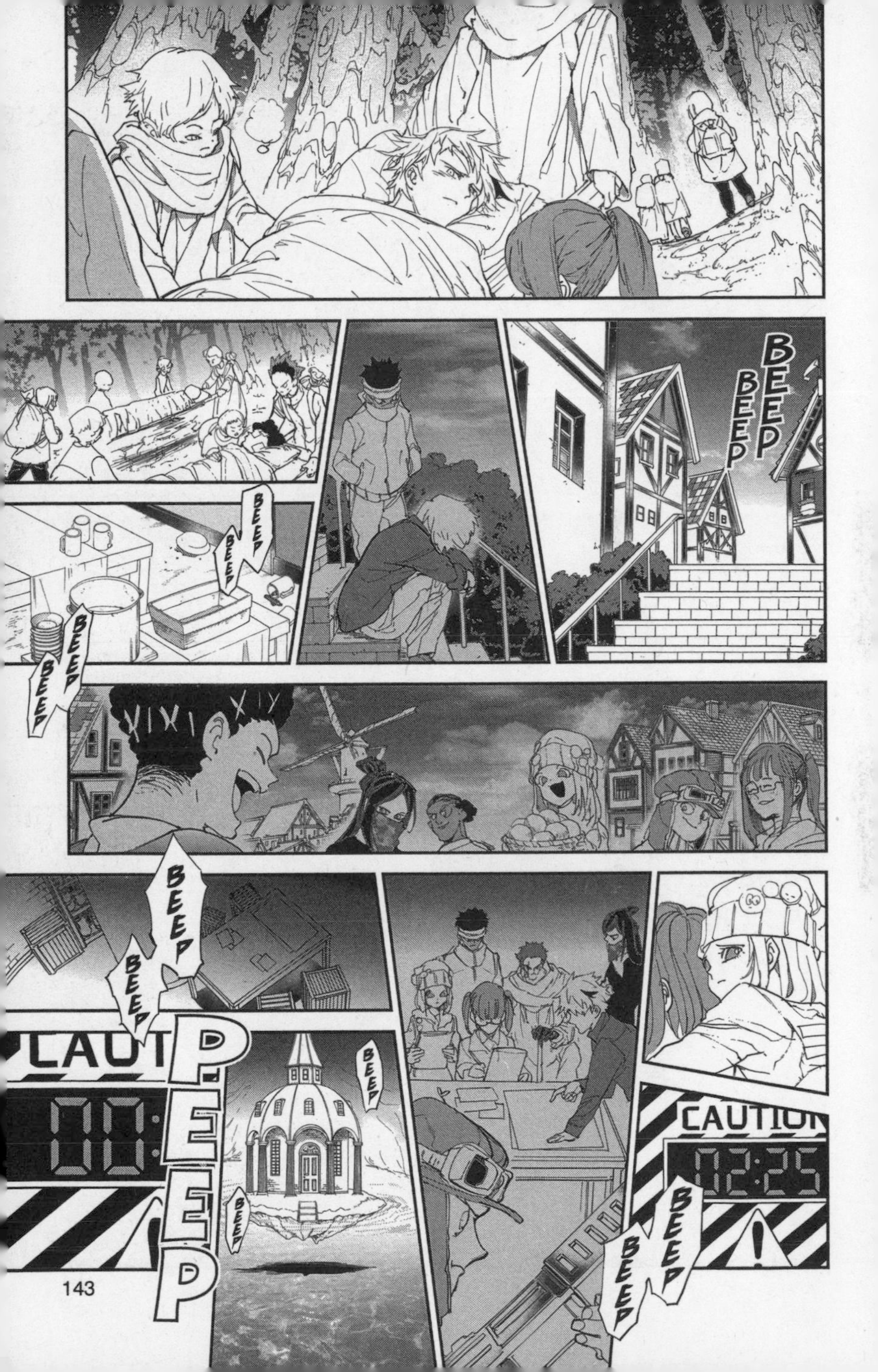
BEEP
BEEP
BEEP
BEEP
BEEP
BEEP
CAUTION
02:25
BEEP
BEEP
BEEP
BEEP
LAUT
00:
PEEP
BEEP
BEEP

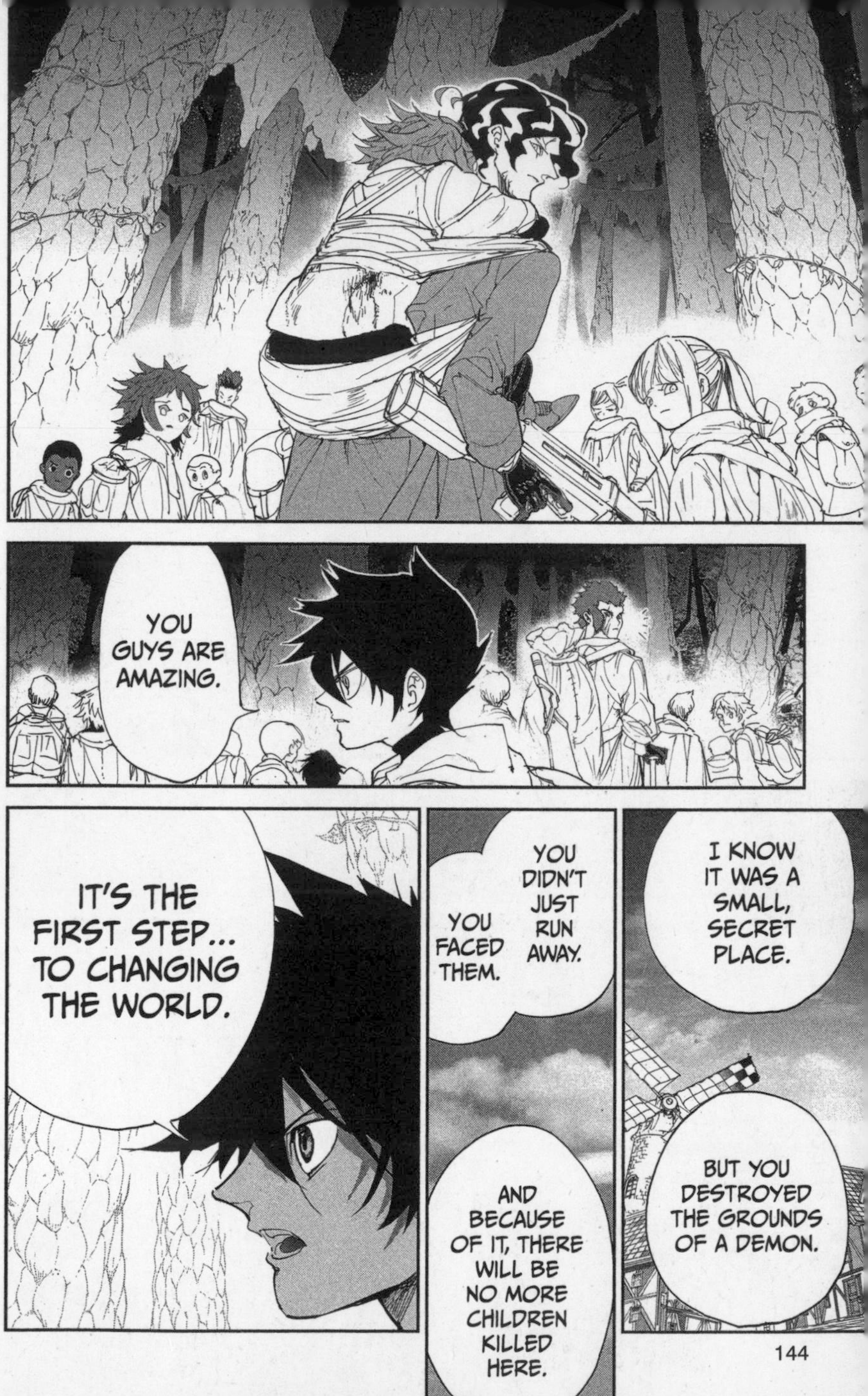
YOU GUYS ARE AMAZING.
I KNOW IT WAS A SMALL, SECRET PLACE.
BUT YOU DESTROYED THE GROUNDS OF A DEMON.
YOU DIDN'T JUST RUN AWAY.
YOU FACED THEM.
AND BECAUSE OF IT, THERE WILL BE NO MORE CHILDREN KILLED HERE.
IT'S THE FIRST STEP... TO CHANGING THE WORLD.

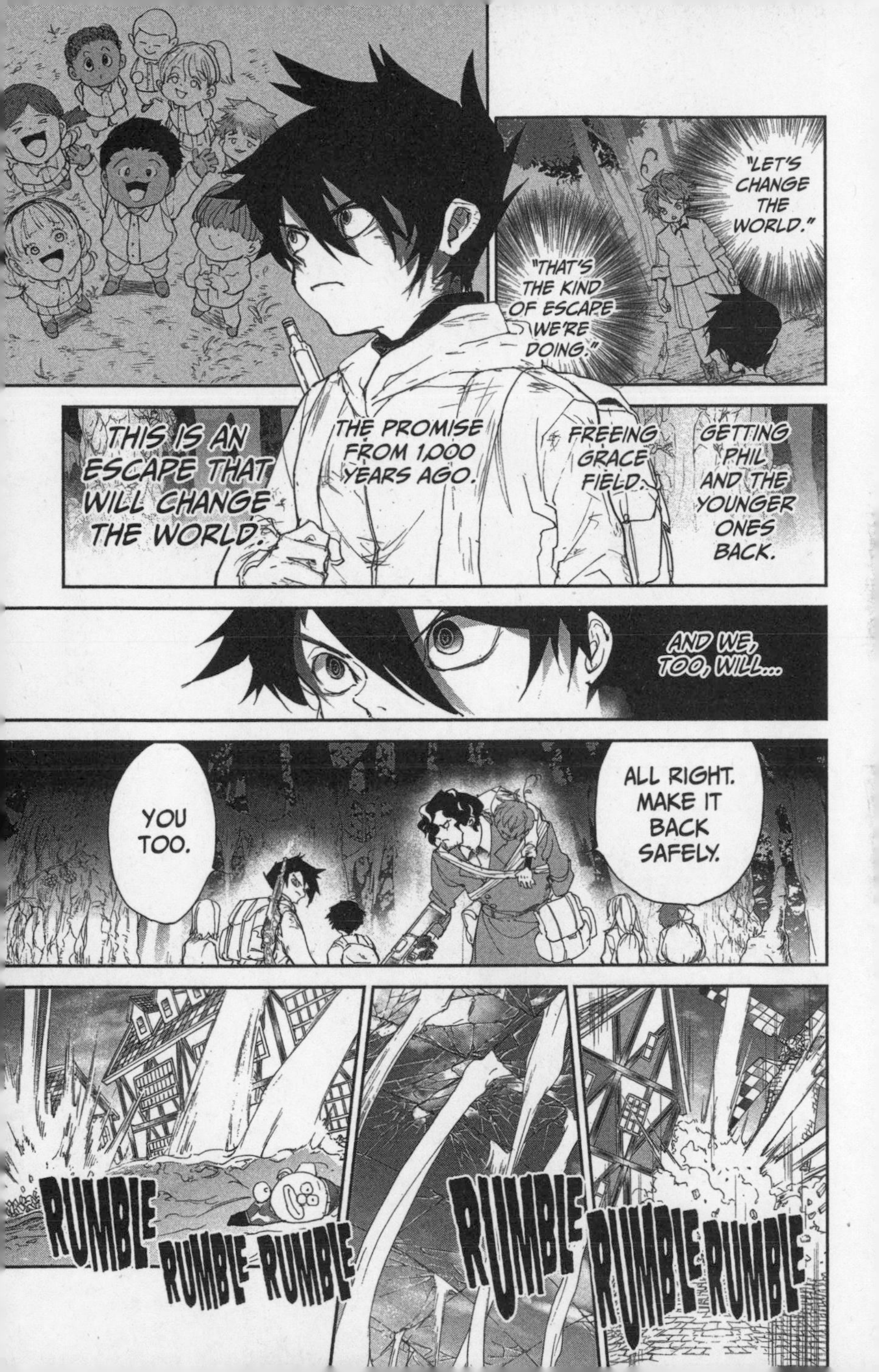
"LET'S CHANGE THE WORLD."
"THAT'S THE KIND OF ESCAPE WE'RE DOING."
GETTING PHIL AND THE YOUNGER ONES BACK.
FREEING GRACE FIELD.
THE PROMISE FROM 1,000 YEARS AGO.
THIS IS AN ESCAPE THAT WILL CHANGE THE WORLD.
AND WE, TOO, WILL...
ALL RIGHT. MAKE IT BACK SAFELY.
YOU TOO.
RUMBLE RUMBLE
RUMBLE
RUMBLE
RUMBLE RUMBLE
RUMBLE

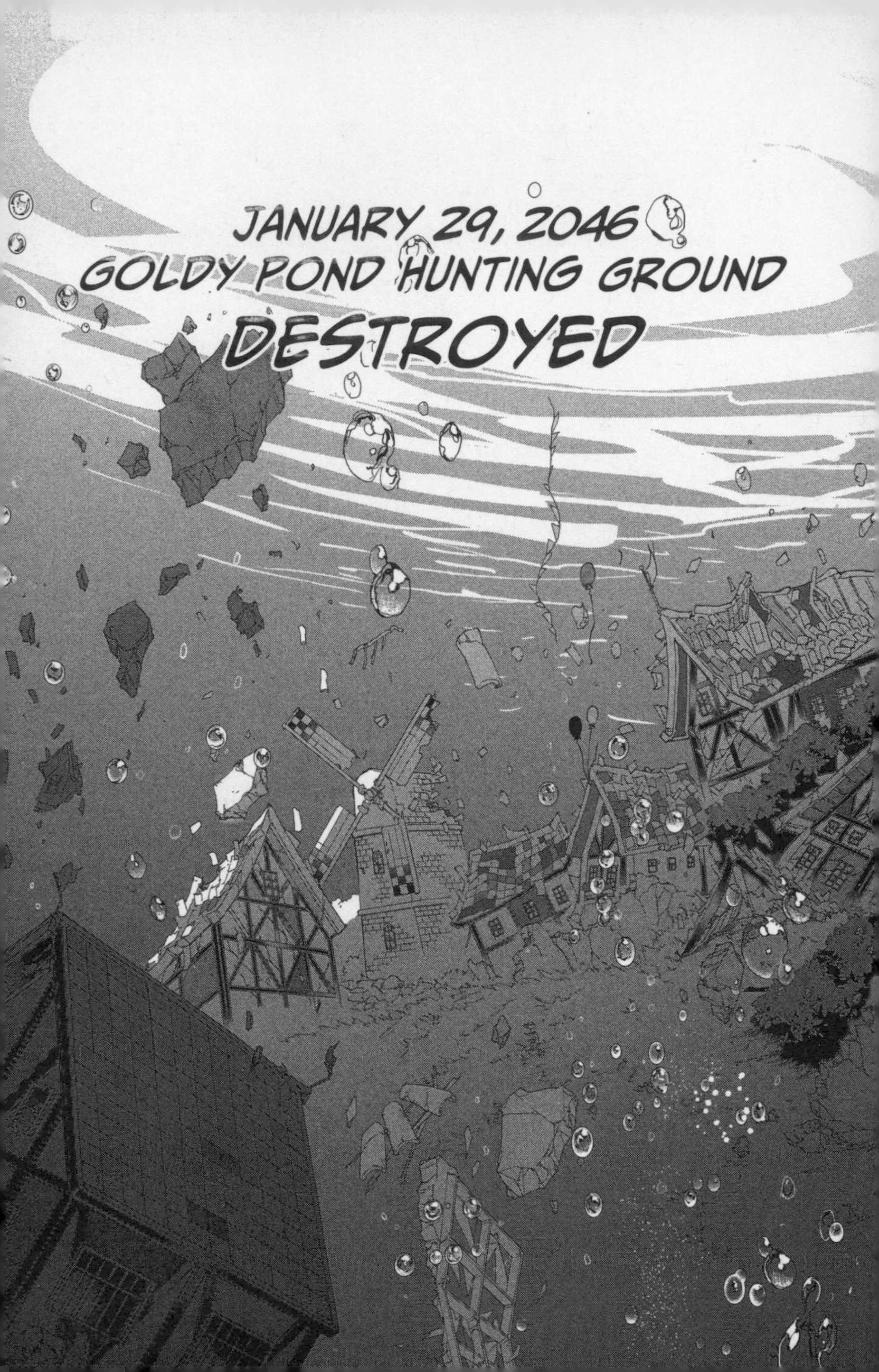
JANUARY 29, 2046
GOLDY POND HUNTING GROUND
DESTROYED

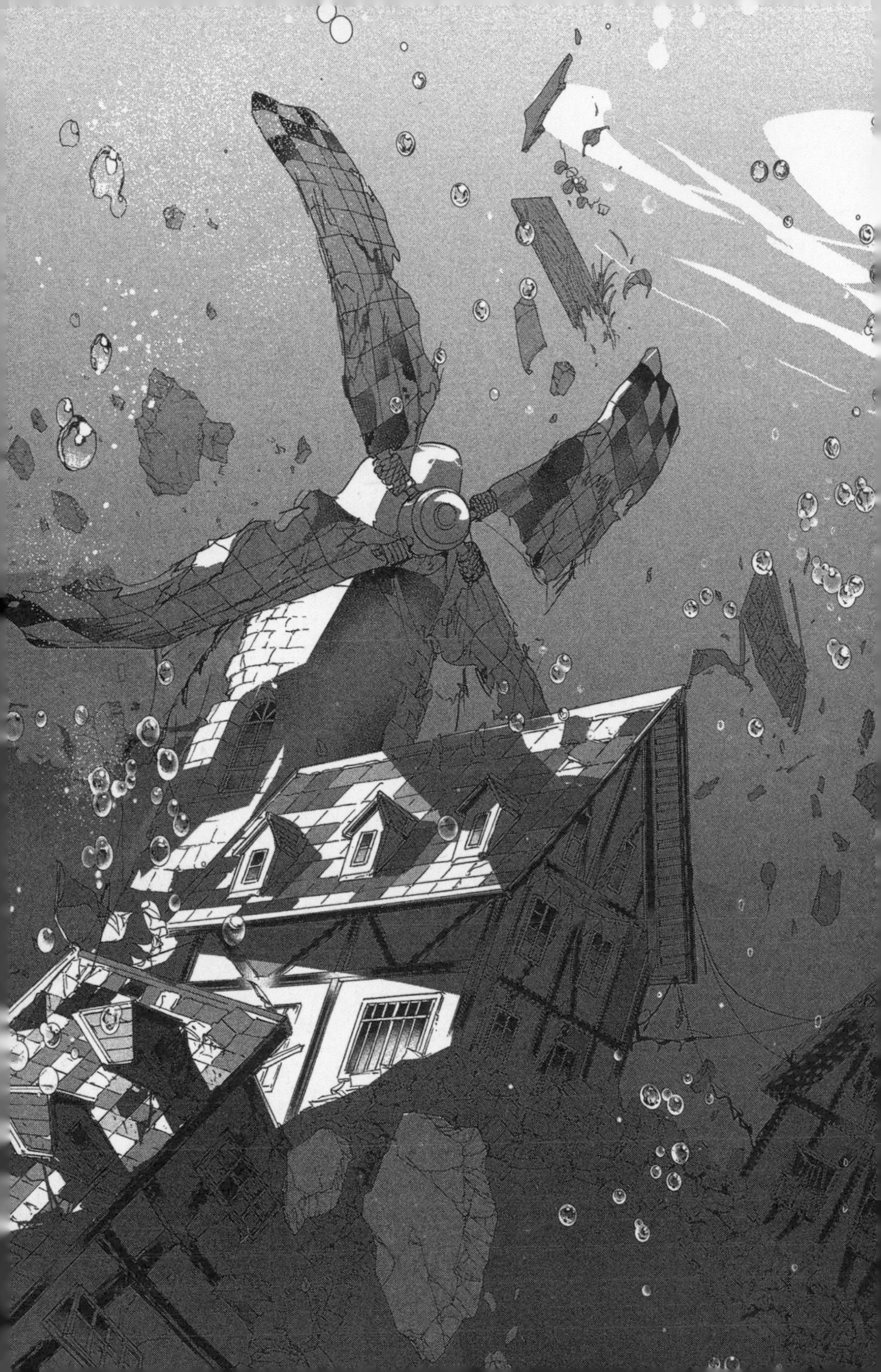

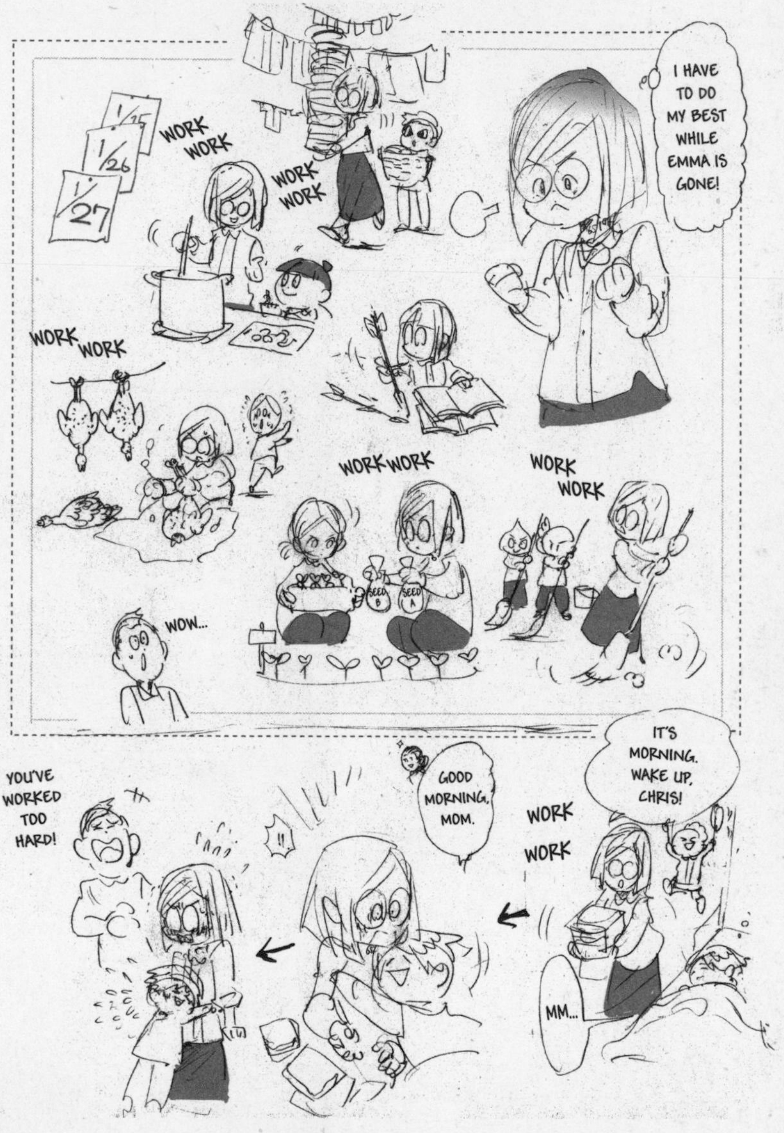
I HAVE TO DO MY BEST WHILE EMMA IS GONE!
WORK WORK
WORK WORK
1/25
1/26
1/27
WORK WORK
WORK WORK
SEED B
SEED A
WORKWORK
WOW...
IT'S MORNING. WAKE UP, CHRIS!
WORK WORK
MM...
GOOD MORNING, MOM.
!!
YOU'VE WORKED TOO HARD!

CHAPTER 96: WELCOME HOME

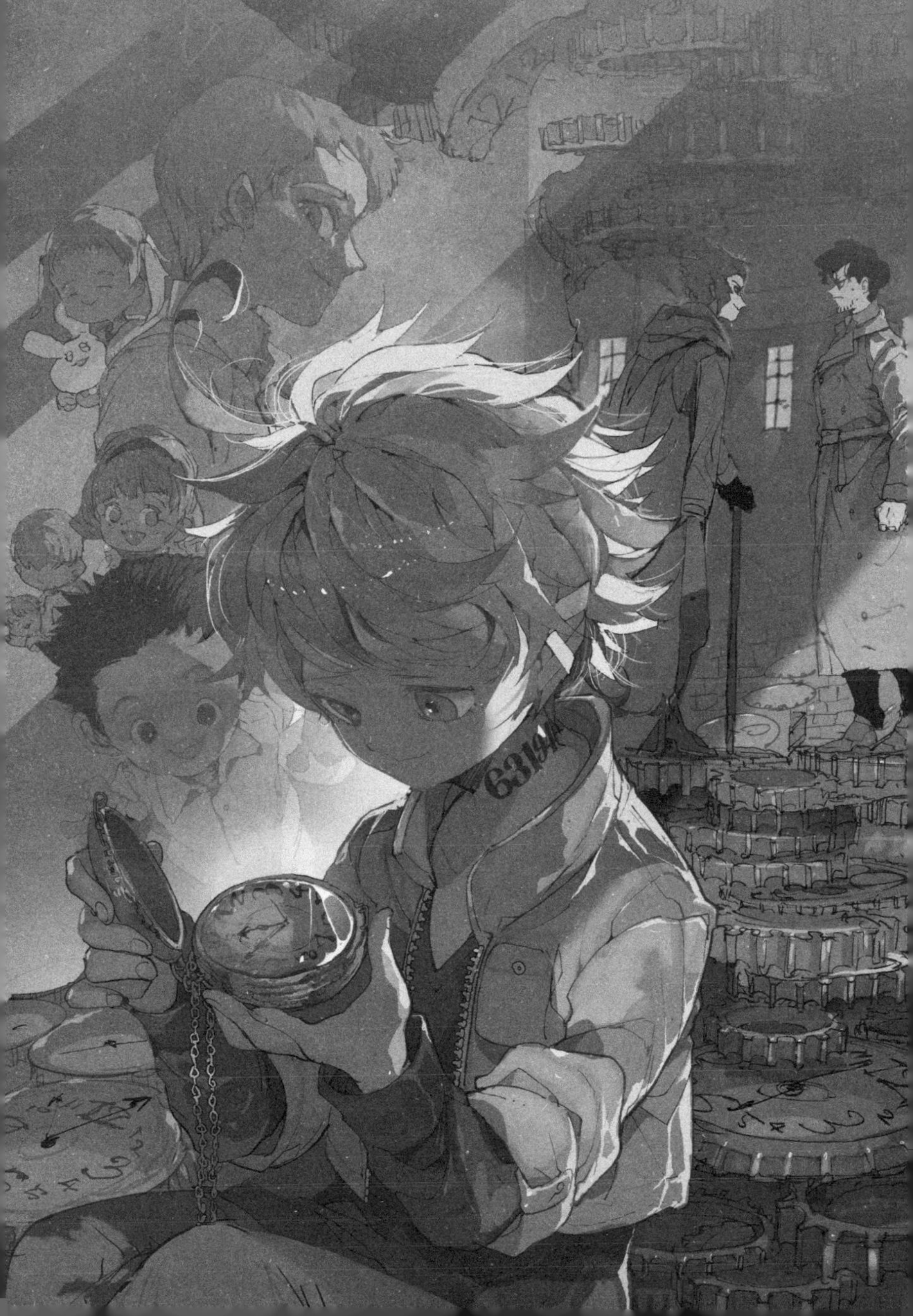

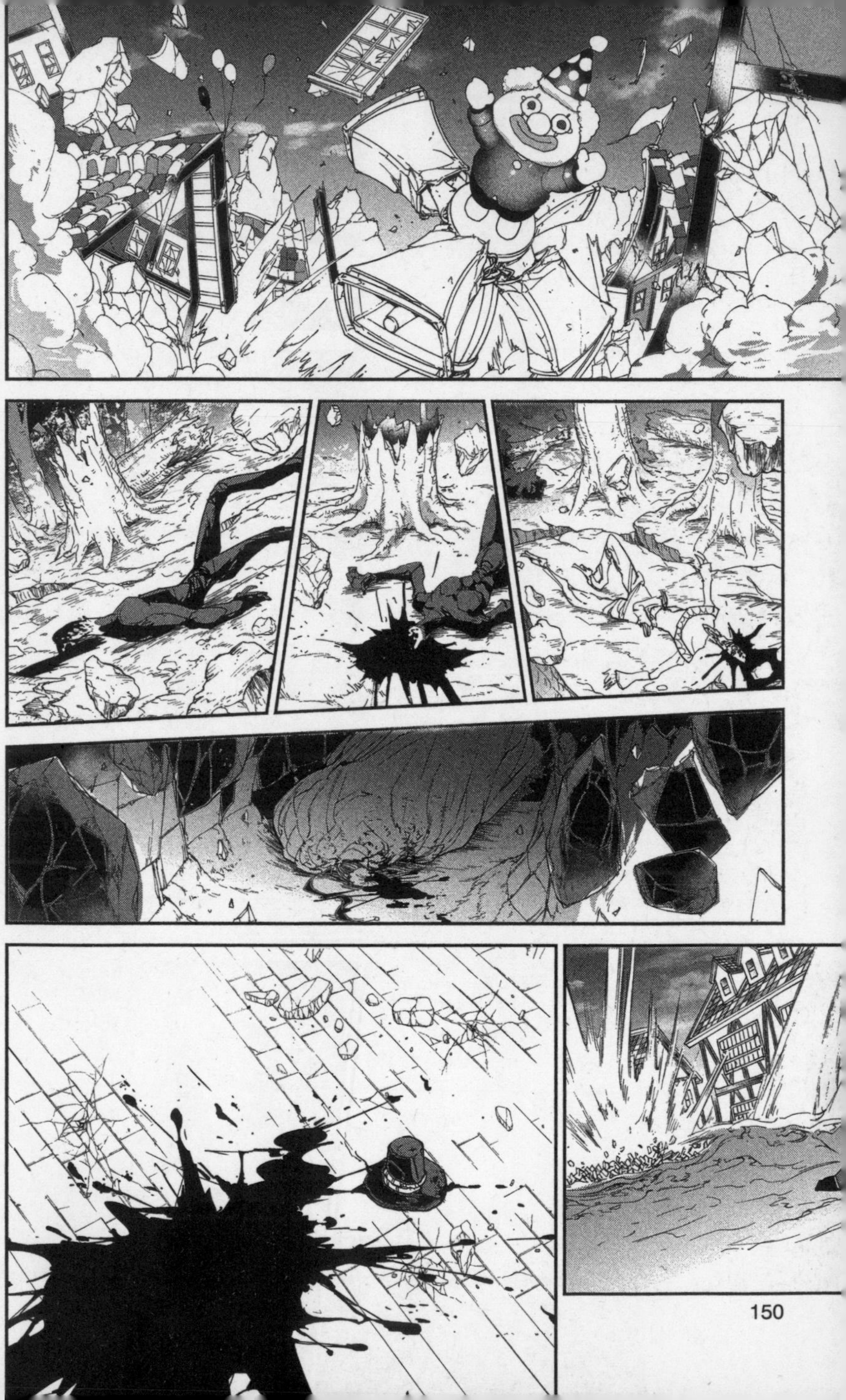

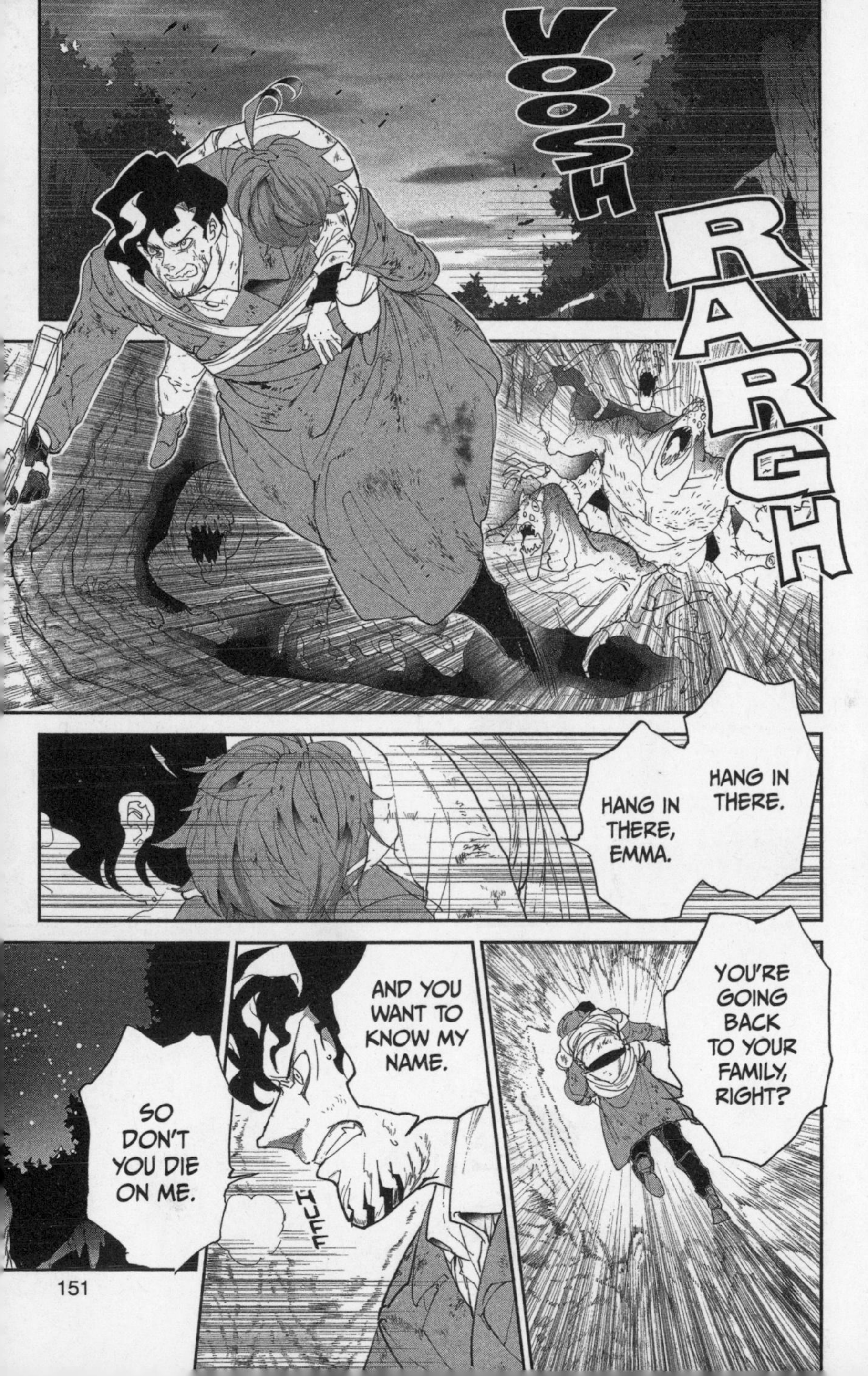
VOOSH
RARGH
HANG IN THERE.
HANG IN THERE, EMMA.
YOU'RE GOING BACK TO YOUR FAMILY, RIGHT?
AND YOU WANT TO KNOW MY NAME.
SO DON'T YOU DIE ON ME.
HUFF

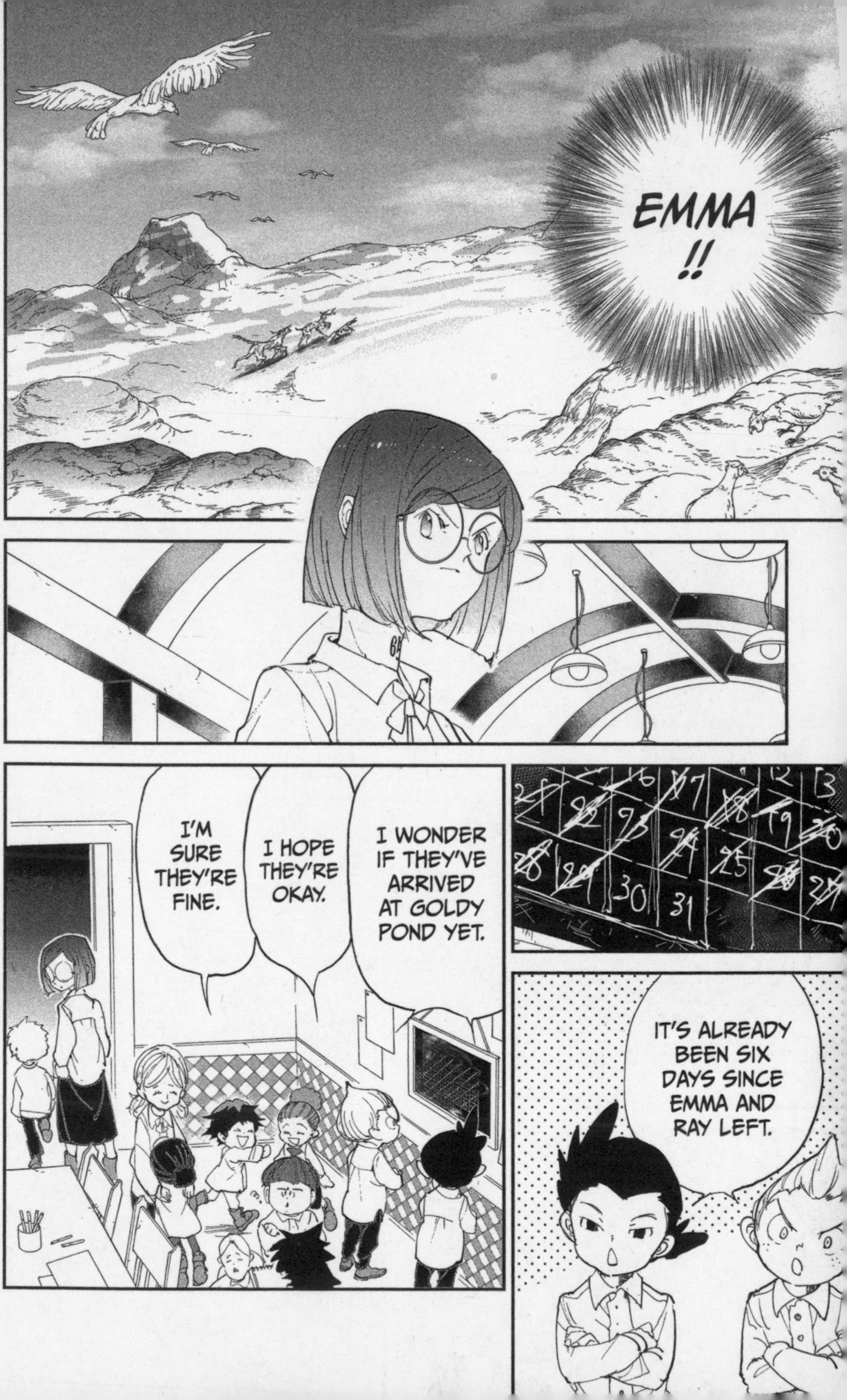
EMMA !!
IT'S ALREADY BEEN SIX DAYS SINCE EMMA AND RAY LEFT.
I WONDER IF THEY'VE ARRIVED AT GOLDY POND YET.
I HOPE THEY'RE OKAY.
I'M SURE THEY'RE FINE.

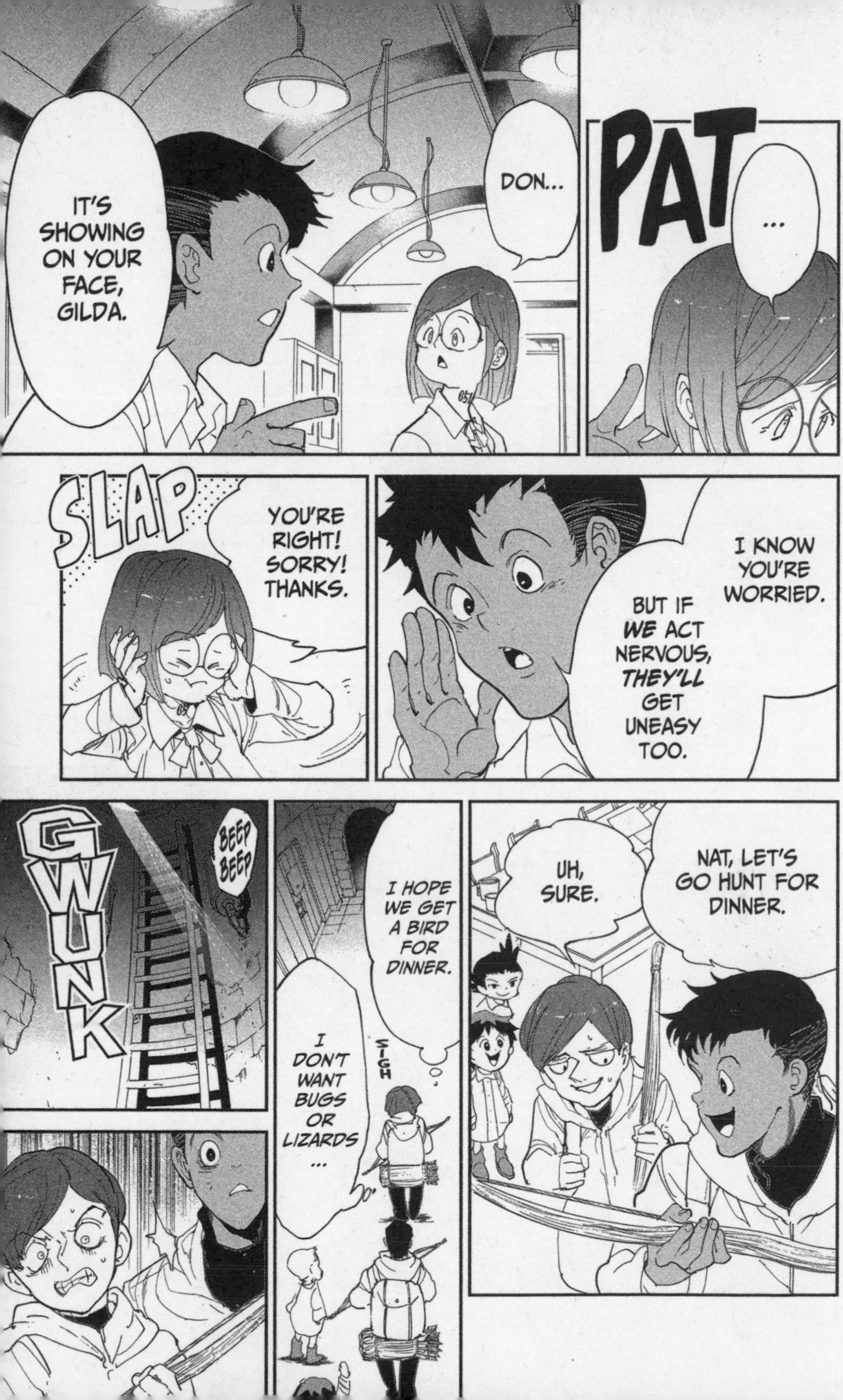
PAT
...
DON...
IT'S SHOWING ON YOUR FACE, GILDA.
I KNOW YOU'RE WORRIED.
BUT IF WE ACT NERVOUS, THEY'LL GET UNEASY TOO.
SLAP
YOU'RE RIGHT! SORRY! THANKS.
NAT, LET'S GO HUNT FOR DINNER.
UH, SURE.
I HOPE WE GET A BIRD FOR DINNER.
SIGH
I DON'T WANT BUGS OR LIZARDS ...
BEEP BEEP
GWUNK

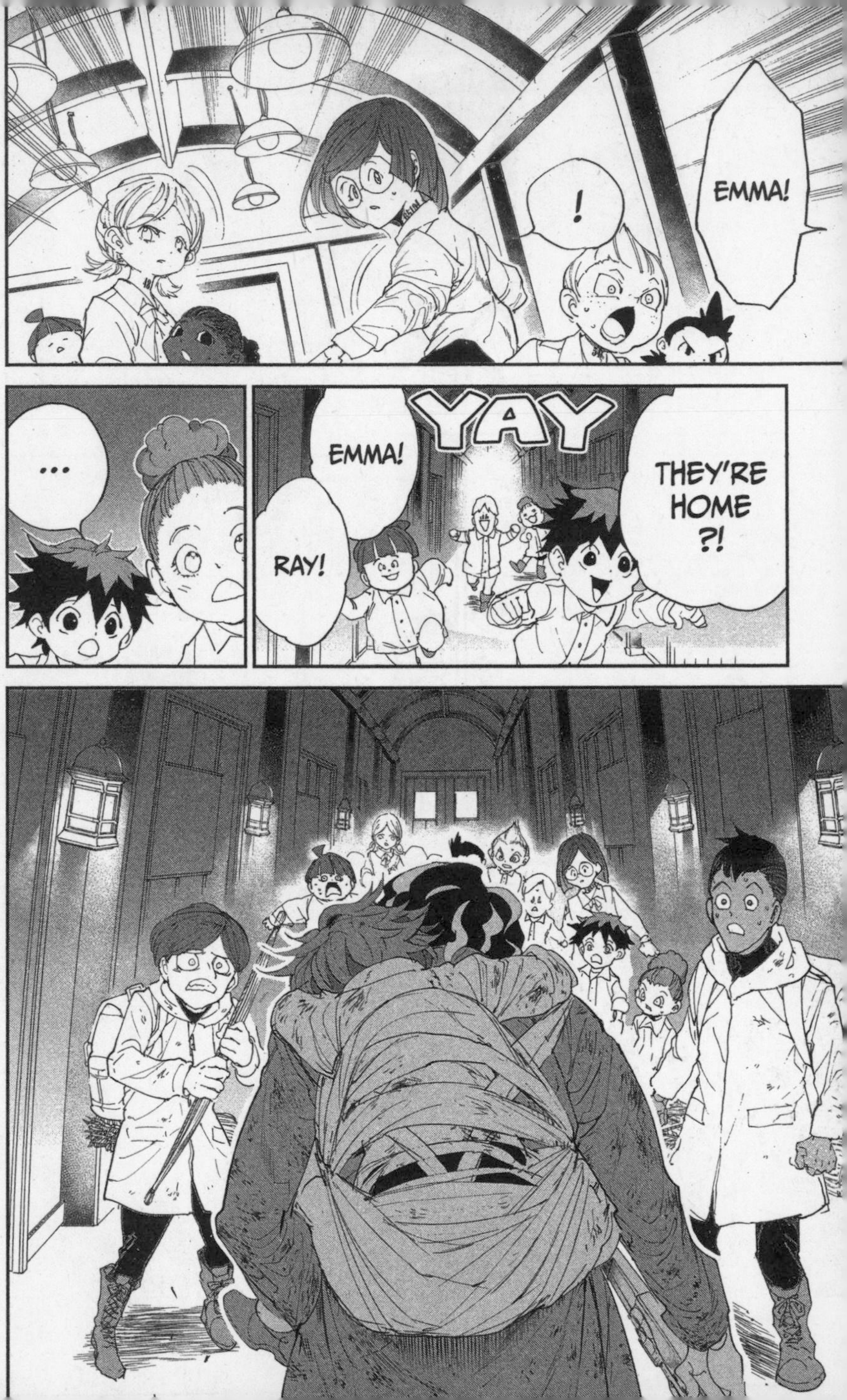
EMMA!
!
THEY'RE HOME ?!
YAY
EMMA!
RAY!
...

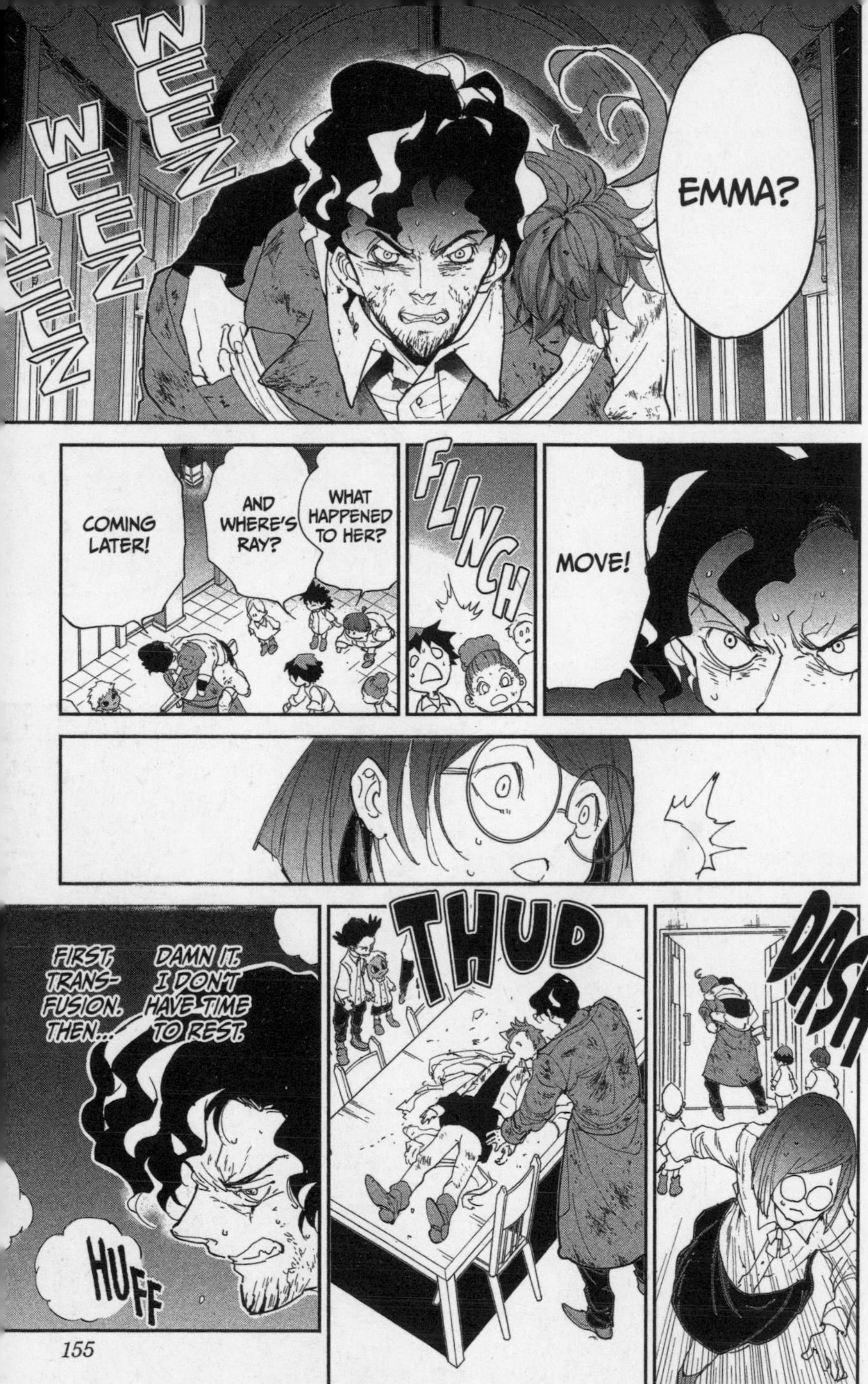
EMMA?
WEEN
WEEN
WEEN
MOVE!
FLINCH
WHAT HAPPENED TO HER?
AND WHERE'S RAY?
COMING LATER!
DASH
THUD
DAMN IT. I DON'T HAVE TIME TO REST.
FIRST, TRANS-FUSION. THEN...
HUFF

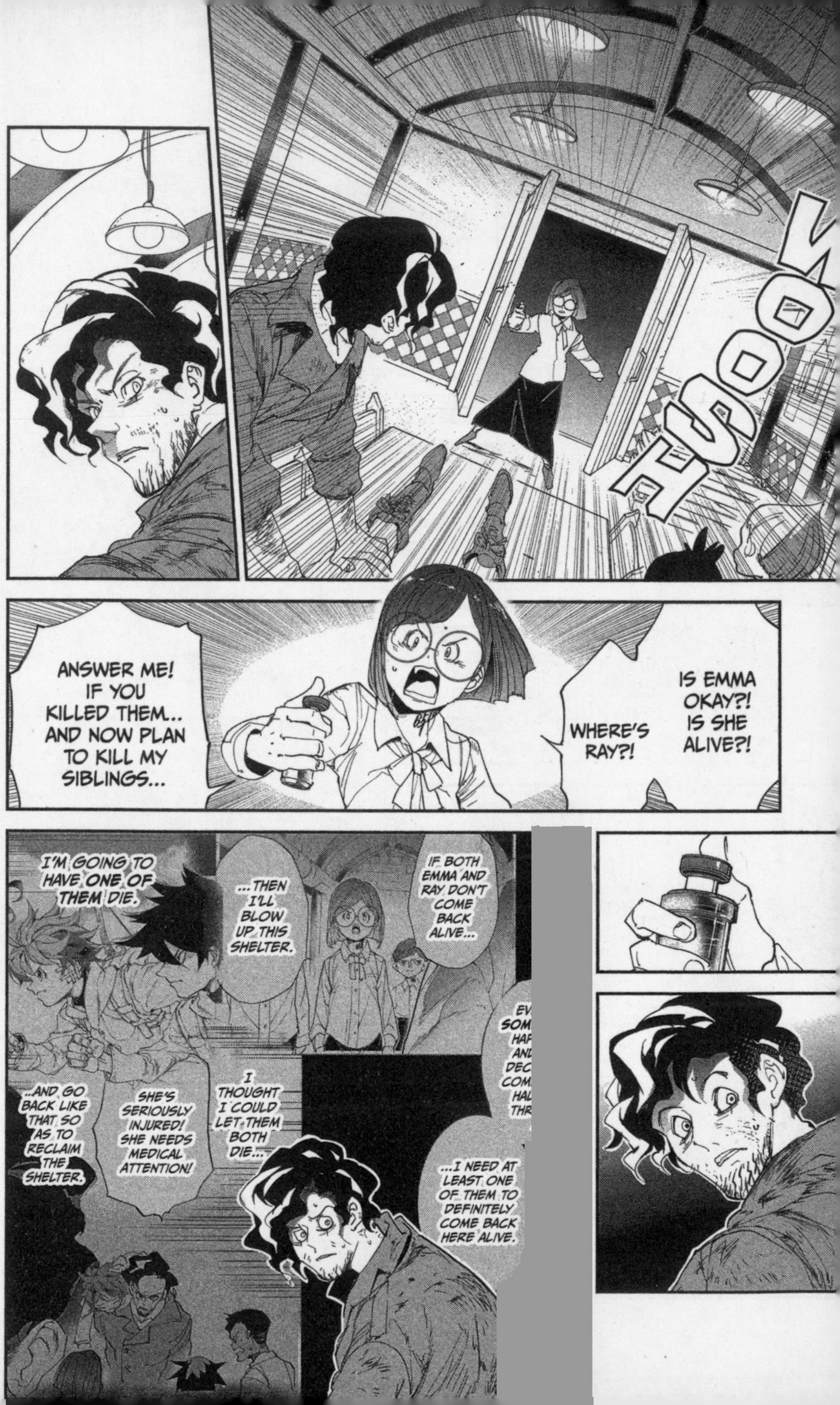
WOOSH
IS EMMA OKAY?! IS SHE ALIVE?!
WHERE'S RAY?!
ANSWER ME! IF YOU KILLED THEM... AND NOW PLAN TO KILL MY SIBLINGS...
IF BOTH EMMA AND RAY DON'T COME BACK ALIVE...
...THEN I'LL BLOW UP THIS SHELTER.
I'M GOING TO HAVE ONE OF THEM DIE.
...I NEED AT LEAST ONE OF THEM TO DEFINITELY COME BACK HERE ALIVE.
I THOUGHT I COULD LET THEM BOTH DIE...
SHE'S SERIOUSLY INJURED! SHE NEEDS MEDICAL ATTENTION!
...AND GO BACK LIKE THAT SO AS TO RECLAIM THE SHELTER.

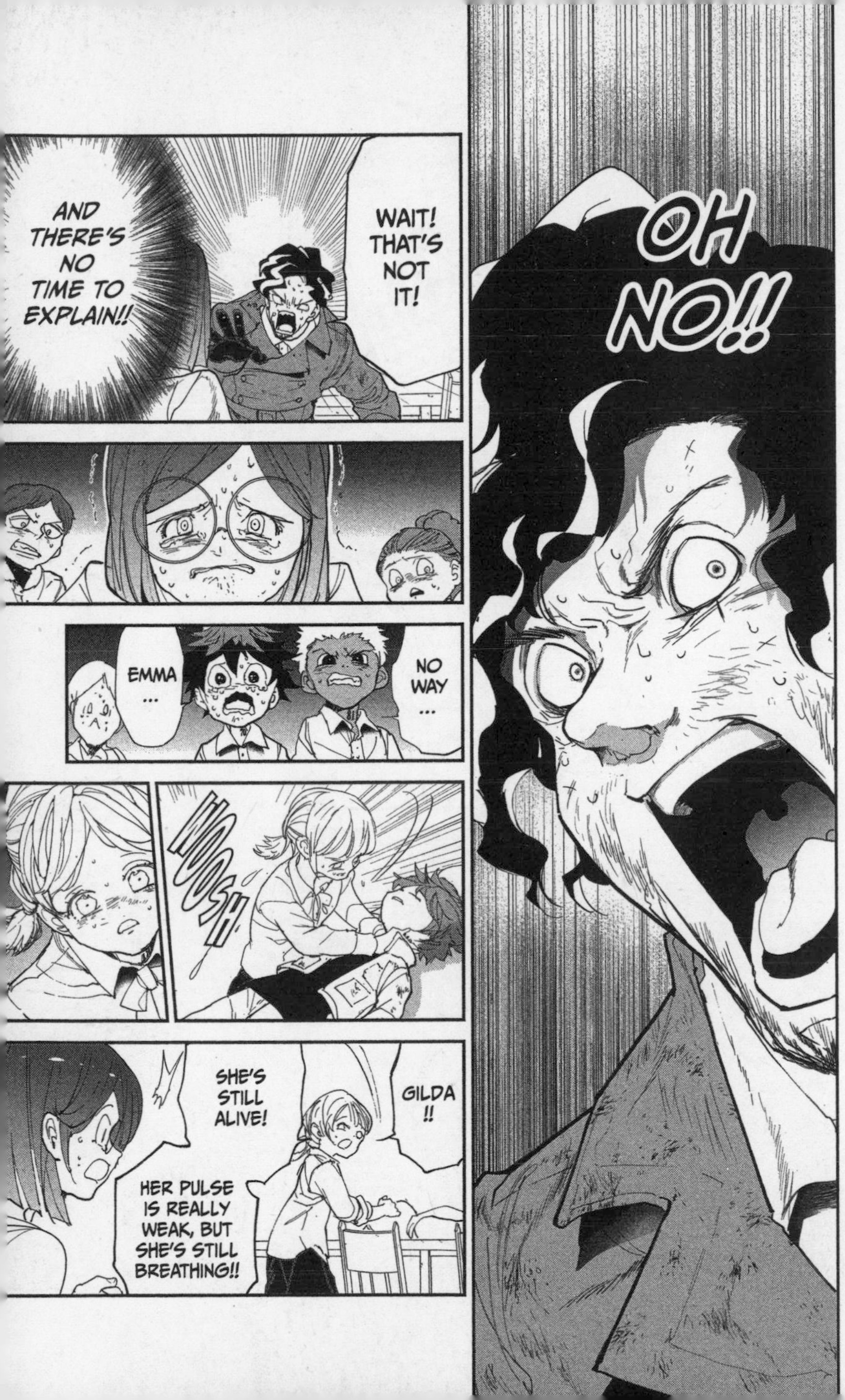
OH NO!!
WAIT! THAT'S NOT IT!
AND THERE'S NO TIME TO EXPLAIN!!
NO WAY ...
EMMA ...
WHOOSH
GILDA !!
SHE'S STILL ALIVE!
HER PULSE IS REALLY WEAK, BUT SHE'S STILL BREATHING!!

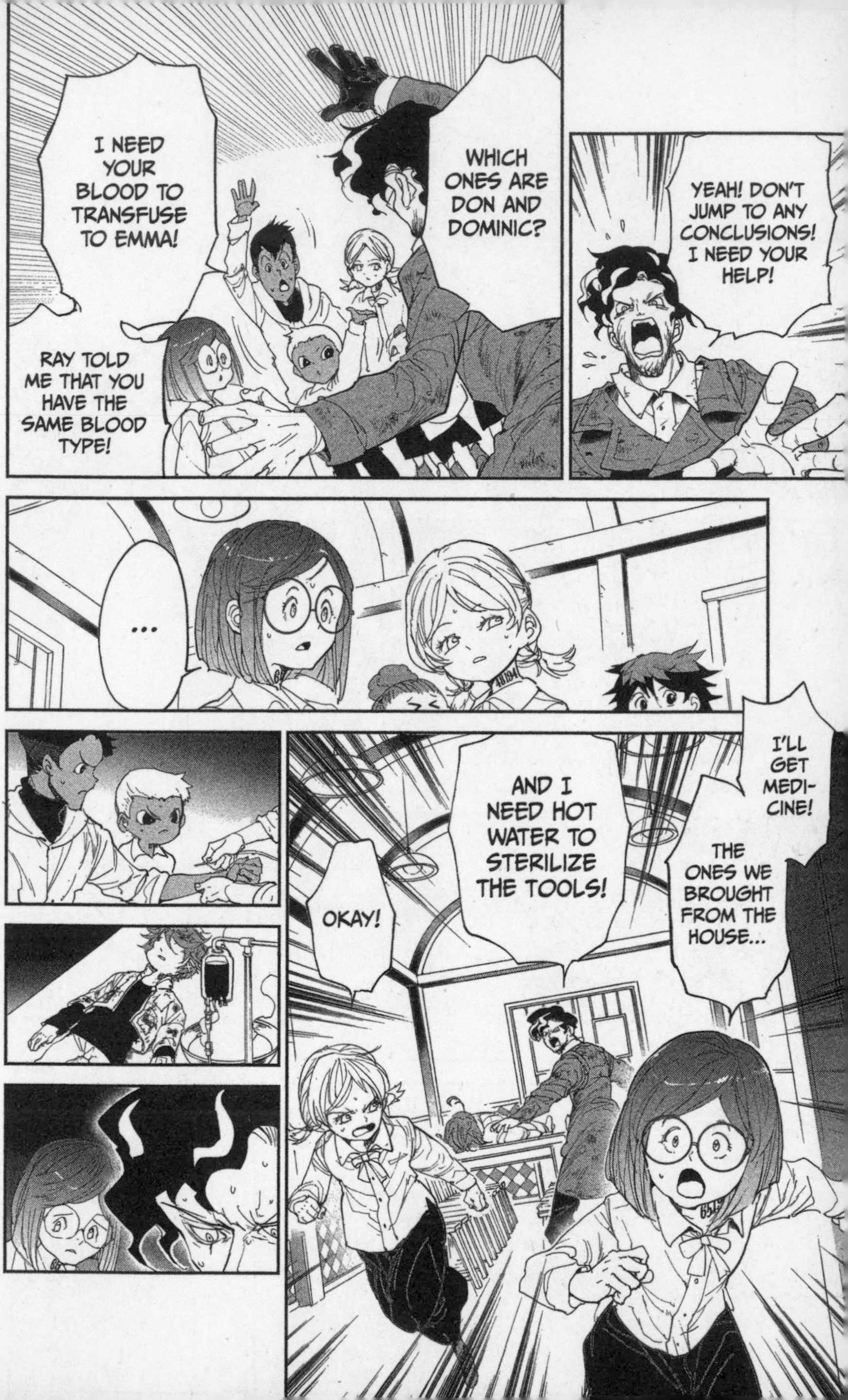
YEAH! DON'T JUMP TO ANY CONCLUSIONS! I NEED YOUR HELP!
WHICH ONES ARE DON AND DOMINIC?
I NEED YOUR BLOOD TO TRANSFUSE TO EMMA!
RAY TOLD ME THAT YOU HAVE THE SAME BLOOD TYPE!
...
I'LL GET MEDI-CINE!
THE ONES WE BROUGHT FROM THE HOUSE...
AND I NEED HOT WATER TO STERILIZE THE TOOLS!
OKAY!

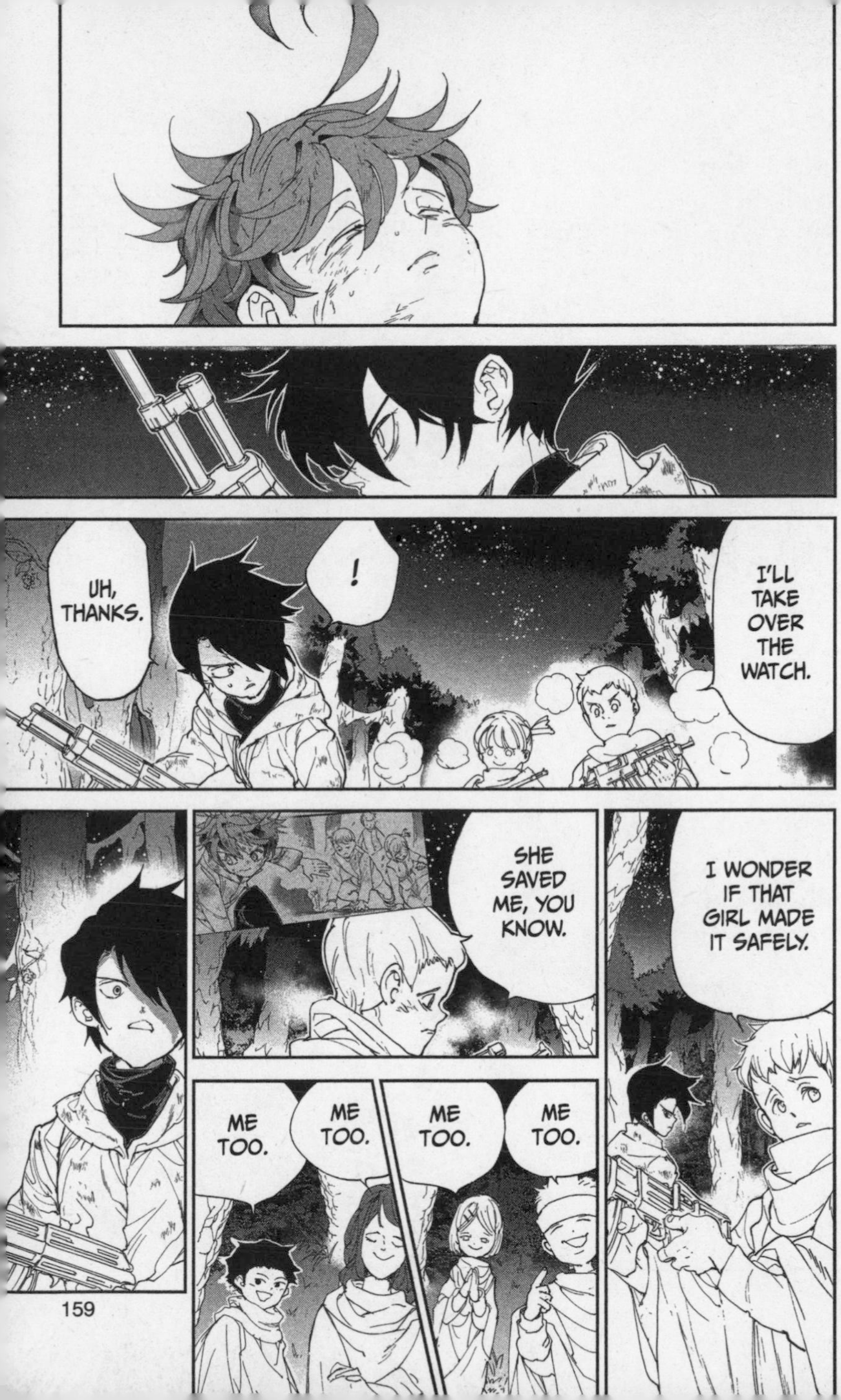
I'LL TAKE OVER THE WATCH.
!
UH, THANKS.
I WONDER IF THAT GIRL MADE IT SAFELY.
SHE SAVED ME, YOU KNOW.
ME TOO.
ME TOO.
ME TOO.
ME TOO.

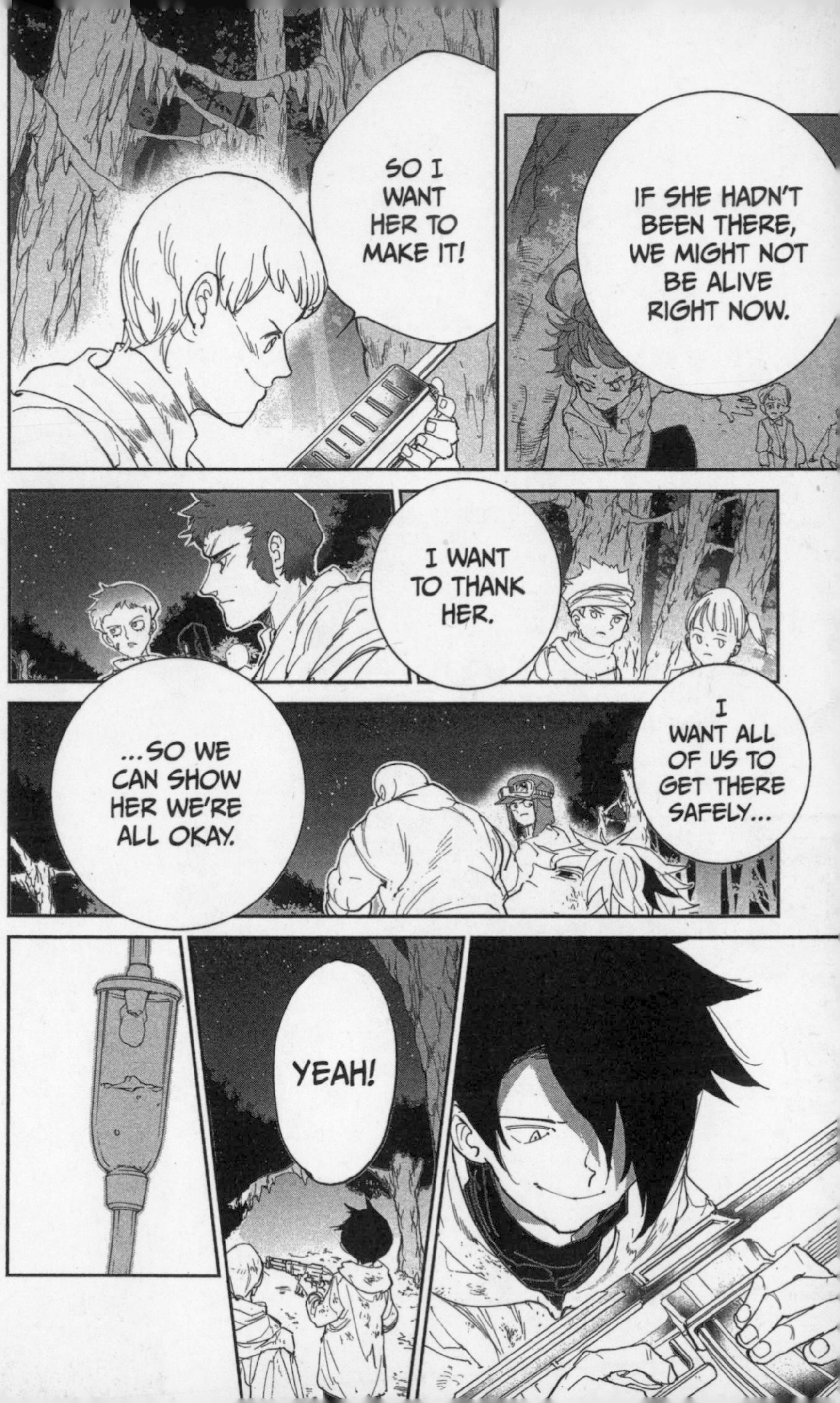
IF SHE HADN'T BEEN THERE, WE MIGHT NOT BE ALIVE RIGHT NOW.
SO I WANT HER TO MAKE IT!
I WANT TO THANK HER.
I WANT ALL OF US TO GET THERE SAFELY...
...SO WE CAN SHOW HER WE'RE ALL OKAY.
YEAH!

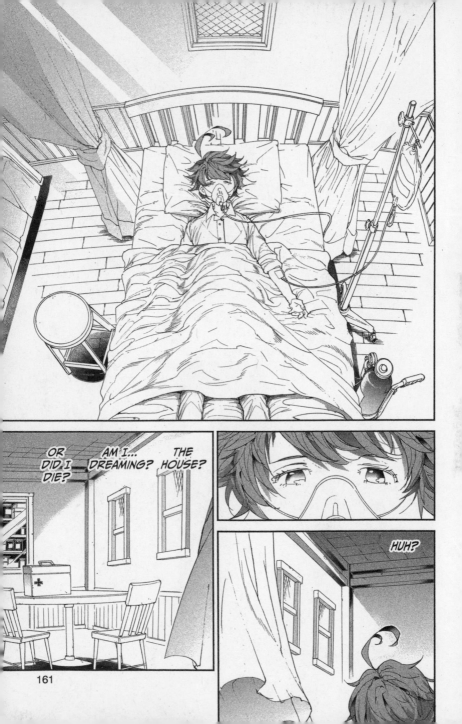

OR
DID I
DIE?

AM I...
DREAMING?

THE
HOUSE?

HUH?

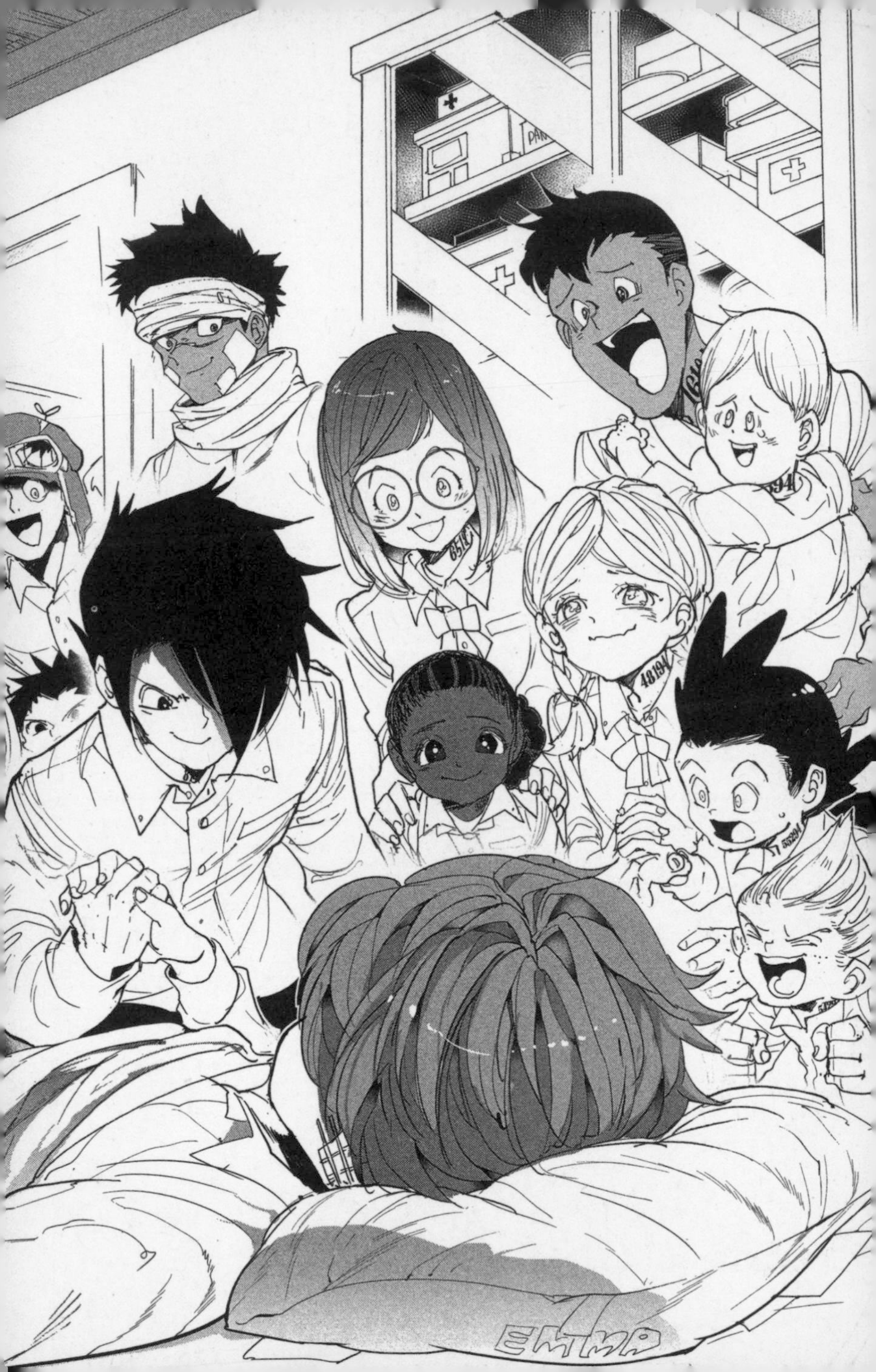
EMMA

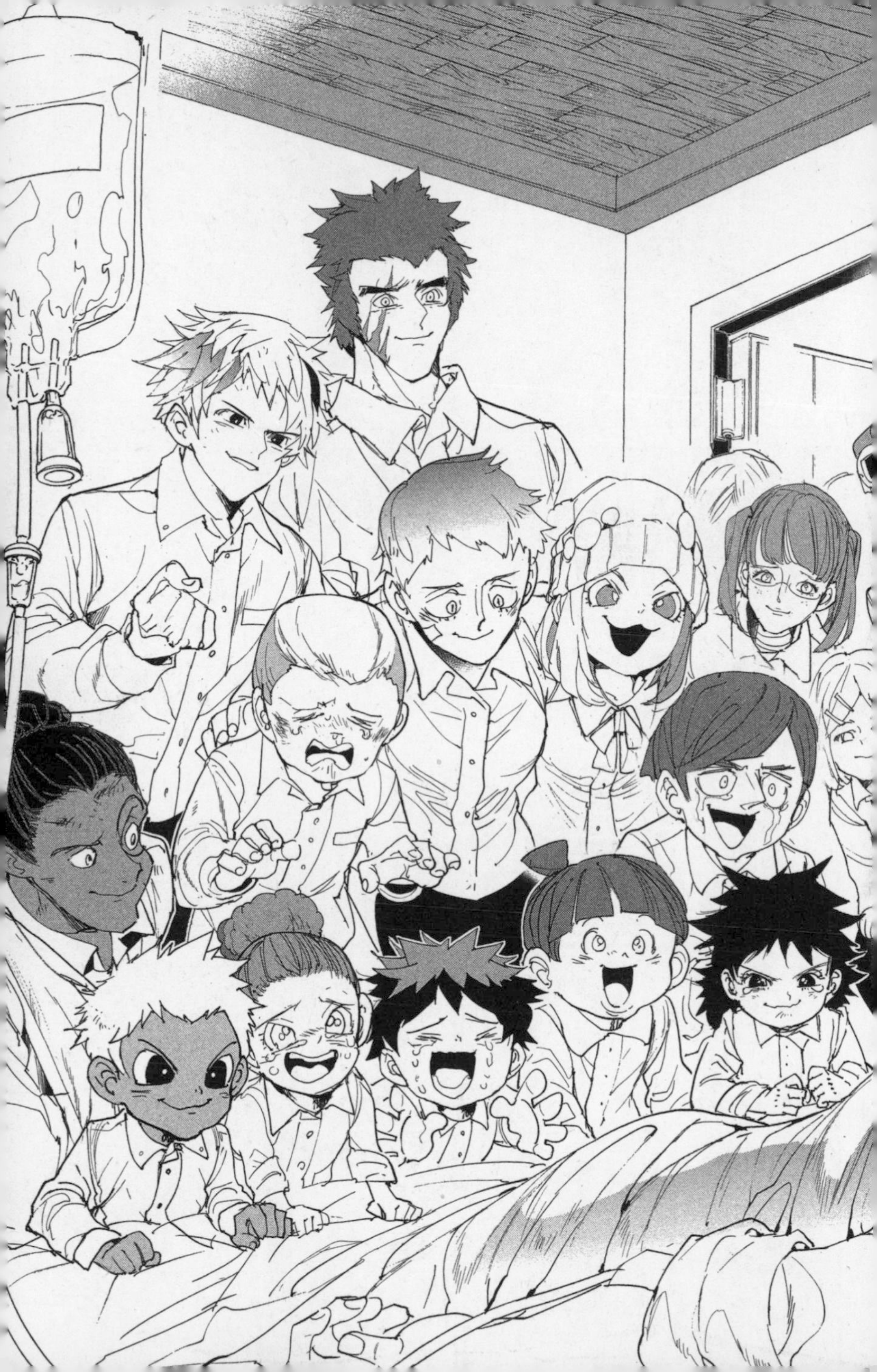

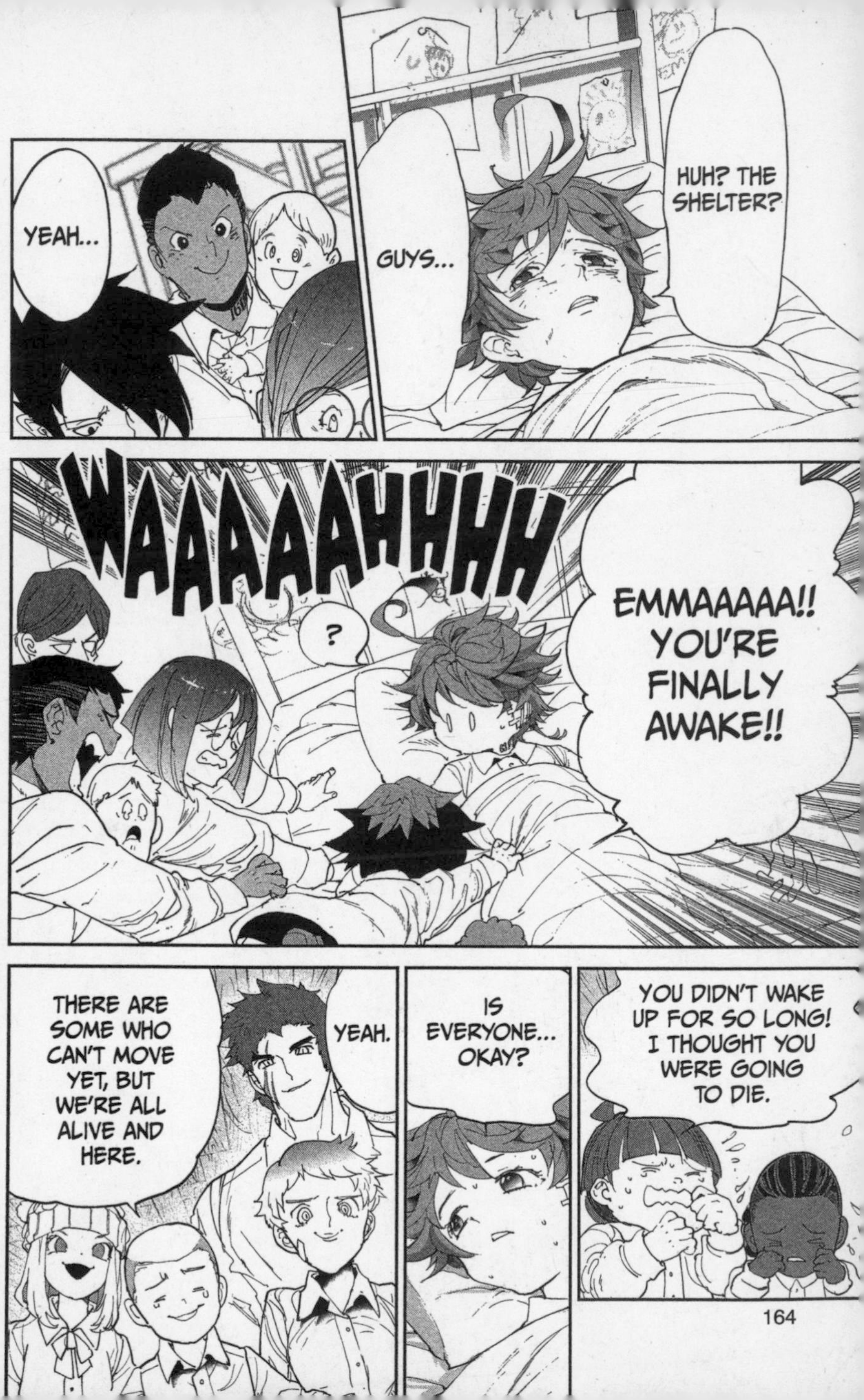
HUH? THE SHELTER?
GUYS...
YEAH...
WAAAAAHHHH
EMMAAAAA!! YOU'RE FINALLY AWAKE!!
?
YOU DIDN'T WAKE UP FOR SO LONG! I THOUGHT YOU WERE GOING TO DIE.
IS EVERYONE... OKAY?
YEAH.
THERE ARE SOME WHO CAN'T MOVE YET, BUT WE'RE ALL ALIVE AND HERE.

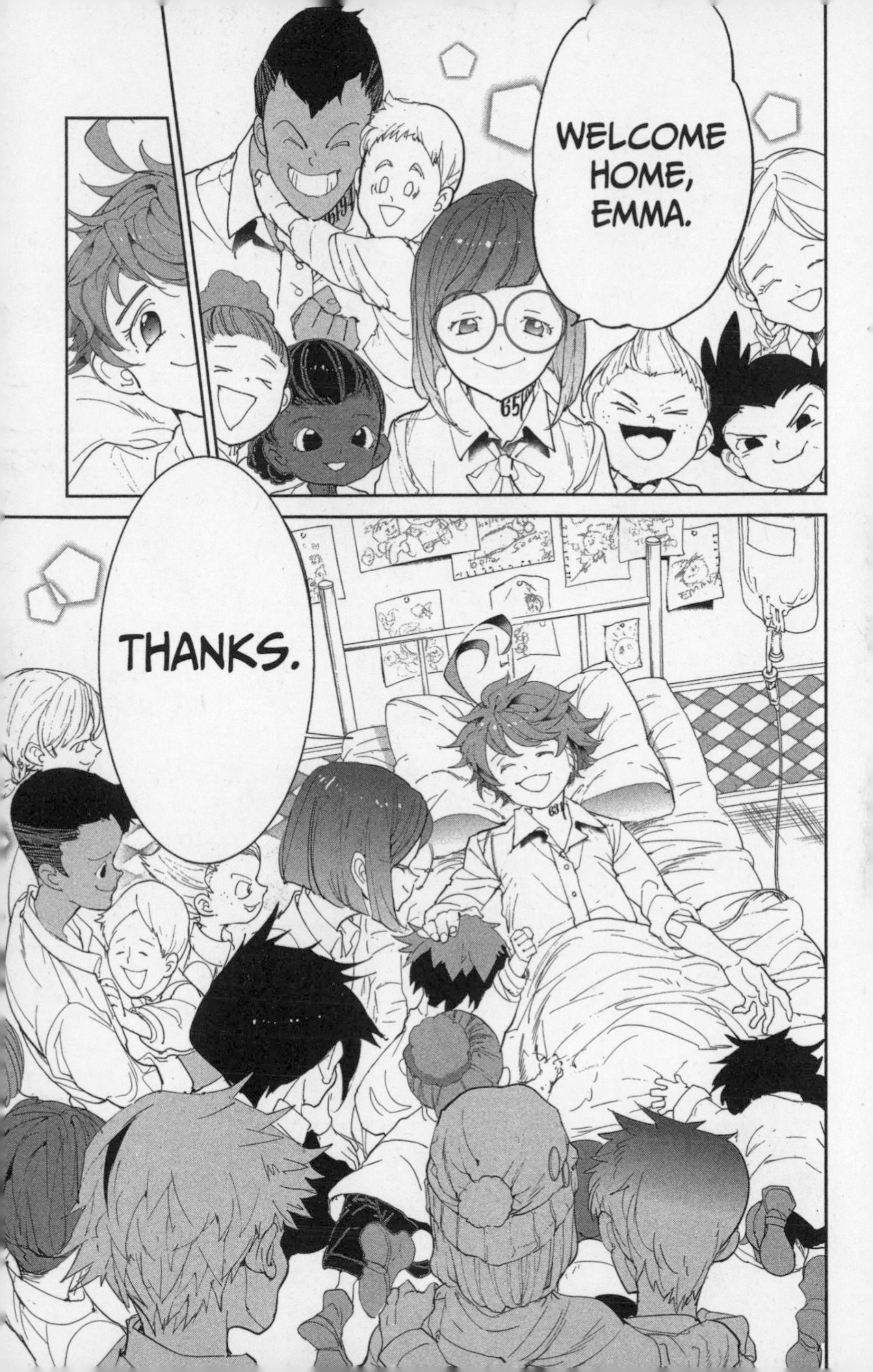
WELCOME HOME, EMMA.
THANKS.

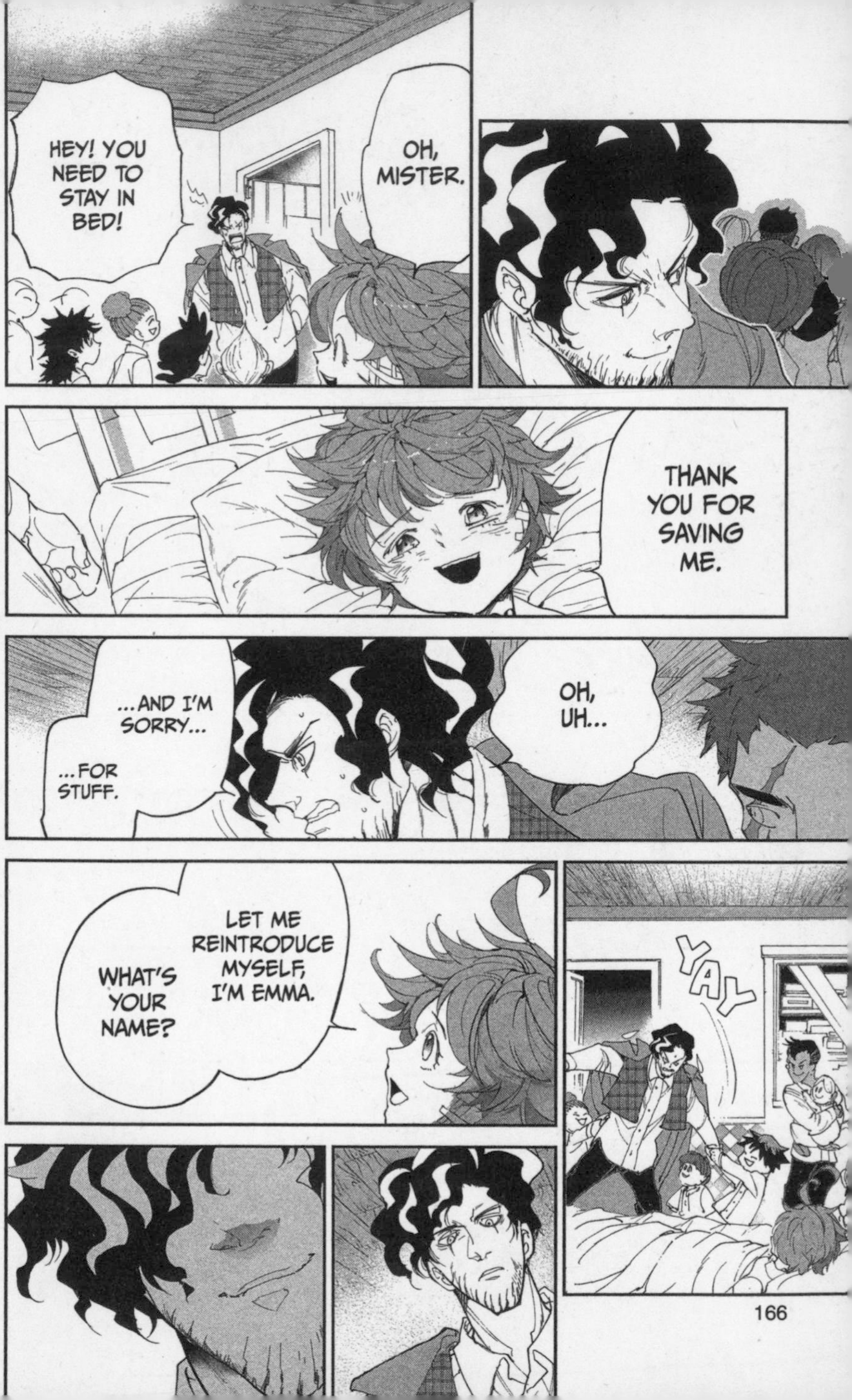
OH, MISTER.
HEY! YOU NEED TO STAY IN BED!
THANK YOU FOR SAVING ME.
OH, UH...
...AND I'M SORRY...
...FOR STUFF.
YAY
LET ME REINTRODUCE MYSELF, I'M EMMA.
WHAT'S YOUR NAME?

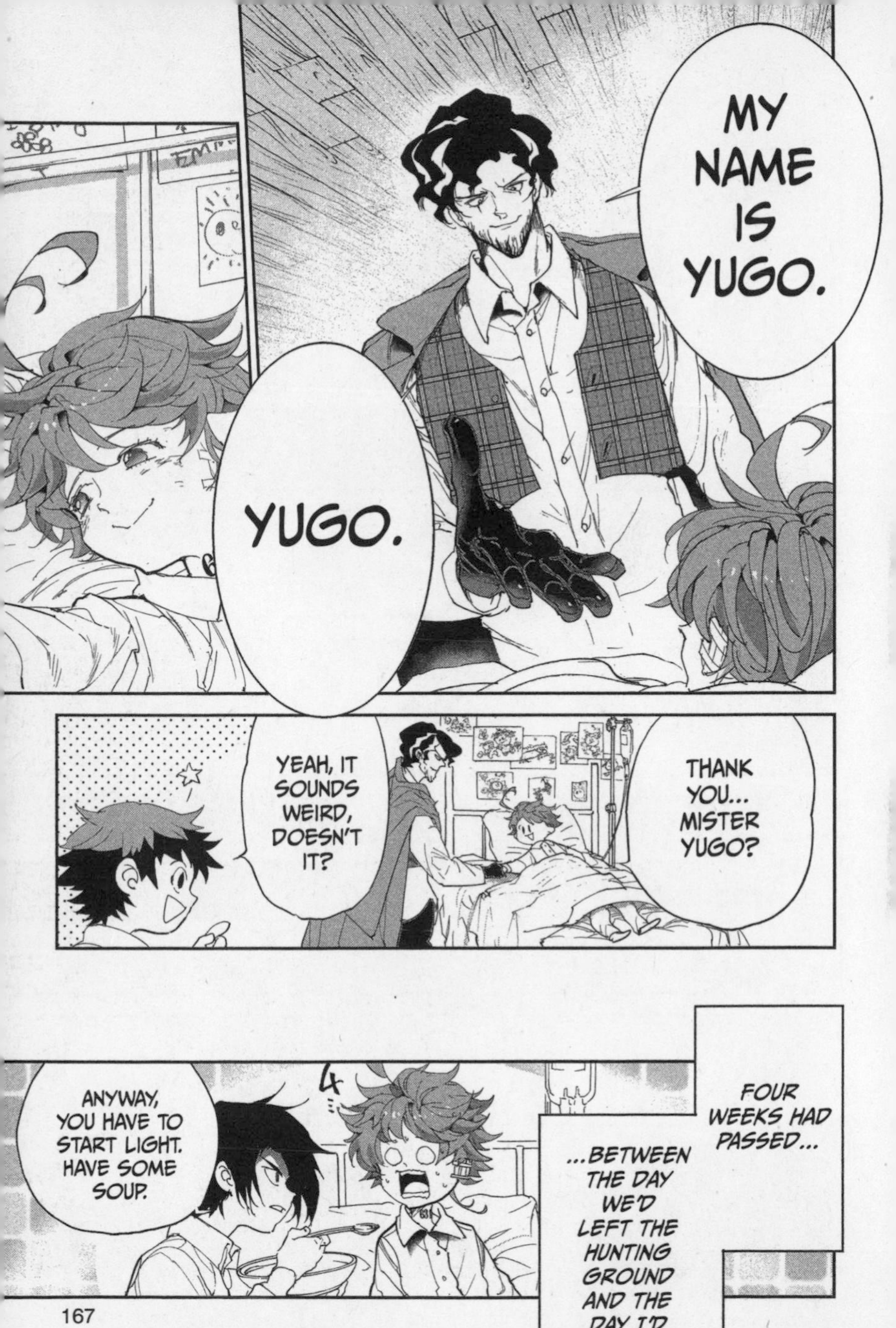
MY NAME IS YUGO.
YUGO.
THANK YOU... MISTER YUGO?
YEAH, IT SOUNDS WEIRD, DOESN'T IT?
FOUR WEEKS HAD PASSED...
...BETWEEN THE DAY WE'D LEFT THE HUNTING GROUND AND THE DAY I'D WOKEN UP.
ANYWAY, YOU HAVE TO START LIGHT. HAVE SOME SOUP.

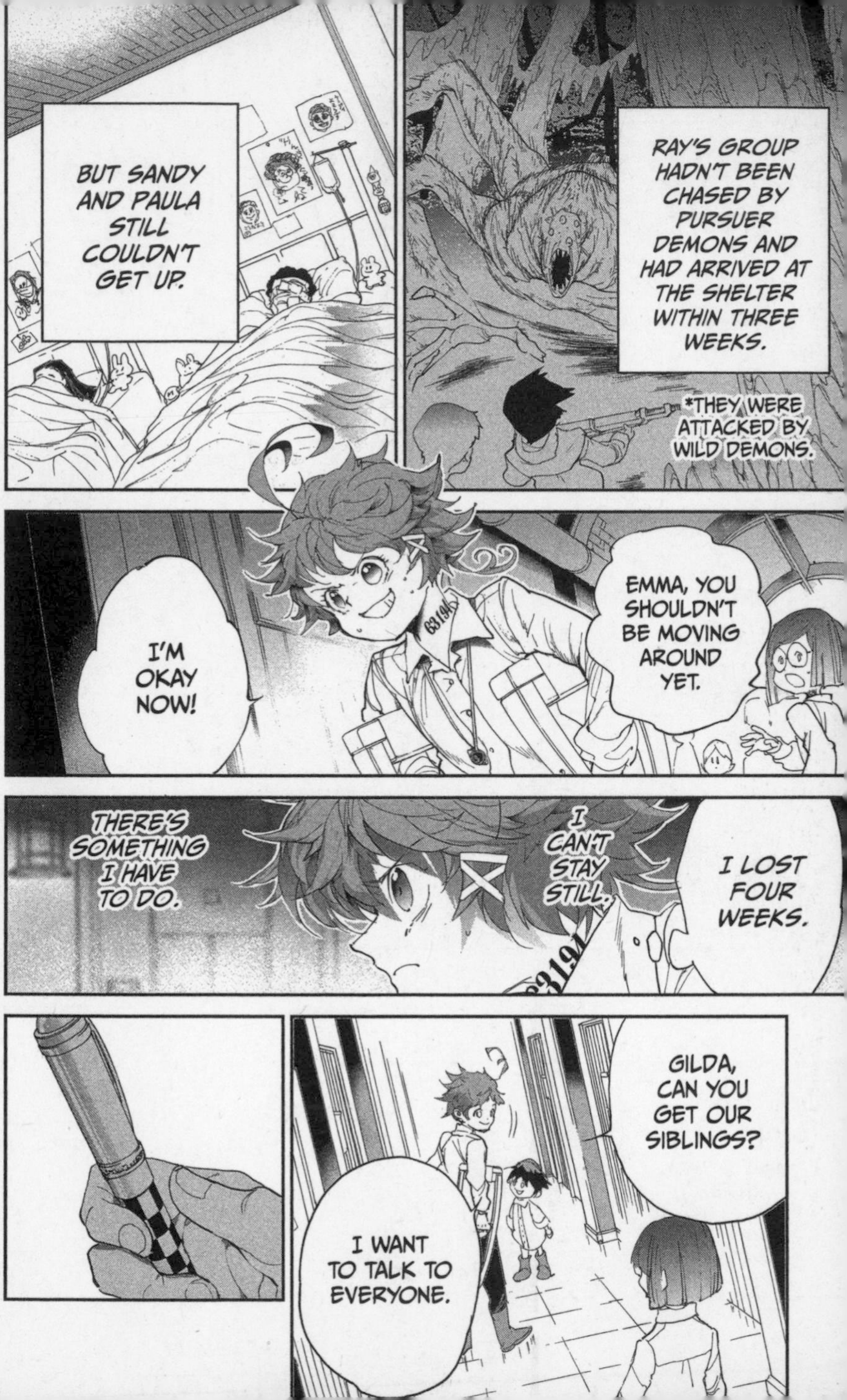
RAY'S GROUP HADN'T BEEN CHASED BY PURSUER DEMONS AND HAD ARRIVED AT THE SHELTER WITHIN THREE WEEKS.
*THEY WERE ATTACKED BY WILD DEMONS.
BUT SANDY AND PAULA STILL COULDN'T GET UP.
EMMA, YOU SHOULDN'T BE MOVING AROUND YET.
I'M OKAY NOW!
I LOST FOUR WEEKS.
I CAN'T STAY STILL.
THERE'S SOMETHING I HAVE TO DO.
GILDA, CAN YOU GET OUR SIBLINGS?
I WANT TO TALK TO EVERYONE.

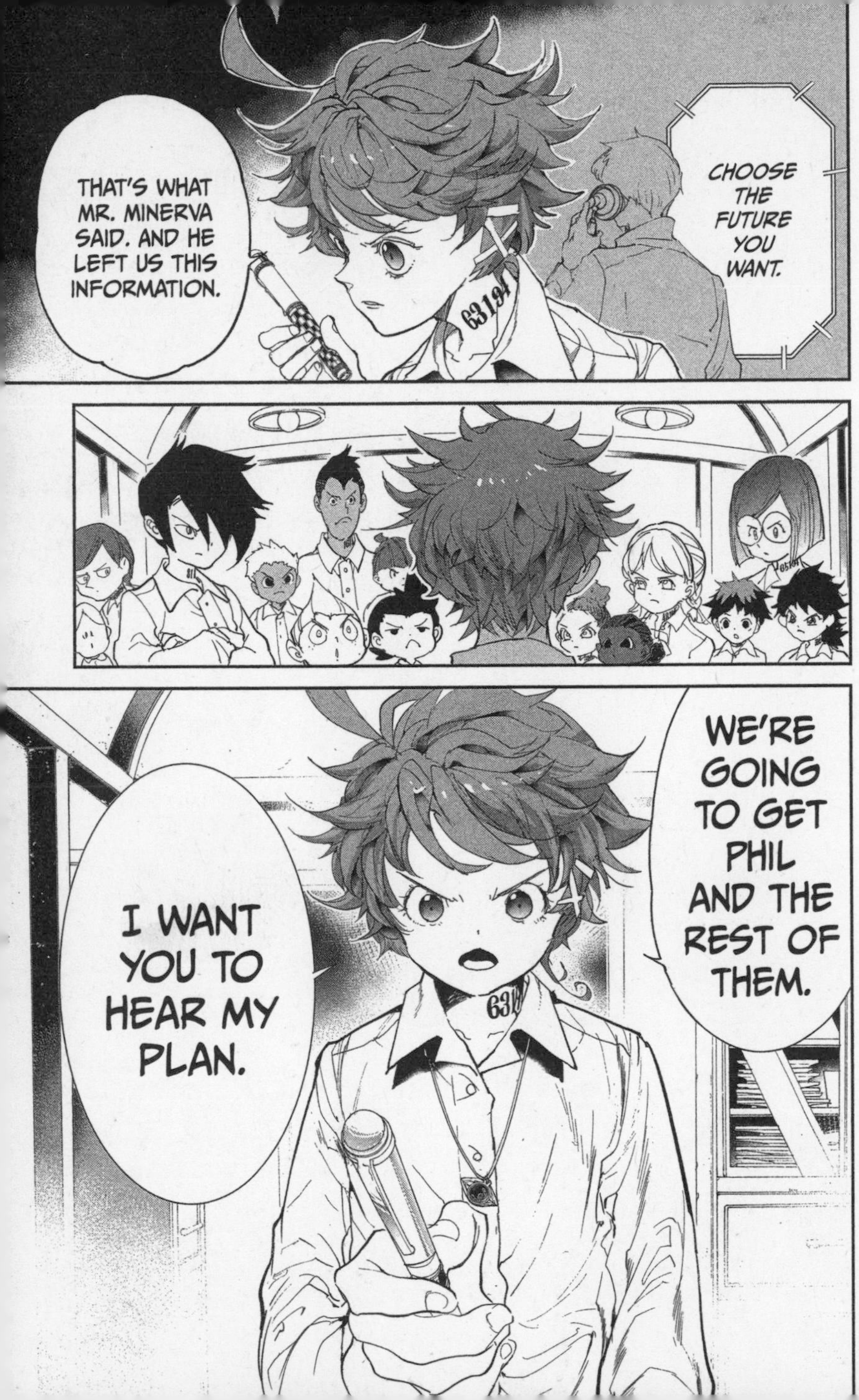
CHOOSE THE FUTURE YOU WANT.
THAT'S WHAT MR. MINERVA SAID. AND HE LEFT US THIS INFORMATION.
WE'RE GOING TO GET PHIL AND THE REST OF THEM.
I WANT YOU TO HEAR MY PLAN.

FOUND OUT

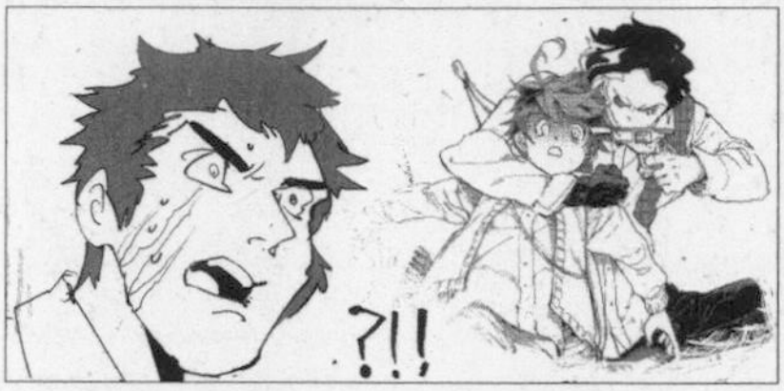
?!!

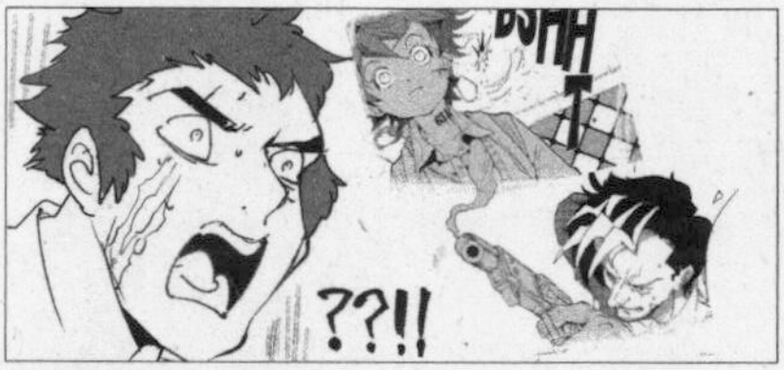
??!!

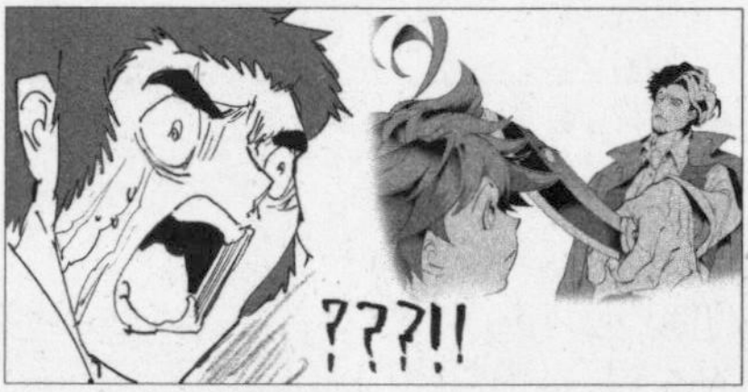
???!!

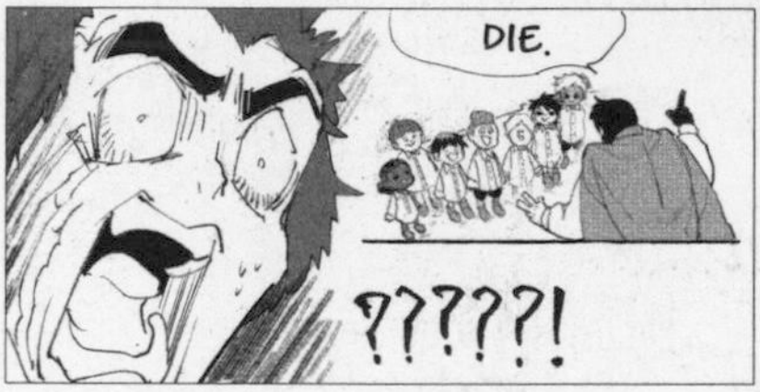
DIE.
?????!

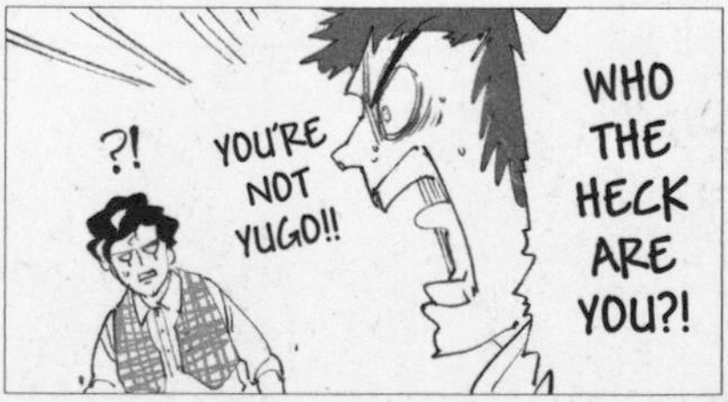
WHO THE HECK ARE YOU?!
YOU'RE NOT YUGO!!
?!

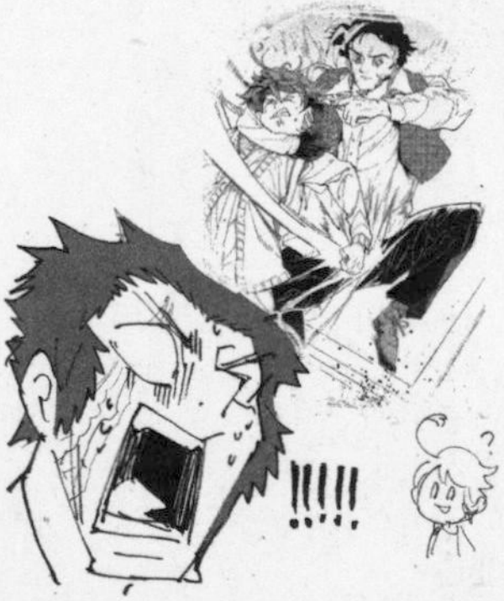
!!!!!

SIDE STORY 8 FIN

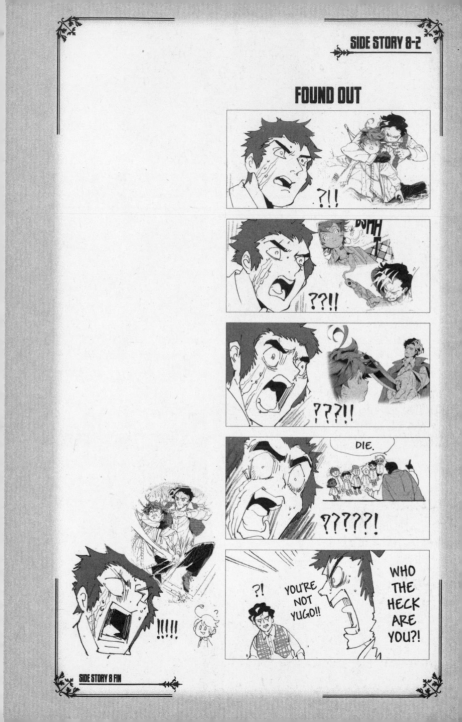

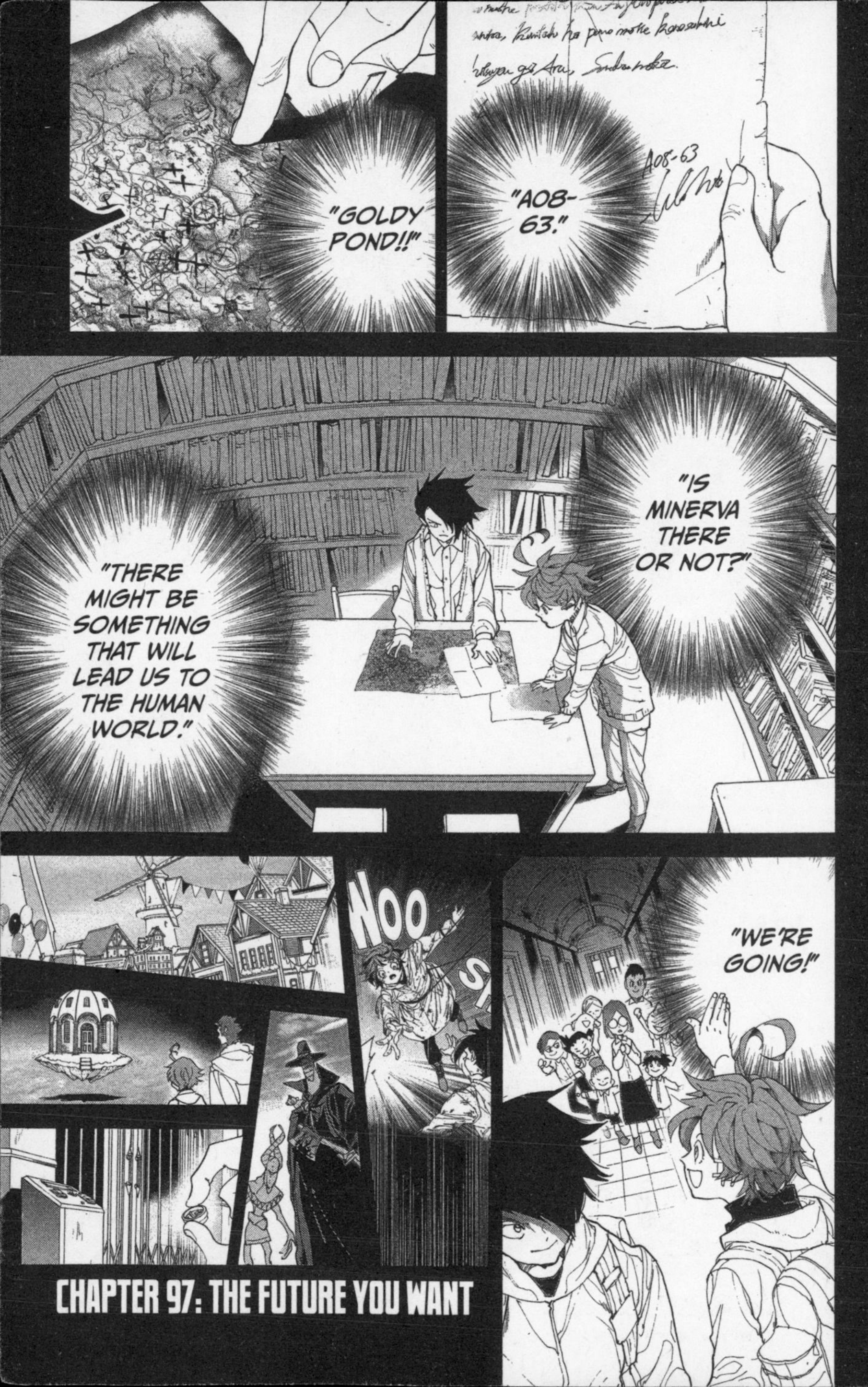

A08-63
"A08-63."
"GOLDY POND!!"
"IS MINERVA THERE OR NOT?"
"THERE MIGHT BE SOMETHING THAT WILL LEAD US TO THE HUMAN WORLD."
"WE'RE GOING!"
NOO

CHAPTER 97: THE FUTURE YOU WANT

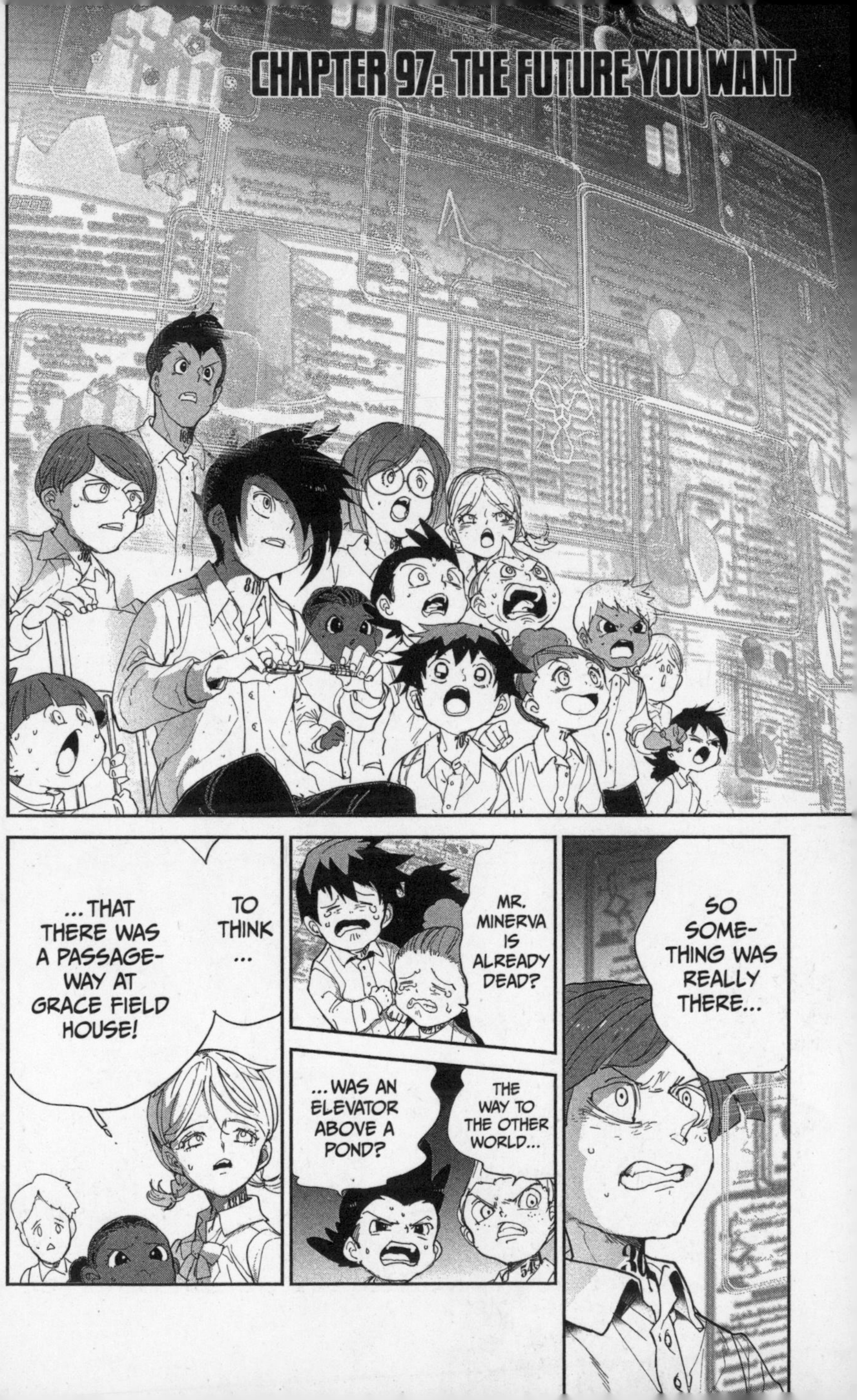
CHAPTER 97: THE FUTURE YOU WANT
SO SOMETHING WAS REALLY THERE...
MR. MINERVA IS ALREADY DEAD?
THE WAY TO THE OTHER WORLD...
...WAS AN ELEVATOR ABOVE A POND?
TO THINK ...
...THAT THERE WAS A PASSAGEWAY AT GRACE FIELD HOUSE!

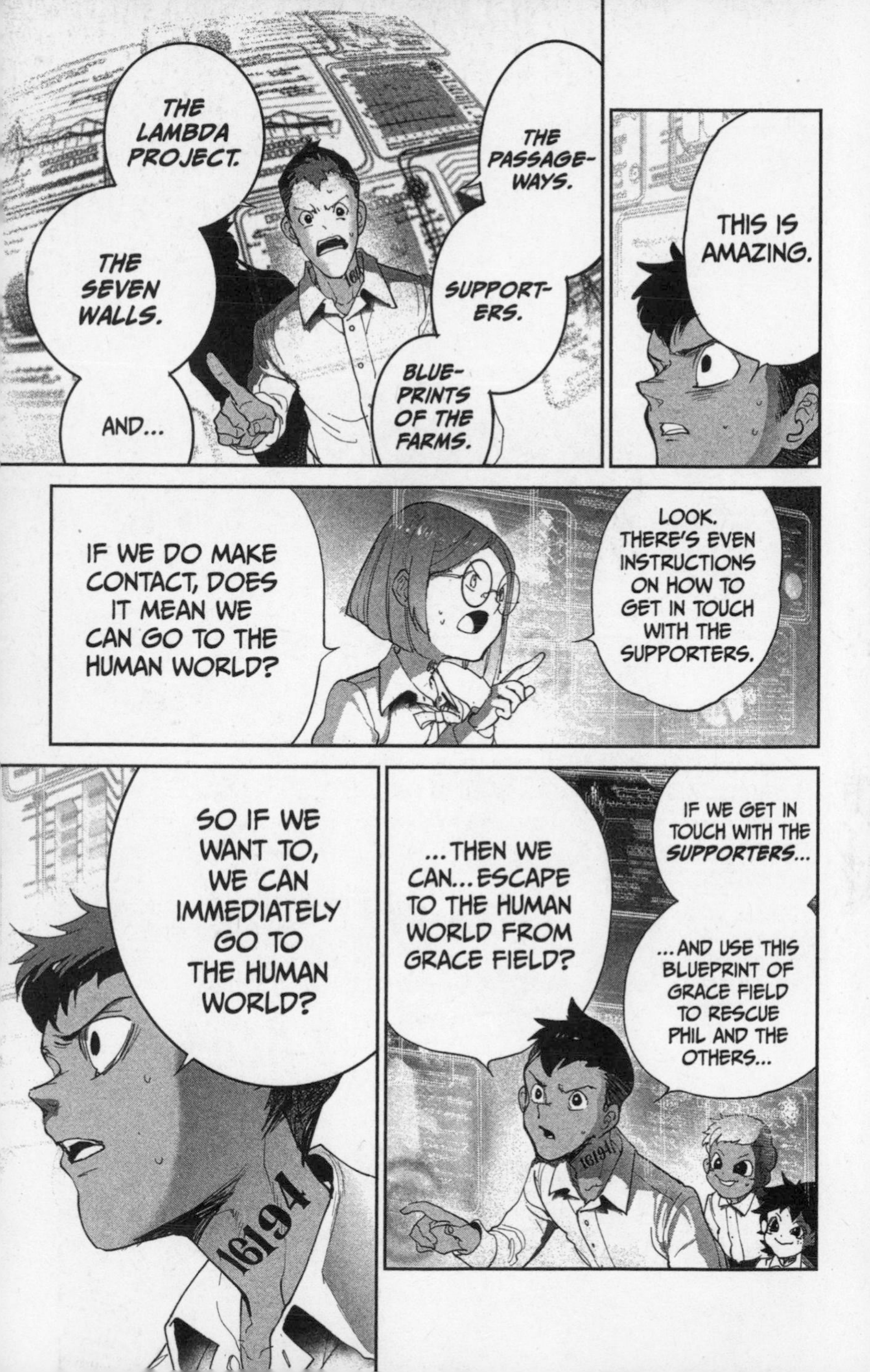
THIS IS AMAZING.
THE PASSAGE-WAYS.
SUPPORT-ERS.
BLUE-PRINTS OF THE FARMS.
THE LAMBDA PROJECT.
THE SEVEN WALLS.
AND...
LOOK. THERE'S EVEN INSTRUCTIONS ON HOW TO GET IN TOUCH WITH THE SUPPORTERS.
IF WE DO MAKE CONTACT, DOES IT MEAN WE CAN GO TO THE HUMAN WORLD?
IF WE GET IN TOUCH WITH THE *SUPPORTERS*...
...AND USE THIS BLUEPRINT OF GRACE FIELD TO RESCUE PHIL AND THE OTHERS...
...THEN WE CAN...ESCAPE TO THE HUMAN WORLD FROM GRACE FIELD?
SO IF WE WANT TO, WE CAN IMMEDIATELY GO TO THE HUMAN WORLD?

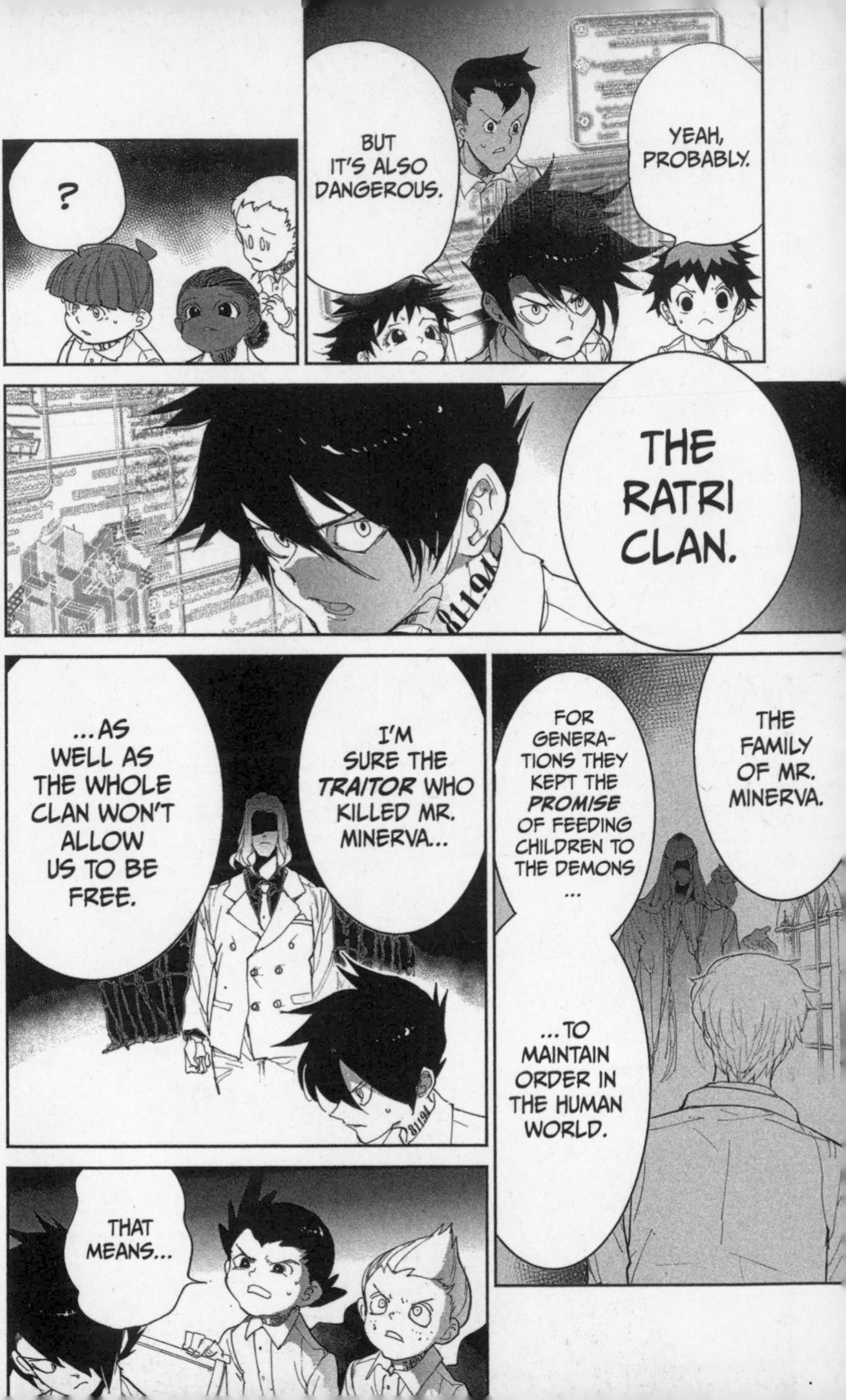
YEAH, PROBABLY.
BUT IT'S ALSO DANGEROUS.
?
THE RATRI CLAN.
THE FAMILY OF MR. MINERVA.
FOR GENERATIONS THEY KEPT THE *PROMISE* OF FEEDING CHILDREN TO THE DEMONS...
...TO MAINTAIN ORDER IN THE HUMAN WORLD.
I'M SURE THE *TRAITOR* WHO KILLED MR. MINERVA...
...AS WELL AS THE WHOLE CLAN WON'T ALLOW US TO BE FREE.
THAT MEANS...

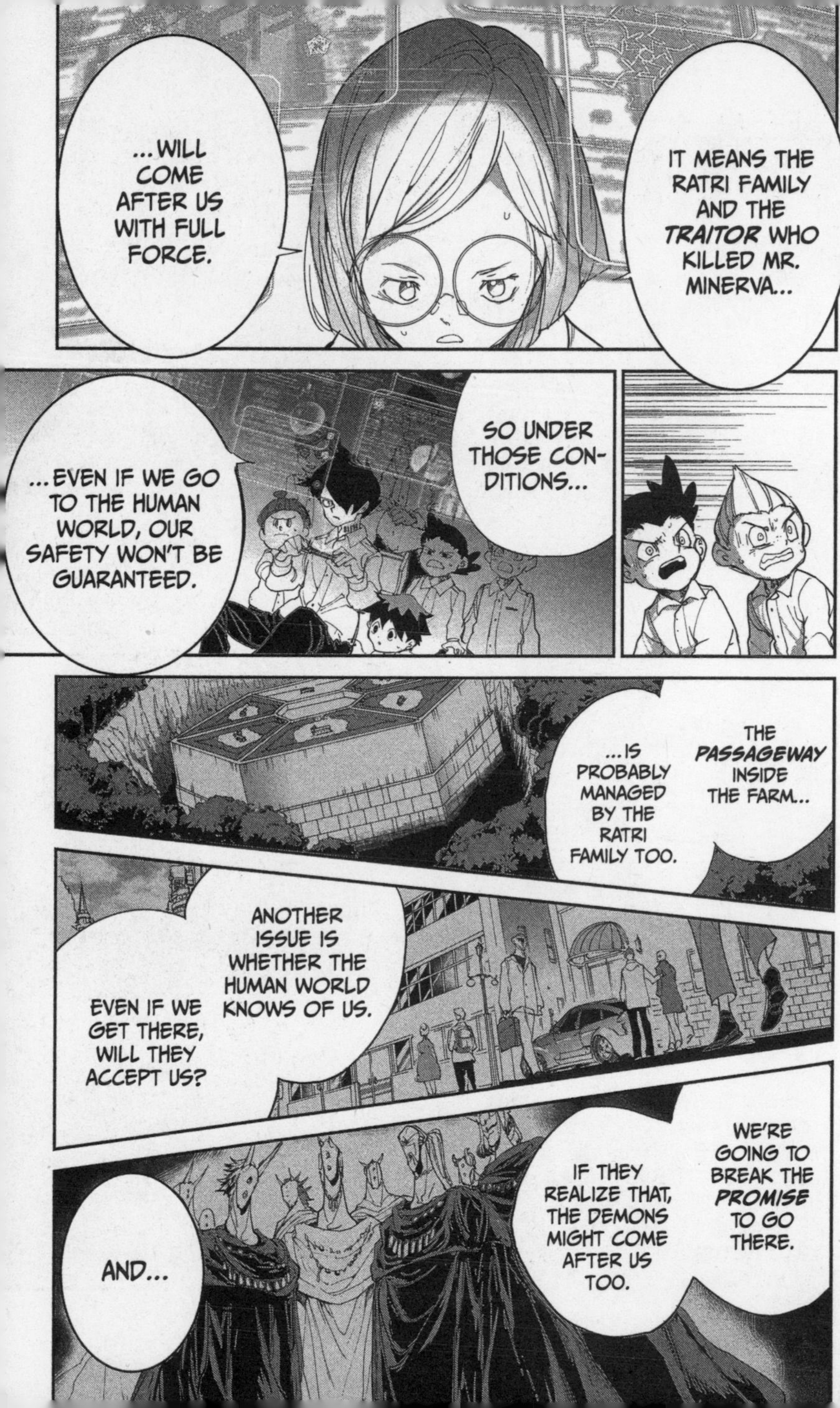
IT MEANS THE RATRI FAMILY AND THE *TRAITOR* WHO KILLED MR. MINERVA...
...WILL COME AFTER US WITH FULL FORCE.
SO UNDER THOSE CON-DITIONS...
...EVEN IF WE GO TO THE HUMAN WORLD, OUR SAFETY WON'T BE GUARANTEED.
THE *PASSAGEWAY* INSIDE THE FARM...
...IS PROBABLY MANAGED BY THE RATRI FAMILY TOO.
ANOTHER ISSUE IS WHETHER THE HUMAN WORLD KNOWS OF US.
EVEN IF WE GET THERE, WILL THEY ACCEPT US?
WE'RE GOING TO BREAK THE *PROMISE* TO GO THERE.
IF THEY REALIZE THAT, THE DEMONS MIGHT COME AFTER US TOO.
AND...

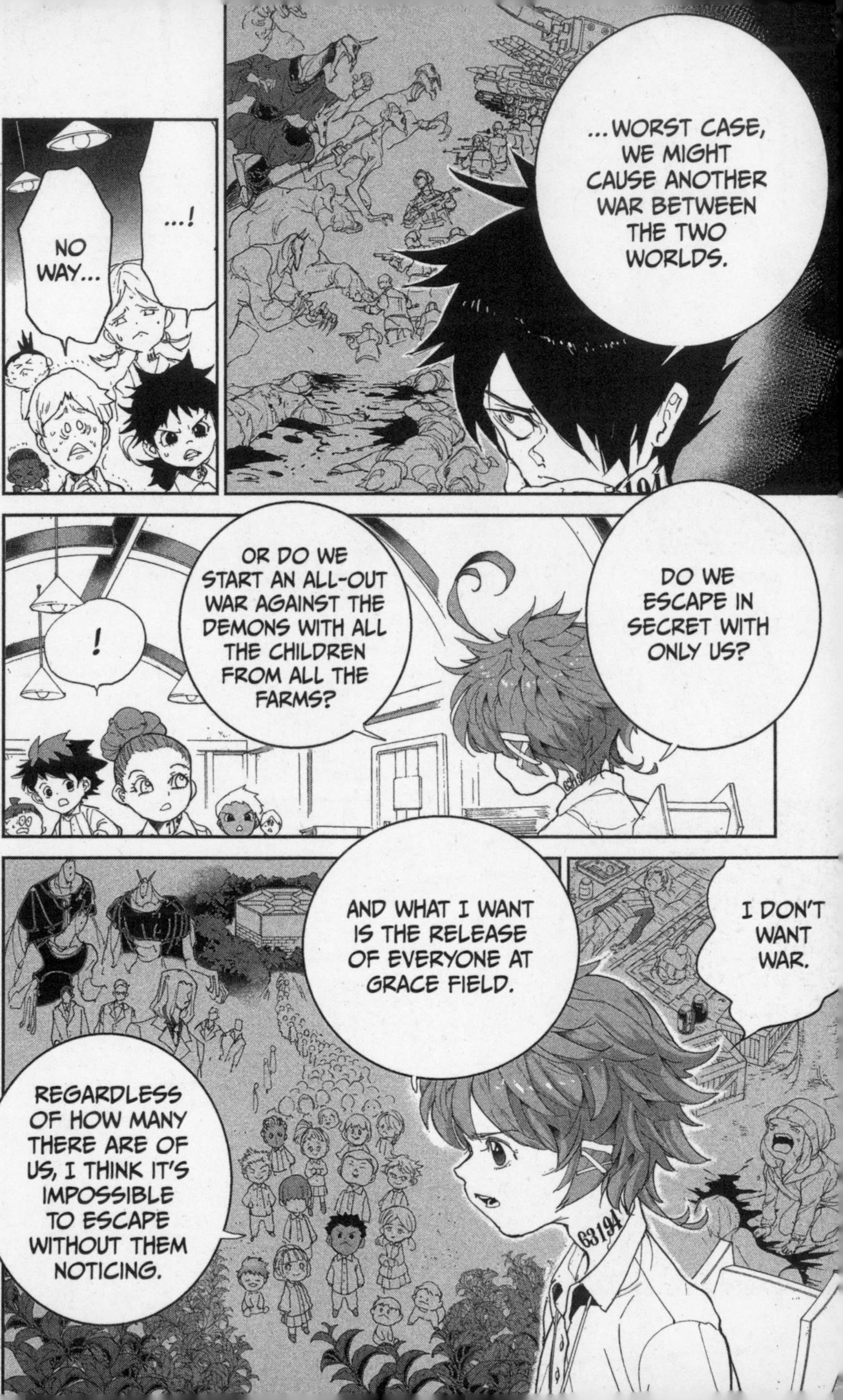
...WORST CASE, WE MIGHT CAUSE ANOTHER WAR BETWEEN THE TWO WORLDS.
...!
NO WAY...
DO WE ESCAPE IN SECRET WITH ONLY US?
OR DO WE START AN ALL-OUT WAR AGAINST THE DEMONS WITH ALL THE CHILDREN FROM ALL THE FARMS?
!
I DON'T WANT WAR.
AND WHAT I WANT IS THE RELEASE OF EVERYONE AT GRACE FIELD.
REGARDLESS OF HOW MANY THERE ARE OF US, I THINK IT'S IMPOSSIBLE TO ESCAPE WITHOUT THEM NOTICING.

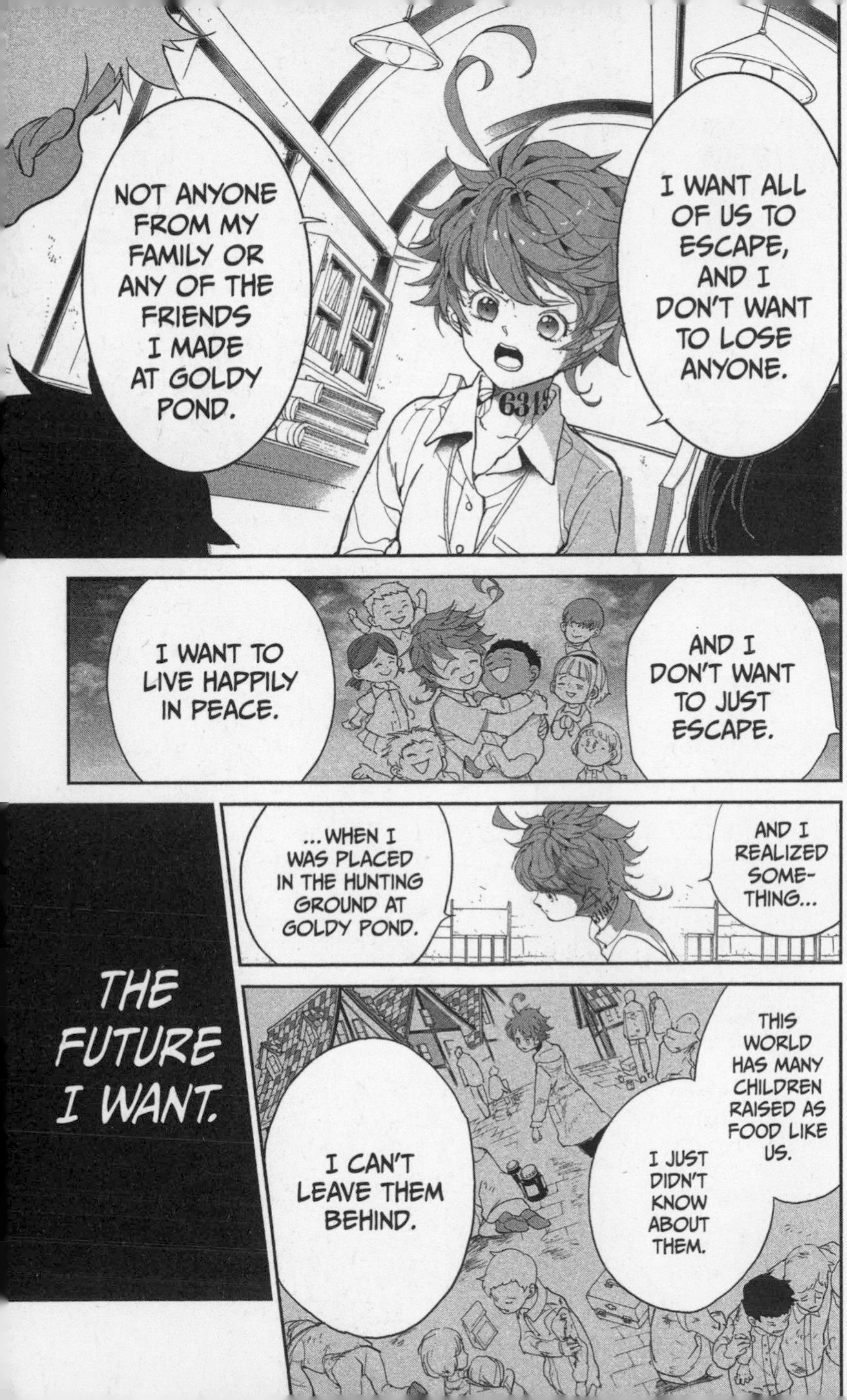
I WANT ALL OF US TO ESCAPE, AND I DON'T WANT TO LOSE ANYONE.
NOT ANYONE FROM MY FAMILY OR ANY OF THE FRIENDS I MADE AT GOLDY POND.
AND I DON'T WANT TO JUST ESCAPE.
I WANT TO LIVE HAPPILY IN PEACE.
AND I REALIZED SOME-THING...
...WHEN I WAS PLACED IN THE HUNTING GROUND AT GOLDY POND.
THIS WORLD HAS MANY CHILDREN RAISED AS FOOD LIKE US.
I JUST DIDN'T KNOW ABOUT THEM.
I CAN'T LEAVE THEM BEHIND.
THE FUTURE I WANT.

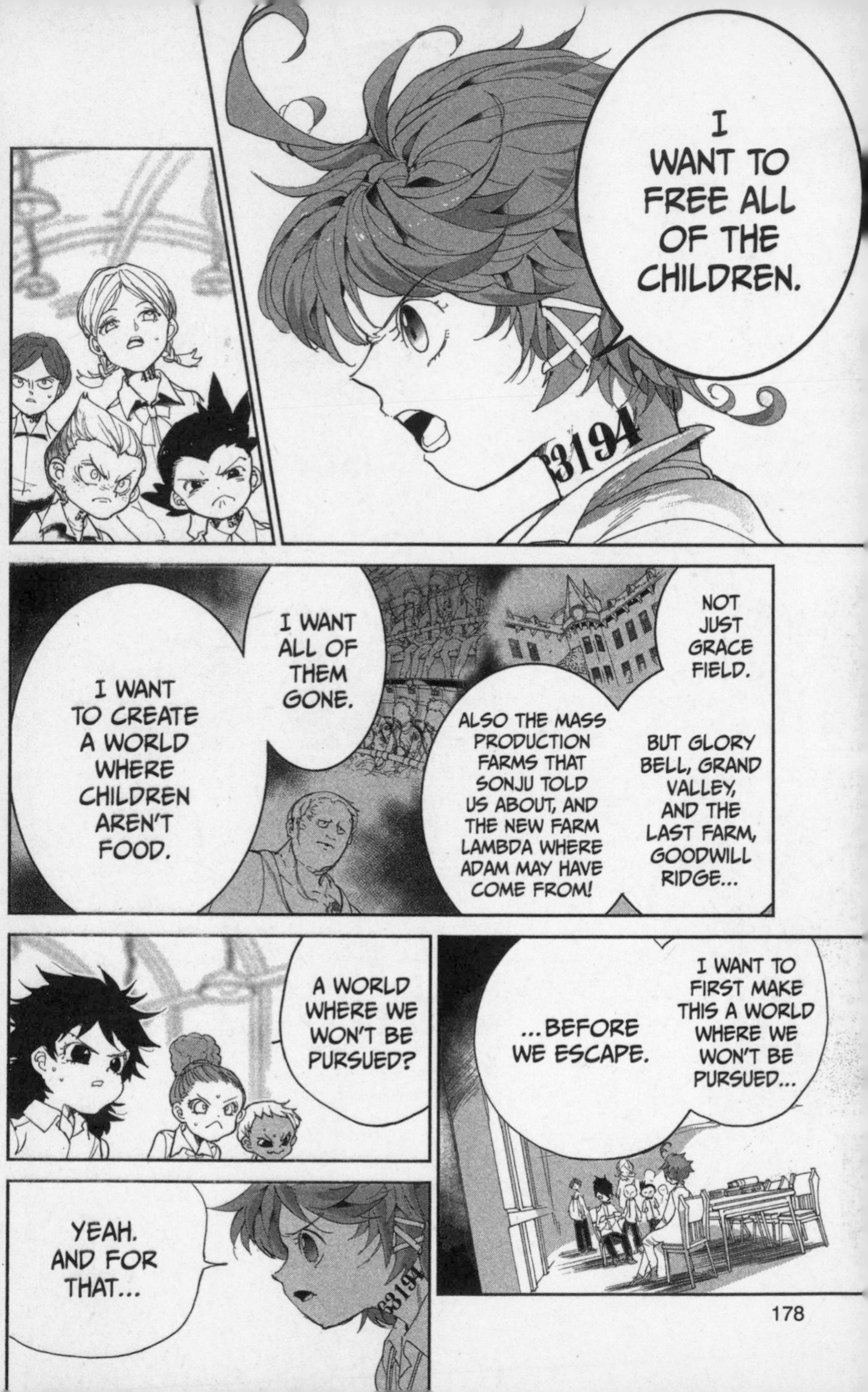
I WANT TO FREE ALL OF THE CHILDREN.
NOT JUST GRACE FIELD.
BUT GLORY BELL, GRAND VALLEY, AND THE LAST FARM, GOODWILL RIDGE...
ALSO THE MASS PRODUCTION FARMS THAT SONJU TOLD US ABOUT, AND THE NEW FARM LAMBDA WHERE ADAM MAY HAVE COME FROM!
I WANT ALL OF THEM GONE.
I WANT TO CREATE A WORLD WHERE CHILDREN AREN'T FOOD.
I WANT TO FIRST MAKE THIS A WORLD WHERE WE WON'T BE PURSUED...
...BEFORE WE ESCAPE.
A WORLD WHERE WE WON'T BE PURSUED?
YEAH. AND FOR THAT...

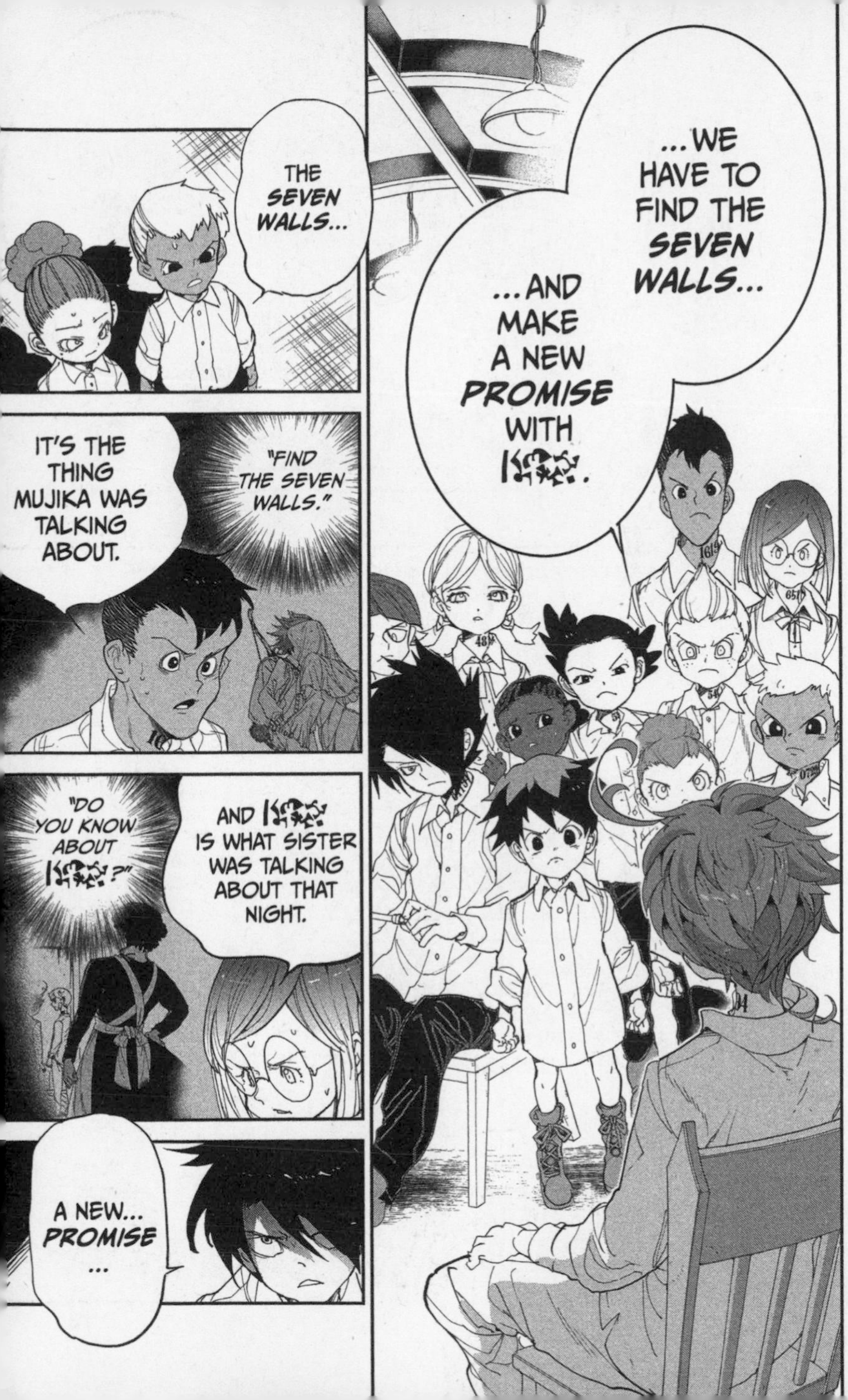
...WE HAVE TO FIND THE SEVEN WALLS...
...AND MAKE A NEW PROMISE WITH .
THE SEVEN WALLS...
"FIND THE SEVEN WALLS."
IT'S THE THING MUJIKA WAS TALKING ABOUT.
AND IS WHAT SISTER WAS TALKING ABOUT THAT NIGHT.
"DO YOU KNOW ABOUT ?"
A NEW... PROMISE ...

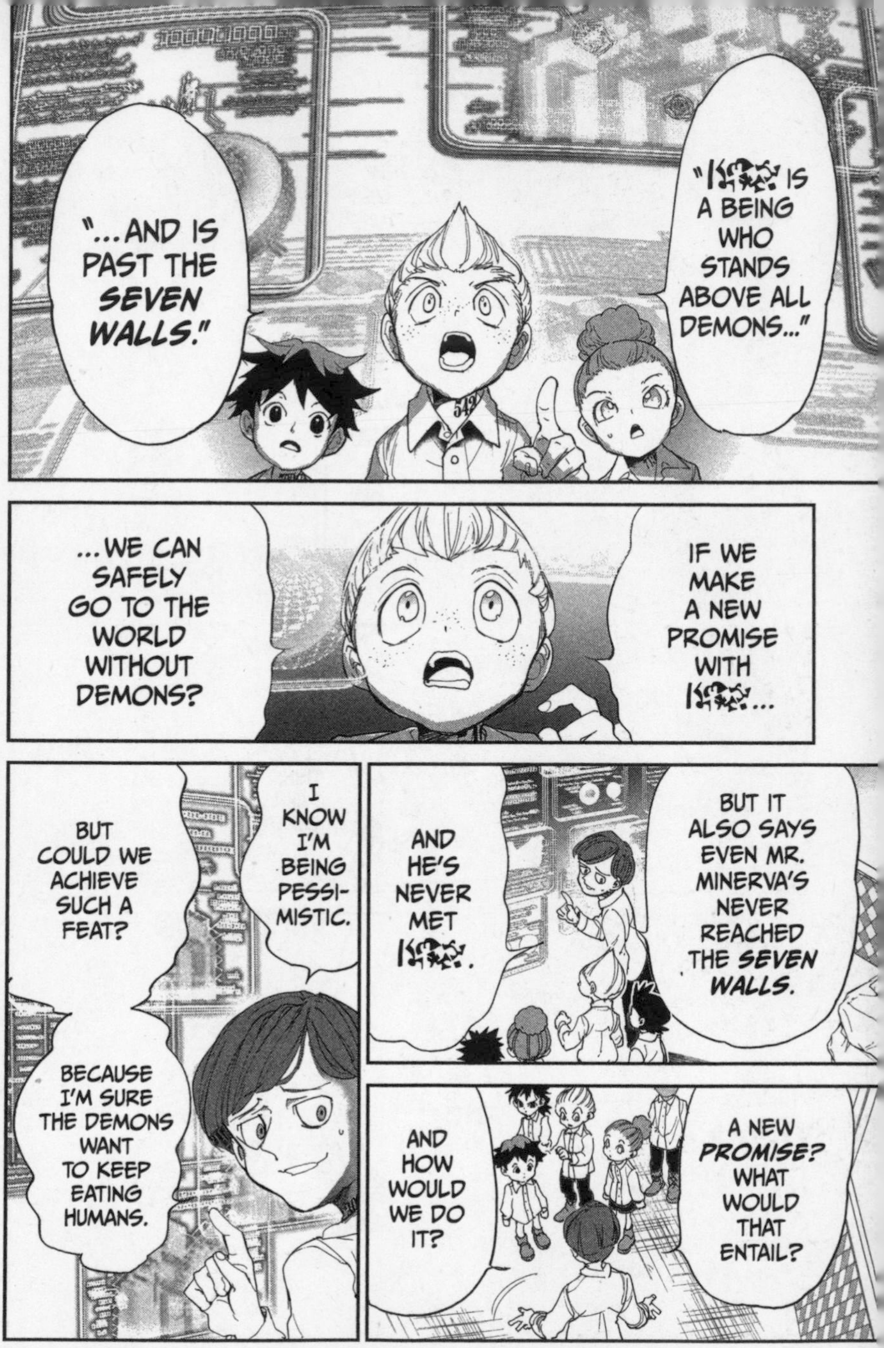
“IS A BEING WHO STANDS ABOVE ALL DEMONS...”
“...AND IS PAST THE SEVEN WALLS.”
IF WE MAKE A NEW PROMISE WITH ...
...WE CAN SAFELY GO TO THE WORLD WITHOUT DEMONS?
BUT IT ALSO SAYS EVEN MR. MINERVA'S NEVER REACHED THE SEVEN WALLS.
AND HE'S NEVER MET .
A NEW PROMISE? WHAT WOULD THAT ENTAIL?
AND HOW WOULD WE DO IT?
I KNOW I'M BEING PESSIMISTIC.
BUT COULD WE ACHIEVE SUCH A FEAT?
BECAUSE I'M SURE THE DEMONS WANT TO KEEP EATING HUMANS.

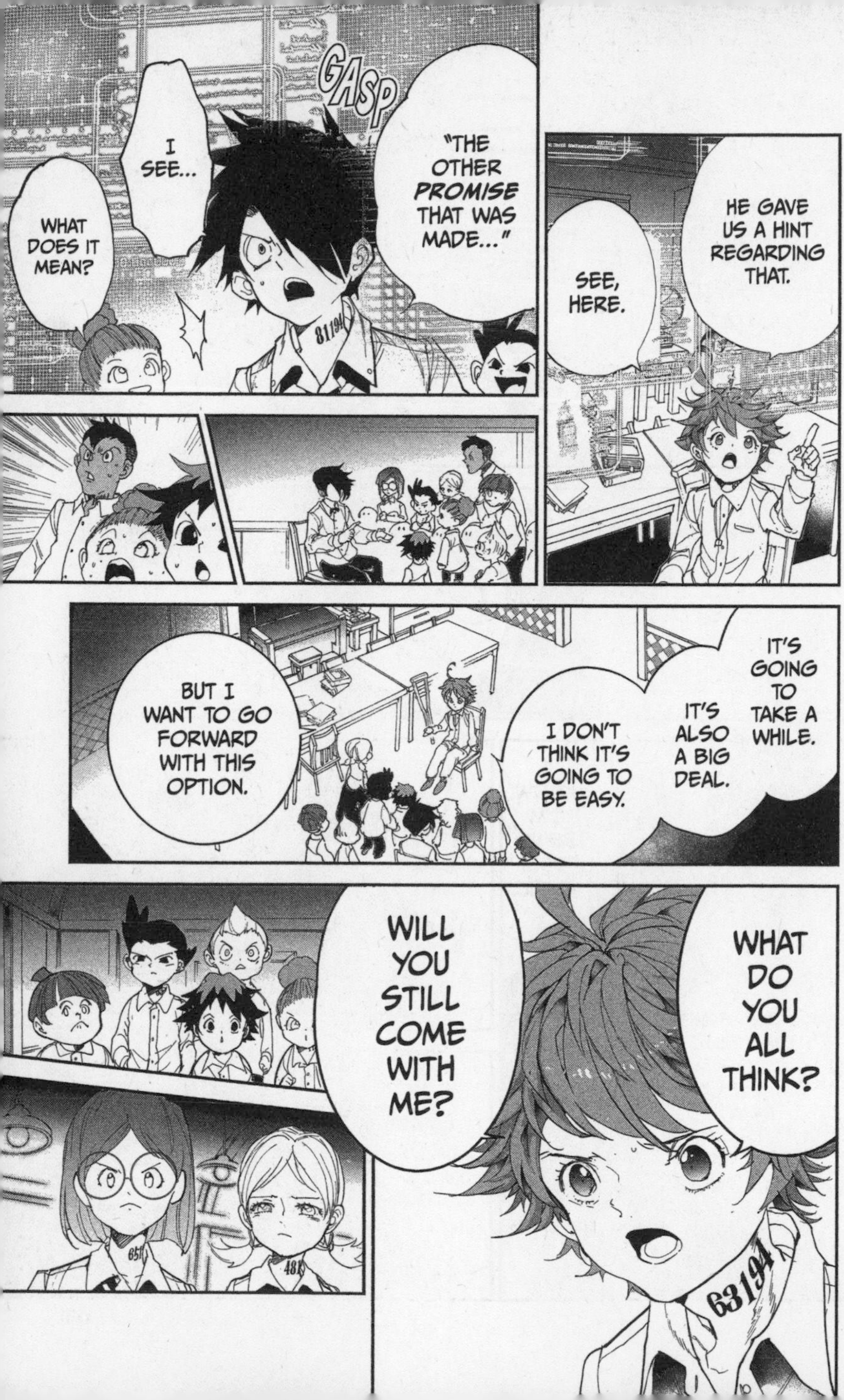
HE GAVE US A HINT REGARDING THAT.
SEE, HERE.
GASP
"THE OTHER PROMISE THAT WAS MADE..."
81194
I SEE...
WHAT DOES IT MEAN?
IT'S GOING TO TAKE A WHILE.
IT'S ALSO A BIG DEAL.
I DON'T THINK IT'S GOING TO BE EASY.
BUT I WANT TO GO FORWARD WITH THIS OPTION.
WHAT DO YOU ALL THINK?
63194
WILL YOU STILL COME WITH ME?

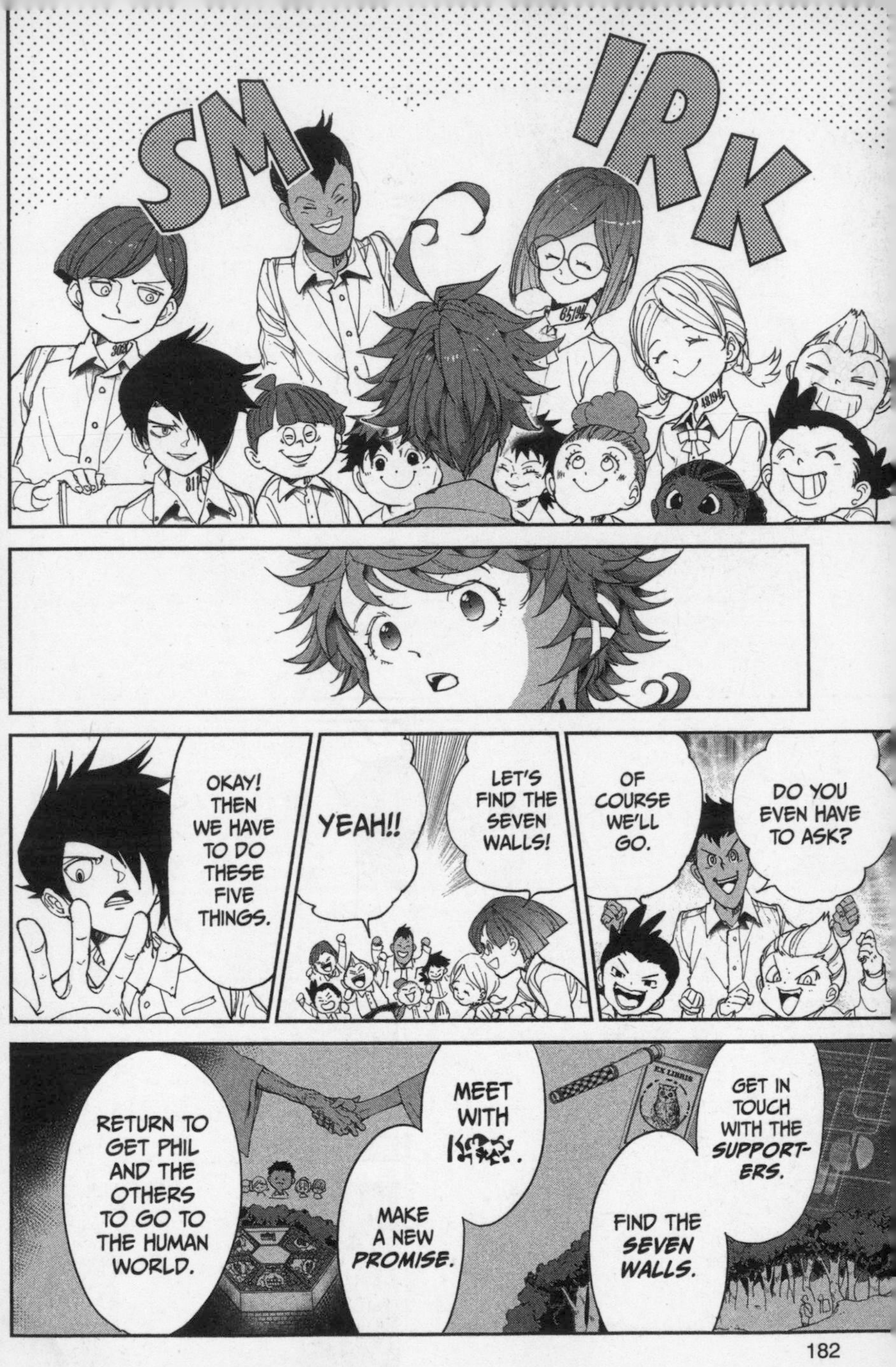
SMIRK
DO YOU EVEN HAVE TO ASK?
OF COURSE WE'LL GO.
LET'S FIND THE SEVEN WALLS!
YEAH!!
OKAY! THEN WE HAVE TO DO THESE FIVE THINGS.
GET IN TOUCH WITH THE SUPPORTERS.
EX LIBRIS
FIND THE SEVEN WALLS.
MEET WITH
MAKE A NEW PROMISE.
RETURN TO GET PHIL AND THE OTHERS TO GO TO THE HUMAN WORLD.

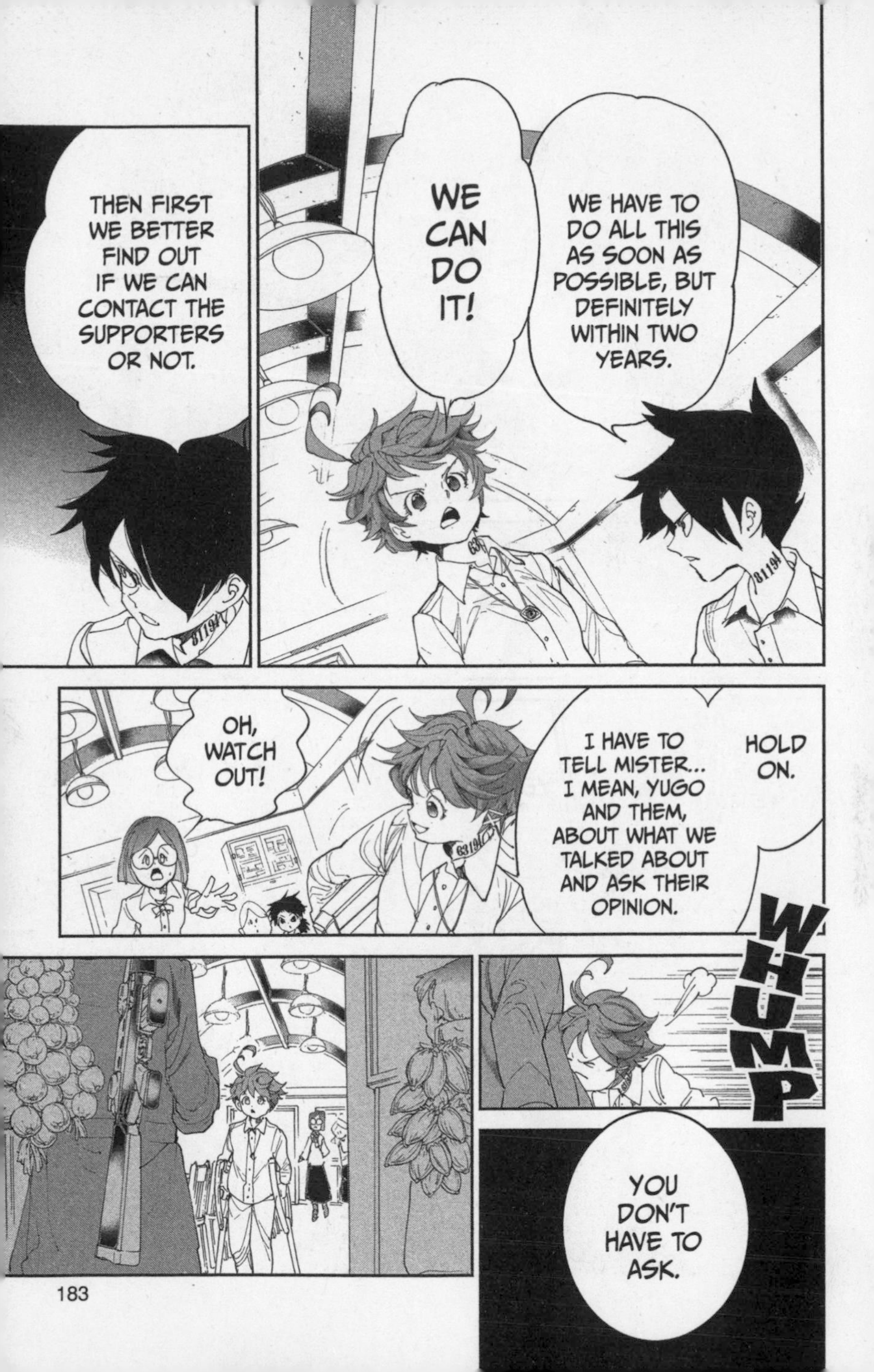
WE HAVE TO DO ALL THIS AS SOON AS POSSIBLE, BUT DEFINITELY WITHIN TWO YEARS.
WE CAN DO IT!
THEN FIRST WE BETTER FIND OUT IF WE CAN CONTACT THE SUPPORTERS OR NOT.
HOLD ON.
I HAVE TO TELL MISTER... I MEAN, YUGO AND THEM, ABOUT WHAT WE TALKED ABOUT AND ASK THEIR OPINION.
OH, WATCH OUT!
WHUMP
YOU DON'T HAVE TO ASK.

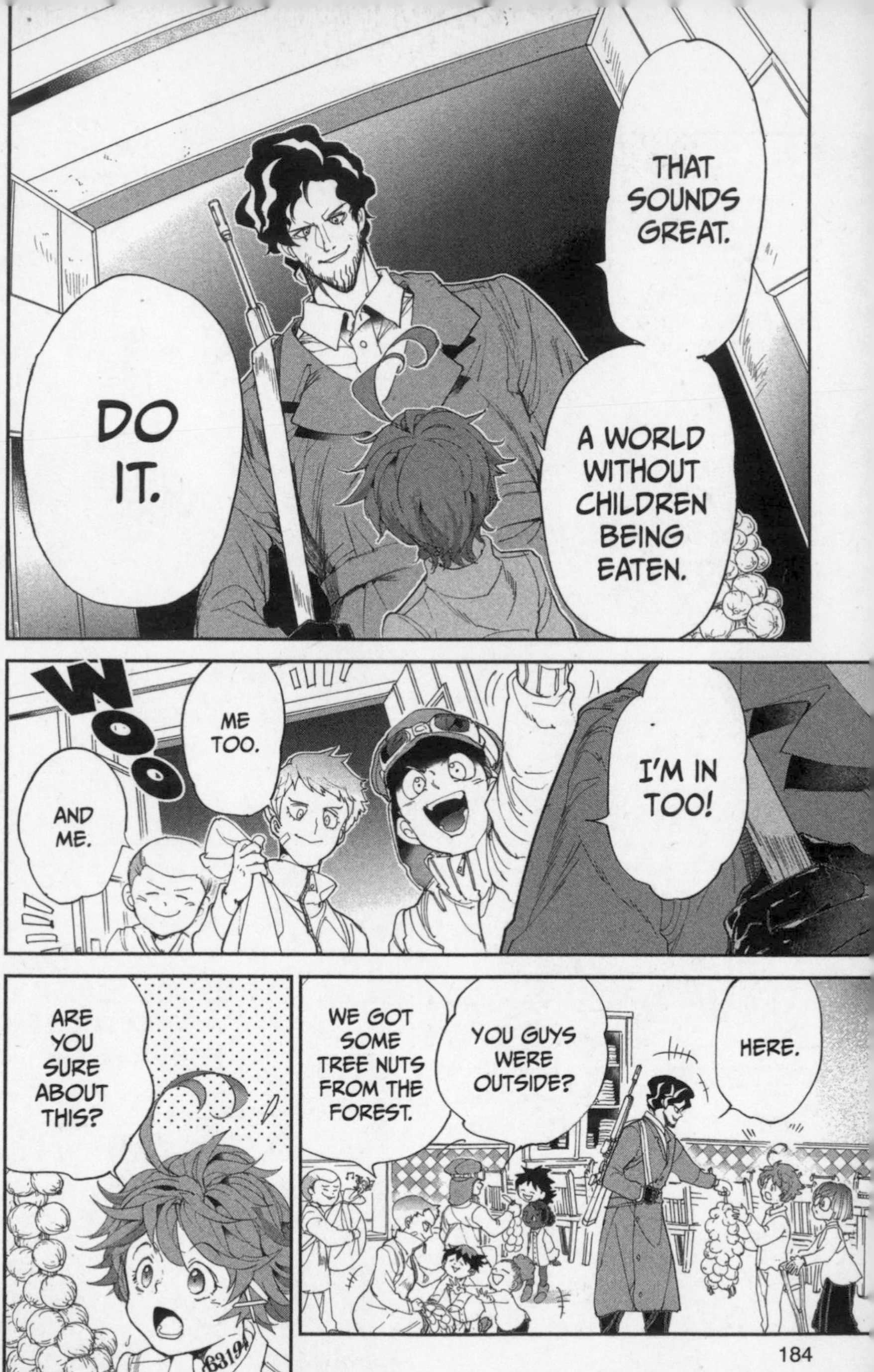
THAT SOUNDS GREAT.
A WORLD WITHOUT CHILDREN BEING EATEN.
DO IT.
I'M IN TOO!
ME TOO.
WOO
AND ME.
HERE.
YOU GUYS WERE OUTSIDE?
WE GOT SOME TREE NUTS FROM THE FOREST.
ARE YOU SURE ABOUT THIS?

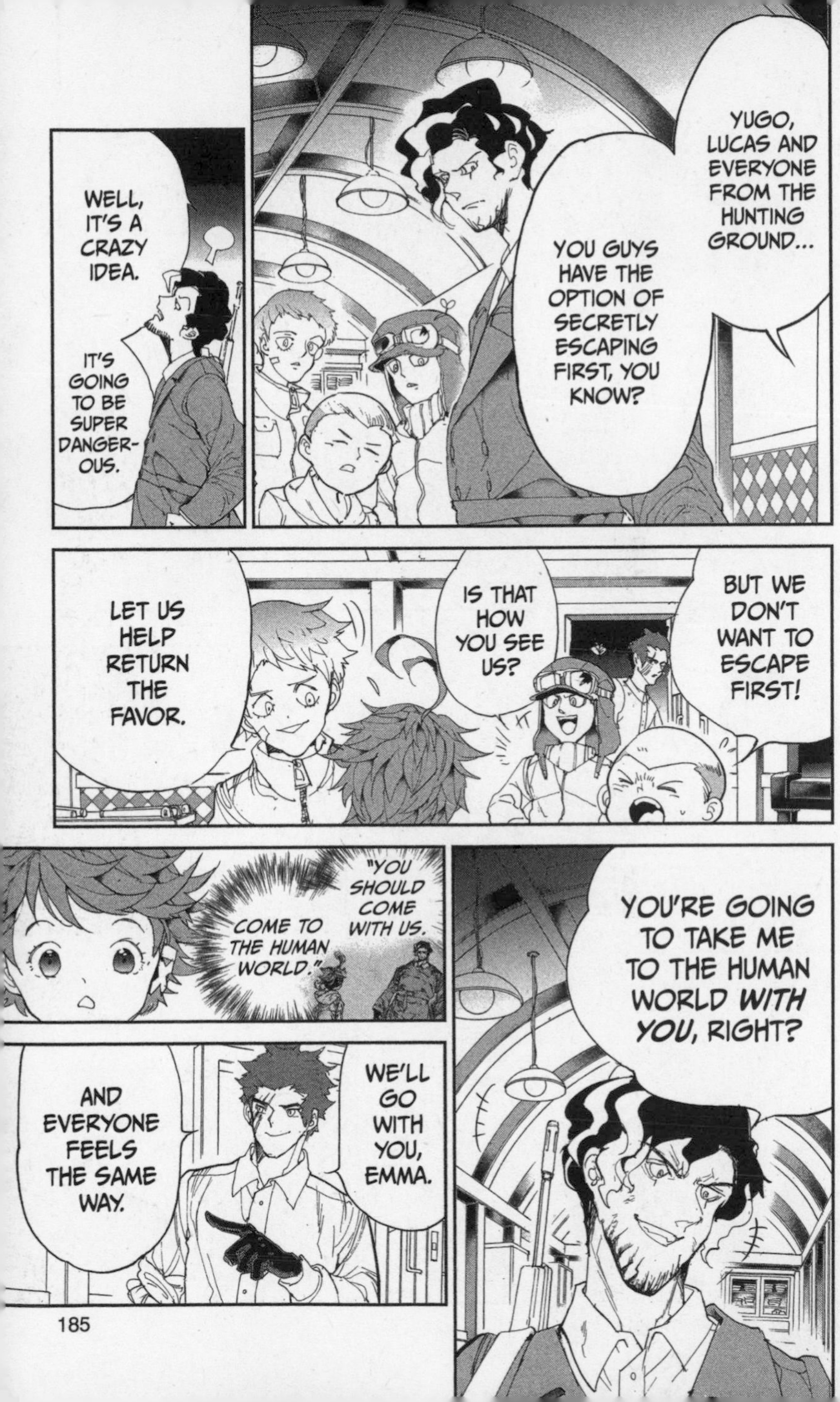
YUGO, LUCAS AND EVERYONE FROM THE HUNTING GROUND...
YOU GUYS HAVE THE OPTION OF SECRETLY ESCAPING FIRST, YOU KNOW?
WELL, IT'S A CRAZY IDEA.
IT'S GOING TO BE SUPER DANGER-OUS.
BUT WE DON'T WANT TO ESCAPE FIRST!
IS THAT HOW YOU SEE US?
LET US HELP RETURN THE FAVOR.
YOU'RE GOING TO TAKE ME TO THE HUMAN WORLD *WITH YOU*, RIGHT?
"YOU SHOULD COME WITH US.
COME TO THE HUMAN WORLD."
WE'LL GO WITH YOU, EMMA.
AND EVERYONE FEELS THE SAME WAY.

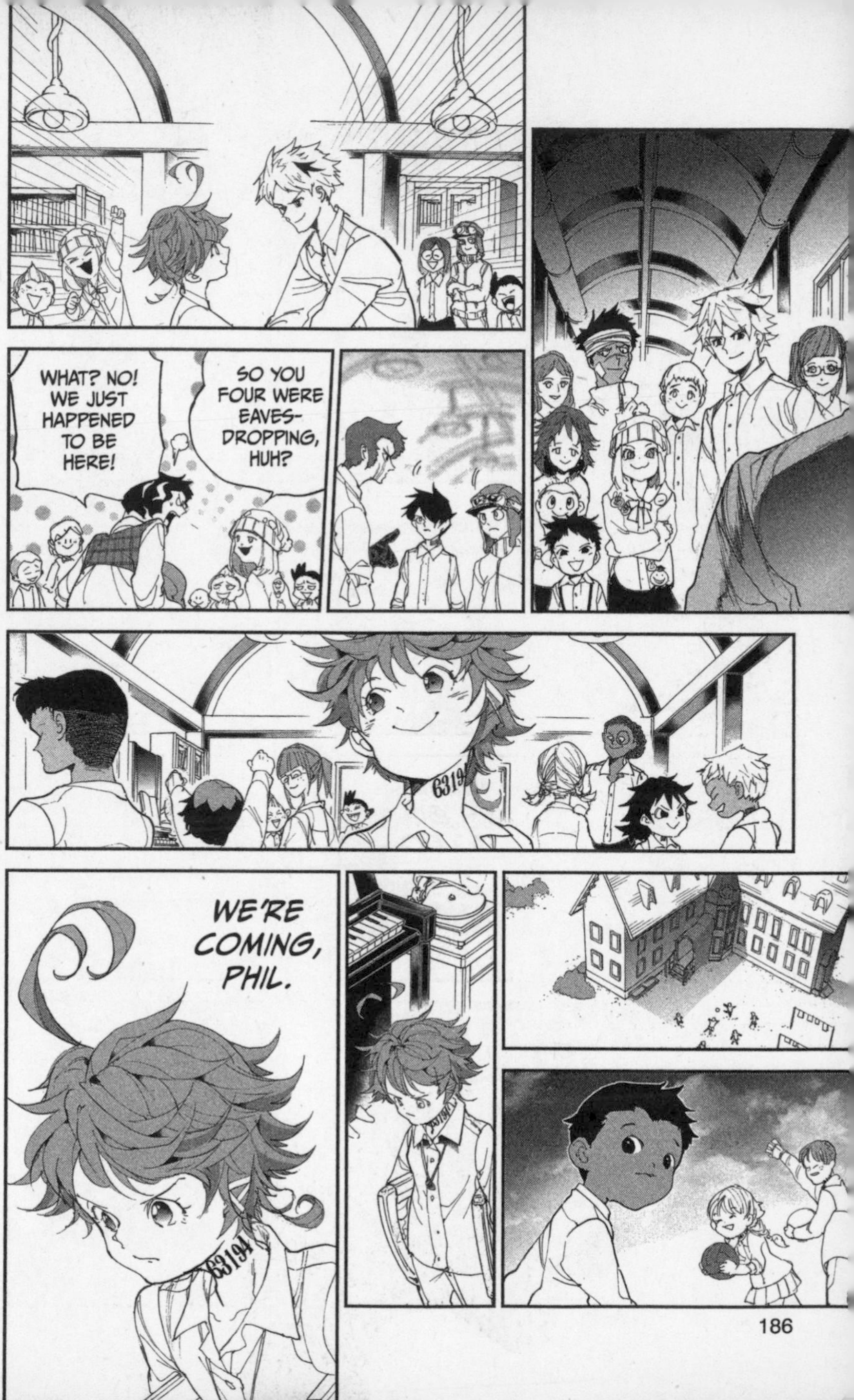

SO YOU FOUR WERE EAVES-DROPPING, HUH?
WHAT? NO! WE JUST HAPPENED TO BE HERE!
WE'RE COMING, PHIL.

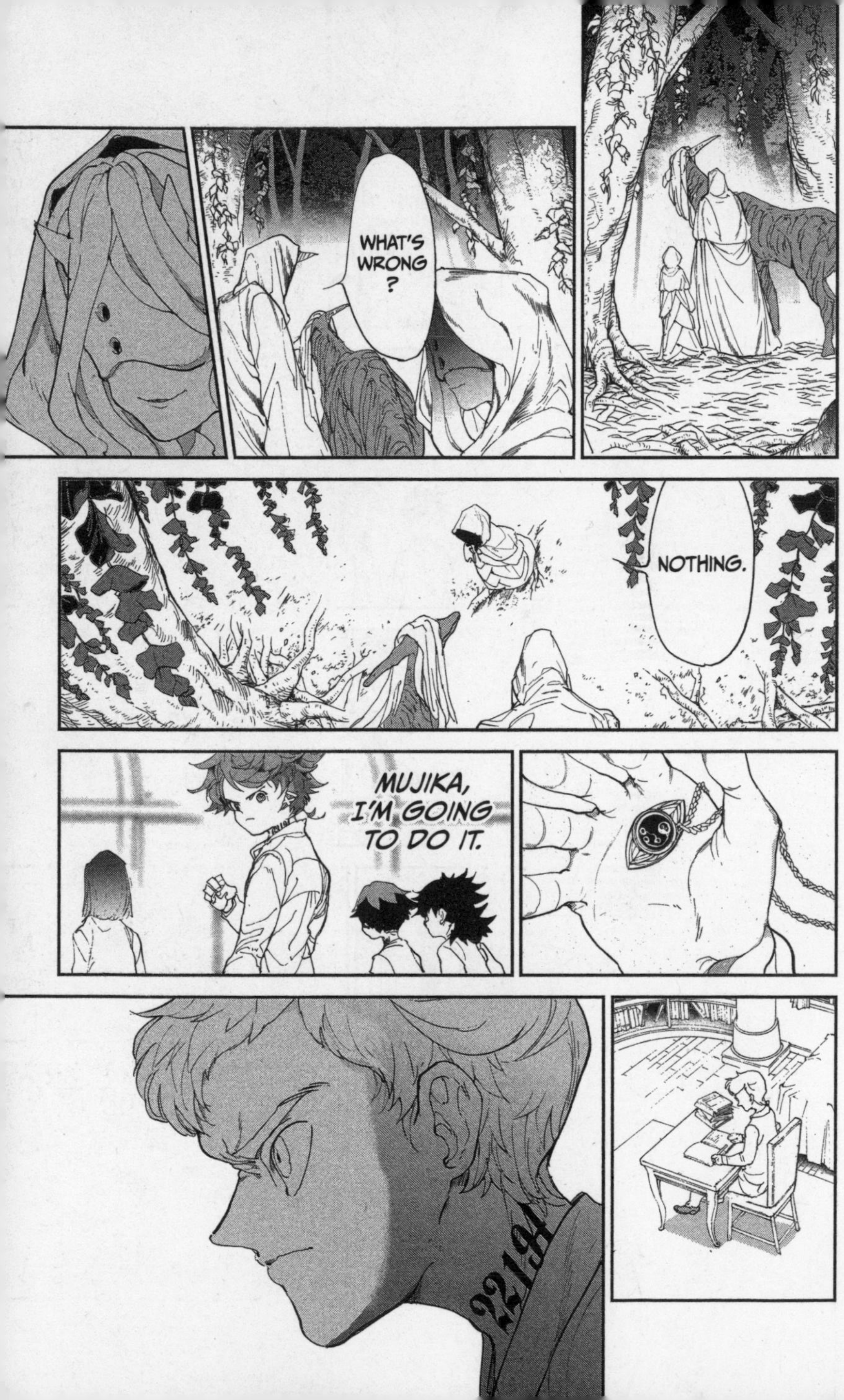
WHAT'S WRONG?
NOTHING.
MUJIKA, I'M GOING TO DO IT.

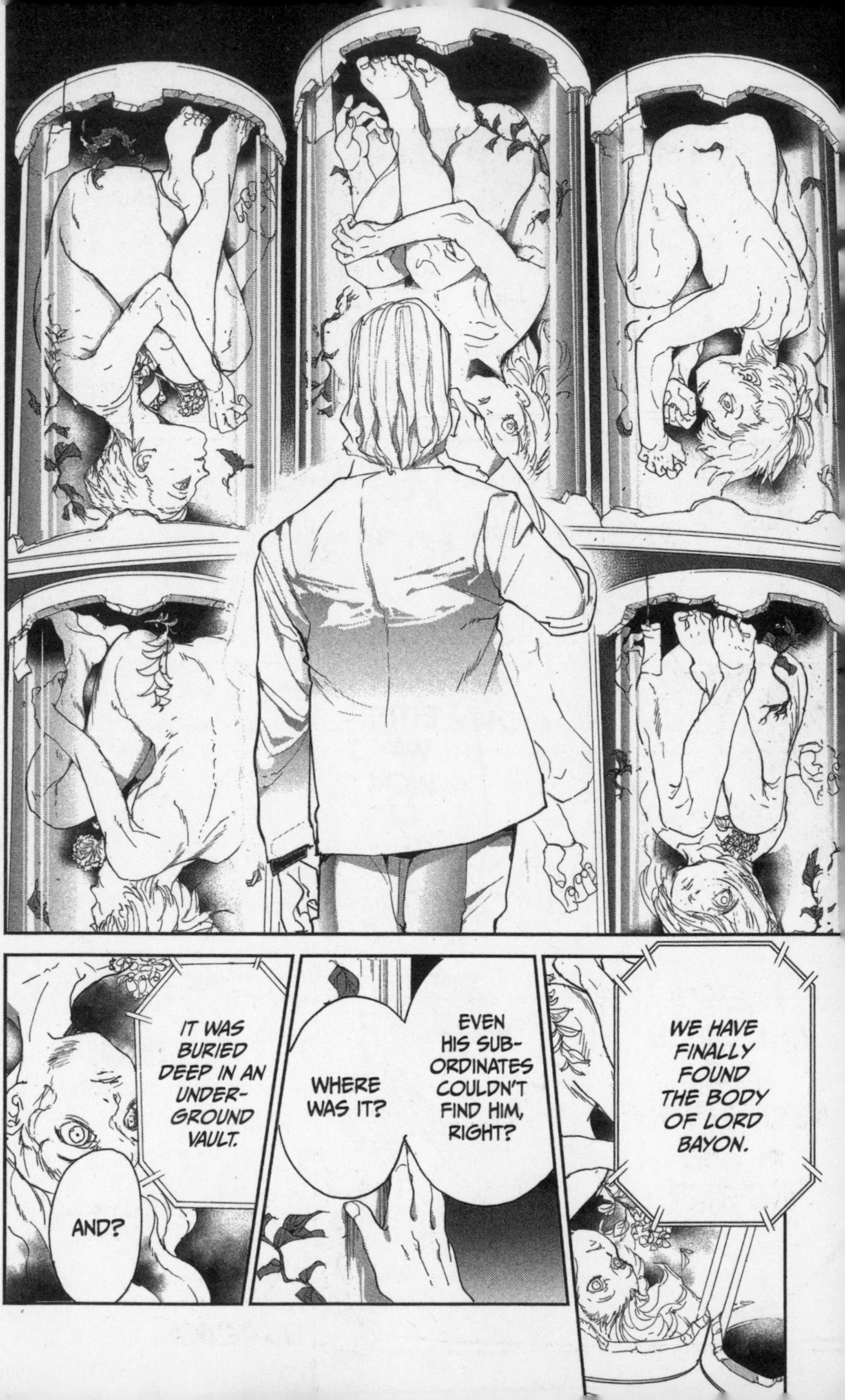
WE HAVE FINALLY FOUND THE BODY OF LORD BAYON.
EVEN HIS SUB-ORDINATES COULDN'T FIND HIM, RIGHT?
WHERE WAS IT?
IT WAS BURIED DEEP IN AN UNDER-GROUND VAULT.
AND?

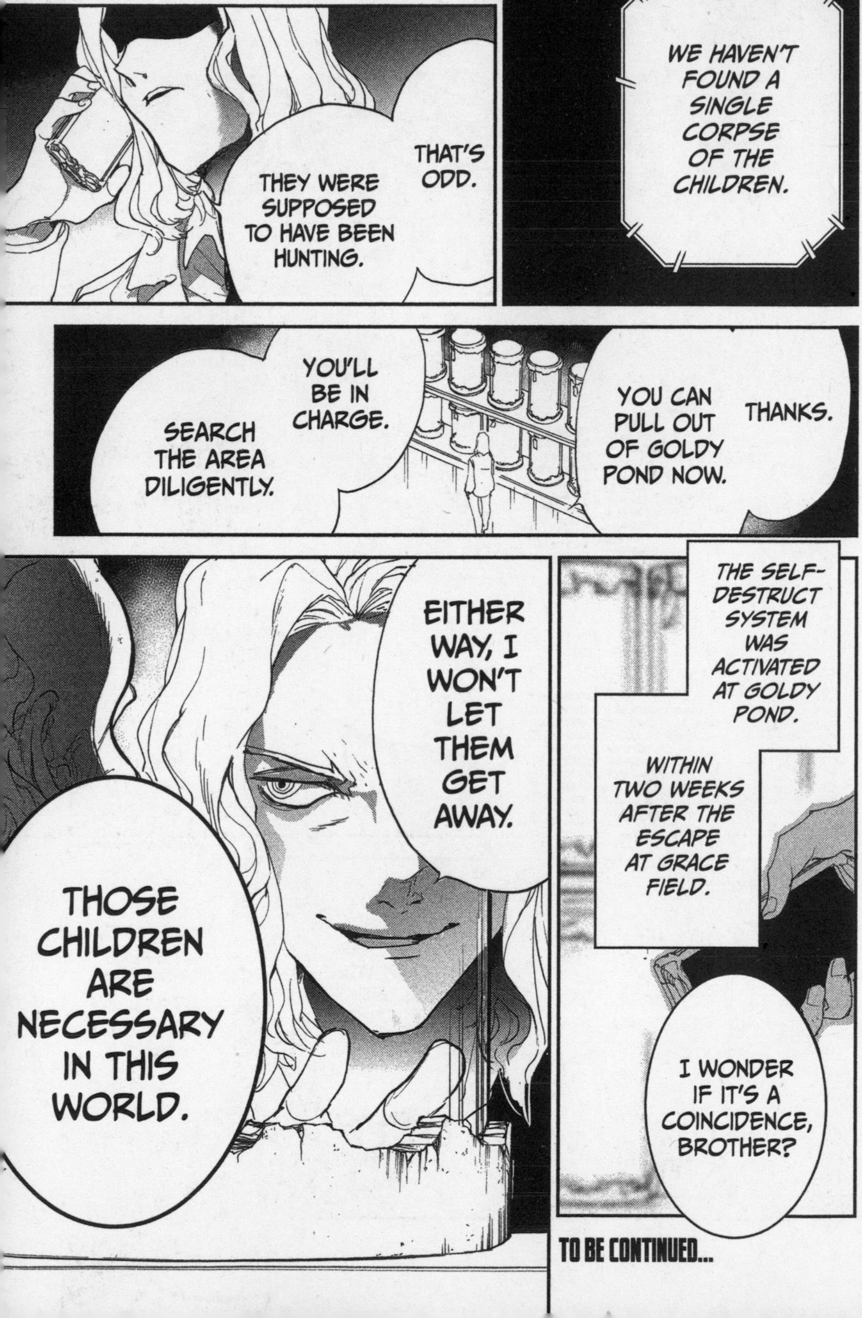
WE HAVEN'T FOUND A SINGLE CORPSE OF THE CHILDREN.
THAT'S ODD.
THEY WERE SUPPOSED TO HAVE BEEN HUNTING.
THANKS.
YOU CAN PULL OUT OF GOLDY POND NOW.
YOU'LL BE IN CHARGE.
SEARCH THE AREA DILIGENTLY.
THE SELF-DESTRUCT SYSTEM WAS ACTIVATED AT GOLDY POND.
WITHIN TWO WEEKS AFTER THE ESCAPE AT GRACE FIELD.
I WONDER IF IT'S A COINCIDENCE, BROTHER?
EITHER WAY, I WON'T LET THEM GET AWAY.
THOSE CHILDREN ARE NECESSARY IN THIS WORLD.
TO BE CONTINUED...

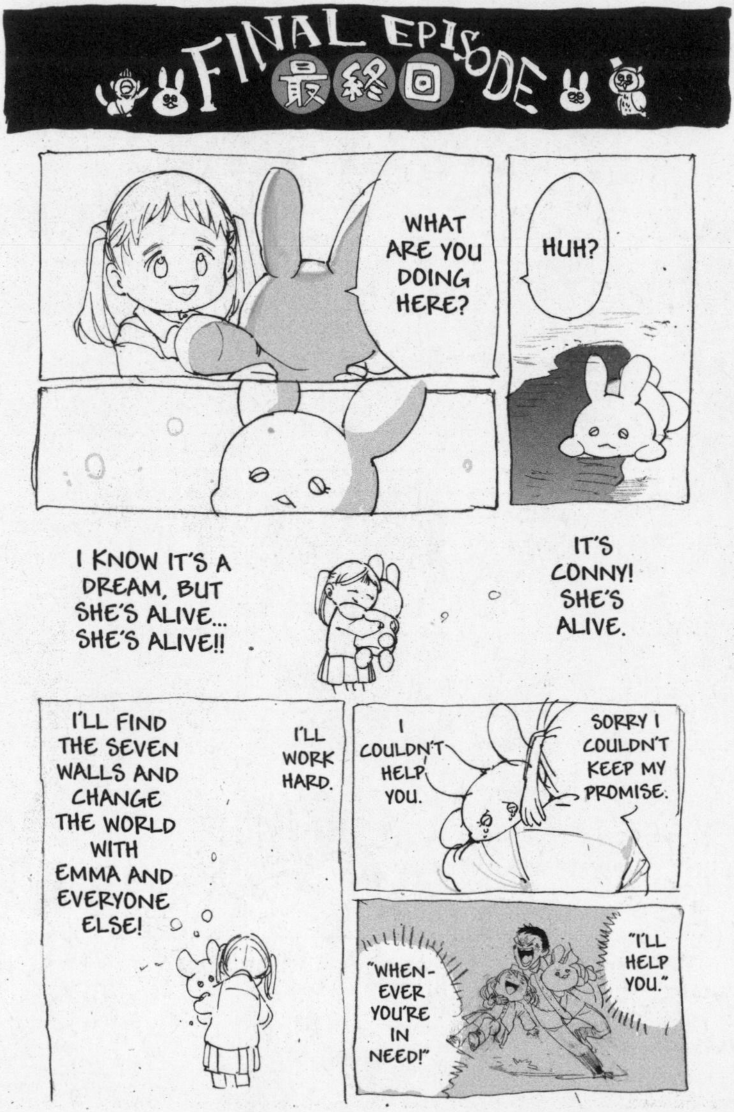
FINAL EPISODE
最終回
HUH?
WHAT ARE YOU DOING HERE?
IT'S CONNY! SHE'S ALIVE.
I KNOW IT'S A DREAM, BUT SHE'S ALIVE... SHE'S ALIVE!!
SORRY I COULDN'T KEEP MY PROMISE.
I COULDN'T HELP YOU.
"I'LL HELP YOU."
"WHEN-EVER YOU'RE IN NEED!"
I'LL WORK HARD.
I'LL FIND THE SEVEN WALLS AND CHANGE THE WORLD WITH EMMA AND EVERYONE ELSE!

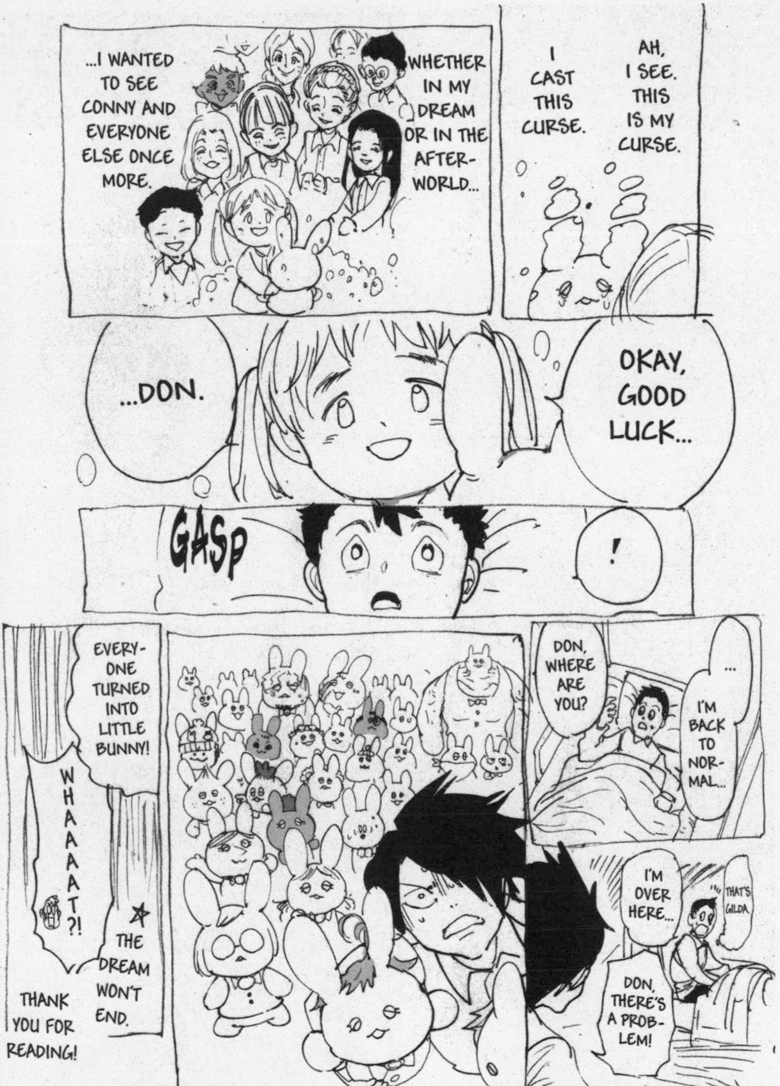
AH, I SEE. THIS IS MY CURSE.
I CAST THIS CURSE.
WHETHER IN MY DREAM OR IN THE AFTER-WORLD...
...I WANTED TO SEE CONNY AND EVERYONE ELSE ONCE MORE.
OKAY, GOOD LUCK...
...DON.
!
GASP
...
I'M BACK TO NOR-MAL...
DON, WHERE ARE YOU?
THAT'S GILDA.
I'M OVER HERE...
DON, THERE'S A PROB-LEM!
EVERY-ONE TURNED INTO LITTLE BUNNY!
WHAAAAAT?!
THE DREAM WON'T END.
THANK YOU FOR READING!

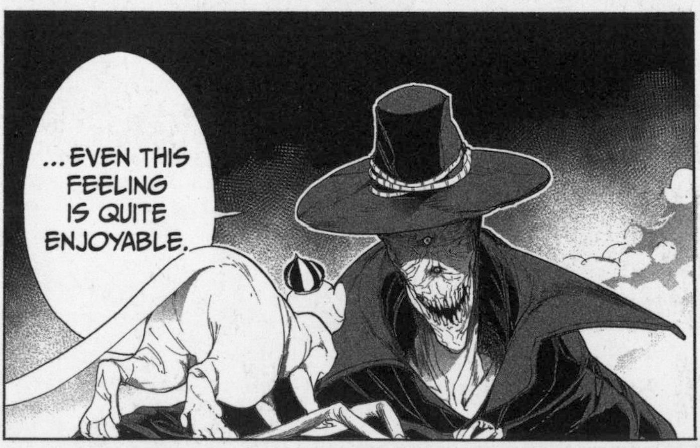
...EVEN THIS FEELING IS QUITE ENJOYABLE.

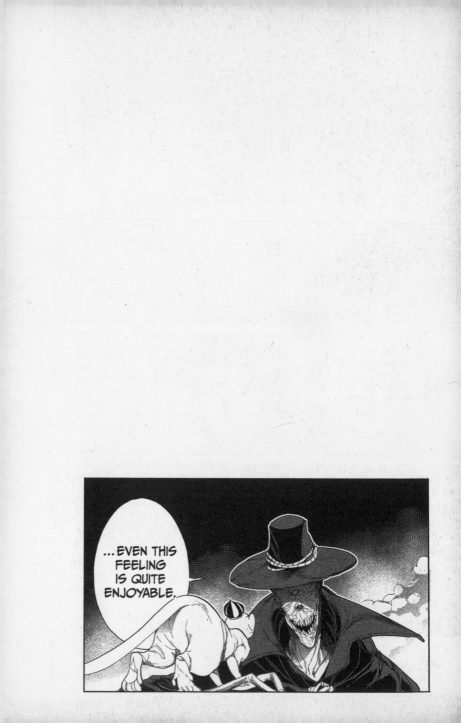

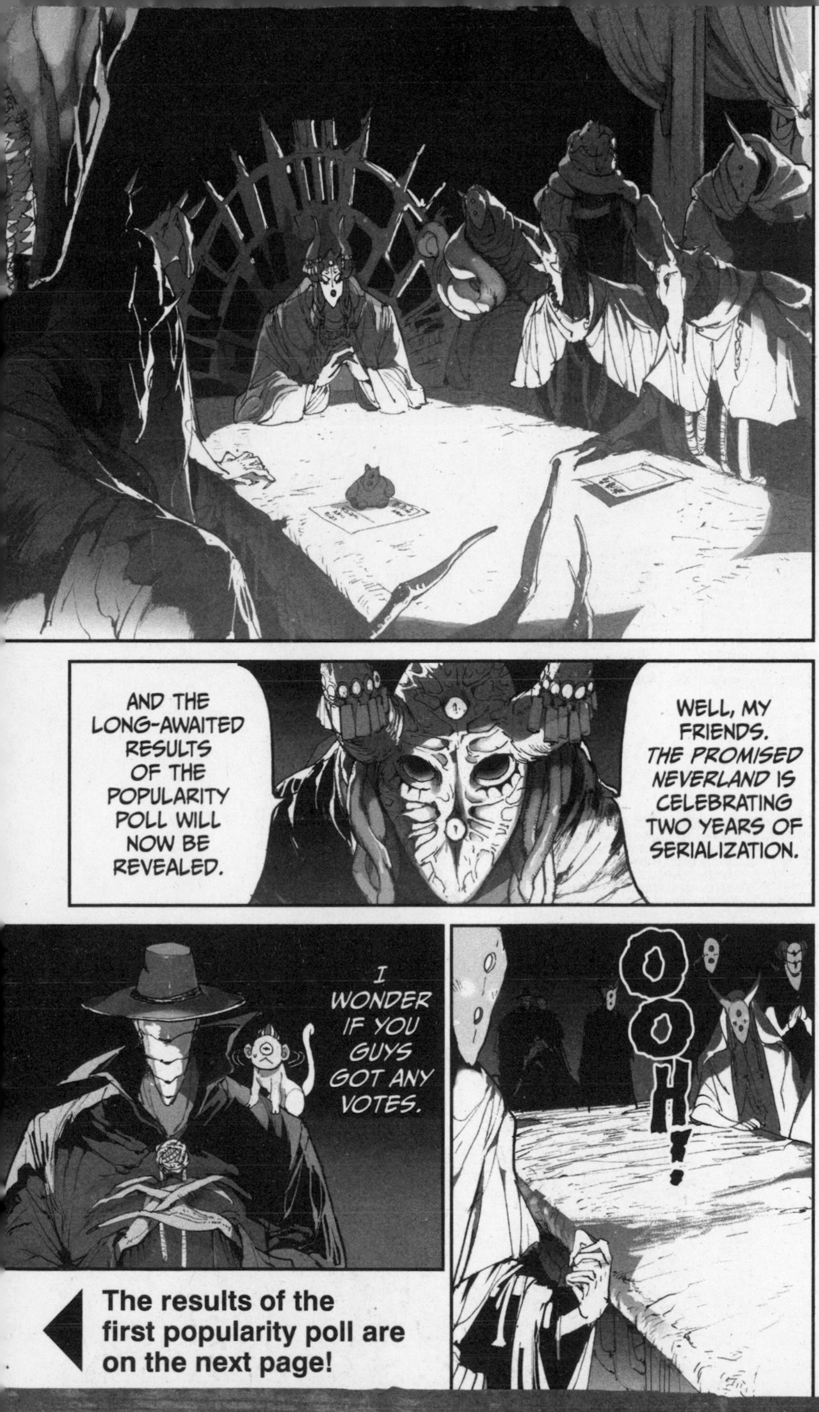
WELL, MY FRIENDS. THE PROMISED NEVERLAND IS CELEBRATING TWO YEARS OF SERIALIZATION.
AND THE LONG-AWAITED RESULTS OF THE POPULARITY POLL WILL NOW BE REVEALED.
OOOH!!
I WONDER IF YOU GUYS GOT ANY VOTES.

◀ **The results of the first popularity poll are on the next page!**

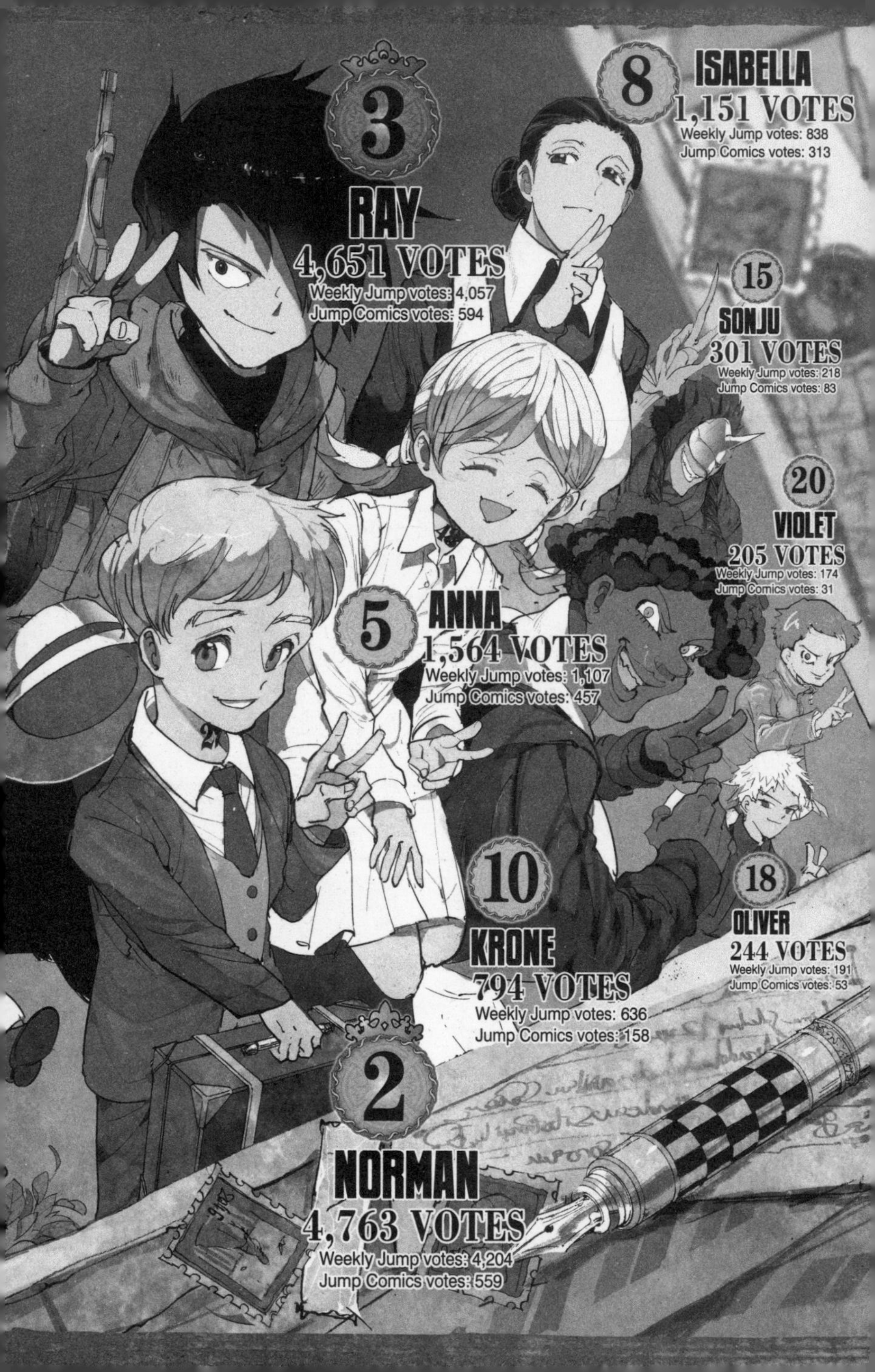
8
ISABELLA
1,151 VOTES
Weekly Jump votes: 838
Jump Comics votes: 313
3
RAY
4,651 VOTES
Weekly Jump votes: 4,057
Jump Comics votes: 594
15
SONJU
301 VOTES
Weekly Jump votes: 218
Jump Comics votes: 83
20
VIOLET
205 VOTES
Weekly Jump votes: 174
Jump Comics votes: 31
5
ANNA
1,564 VOTES
Weekly Jump votes: 1,107
Jump Comics votes: 457
18
OLIVER
244 VOTES
Weekly Jump votes: 191
Jump Comics votes: 53
10
KRONE
794 VOTES
Weekly Jump votes: 636
Jump Comics votes: 158
2
NORMAN
4,763 VOTES
Weekly Jump votes: 4,204
Jump Comics votes: 559

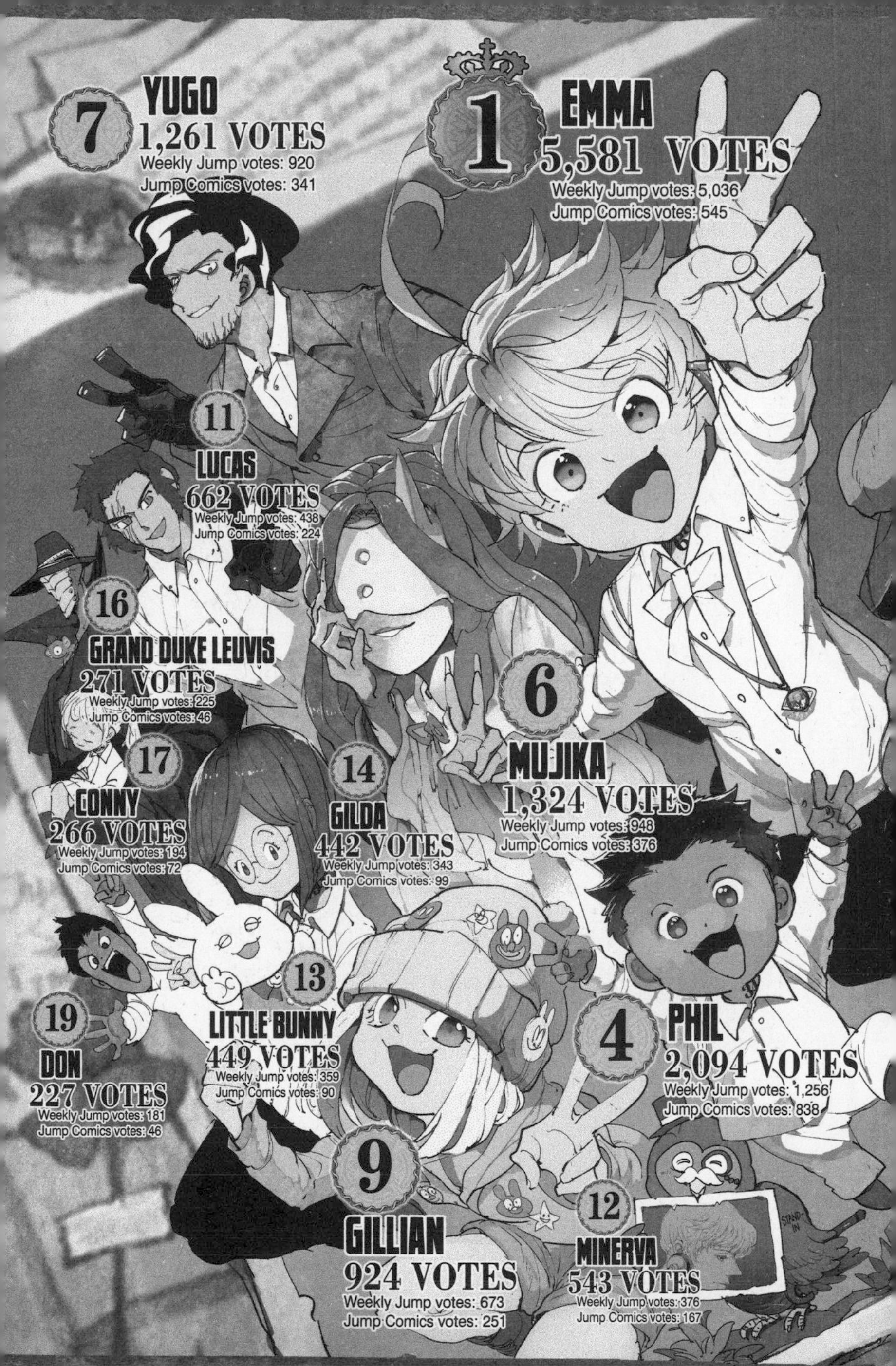
1
EMMA
5,581 VOTES
Weekly Jump votes: 5,036
Jump Comics votes: 545
7
YUGO
1,261 VOTES
Weekly Jump votes: 920
Jump Comics votes: 341
11
LUCAS
662 VOTES
Weekly Jump votes: 438
Jump Comics votes: 224
6
MUJIKA
1,324 VOTES
Weekly Jump votes: 948
Jump Comics votes: 376
16
GRAND DUKE LEUVIS
271 VOTES
Weekly Jump votes: 225
Jump Comics votes: 46
14
GILDA
442 VOTES
Weekly Jump votes: 343
Jump Comics votes: 99
17
CONNY
266 VOTES
Weekly Jump votes: 194
Jump Comics votes: 72
4
PHIL
2,094 VOTES
Weekly Jump votes: 1,256
Jump Comics votes: 838
13
LITTLE BUNNY
449 VOTES
Weekly Jump votes: 359
Jump Comics votes: 90
19
DON
227 VOTES
Weekly Jump votes: 181
Jump Comics votes: 46
12
MINERVA
543 VOTES
Weekly Jump votes: 376
Jump Comics votes: 167
STAND-IN
9
GILLIAN
924 VOTES
Weekly Jump votes: 673
Jump Comics votes: 251

THE PROMISED NEVERLAND'S SECONDARY GROUP?!

21st and below are these characters!!!

21st
114 votes
WJ votes: 114
JC votes: 0
LESLIE

22nd
97 votes
WJ votes: 96
JC votes: 1
DOMINIC

23rd
84 votes
WJ votes: 64
JC votes: 20
THOMA

24th
62 votes
WJ votes: 55
JC votes: 7
CHRISTIE

25th
55 votes
WJ votes: 53
JC votes: 2
SHERRY

THANK YOU...

25th
55 votes
WJ votes: 55
JC votes: 0
DINAH

27th
46 votes
WJ votes: 40
JC votes: 6
ZACK

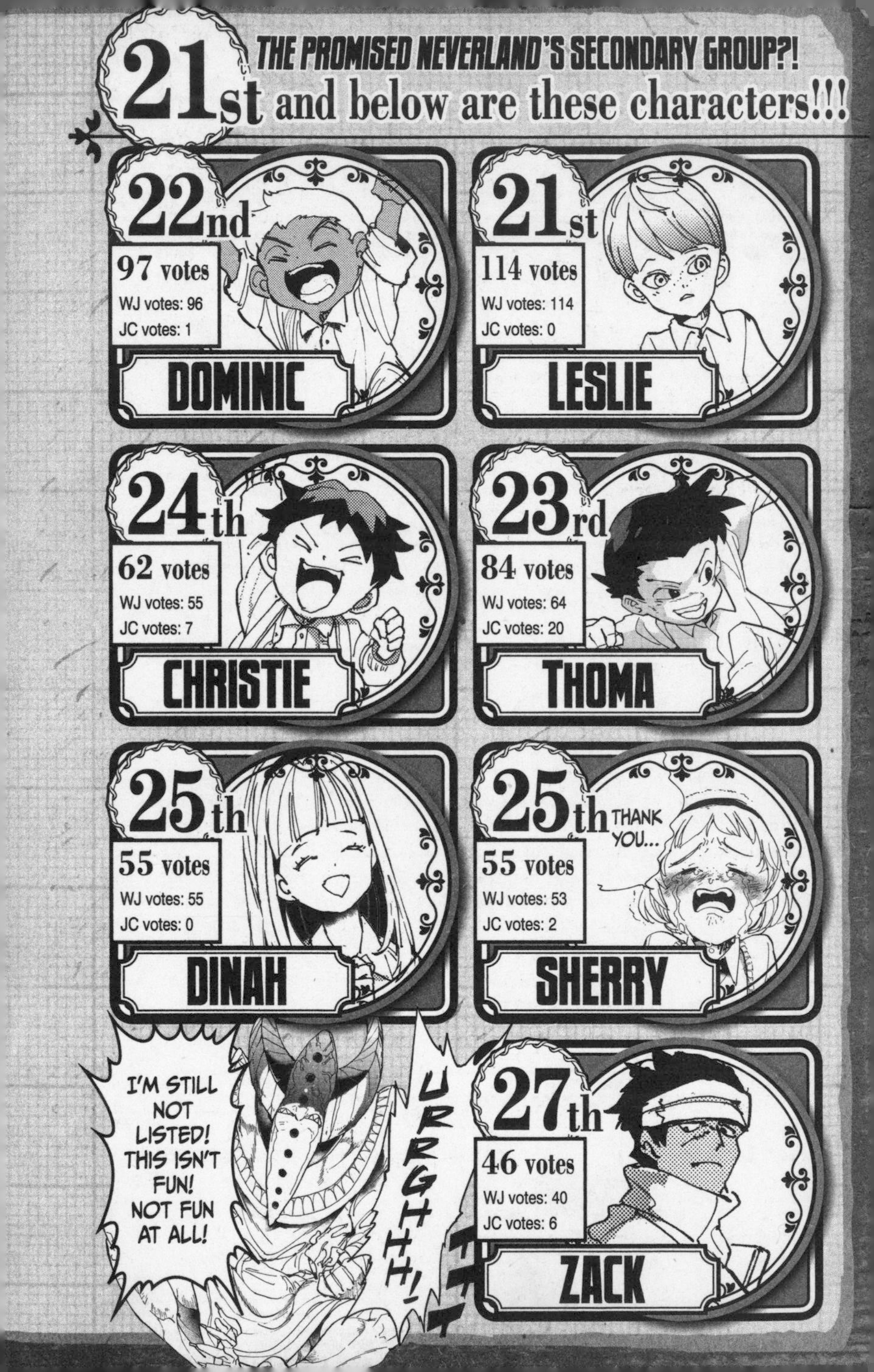
I'M STILL NOT LISTED! THIS ISN'T FUN! NOT FUN AT ALL!
URRGHHH!!

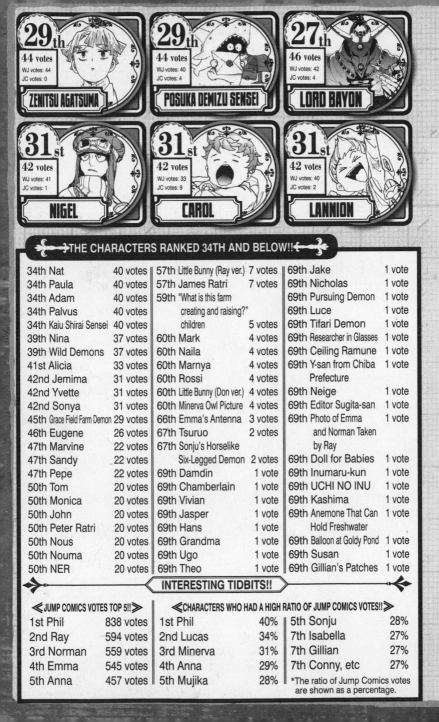

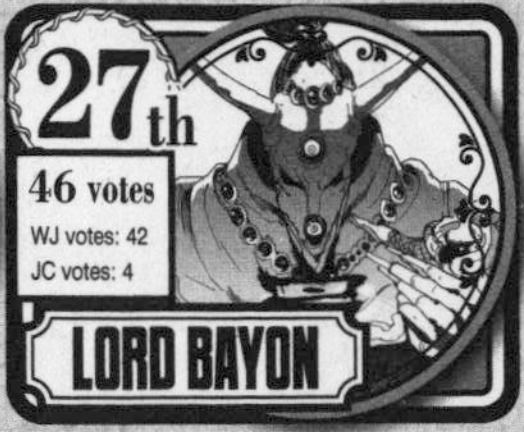
27th
46 votes
WJ votes: 42
JC votes: 4
LORD BAYON

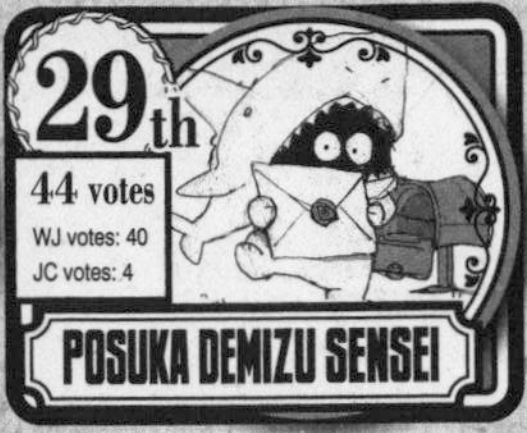
29th
44 votes
WJ votes: 40
JC votes: 4
POSUKA DEMIZU SENSEI

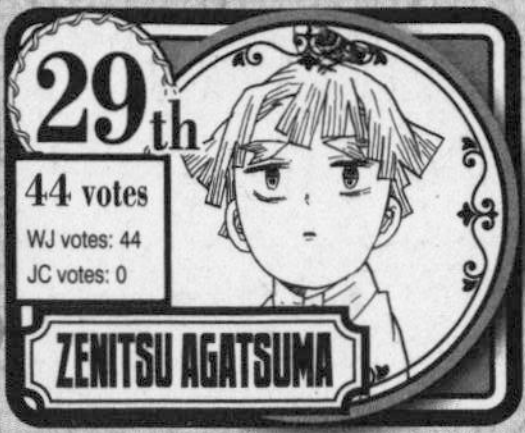
29th
44 votes
WJ votes: 44
JC votes: 0
ZENITSU AGATSUMA

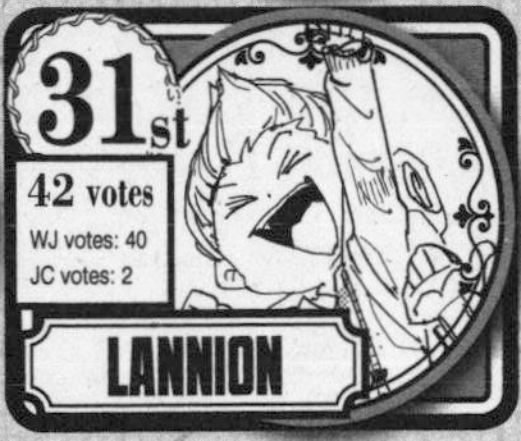
31st
42 votes
WJ votes: 40
JC votes: 2
LANNION

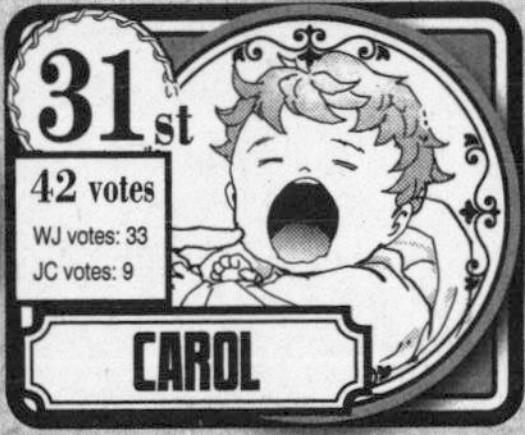
31st
42 votes
WJ votes: 33
JC votes: 9
CAROL

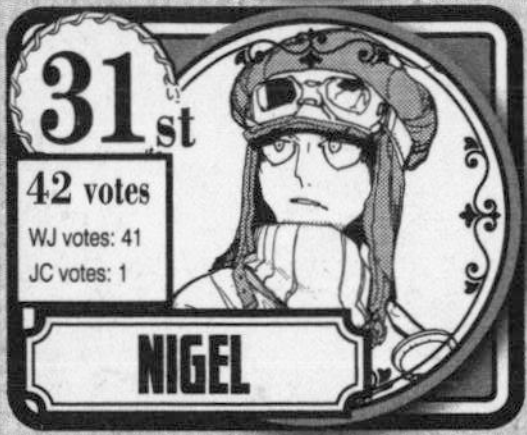
31st
42 votes
WJ votes: 41
JC votes: 1
NIGEL

THE CHARACTERS RANKED 34TH AND BELOW!!

34th Nat	40 votes
34th Paula	40 votes
34th Adam	40 votes
34th Palvus	40 votes
34th Kaiu Shirai Sensei	40 votes
39th Nina	37 votes
39th Wild Demons	37 votes
41st Alicia	33 votes
42nd Jemima	31 votes
42nd Yvette	31 votes
42nd Sonya	31 votes
45th Grace Field Farm Demon	29 votes
46th Eugene	26 votes
47th Marvine	22 votes
47th Sandy	22 votes
47th Pepe	22 votes
50th Tom	20 votes
50th Monica	20 votes
50th John	20 votes
50th Peter Ratri	20 votes
50th Nous	20 votes
50th Nouma	20 votes
50th NER	20 votes
57th Little Bunny (Ray ver.)	7 votes
57th James Ratri	7 votes
59th "What is this farm creating and raising?" children	5 votes
60th Mark	4 votes
60th Naila	4 votes
60th Marnya	4 votes
60th Rossi	4 votes
60th Little Bunny (Don ver.)	4 votes
60th Minerva Owl Picture	4 votes
66th Emma's Antenna	3 votes
67th Tsuruo	2 votes
67th Sonju's Horselike Six-Legged Demon	2 votes
69th Damdin	1 vote
69th Chamberlain	1 vote
69th Vivian	1 vote
69th Jasper	1 vote
69th Hans	1 vote
69th Grandma	1 vote
69th Ugo	1 vote
69th Theo	1 vote
69th Jake	1 vote
69th Nicholas	1 vote
69th Pursuing Demon	1 vote
69th Luce	1 vote
69th Tifari Demon	1 vote
69th Researcher in Glasses	1 vote
69th Ceiling Ramune	1 vote
69th Y-san from Chiba Prefecture	1 vote
69th Neige	1 vote
69th Editor Sugita-san	1 vote
69th Photo of Emma and Norman Taken by Ray	1 vote
69th Doll for Babies	1 vote
69th Inumaru-kun	1 vote
69th UCHI NO INU	1 vote
69th Kashima	1 vote
69th Anemone That Can Hold Freshwater	1 vote
69th Balloon at Goldy Pond	1 vote
69th Susan	1 vote
69th Gillian's Patches	1 vote

INTERESTING TIDBITS!!

JUMP COMICS VOTES TOP 5!!

1st Phil	838 votes
2nd Ray	594 votes
3rd Norman	559 votes
4th Emma	545 votes
5th Anna	457 votes

CHARACTERS WHO HAD A HIGH RATIO OF JUMP COMICS VOTES!!

1st Phil	40%
2nd Lucas	34%
3rd Minerva	31%
4th Anna	29%
5th Mujika	28%
5th Sonju	28%
7th Isabella	27%
7th Gillian	27%
7th Conny, etc	27%

*The ratio of Jump Comics votes are shown as a percentage.

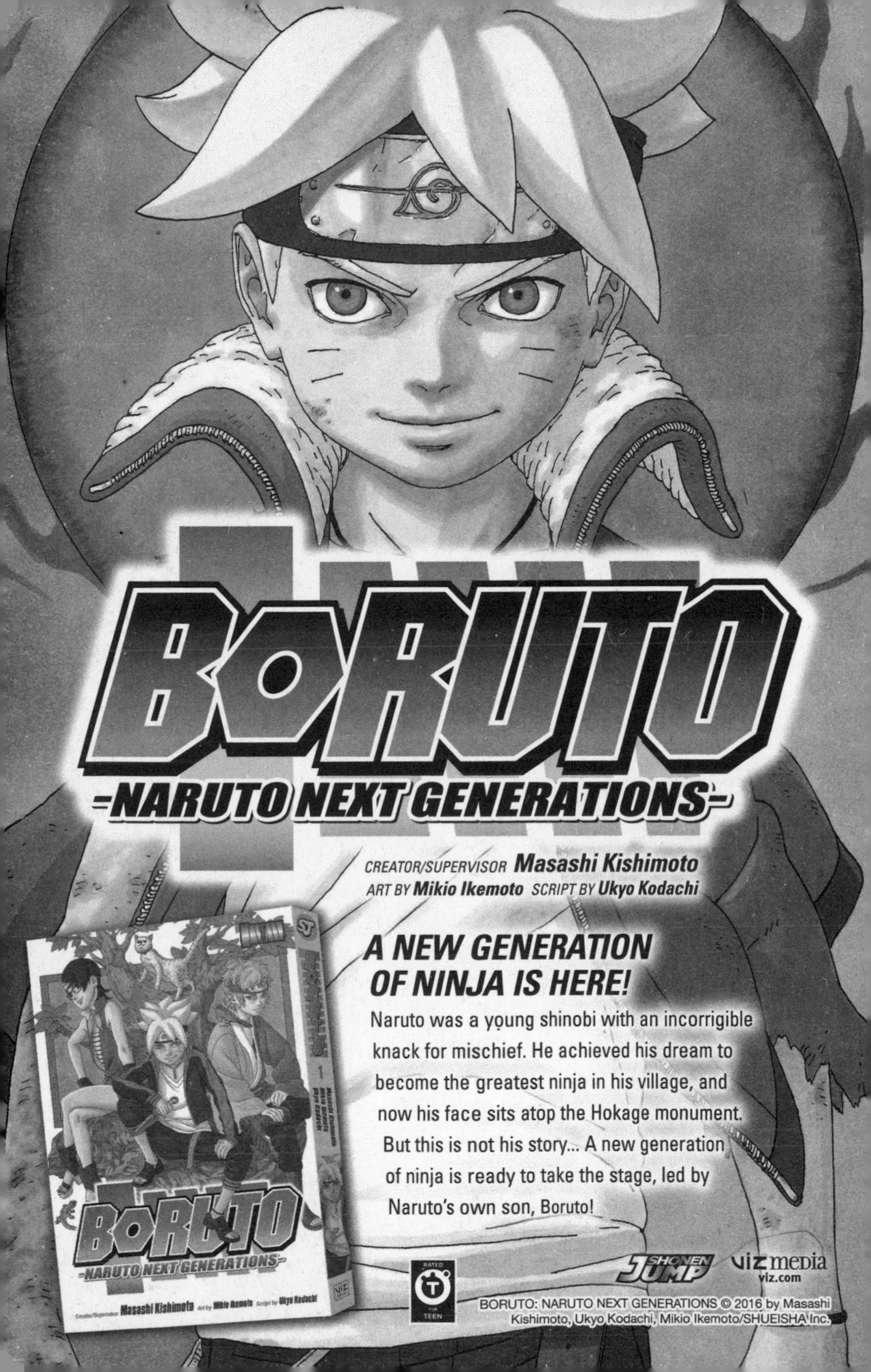
BORUTO
-NARUTO NEXT GENERATIONS-
CREATOR/SUPERVISOR Masashi Kishimoto
ART BY Mikio Ikemoto SCRIPT BY Ukyo Kodachi
A NEW GENERATION OF NINJA IS HERE!
Naruto was a young shinobi with an incorrigible knack for mischief. He achieved his dream to become the greatest ninja in his village, and now his face sits atop the Hokage monument. But this is not his story... A new generation of ninja is ready to take the stage, led by Naruto's own son, Boruto!
RATED T FOR TEEN
SHONEN JUMP
VIZ media
viz.com
BORUTO: NARUTO NEXT GENERATIONS © 2016 by Masashi Kishimoto, Ukyo Kodachi, Mikio Ikemoto/SHUEISHA Inc.

YOU'RE READING THE **WRONG WAY!**

The Promised Neverland reads from right to left, starting in the upper-right corner. Japanese is read from right to left, meaning that action, sound effects and word-balloon order are completely reversed from English order.

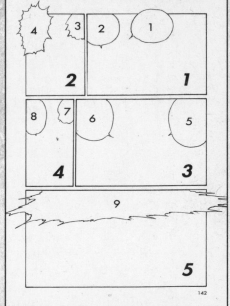